AF207871

READY

FOR MY

CLOSE-UP

READY
FOR MY
CLOSE-UP

THE MAKING OF *SUNSET BOULEVARD* AND THE DARK SIDE OF THE HOLLYWOOD DREAM

DAVID M. LUBIN

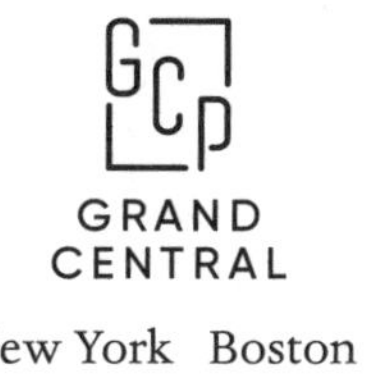

GRAND CENTRAL

New York Boston

Grand Central Publishing
Hachette Book Group
1290 Avenue of the Americas, New York, NY 10104
grandcentralpublishing.com
@grandcentralpub

First edition: August 2025

Grand Central Publishing is a division of Hachette Book Group, Inc. The Grand Central Publishing name and logo is a registered trademark of Hachette Book Group, Inc.

The publisher is not responsible for websites (or their content) that are not owned by the publisher.

The Hachette Speakers Bureau provides a wide range of authors for speaking events. To find out more, go to hachettespeakersbureau.com or email HachetteSpeakers@hbgusa.com.

Grand Central Publishing books may be purchased in bulk for business, educational, or promotional use. For information, please contact your local bookseller or the Hachette Book Group Special Markets Department at special.markets@hbgusa.com.

Print book interior designed by Bart Dawson

Library of Congress Cataloging-in-Publication Data

Names: Lubin, David M. author
Title: Ready for my close-up : the making of Sunset Boulevard and the dark side of the Hollywood dream / David M. Lubin.
Description: First edition. | New York : Grand Central Publishing, 2025.
Identifiers: LCCN 2025009461 | ISBN 9781538739297 hardcover | ISBN 9781538739310 ebook
Subjects: LCSH: Sunset Blvd. (Motion picture) | Wilder, Billy, 1906–2002—Criticism and interpretation | Motion picture industry—California—Los Angeles—History | LCGFT: Film criticism
Classification: LCC PN1997.S845 L82 2025 | DDC 791.43/72—dc23/eng/20250313
LC record available at https://lccn.loc.gov/2025009461

ISBNs: 9781538739297 (hardcover), 9781538739310 (ebook)

Printed in the United States of America

LSC-C

Printing 1, 2025

To Norma, Joe, and Max

CONTENTS

PROLOGUE: The Early Hours — ix

1. The Man in the Pool — 1
2. Glorious Gloria — 19
3. Writers in Wonderland — 38
4. "The Happiest Couple in Hollywood" — 53
5. Adultery, Addiction, and Mass Murder — 65
6. "The Foolishness of This Foolish Town" — 77
7. Finding Norma — 85
8. The Man You Love to Hate — 101
9. "Hello, Young Fellow" — 115
10. "Do You Know Bill Holden?" — 127
11. Locations: Real and Imagined — 137
12. A New Monkey for Norma — 148
13. Out with the Old, In with the New — 175
14. Getting Ready for Her Close-Up — 183
15. Reactions to *Sunset* — 199
16. What Became of . . . ? — 215

EPILOGUE: The Legacy of *Sunset Boulevard* — 239

ACKNOWLEDGMENTS — 243
NOTES — 245
PHOTO CREDITS — 291
INDEX — 293

THE EARLY HOURS

MONDAY, APRIL 18, 1949

Billy Wilder had reason to be anxious. He was about to start shooting his new film, *Sunset Boulevard*. A lot was riding on its success. An immigrant from Vienna by way of Berlin and Paris, he had finally found a niche in Hollywood as a writer and director, enough to afford a modest one-story home on a gently curving tree-lined road in Beverly Hills. But this new film was a gamble, even more so than usual. The sordid tale of Norma Desmond, a reclusive former movie star, and Joe Gillis, an unemployed screenwriter nearly half her age, whom she hires, takes as a lover, and murders in a jealous rage, it was also a movie about moviemaking, a genre that rarely did well at the box office. Moreover, the film starred Gloria Swanson, an erstwhile star of the silent screen who had not had a hit in two decades. Her costar, William Holden, was also a risky prospect, having been in the movie business for more than a decade without attaining prominence.

In recent years, Wilder had cowritten and directed two critically acclaimed hits: the groundbreaking film noir *Double Indemnity* and *The*

Lost Weekend, a searing drama about alcoholism that won two major Academy Awards. His next two films, however, were disappointments. *The Emperor Waltz*, a lightweight musical set in turn-of-the-century Vienna, had done well enough at the box office, though mostly on account of the popularity of its star, Bing Crosby. The other film, a sour satire titled *A Foreign Affair*, had caused a ripple of controversy by depicting the black-market activities of American army officers in occupied Berlin, but it did not live up to the studio's or Wilder's expectations.

In Hollywood, memories are short. Indeed, that was a major theme of the movie about to be shot: the agony of being overlooked or, worse, forgotten. Perhaps Norma Desmond, unwilling to accept the harsh Hollywood dictum that you're only as good as your last picture, was an avatar for Wilder himself, a projection of his own fear of being overlooked. He needed a comeback film. In an early scene, Joe Gillis tells Norma that he didn't know she was planning a comeback. "*I hate that word,*" she protests, scrunching her face: "It's a return, a return to the millions of people who have never forgiven me for deserting the screen." Whatever she might call it, she was in fact planning a comeback, and so, too, we might conjecture, was Billy Wilder.

A few miles away from Wilder's home on Beverly Glen, in a well-proportioned mansion on Bellagio Road in Bel Air, the movie's producer and cowriter, Charles Brackett, had concerns of his own. He and Wilder were the most celebrated writing-directing-producing team in the movie business, having received an Academy Award nomination in 1940 for cowriting Ernst Lubitsch's famous Greta Garbo comedy *Ninotchka* and for bringing home a pair of Oscars for *The Lost Weekend*. But the ground was shifting. Five months earlier, Billy had announced that *Sunset Boulevard* would be their final film together. Brackett was shattered by the news. In his diary, he wrote that he found himself depressed at the thought of "being alone in the cinema world for the first time in twelve years." Now no longer a young man, he doubted he'd ever work with another filmmaker as brilliant as Wilder. *Sunset*

Boulevard might well be his last chance at greatness, a chance he couldn't afford to squander.

Ultimately, the success of the new film would rest on the shoulders of its star, a woman twice the age of Hollywood's typical female lead. Having traveled by train from her home in Manhattan, Gloria Swanson had set up shop in a rented house on Horn Avenue in West Hollywood. Back in the town she had left behind some fifteen years earlier, she couldn't help but reflect on her past. She had led a dramatic life, both personally and professionally. Her career had begun in obscurity, reached its peak in the 1920s, and then, with the advent of talking pictures, faded into oblivion. In 1926, she was the highest-paid female performer in the world, earning nearly $20,000 a week as Paramount Pictures' biggest box-office draw. Twenty-two years later she was hosting an afternoon television talk show for less than $20,000 a year. Her last film, *Father Takes a Bride* (1941), had been a humiliating flop. Would *Sunset Boulevard* be yet another? Or would it provide the vehicle for her "return"?

That same morning on April 18, in suburban Toluca Lake, William Holden woke in a two-story, Georgian-style home with a mortgage that overshot his income. He knew he had not been Brackett and Wilder's first choice for Joe Gillis. Better-known actors had refused the role, fearing they would alienate their fans by playing a down-and-out gigolo. Holden, too, worried that playing love scenes with a much older woman would erode his already dwindling fan base. After an auspicious start to his career in 1939, when he won the coveted lead in a prestige picture called *Golden Boy*, Holden had failed to live up to expectations. Would *Sunset Boulevard* boost his flagging career or put an end to it?

Leaving behind his permanent residence outside Paris, Erich von Stroheim had rented a hillside villa on winding Oporto Drive in North Hollywood. No one in the cast or crew of *Sunset Boulevard* knew better the perverse cruelty of life—or, more specifically, that of Hollywood—than Stroheim, cast as a former filmmaker who had directed Norma

Desmond in the 1920s and was now her butler. Stroheim had in fact directed Gloria Swanson in the 1920s, when they were both at the peak of their powers, but the filming of *Queen Kelly* had gone terribly wrong, leading to the abrupt termination of his career as a director. Twenty years later, he still held Swanson responsible for the fiasco. As both the movie's star and its coproducer, Swanson had fired him before filming was completed. And now, ignominiously, he was to play her servant.

Living with an aunt and uncle in posh Pacific Palisades, Nancy Olson, twenty years old, was anxious to do a good job in the role of William Holden's love interest. But she was also giddy with excitement. Her future in movies looked bright. As a sophomore at the University of Wisconsin, she had impressed her acting instructors and, on their advice, transferred to the theater department at UCLA, where a talent scout from Paramount discovered her. Since then, she had appeared in one feature film: a forgettable western called *Canadian Pacific*. Innocent and girl-next-door-ish, she was known to her friends as "wholesome Olson." Thrilled to be cast in the latest film by the much-lauded Billy Wilder, she felt as though, to use a Wisconsin idiom, she had "fallen into a tub of butter." She knew Bill Holden by reputation to be a ladies' man. She knew Erich von Stroheim to have been a legendary director of the silent era. But she had never heard of Gloria Swanson. Her mother had to explain to her that Swanson was one of the most dazzling stars of the silent era.

A movie about has-beens and also-rans, about failed comebacks, misguided dreams, and murderous delusions, *Sunset Boulevard* was made by a raft of exceptionally creative individuals, all at critical junctures in their careers, several of them playing roles that seemed drawn from their actual lives. It wasn't merely their personal dreams and worries that would find such brilliant expression in this meta-film. It was also the anxieties of an entire industry on the edge of collapse or reinvention, depending on whom you asked. The old studio system was crumbling, a draconian blacklist was in effect, and a new medium was threatening to supplant movies, as talkies had supplanted silent films. Television was revolutionizing popular culture, and in only a few short years, half of all American homes would have one.

Clearly Hollywood was on the brink, but of what no one could safely say. The tensions of the principal actors and creators of the film that was about to go into production mirrored those of the industry at large. Yet these all had to be set aside early on a sunny morning in mid-April 1949. The makeup artists unpacked their brushes, and the electricians tested their lights. The well-oiled gears of the Hollywood studio system had begun to whir. *Sunset Boulevard* was at last under way.

In the summer of 1948, when Charles Brackett and Billy Wilder had their first inkling of the movie that would become *Sunset Boulevard*, all they knew was that it would involve a swimming pool in a Beverly Hills mansion owned by an aging movie star. Lacking a title, they referred to the germinating idea as both "the Hollywood story" and "the swimming pool story." The film they completed nearly two years later is indeed a swimming pool story. It opens with a dead man floating in a pool. The rest of the picture explains how he got there.

CHAPTER ONE

THE MAN IN THE POOL

He stood at the edge of the swimming pool. Heat radiated from the pavement. Laying aside his hat and shoes, he dove into the water and, with long even strokes, swam to the far end. It was a Sunday afternoon in July, the year 1934. Millions of Americans were suffering from joblessness, poverty, and hunger, although you wouldn't know it from this distinguished Beverly Hills gathering, attended by wealthy and influential German and Austrian exiles from the fatherland. He was not wealthy. Billie Wilder—who hadn't yet Americanized his name to Billy—was, in fact, poor, very poor. He had known poverty previously, when he left his home in Vienna for Berlin in 1926, at the age of twenty, but since coming to Hollywood in February, a refugee from Nazi Germany, he had sunk to a new level of penury, one that lacked the traditional nobility of a young man venturing forth to seek fame and fortune. He had been young when he first arrived in Berlin. Now, eight years later, he was no longer young.

Worse, he was trying—and dismally failing—to write screenplays in a language he could barely speak. The man who owned the pool and mansion, an expatriate German movie producer named Erich Pommer, had offered the out-of-work screenwriter $50 if he would dive fully clothed into the pool and swim to the other side. Another guest might have laughed off the offer. Not Billie Wilder. He needed the money. He also needed to be noticed amid this gathering of Hollywood swells.

★ ★ ★

Did this actually happen? Perhaps. And why not? Wilder was a showman with a flair for self-invention. The pool story is one of the many acerbic anecdotes about himself he loved to trot out in his rich Viennese accent. It made good copy, despite its ring of self-mythification. "When the legend becomes fact," says the newspaper editor in John Ford's western *The Man Who Shot Liberty Valance* (1962), "print the legend." Wilder made his early life into a series of legends, and, for the most part, he was the only surviving witness, which makes for difficulties in corroborating them. Whether or not they are true, the stories offer insight into Wilder, his worldview, and the emotional truths woven through his work.

First, the name: Billie. Wilder was born Samuel Wilder on June 22, 1906, in Sucha, a small town in the remote Austro-Hungarian province of Galicia, in what today is western Poland. As Wilder liked to say, he was born "half-an-hour from Vienna—by telegraph." His father, Max, the manager of a railway station café, had moved up the social ladder by marrying Eugenia Baldinger, a fellow Galician Jew whose widowed mother, Frau Baldinger, owned a resort hotel in the Carpathian Mountains. As a teenager, Genia, as she was known, had spent three years in New York living in a spacious apartment on Madison Avenue with the family of her mother's brother, a well-to-do jeweler. The highlight of her sojourn was a visit to the Buffalo Bill Wild West Show at Madison Square Garden. After returning to Galicia, she met and married Max Wilder. They named their second child Samuel after Max's deceased father, but Genia intended all along to call him Billie in tribute to Buffalo Bill. Bill was a resonant name in American popular culture of the Wild West: In addition to Buffalo Bill, heroic good guys and bad boys of western lore included Wild Bill Hickock, Billy the Kid, and the first western hero of the movies, Bronco Billy Anderson. As such, Billy was groomed from birth to be an appreciator of American popular culture, like his mother. After the Wilder family moved to Vienna in 1914, when Billy was eight and the Great War had just begun, he and his mother frequented the local cinemas, laughing at the slapstick comedies of Charlie Chaplin and Buster Keaton and thrilling to the exciting westerns of Tom Mix and other rope-twirling cowboys in white hats.

When Billy was ten, Max, who now owned a small hotel in the Jewish quarter of Vienna, took him to the Café Einstein on the Ringstrasse to watch the funeral procession of the Austro-Hungarian emperor, Franz Josef, who had occupied the throne for three-quarters of a century. Max Wilder venerated the sovereign because he had vigorously opposed antisemitic legislation. Max lifted Billy onto one of the café's marble tables for a better view of the street below. Under dark skies and roiling winds, imperial horsemen clad in ceremonial black uniforms, their mounts' heads topped with black plumes, advanced to the cadence of muffled drums. Franz Josef's coffin passed by, followed by an open-air carriage that displayed the new emperor, Karl von Habsburg, and his empress. Riding behind them, mounted on a pristine white pony and attired in an immaculate white uniform, his helmet topped by a white feather, was their son, Otto von Habsburg, a child of four.

Pointing to the boy in white, Max said to his son, "There is your future emperor.... Someday you will come here with *your* son and that boy will be your emperor." History proved Max wrong. The Habsburg monarchy did not survive the Great War. Twenty-five years later, Wilder, now among the highest-paid screenwriters in Hollywood, was having lunch in Paramount's commissary when a front-office executive in charge of foreign distribution asked him to give a private tour of the studio to a visitor whom he thought Wilder would enjoy meeting. The visitor, a nondescript middle-aged man in a rumpled gray suit, was none other than Otto von Habsburg, the little boy on the white horse, now eking out a living as a college lecturer on international relations. Their chance encounter drove home to Wilder the *vanitas* theme that he, along with his writing partner, Charles Brackett, would explore in *Sunset Boulevard*: Fame is fleeting, accolades transient, and dreams of glory easily foiled. This is one of the great preoccupations of world literature, from the Bible and the ancient Greeks to Shakespeare, Shelley, and beyond. But it was rarely broached in the feel-good cinema of Hollywood's golden age. *Sunset Boulevard* would prove an exception.

★ ★ ★

If one of the key themes of *Sunset Boulevard* is the ultimate futility of human endeavor, so too is the transactional nature of love, a topic Wilder explored almost obsessively. He had a lifelong fascination with love-for-hire in its many forms, one that was no doubt prompted by the milieu in which he was raised. In his posthumously published memoir, *The World of Yesterday* (1942), the Austrian novelist and historian Stefan Zweig recalled that in fin de siècle Vienna, "The sidewalks were so sprinkled with women for sale that it was more difficult to avoid them than find them....At that time female wares were offered for sale at every hour and at every price, and it cost a man as little time and trouble to purchase a woman for a quarter of an hour, an hour, or a night, as it did to buy a package of cigarettes or a newspaper." Likewise, Salka Viertel, an expatriate Austrian actress, screenwriter, and memoirist who hosted a weekly salon for fellow Austro-German expatriates in Hollywood, recalled that "Imperial Vienna exuded an intense erotic atmosphere. It was impossible for a young woman to walk alone without being followed. Alternating between the sentimental and the rudely obscene approach, men pursued one with undaunted persistence."

Not surprisingly, this atmosphere fostered in Wilder a cynicism toward romance. In high school, he spent several years looking out the classroom window at the pay-by-the-hour hotel across the street, where men and women entered together, only to leave separately a short time later. Imagining what went on inside inflamed Wilder's adolescent desires. Unable to afford the luxury of a room in even the cheapest of hotels, he opted, of necessity, for furtive back-alley sex.

Further disillusioning the young Wilder was his failed romance with Ilse, a "modern girl" who smoked cigarettes, wore short skirts, and shimmied to the syncopations of American-style jazz. He planned to marry her, until a friend tipped him off that he had seen her leaning on a lamppost in Vienna's red-light district. Years later, perhaps to save face, Wilder insisted to a biographer that he had known all along that his girlfriend was a sex worker: "She was very pretty, and I paid her. There were hookers in my life, but I was never in love with a hooker."

If Billy ever believed sex was meant to be an outgrowth of love and mutual respect, his affair with Ilse cured him of that illusion. It is hardly surprising, then, that a cynical view of heterosexual love characterizes many of his future films, including *Sunset Boulevard*, where Norma, desperate for companionship, shamelessly showers her paramour with expensive gifts and tailored outfits. Despite its ambiguously happy ending ("nobody's perfect"), *Some Like It Hot* is similarly driven by desperate characters seeking to exploit other characters for personal gain: Tony Curtis schemes to deceive and seduce Marilyn Monroe, who in turn aims to reel in a millionaire, while Jack Lemmon dons stockings and high heels in order to evade gangsters who are after him and later to woo a sugar-daddy millionaire who mistakes him for a woman. Wilder's characters do whatever it takes.

While still in high school, Wilder inadvertently opened a letter addressed to Max, whom, he discovered on reading it, had fathered an illegitimate son nearly Billy's age. When Billy confronted his father with this disturbing revelation, Max begged him not to divulge the secret to his mother. Billy agreed. But the knowledge festered in him, creating an emotional gap between son and father—and possibly between son and mother as well, since now he was colluding in her betrayal. Once again, young Wilder experienced love as fundamentally a source of pain, not pleasure. The encounter corrupted his faith in the family—his own, everyone's—and destroyed what remained of his childhood innocence. The film historian Charles Higham summarized Wilder's characteristically bitter view of humanity thus: "The world is ugly and vicious, selfishness and cruelty are dominant in men's lives. Greed is the central impetus of the main characters, and even the walk-ons . . . are cruel."

* * *

Though Billy himself preferred dancing and sports to academic endeavors, he was a bright young man whose impressionable mind could not help but absorb the potent atmosphere of post–World War I Vienna, where art, literature, drama, music, architecture, politics, and psychoanalysis all bubbled in fermentation. On finishing high school, Wilder took a job with the tabloid newspaper *Die Stunde* (*The Hour*), reporting on sporting events, thefts, murders, and the occasional double suicide. For a special December issue of the paper, Wilder was assigned to ask some of Vienna's most prominent citizens their views of Italian fascism. In a single morning he managed to converse with the composer Richard Strauss, psychotherapist Alfred Adler, playwright Arthur Schnitzler, and the founder of psychoanalysis, Sigmund Freud. Well, almost Sigmund Freud. Wilder caught a streetcar to Berggasse 19, where Freud both lived and worked. A maid answered the door and explained that the doctor was having lunch. Rising from the table to see who was calling, the Great Man came to the door with a napkin tucked under his chin. Annoyed by the interruption and contemptuous of journalists, he sent Wilder packing before the eager reporter could even pose his question.

While Wilder came of age in a Vienna populated with writers, artists, and intellectuals of what the historian Hilde Spiel called "Vienna's Golden Autumn," it seems likely that his taste in literature veered more toward the satirical journals that filled Vienna's newsstands. *Die Fackel* (*The Torch*) was edited by the humorist Karl Kraus, a master of the putdown. He accused psychoanalysts of picking "our dreams as if they were our pockets." He defined education as "what most people receive, many pass on [to others], and few have." More misanthrope than misogynist, Kraus wrote, "Women at least have elegant dresses. But what can men use to cover their emptiness?" The witticisms of Kraus, rather than the analyses of Freud, left their mark on young Wilder.

It was not only the pithiness of Kraus's aphorisms that would have impressed a youth such as Wilder, but also the coruscating cynicism behind them, which held nothing sacred. A Jew who converted to and then renounced Catholicism, Kraus mocked all religious faiths, the monarchy, the state, the courts, the schools, business, and the press. He mocked himself, and he mocked his readers. He was Vienna's most read and most debated author, and his one-liners clearly informed Wilder's future career as a master of sharp-edged dialogue. Wilder was also drawn to the drama and fiction of Arthur Schnitzler and the poetry of Strauss's librettist Hugo von Hofmannsthal. Both writers, like Kraus, attacked conventional bourgeois morality and viewed humanity with a jaundiced eye. Their writings appealed to young Wilder because they reinforced his own burgeoning realization that men and women were hypocrites by nature, hiding from others—and from themselves—their true beliefs and socially unacceptable desires.

Wilder thrived in this vibrant atmosphere in which no gods were held sacred. (In a different context, Norma Desmond would complain that the captains of the new Hollywood "took all the idols [of the silent era] and smashed them.") While vitriolic social critics such as Kraus deconstructed pretentiousness with epigrammatic precision, the modern architect Adolf Loos, whose anticonventional thinking Wilder admired, accomplished something similar in the realm of three-dimensional space. In 1910, Loos designed a small building for a tailor's shop on the square adjacent to the façade of Franz Josef's imperial palace. Fed up with the palace's gaudy Baroque ornamentation, Loos envisioned a building devoid of ornament. No squiggly moldings, no gaudy window trim, no nonfunctional dormers or picturesque peaked roofs. Viennese were outraged by what they considered an insult to their city's storied architectural grandeur. Coming and going from his palace, old Franz Josef allegedly closed the curtains on his carriage so that he wouldn't have to face Herr Loos's brutal minimalism. In defense of his controversial aesthetic, Loos gave a lecture titled "Ornament and Crime" to the local society of architects, stating that modern architecture should favor function over form; that gratuitous ornamentation was a "crime" against the purity and honesty of unadorned lines.

Wilder absorbed this anti-ornamental attitude, which was the bedrock of his later work as a filmmaker: He disdained camerawork, lighting, and editing that screamed for the viewer's attention. He regarded such techniques as arty and pretentious tricks. As he was fond of observing, "The best director is the one you don't see." In an interview, he once told a journalist, "You will not find in my pictures any phony camera moves or fancy setups to prove that I am a moving-picture director." Furthering the point, he added, "I like to believe that movement can be achieved eloquently, elegantly, economically and logically without shooting from a hole in the ground." (Here he seemed to have forgotten about the flamboyant shot of Joe Gillis's floating corpse taken from the bottom of a literal hole in the ground—a swimming pool.)

By the time Billy graduated from high school, the Loosian doctrine of minimalism was in the forefront of architectural theory, soon to be applauded by the likes of Le Corbusier in France and the International

Style architects Walter Gropius and Ludwig Mies van der Rohe in Germany. Young Billy imbibed this aesthetic in his personal as well as his professional life. Many years later, he and his wife, Audrey, would commission their modern designer friends Ray and Charles Eames to create a modernist glass-box home for them in the Hollywood Hills, but the projected costs proved prohibitive. Instead, they would move into an International Style apartment complex at 10375 Wilshire Boulevard in Westwood. The fourteen-story tower was designed by Victor Gruen (Grünbaum), an Austrian, Loos-trained architect who, like Billy, had escaped from the Nazis.

But that was decades into the young man's future. For now, he could only dream of escaping moribund Vienna, a city that, with the travails of the war and the demise of the Habsburg empire, had lost its glitter. With hyper-inflation choking the economy, Max Wilder lost ownership of his hotel and cycled through a series of downwardly mobile jobs and foolish get-rich schemes. His household was mired in disillusionment, secrets, and failure. Billy needed to get out of town.

In May 1926, an exit materialized. Paul Whiteman, the American bandleader known as the King of Jazz, was on a concert tour of Europe with his twenty-eight-piece jazz orchestra. Wilder interviewed him for *Die Stunde* at the elegant Hotel Bristol. Whiteman didn't speak German, and Wilder's English was barely serviceable, but Billy was immensely knowledgeable about jazz and offered to show the American musician the best jazz spots in town. After a night of eating, drinking, and listening to music at Billy's favorite establishments, Whiteman invited him to tag along when the band traveled to Berlin, the next stop on their concert tour. Wilder leapt at the opportunity. With no savings and no job in hand, the precocious young journalist, not yet twenty, followed Whiteman to Berlin, the capital of the deeply turbulent, politically divided, culturally explosive Weimar Republic. To Wilder, Vienna was the past, Berlin the future. Apart from one brief trip in 1935, he never returned home.

★ ★ ★

Wilder felt accepted in Berlin as he had never been in xenophobic Vienna, where he was twice-over a foreigner: a Galician and a Jew. In Weimar Berlin, people who were outsiders in their own lands were treated as insiders. Entirely different from the Austrian capital, the cosmopolitan and magnificently tolerant Berlin was a kaleidoscope of ethnicities and sexualities, a city that embraced the nonnative, that thrived on difference, where it didn't matter if Wilder was a Galician, an Austrian, a Jew, a tabloid journalist, or a young man whose pockets were perpetually empty. "Above all," wrote the journalist and historian Otto Friedrich, "Berlin in the 1920's [*sic*] represented a state of mind, a sense of freedom and exhilaration." Here the restless and ambitious filmmaker-to-be found his spiritual home.

Economically devastated by allied blockades during the First World War and the hyper-inflation that followed, Berlin had by 1926 roared back into its primacy, pulsating to the rhythms of nonstop industry and round-the-clock entertainment. Carl Zuckmayer, a playwright, remarked that Berlin sucked up human talents and energies "with tornado-like powers." He likened it to a "hugely desirable woman" whom everyone wanted and no one could resist: "The man who owned Berlin owned the world." Eric Weitz, the distinguished historian of Weimar Germany, contended that the frenetic social and cultural energy of the German metropolis—"its heady enthusiasms, its artistic experimentation, its flaunting of sexuality and unconventional relations, its vibrant, kinetic energy"—resulted from the vast disruptions of World War I: "An intense desire to grasp life in all its manifold dimensions, to experience love, sex, beauty, and power, fast cars and airborne flight, theatre and dance crazes, arose out of the strong sense of the ephemeral character of life, of lives so quickly snuffed out or forever maimed by bullet wounds and gas attacks."

Billy was confident he could live by his wits and end up rich. His plan was to support himself as a journalist while writing film scripts on speculation and eventually breaking into the movie business. Berlin boasted 120 newspapers and forty-five magazines, so finding work as a reporter was not difficult. Moreover, there were forty legitimate theaters and 360 movie production companies, most of them small, some enormous, like the world-famous UFA (*Universum-Film Aktiengesellschaft*) created by the German government during the Great War to counter Allied propaganda movies with films of its own. Wilder parlayed his expertise as a Viennese crime reporter, sports journalist, and celebrity interviewer into a job with one of the more popular Berlin dailies, the *Berliner Zeitung am Mittag*, known locally as the *B.Z.* He also wrote and occasionally sold twenty- to thirty-page scenarios for German silent films.

Neither reporting nor screenwriting paid well, and he supplemented his paltry income by working at Berlin's two most fashionable grand hotels, the Eden and the Adlon, as a "tea dancer" or "taxi dancer." Both terms were euphemisms for a dance partner or social (and perhaps sexual) companion available for hire: a gigolo (the term was coined in the 1920s). A smooth dancer with an even smoother wit, young Wilder was adored by the women, both American and otherwise, who sought male companionship. Being a gigolo was hard work with long hours, but he found it amusing. In 1927, when he was still twenty, he managed to capitalize on the experience by publishing a lighthearted, four-part series of magazine articles titled "'Waiter, A Dancer Please!'"

In 1928, when Billy was twenty-two, his father, who had come to visit him in Berlin, was suddenly struck down with an abdominal illness. He died a few days later. Billy and the rabbi who said kaddish in the Jewish cemetery in the Schönhauser Allee were the only mourners present. Years later, Billy named the long-suffering butler in *Sunset Boulevard* Max von Mayerling, perhaps in homage to his father. The butler's surname alludes to the notorious Mayerling incident from 1889 in which the thirty-year-old crown prince of Austria and his seventeen-year-old mistress committed a double suicide in a royal hunting lodge near the village of Mayerling; it gave Norma's lugubrious butler an appropriately character-specific association with scandal, tragedy, and *amour fou.*

Wilder's big break came when he was invited by several of his fledgling filmmaker friends, including the later-celebrated directors Robert Siodmak, Edgar G. Ulmer, and Fred Zinnemann, to write the script for what turned out to be one of the last classic motion pictures of German silent cinema: *Menschen am Sonntag,* or *People on Sunday.* The movie was part of a wider reaction in German filmmaking against the stylized gothic melodramas of German expressionism, as seen in films such as *The Cabinet of Dr. Caligari, Nosferatu,* and *Metropolis.* By the mid-1920s, a countervailing force in the German arts was the *Neue Sachlichkeit,* or New Objectivity, a serious effort to show daily life as it was, plain and ordinary, rather than ratcheted up to visual and emotional extremes. *Neue Sachlichkeit,* partially descended from the anti-ornamental and anti-rhetorical aesthetics of Adolf Loos and his followers, has also been translated as the New Sobriety or New Matter-of-Factness. It was not a uniquely German phenomenon, but it was understandably more prevalent among the losers of World War I than the victors. *People on Sunday* exhibits the spirit of this new objectivity, with its nonjudgmental, non-moralistic documentation of everyday life. Cast with nonprofessional actors, it's the simple, uneventful tale of two young men who spend a carefree afternoon in a park on the outskirts of Berlin with two young women they have just met. They talk, swim, picnic, listen to music on a portable gramophone, and find time for romance.

Shot with the spontaneity, flair, and good humor that became familiar to filmgoers some thirty years later with the rise of the French New Wave, *People on Sunday* is charmingly unplotted. It simply flows, thanks in large part to Wilder's unobtrusive writing. It might be regarded as his most light-handed script, modern not only in its lack of plot but also in its casual amorality. One of the men, a wine salesman, supplements his income by tea dancing, while the other, a two-timing cabdriver, leaves his sleepy-headed girlfriend back in his apartment while he cavorts with his new female acquaintance. Romance, it seems, is a whim of the moment. An amorous encounter in the bushes culminates drolly with the woman pulling a pinecone out from beneath her bottom, too caught up in the ardor of the moment to have removed it sooner. As was to be characteristic of Wilder's subsequent career, chivalric codes of love and romance go out the window. The sexual urge is ultimately biological, his films maintain, and in accordance with nature, despite the selfish or power-playing ends to which any attempt to satisfy that urge may lead.

The movie, which opened at the cavernous U. T. Kurfürstendamm Theater in the spring of 1930, ran continuously for six months. Scriptwriting offers poured in. Billy could pick and choose at will, no longer needing to dance with wealthy older women for pay. Instead he took up with a wealthy younger woman, Hella Hartwig, whose family owned a pharmaceutical company. They moved in together, and Billy indulged himself as only the formerly deprived could do. He purchased an expensive convertible, collected modern art (this was to become a lifelong passion), and ordered bespoke suits. Everything he had dreamed of was now within his grasp.

Three years after the premier of *People on Sunday*, Adolf Hitler swept into power as chancellor of Germany. Billy knew he would have to leave as soon as possible. The morning after the German Parliament building, the Reichstag, burned to the ground, effectively bringing the Weimar Republic to a rude termination, he and Hella set off for Paris, all their savings converted into gold coins hidden in the band of his hat.

With a modicum of high school French at his disposal, Wilder made his way in the French film industry, cowriting and codirecting his first film, a fast-moving caper called *Mauvaise Graine* (*Bad Seed*). It's the story of a rich playboy who takes up with a ring of car thieves on the French Riviera and falls in love with the gang leader's sister, played by Danielle Darrieux in her first starring role. It has car chases, romance, and a climactic shoot-out with the police, but not the acerbic wit and incisive characterization that would later make Wilder famous. Still, it was an impressive directorial debut. It would be another eight years before he was behind the camera again, this time in Hollywood.

In early 1934, Wilder's friend Joe May (born Josef Otto Mandl), a fellow Austrian who had achieved considerable success as a filmmaker in German silent cinema before relocating to Hollywood at the rise of Hitler, used his connections to get Billy a six-week contract with Columbia Pictures. Columbia was one of the smaller of the eight major film studios, run autocratically by mogul Harry Cohn, who, together with his trusted lieutenant Sam Briskin, approved the idea of bringing in this reputedly clever Austrian to write the script for a backstage musical called *Pam-Pam*. It was to be along the lines of Warner Bros.' hit Busby Berkeley musicals *Footlight Parade* and *Gold Diggers of 1933*, but with the addition of criminals. Joe May would direct. Columbia wired funds to Wilder to pay for his one-way passage on the *Aquitania*. Promising Hella he would send for her at the earliest opportunity (which he never did; she quickly receded into his past), Wilder crossed the Atlantic in late January 1934.

When he reported for duty in early March, Columbia was basking in the extraordinary success of its new release, *It Happened One Night*, a delirious comedy directed by Frank Capra, with Claudette Colbert as a runaway heiress traveling incognito and Clark Gable as the hard-boiled reporter who discovers her on a night bus to New York and protects her identity for the sake of an exclusive story. Despite constant bickering and a series of misadventures, they fall in love. Cohn and Briskin were eager for more stories of a similar nature, and perhaps *Pam-Pam* would fit the bill. Unfortunately, when they met Wilder, they were outraged. Their new hire couldn't speak proper English: "I—I—been—Austrian," he stammered, when introducing himself. If he couldn't speak the language, how was he going to write credible dialogue? Only five or six years earlier, before the advent of talking pictures, a nonnative speaker like Wilder could have made a good living by inventing stories and devising incidents, but talkies required talk, the more colloquial and fast-paced, the better. Billy tried to explain that he would compose in his native language and then be translated, but Wilder wasn't Ibsen. The project died.

With little money at his disposal, the hapless immigrant rented a room in Joe May's house and purchased a used car—a 1927 DeSoto. Like Joe Gillis at the start of *Sunset Boulevard*, he needed a car to look for work, but, also like Gillis, he couldn't find anyone to hire him. He had the additional problem of an expiring visa. He crossed the border to Mexico, where he joined thousands of other refugees waiting for visas, some of them stranded for months. For Billy, it happened to be only a matter of days, since he convinced a US border official that he was already an established Hollywood screenwriter. The official, an avid filmgoer, stamped his documents and urged the young Austrian to write some good movies in his new homeland. Or so Wilder recounted in 1988, when accepting the prestigious Irving G. Thalberg Memorial Award from the Academy of Motion Picture Arts and Sciences.

Returning to Los Angeles still without a job, Wilder secured a cheap room adjacent to the women's toilets at the Chateau Marmont, a relatively new and at that time inexpensive residential hotel perched on a hillside above Sunset Boulevard. He subsisted by living on canned beans, and his sleep was punctuated by the flushing of commodes. He said he could trick himself back to sleep by pretending he was staying in an expensive spa, hearing the magical sounds of a waterfall outside his window. Years later, when he was rich and famous, he stayed at exactly such a spa in Germany, only now he couldn't sleep because the waterfall outside his window sounded to him too much like those flushing toilets. Or so he said.

Displaying a fanatical desire to learn English, Wilder quickly realized that spending too much time with Joe May and his wife and other German and Austrian émigrés to Southern California was not going to make this happen; "I learned by not associating myself with the European refugee colony," he later explained. Instead he preferred to chew the fat with bartenders, taxi drivers, hotel clerks, and, above all, the young American women living alongside him at the Chateau Marmont. Finding them eager to provide free after-hours instruction, he pursued them with eagerness and charm. According to Wilder, the Chateau Marmont night clerk noticed the nocturnal comings and goings and expressed amazement that the foreigner with the thick accent and thinning hair was such a hit with the ladies.

By day, Billy's radio broadcast the patter he longed for. He especially liked listening to soap operas, with their convoluted narratives but clearly enunciated dialogue, and baseball games, where the announcers' animated play-by-play descriptions transformed his shabby hotel bedroom into a breezy grandstand on a splendid, sun-filled afternoon. (This was long before the Brooklyn Dodgers moved to Los Angeles, but LA abounded with minor- and sub-minor-league teams that a listener could choose among.) For the rest of his life, he preferred hearing baseball on the radio to attending a game in person or watching it on TV, because that method, he believed, gave his mind and imagination the greatest scope.

Still, he maintained intermittent ties with the colony of German and Austrian writers, composers, artists, and filmmakers who had taken refuge in Los Angeles. The more highbrow of these expatriates, such as Thomas Mann, Arnold Schoenberg, Otto Klemperer, and Theodor Adorno, gathered frequently at 165 Mabery Road in Santa Monica. Two blocks from the Pacific Ocean, this was the address of Salka Viertel, who cultivated a German-language salon that also included European artists such as Igor Stravinsky and Greta Garbo for whom Deutsch was not a native language. Wilder was rankled by what he regarded as the pretentions of intellectuals who, by and large, disdained the culture industry (Adorno's derogatory term) that Hollywood epitomized— and that the young Austrian was eager to crack. One filmmaker the movie-averse intellectuals at Viertel's salon did admire was Erich Pommer, who had produced several classics of the German screen, including *The Cabinet of Dr. Caligari*, *Metropolis*, *The Last Laugh*, and *The Blue Angel*.

These last two films, both starring the famed actor Emil Jannings, recount tales of humiliation. In *The Last Laugh*, Jannings plays the head doorman at a grand Berlin hotel. Wearing a military-style greatcoat with epaulets and brass buttons, he takes inordinate pride in his position, until one day the manager declares him too old for the job. Without the impressive coat and now relegated to cleaning toilets, Jannings spirals into despair. In *The Blue Angel*, Jannings has a similar role, this time as a pedantic and middle-aged high school teacher who becomes desperately infatuated with a young nightclub singer (Marlene Dietrich). Making a fool of himself during her cabaret act, he loses his job and ultimately the last vestiges of his self-respect.

Now settled in Hollywood, Pommer, the master of on-screen humiliation, amused his poolside guests one summer afternoon in 1934 with a live scene of humiliation: offering Wilder cash for diving into the pool fully clothed. Of course, maybe neither Pommer nor Wilder thought the offer humiliating. By all accounts, Pommer was a genial man who had occasionally given film work to Wilder during their Weimar days. Perhaps his motivation was to help the impoverished young writer without embarrassing him with an outright cash gift, or maybe he simply wished to amuse his guests. Wilder did not hesitate. It was a paying opportunity, and his cash supply was lower than low. If this was how Hollywood worked, if gratifying the whims of the wealthy was the game he had to play, the former gigolo would do whatever it took.

✶ ✶ ✶

Sunset Boulevard opens with a fully clothed man in a swimming pool, only this time the man is dead. Joe Gillis, a thirty-year-old failed screenwriter, isn't going anywhere. He's stuck in place. Not so "Billie" Wilder, who easily reached the opposite end of the pool. Not long after this baptismal dunk into the waters of Beverly Hills, he christened himself "Billy" Wilder.

Pommer hired him to help adapt the lighthearted Broadway musical *Music in the Air*, written by the popular songwriting team of Jerome Kern and Oscar Hammerstein II. Joe May was to direct. Pommer also hired Billy's fellow refugee from Nazi Germany, a young composer named Franz Waxman, to adapt the music. The actress whom Pommer had in mind for the lead, Gloria Swanson, had been one of the great movie stars of the 1920s, though her career had faltered with the coming of sound. Pommer believed she was up to the task. The story concerns an opera singer in Munich who, to make her romantic partner jealous, unsuccessfully seduces a much younger man, a songwriter from the Bavarian Alps. Swanson herself had trained as an opera singer and possessed a natural comic touch. It was Wilder's job to write sparkling dialogue for her. He did his best, but the movie failed at the box office. Indeed, it was Fox Pictures' greatest flop of 1934. Audiences who had loved Swanson as a pert young thing in the 1920s could not warm to her in the role of a jealous older woman seeking the attentions of a younger man. The film killed what was left of her Hollywood career and didn't do much for Wilder's, either.

Fifteen years later, he cast her as Norma Desmond.

CHAPTER TWO

GLORIOUS GLORIA

Wait a minute," says Joe Gillis as he is kicked out of the bedroom of an imperious woman in black who has realized her error in thinking him the pet undertaker she had summoned, "haven't I seen you—?"

She threatens to call her servant. "I know your face," Gillis continues, combing his memory. "You're Norma Desmond. You used to be in pictures. You used to be big."

Her eyes locking with his in fuming indignation, she snarls, "I *am* big. It's the pictures that got small."

The same could be said of the actress who played Norma Desmond: Gloria Swanson, who in the 1920s was the most-photographed woman in the world. At her death in 1983, the *New York Times* noted that she "was young when the movies were young, and has to be mentioned in the same breath with Douglas Fairbanks, Charlie Chaplin, Mary Pickford, Rudolph Valentino. Unlike her peers, however, she eclipsed the successes of her youth with one remarkable performance in middle age"—as Norma Desmond, that is, in *Sunset Boulevard*. In a movie that plays with levels of reality, mixing real people and places with fictitious ones, Gloria Swanson seemed to be Norma Desmond in the flesh.

At the zenith of her career, Swanson was among Hollywood's greatest celebrities, beloved by legions of fans who were whipped into a constant state of adoration by a popular new medium, the movie magazine, *Photoplay* being the best known. These slick, inexpensive, amply illustrated, gossip-filled, mythmaking periodicals proliferated in the 1920s and attained nationwide circulation by breathlessly reporting the off-screen behavior of movie folk, especially that of mega-celebrities such as Swanson.

A reciprocal relationship evolved: Fan magazines couldn't thrive without movie stars, and movie stars couldn't maintain their hold on the public without fan magazines. The studios encouraged viewers who favored one star or another to establish fan clubs, which proliferated nationally and internationally. The stars (or, more likely, their personal assistants) scrawled signatures on glossy headshots and sent them out to worshipping fans (short for "fanatics"), who treated them like holy icons. Studio publicity departments, as well as fashionable magazines such as *Vogue* and *Vanity Fair*, hired glamour photographers including Clarence Sinclair Bull, George Hurrell, and Ruth Harriet Louise—who themselves became minor celebrities—to use state-of-the-art lighting techniques, camera lenses, and film emulsions to endow movie stars with an aura of mystery and beauty, making them irresistible objects of both desire and veneration.

In a particularly striking glamour photo, Edward Steichen portrayed Swanson with her face hidden behind a patterned veil. As he recounted in *A Life in Photography*, "At the end of the session, I took a piece of black lace veil and hung it in front of her face. She recognized the idea at once. Her eyes dilated, and her look was that of a leopardess lurking behind leafy shrubbery, watching her prey. You don't have to explain things to Miss Swanson. Her mind works swiftly and intuitively." Cecil B. DeMille, who knew all about glamour, said of Swanson, "When you put them all together and add them up, Gloria Swanson comes out the movie star of all movie stars. She had something that none of the rest of them had."

The star system itself was a modern invention. In the early days of cinema, movies were made with anonymous performers, but audiences began clamoring to know the names of the actors they wished to see more of. Afraid of having to raise actors' salaries, studios enforced anonymity instead. Biograph Studios, for example, made numerous movies in the early 1910s with a young Canadian actress whom they identified only as "the Biograph Girl." Intrigued, the public demanded to know her actual name. It was Florence Lawrence, and she is often regarded as the first non-anonymous movie star. By the early 1920s, with the increased sophistication of the star-making apparatus, Gloria Swanson became a household name.

Swanson detailed the ups and downs of her acting career, and those of her personal life, in her bestselling autobiography, *Swanson on Swanson*, published in 1980, three years before her death. The movie star's sensational memoir is filled with old-time melodrama, not unlike the movies she made during the silent era. Swanson described the privations of her childhood, a secret abortion at the height of her fame, her six marriages and numerous love affairs, her extraordinary popularity with movie audiences and film fans, and her several reversals of financial fortune. In *Sunset Boulevard*, Norma says she hates the word *comeback*, but the truth is that Swanson had four or five comebacks after costly flops had seemingly ended her career. With *Sunset Boulevard*, made when she was fifty and long out of the public eye, she staged the greatest comeback in film history.

★ ★ ★

Swanson got her start in movies by accident. At fifteen, she toured Chicago's Essanay film studio, best known for producing slapstick comedies, and made an unexpected impression on the resident filmmakers. Struck by the girl's appearance, a director offered her employment as an extra. Her mother, Addie, who was separated from Gloria's father, approved, and, within weeks, Gloria went from extra to bit player to stock player. At first, Essanay did not identify her by name, but her dark good looks caught the attention of moviegoers—as well as that of Essanay's star attraction, Charlie Chaplin, who had temporarily left Los Angeles for the lucrative contract Essanay offered him. The British comedian, who was not yet world-famous, considered casting her as the leading lady in *His New Job* (1915) and spent a morning rehearsing with her. Gloria couldn't mesh Charlie's sense of humor with her own: "I felt like a cow trying to dance with a toy poodle." Exasperated, he told her she lacked comic timing. In turn, she informed *him* that his pratfalls were vulgar. Impressed with her spirit, Chaplin gave her an uncredited bit part in the film, where, with copious hair piled atop her head, she appears as a stenographer unobtrusively typing at a desk in the back of the shot; look too quickly, and you'll miss her altogether.

If Chaplin, an inveterate womanizer, had romantic designs on this fetching adolescent, he appears not to have pursued them. Not so a rough and burly second-banana Essanay actor named Wallace Beery, who was primarily known for cross-dressing as Sweedie, a Swedish housemaid, in a series of buffoonish comedies. In *Sweedie Goes to College* (1915), the sixteen-year-old Swanson received screen credit for playing a stylish coed. She thought the movie "vulgar, disgusting and stupid," but, like other young female players at the studio, she developed a crush on Beery. At the end of a day's filming, he would drive her around town in his speedy roadster. Gloria was infatuated with him, even though—or because—he was nearly twice her age.

When the irate parents of another underage girl at the studio accused Beery of inappropriate behavior, he moved to the West Coast branch of Essanay outside San Francisco and resumed his acting career with little interruption. Shortly after, Gloria persuaded her mother to accompany her to Los Angeles, where she hoped to become a star. As ambitious for her daughter as her daughter was for herself, Addie agreed. Gloria secured an audition with Mack Sennett, the head of Keystone Studios, famed for short comedies including those of the lovably incompetent Keystone Cops. The producer was a notorious philanderer. Years later, an associate recalled that the studio boss's "door and his fly were always open. No girl ever got on the lot if she hadn't first been on his casting couch." In his own memoir, Sennett remembered that Swanson's audition took place at night, but if it involved sex, he never said as much, nor did she. He recalled being struck by Gloria's magnificent light-blue eyes: "It isn't a trick of make-up that beams them at you from the screen."

Nicknamed "Baby Gloria" because of her chubby cheeks and diminutive stature (approximately five feet), Swanson created an on-screen stir. Meanwhile, Beery, who had left Essanay and was now himself working for Sennett, wooed Gloria in a lightning-fast campaign that culminated in marriage. Their wedding, attended by Addie and officiated by a justice of the peace, took place on the bride's seventeenth birthday. In her autobiography, Swanson claimed that her thirty-year-old groom raped her on their wedding night: "I was brutalized in pitch-blackness by a man who whispered filth in my ear while he ripped me almost in two." Afterward, while he snored away, Swanson cowered in the bathroom, where she tried to stanch the bleeding. Her pain was excruciating—physically, but also emotionally. Disgusted by his crude and violent behavior, she told herself it was only to be expected, for, as she wrote, "It's a man's world." Nevertheless, she was determined to make a good wife for him.

And so she did—until she discovered she was pregnant. According to her account, Beery gave her a morning-sickness drug that she later discovered was an abortifacient. The under-the-counter drug put an end to the pregnancy and landed her in the hospital. With that, the marriage was over, as far as she was concerned, and she moved back in with Addie. Beery begged her to return to him, and ultimately she did. Yet she continued to loathe everything about him, including his touch, which revolted her.

More surprising still, she agreed to act with him in a series of lightweight but popular Keystone comedies. This being an era in which dialogue could only be relayed through intertitles, comedies had to rely instead on nonstop action; humor was to be found in comic timing and amusing situations. *Teddy at the Throttle* (1917), for example, earned laughs by parodying the popular railroad-rescue serials from earlier cinema; here the villain is played by Beery and the heroine by Swanson. Resourcefully, Gloria's character, tied to the tracks, scribbles a plea for rescue and gives it to her Great Dane, Teddy, who leaps out a window, jumps from a cliff into a river, dog-paddles against the current, bounds over the tracks, catapults himself onto the speeding train, and delivers the note to the engineer, who tries but fails to stop the locomotive in time to save his beloved owner. She, meanwhile, has dug a hole into which she lowers herself moments before the slowed-down train passes over her head. Swanson insisted on doing the beneath-the-tracks stunt herself; it may have been the first, but wouldn't be the last, time she did her own stunts.

The essence of the film lies in its speed, not its story. *Teddy at the Throttle* capitalizes on one of the signal fascinations of the early twentieth century. In Italy, the futurists extolled fast bicycles, hurtling automobiles, and soaring biplanes as mechanical symbols of modernity. Transportation was not the only conductor of speed; so, too, were new modes of communication, including one-, two-, or three-reel movies that appeared to have been filmed only yesterday (a reel lasted approximately twelve to fifteen minutes, depending on the speed of projection). The breakneck speed of *Teddy at the Throttle* suited the velocity-mania of the times.

In another Sennett comedy, *The Danger Girl* (1916), Swanson played a type of liberated young woman that was rapidly emerging in American society. In the 1920s, such women would be called flappers or modern girls: sexy, sophisticated, self-confident authors of their own destiny. A modern girl unabashedly consumed fashion and beauty products to help her attain a level of autonomy not available to previous generations.

Modern girls were politically progressive in the sense that their unconventional, even anti-traditional, ways of carrying themselves amounted to an assault on conservative mores and social values. Flaunting their bodies with short skirts, flimsy dresses, and the newfangled brassiere (invented in 1913), bobbing their hair, drinking bootleg alcohol, smoking cigarettes like a man, driving cars like a man, syncopating their bodies on the dance floor to the hot rhythms of jazz, "dating" (a new term) men without the surveillance of a chaperone, and defiantly claiming control of their sexuality, modern girls were advance troops in the cultural wars of the day between big-city progressive modernity and small-town conservative backlash. Swanson was Hollywood's first modern girl; others to follow included Clara Bow, Louise Brooks, and Joan Crawford.

Danger Girl was rushed into production with virtually no discernible plot, which may madden the current viewer but did not bother audiences of the time, who relished seeing the heroine drive fast, repair her car, and change a flat tire, all activities that were stereotypically ascribed to men. To further the gender-bending, Gloria's character cross-dresses—in white tie and top hat, no less—to seduce and then expose a woman who is trying to steal the affection of her boyfriend. Swanson said she drew on Wally Beery's masculine swagger and other physical mannerisms to make her pseudo-male characterization plausible. Gloria's rival, thinking Gloria is male, falls in love with her, and Gloria, emerging from her disguise, wins back her man. Films such as these put their finger on the pulse of a new world, the so-called Jazz Age, where modern girls rejected the Victorian mores of their mothers and grandmothers as readily as they rejected their foremothers' corsets and crinolines.

By 1919, Swanson had finally divorced Beery, left Keystone Studios, and begun working with Hollywood's leading director, Cecil B.

DeMille. Her first and very successful DeMille film, *Don't Change Your Husband,* was one of six domestic comedy-dramas she would make with him about modern marriage; another was called *Why Change Your Wife?* (1920). Typically, she played a timid housewife who comes to embrace the new consumer ethos of the Jazz Age—that is, to become a modern girl. Captivated by Swanson's youth, beauty, and energy, her fans clamored to see more of her on screen.

In *Why Change Your Wife?,* she played a frumpy housewife who makes no attempt to keep lit the flame of conjugal romance. When she rejects the revealing lingerie that her husband buys for her because she does not find it practical, he takes up with the shopkeeper who modeled it for him. Seeing the error of her ways, Swanson, in an about-face, decides to embrace a host of beauty treatments, along with the latest fashions in both outerwear and underwear, and thus wins back her husband. Lesson learned. The final intertitle of the film makes the nature of the lesson clear: "And now you know what every husband knows, that a man would rather have his wife for his sweetheart than any other woman, but Ladies, if you would be your husband's sweetheart you simply *must* learn to forget when you're his wife."

DeMille's marital comedies may have been humorous, but they touched on a serious social issue of the day: divorce. As the marriage rate rapidly increased in the United States after the First World War, so, too, did the rate of divorce. In 1910, there were 4.5 divorces per one thousand residents; by 1920, the rate had nearly doubled to 7.7. (A century later, in 2020, the divorce rate had dropped to 2.3 per one thousand.) The United States led the world in the annual number of divorces. Fears of abandoning their children had previously prevented women from seeking divorce, but that changed with the advent of family planning; it was easier for women to sue for divorce if children were not involved. In 1914, the birth control activist Margaret Sanger knowingly violated Comstock Laws by distributing contraception information through the mail. In 1916, she opened America's first birth control clinic, and in

1921, she founded the American Birth Control League, the precursor organization to Planned Parenthood. By the 1920s, then, women had legal options available to them for choosing not to produce children, which afforded them a greater degree of control over their destinies than previous generations had known.

Another factor in the rising rate of divorce was the growth of cities. The 1920 census showed that for the first time more Americans lived in big cities than in small towns. In small-town communities, where everyone knew everyone else—and their business—it was more difficult to dissolve conjugal relationships than it was in the cities, where, with increased anonymity and autonomy, young people felt less constrained by the watchful eyes of their neighbors and elders to remain in marriages that no longer satisfied them. In this regard, not only Hollywood movies but also its movie stars made divorce appear to be an acceptable option. Gloria Swanson herself epitomized the multi-married, multi-divorced Hollywood star. She married six husbands over the course of her life and divorced all six of them. Swanson, the ultimate modern girl, seemed to change lovers as frequently as she changed her wardrobe.

In fact, her wardrobe was integral to her stardom. Referring to her latest release, DeMille's *For Better, for Worse* (1919), she told her public, "I have worn about twenty-five or more different gowns, and I know they all cost a lot of money. When I have them on, I am in heaven. Every woman loves to be dressed up in expensive creations." To this she added, "All during the day I am a queen, garbed in all the wonders of the costumer's art; then, when we quit work…I am nothing but a poor actress again, in my simple dress. It's really pathetic. I think it's quite sad." Swanson knew better than anyone how to play the Cinderella card; she portrayed herself as an ordinary woman who, like her fans, dreamed about fashionable clothing but, unlike them, actually got to wear it. If her dreams could come true, why couldn't theirs?

Fans thus went to her movies eager to see what she wore. The plot of *Under the Lash* (1921; not a DeMille picture) called for her to be dressed shabbily throughout. Her devotees were disappointed. Jesse Lasky, the studio's head of production, vowed not to make that mistake twice, and from then on Swanson was always appareled on screen—as well as off screen—with the most fashionable and expensive clothing available. *Photoplay* reported that the star was earning more than $1 million a year and spending it liberally: $500,000 on jewelry, $50,000 on gowns, $25,000 on furs, $10,000 a year on lingerie, $9,600 on silk stockings, $6,000 on perfume, and $5,000 on purses. At that time the average annual household income was $3,269.40.

When at the height of her fame she took the exorbitant costs of her personal wardrobe as a business expense, the Internal Revenue Service balked, demanding $15,000 in back taxes, threatening to charge her with criminal fraudulence. She argued that the public expected her to be always attired as a star and never to be caught wearing the same outfit twice. The IRS dropped the criminal charge against the actress but collected the fifteen grand they insisted she owed.

A 1923 *Photoplay* article captioned, "You've wondered about Gloria Swanson's real personality. Here it is," provided photos of the star posing on the grounds of her twenty-two-room Mediterranean-revival mansion located off Sunset Boulevard. According to *Photoplay*, Swanson had transformed herself into "the most irresistibly beautiful creature on the screen" by means of her superb fashion sense, savvy use of makeup, and charismatic personality. The author of the piece, Adela Rogers St. Johns, a journalist, novelist, and screenwriter who would later become a good friend of Swanson's, gushed, "I would rather look at Gloria than all the rest of them [female stars] put together.... I never have any idea what her pictures are about. I just like to gaze at her."

A great measure of Swanson's appeal came from her idiosyncratic appearance: She simply didn't look like anyone else. Movie-star historian Larry Carr, observing that Swanson "contributed immensely to a new look for women," wrote that she "changed the concept of beauty from one of doll-like pastel prettiness of sugar-spun perfection to one of intelligence, emphasizing bone structure, strong features and a smooth clean line of individuality." By sheer force of personality, Swanson "turned her nonconforming features to advantage by accentuating their unusual, distinctive points: the large almond-shaped eyes, the tilting nose, the dazzling square smile with the Chiclet teeth, set in a face that achieved beauty in its own way, quite unlike anyone else before or since."

Swanson accepted the idiosyncrasies of her body and face. She refused plastic surgery to "correct" what might have been viewed as deficiencies. Cosmetic surgery was a relatively new medical procedure in those years, developed by necessity during the Great War to aid soldiers who came out of trench warfare with severely damaged faces. The intervention gained popularity, especially among movie stars, in the 1920s. Swanson, however, held that the body was sacred and should not be tampered with; instead, it should be treated lovingly, through rest, exercise, and healthy diet. She did indulge herself with massages performed daily by Sylvia Ulback, known to the movie colony as Sylvia of Hollywood, Masseuse to the Stars.

She applied makeup liberally to enhance her facial features. Modern girls were not afraid to wear makeup; indeed, they called attention to it. In this, they defied Victorian and early-twentieth-century codes of female deportment imposed by guardians of public morality who regarded makeup as a tool of the devil. As late as 1915, the Kansas legislature proposed to make it a misdemeanor for women under the age of forty-four to wear cosmetics with the intention of misleading men.

In *True Heart Susie*, a 1919 melodrama by the social and political reactionary D. W. Griffith, Lillian Gish played a pure and simple country lass who wins back her errant boyfriend from a femme fatale who has ensnared him with her abundant use of makeup. An intertitle reads, "Do not men look for the true heart in women? Or are most of them caught by the net of paint, powder and suggestive clothes?" At no point during *True Heart Susie* does Gish appear on screen *without* makeup, even though the movie takes a stand against the vanity that its usage is said to imply. DeMille also tried to have it both ways. His movies, unlike Griffith's, overtly glamorized sex and artifice (makeup, lingerie, coquettishness, et cetera), but in the end they, too, proclaimed patriarchal family values: His women might walk on the wild side for much of the picture, thus satisfying viewers who were eager to ogle the latest fashions and hairstyles, but the heroine's fulfillment required her to return to the nest properly chastened for her wayward behavior.

★ ★ ★

The biggest hit of DeMille's marriage series and the film that elevated Swanson to stardom was *Male and Female* (1919), a movie in which the protagonists are married neither to each other nor to anyone else. A very loose adaptation of *The Admirable Crichton*, a popular play by Sir James M. Barrie (author of *Peter Pan*), *Male and Female* tells of a party of British aristocrats on a yachting holiday who are marooned on a desert island with their butler, Crichton. Lady Mary Lasenby, played by Swanson, had previously treated the butler with haughty disdain, but not so on the island, where she succumbs to his ultra-masculine, take-charge authority. DeMille titillated audiences at the start of the film, pre-shipwreck, with a scene of Lady Mary disrobing in a bathroom with the assistance of two maids, who help her down the steps to a sunken tub while at the same time obscuring her nakedness from the audience; he then used colored water to hide her breasts. This was one of the first movies ever to show a bathtub, and a luxurious bathtub at that. In 1920, only 1 percent of Americans had indoor plumbing, and certainly not private bathrooms as grand as this. Audiences hungered for glimpses of haute-bourgeois commodities, such as fashionable clothing, yachts, and luxurious indoor plumbing, that they could only dream of acquiring for themselves, and *Male and Female* provided these aplenty: The titillation was not only sexual but also commercial.

Following the shipwreck, Lady Mary emerges from the water in a wet and revealing dress. At the premiere of *Male and Female*, recalled Swanson, the audience collectively gasped "when I walked out of the Santa Cruz surf" wearing a "shredded satin evening dress soaked and clinging to my skin." But her most titillating outfit appeared in a fantasy sequence in which Swanson wears a towering headdress composed of white peacock feathers and a low-cut, formfitting, peekaboo beaded gown, complete with a train. The gown was made entirely of pearls and white beads and was so heavy that two assistants were required to help her move about the set. This highly sexualized costume was created by DeMille's protégé, the young set decorator and costume designer Mitchell Leisen, who in the late 1930s and early 1940s became one of the top directors at Paramount. Brackett and Wilder provided scripts for three of his hit films, and Brackett, without Wilder, wrote and produced a fourth.

At the climax of the fantasy sequence, Lady Mary, imagined by her now dominant butler to be a virgin slave in ancient Babylon, lies facedown and motionless on the floor of a lion's den while a king lion rests his paw on her naked back and snarls in a display of ownership. In *Male and Female*, the shot lasts no more than an instant, but it stunned audiences with its shocking verisimilitude. Swanson was now touted as highly for her bravery as for her costumes.

★ ★ ★

By 1925, at twenty-six, Swanson ranked among the film industry's highest-paid performers and was said to be the world's most-photographed woman. "Every important photographer both in Europe and in America took her portrait," wrote glamour historian John Kobal. "One could mount a survey of great early 20th-century portrait photography and photographers using just her pictures."

Women around the globe imitated her haircuts (which varied widely from film to film), clothing styles, and facial expressions. Theater owners called her the mortgage lifter, because, she explained in her memoir, "beginning with *Male and Female*, all they had to do was put my name on the marquee and watch the money roll in. It didn't matter very much if the pictures I played in were good, bad, or so-so. People went to all of them. They thought of me as part of their families. They liked to visit me regularly; see if I had changed since the last picture."

The outlandish costumes she wore on the screen, at parties, and in the pages of the fan magazines made her unquestionably the most glamourous star of her era. The word *glamour*, originally meant to describe the hypnotic and potentially deadly attractiveness of a sorceress, was little employed before the 1920s, until Swanson came along and brought it into common usage. Her fans were bewitched, rapturously following her every move, on screen and off.

While shooting a film in France, *Madame Sans-Gêne* (1925), a romance of the French Revolution, Swanson, not speaking French, was assigned a full-time translator. His name was Henri de La Falaise, the Marquis de La Coudraye. Strikingly handsome, the marquis had won the Croix de Guerre for heroism during the Great War, but, like many aristocrats of the time, he was landless and penniless. Inevitably, they fell in love.

After the film wrapped, Gloria and Henri made an unannounced visit to the town hall in Passy, a village on the outskirts of Paris, where they married in a civil ceremony attended by a handful of guests. No one, including Henri, knew she was pregnant. It was a secret she guarded carefully, even from him. She feared that if it was discovered she had conceived a child out of wedlock—and worse, that she did so while her divorce from her previous husband, Herbert Somborn, had not yet been finalized—it would ruin her career: "What I knew is that if I had Henri's child in seven months, my career would be finished.

The industry and the public would both reject me as a morally unsound character, unfit to represent them."

In response to a series of shocking sex, drug, and murder scandals in the early 1920s that had shaken the public's faith in Hollywood, the studios had set up a self-censorship bureau commonly referred to as the Hays Office, because it was headed by the former US postmaster general William Hays. To protect their investments further, studios also insisted that their top stars, Swanson included, sign strict morality clauses, which would, it was intended, keep them free of scandal, which at that time was seen as bad for business. These contractual clauses stated that a studio employee would be summarily fired if found to have engaged in indecent or immoral behavior. Swanson's clause specifically stipulated that she could not engage in sexual relations with a man while she was still married to another. In a decision she regretted for the rest of her life, she had an abortion.

According to Swanson's autobiography, the procedure was bungled, and she lapsed into fever. For weeks, she wrote, "I lay between life and death in a Paris hospital, having nightmares about the child I had killed, wishing I were dead myself." She announced to the press that her prolonged hospital stay was the result of internal injuries sustained from a riding accident. Her recovery room was flooded with flowers, letters, and telegrams of affection and concern from friends, acquaintances, and the public at large. Swanson never revealed the name of the doctor who performed the procedure. In France up until the end of World War II, the penalty for providing abortions was execution by guillotine.

As soon as Gloria was strong enough to travel, she and Henri sailed for America. When the ocean liner docked in New York, they were greeted by throngs of fans and reporters. At the New York premiere of *Madame Sans-Gêne*, the streets outside the theater were so clogged with her admirers that traffic had to be rerouted. Paramount booked a private train to transport Gloria, Henri, and a large entourage of studio executives and theater owners to the West Coast. Though dangerously exhausted, Swanson roused herself to greet her fans, many of them adoring schoolchildren, who gathered in wait for her at whistle-stops along the way.

After they reached Los Angeles, which she had not seen in two years, she paid a call at Paramount. The chief executive, Adolph Zukor, had arranged for all his employees to gather inside the studio's gate to greet her. She arrived in a chauffeured, open-air limousine upholstered in faux leopard skin. This made a lasting impression on a young costume department assistant named Edith Head, who a quarter of a century later would design Swanson's leopard-print accessories for *Sunset Boulevard* with that extraordinary day in mind. Paramount's female employees, Head included, flung rose petals at Swanson's tiny feet. In *Sunset Boulevard*, the fictitious Norma Desmond arrives at that same gate, only no one is waiting to greet her, let alone fling rose petals, and the sole person to recognize her is a studio cop even older than she is.

That night, Swanson, now a marquise, and her handsome husband paraded down the aisle of a majestic motion picture palace for the West Coast premiere of *Madame Sans-Gêne*. Its title, roughly translated as "Madame without Embarrassment," was ironic indeed, since she was surfeited with embarrassment and shame. When Gloria, in a silver lamé evening gown, and Henri, in an evening suit festooned with ribbons and medals—including his Croix de Guerre—entered the theater, the audience leapt to its feet and cheered wildly, while an orchestra struck up "Home, Sweet Home."

Gloria's response to such adulation was mixed. "Would they have forgiven me, all these glamorous people? Would they have thought I had sufficiently paid by nearly dying of blood poisoning in a Paris hospital? I honestly didn't care...their hypothetical forgiveness meant nothing to me. The only thing that mattered was whether I would ever be able to forgive myself." She ruminated, "Even if [movie impresario] Sid Grauman built me an Arch of Triumph in California as colossal as the one in Paris, it would always have a tomb under it, the tomb of an unknown baby who had picked Henri and me for parents and was now dead." In this maudlin passage from *Swanson on Swanson*, in which self-pity vies with self-aggrandizement, the former movie star at last revealed her long-held secret. Indeed, the five-hundred-page memoir opened with the incident.

On the heels of her triumph with *Madame Sans-Gêne*, Paramount offered Swanson an astronomical multimillion-dollar annual salary; only a minuscule number of Hollywood stars, male or female, earned that much. Eager to strike out on her own, however, Gloria turned down the offer and instead joined United Artists, a powerful consortium of independent film producers organized in 1919 by Chaplin, Douglas Fairbanks, Mary Pickford, and Griffith. More important to her than making money was making movies, quality movies over which she had full control. And that is what she immediately began to do, forming Gloria Swanson Productions and becoming one of the first female film producers in the history of Hollywood.

Unfortunately, her initial independent production, *The Love of Sunya* (1927), performed poorly at the box office. The second, *Sadie Thompson* (1928)—an adaptation of Somerset Maugham's controversial play *Rain* about a prostitute in the South Seas—did well at the box office and earned Swanson a best actress nomination in the first year, 1929, that the newly established Academy of Motion Picture Arts and Sciences handed out awards. True to form, she arrived at the ceremony in a gown embroidered in puce that matched the tones of her chauffeured limousine. She lost to Janet Gaynor.

Her third production, *Queen Kelly* (1929), directed by the controversial "genius" Erich von Stroheim and coproduced by the Boston financial wizard Joseph P. Kennedy, went so far off course during filming that she pulled the plug halfway through, saddling herself with debts it took decades to pay off. (Kennedy was not only Swanson's business partner but also her lover; she was still married to Henri, and he was married to

Rose Fitzpatrick Kennedy, the mother of his eight children, including his son Jack, a future president of the United States.)

Swanson's first talking picture, *The Trespasser* (1929), showed her making a smooth transition from silent pictures to sound. A tearjerker about maternal self-sacrifice, *The Trespasser* was a box-office and critical success, earning Swanson her second Academy Award nomination. She and Greta Garbo, who starred in *Anna Christie*, both lost to Norma Shearer in *The Divorcee*.

Despite healthy revenues from *The Trespasser*, the insurmountable burden of debt from *Queen Kelly* brought her production company to an end, and Swanson went back to acting as her sole source of income. In a reminiscence about the volatility of Swanson's career, Adela Rogers St. Johns wrote:

No other star ever turned down a contract which agreed to pay $26,000 every week, fifty-two weeks every year for five years. That would have amounted to $6,760,000 in the days before big income tax. La Belle Swanson, at twenty-seven, then the best dressed woman in the world, a public idol, brushed it aside and two years later she was broke—and I mean flat broke....Never did the pendulum of success and failure swing to such violent extremes as it did with Swanson.

Swanson transitioned into talking pictures more successfully than many actors of her generation. Critics praised her strong, clear, and nuanced voice. The film reviewer for the *New York Times*, Mordaunt Hall, applauded her performance in *The Trespasser*: "She is more of an actress than ever, speaking her lines naturally and without unnecessary pantomimic gestures. Her work is restrained, even in the emotional scenes." The historian of early sound cinema Richard Barrios has written that with *The Trespasser*, Swanson made "the most spectacular sound debut of any silent favorite except the white-hot Garbo."

Her sound debut may have been spectacular, but the magic didn't last. Vocal and acting styles were rapidly changing, as characterized by the more modern, street-smart speech of the new generation of female film stars such as Barbara Stanwyck, Jean Harlow, Bette Davis, and Claudette Colbert, actresses who could reel off one-liners with an alacrity and verve that Swanson could not match. By comparison, her voice sounded shrill, and her mannerisms seemed unnatural. In the handful of talking pictures she made from 1929 to 1934, she was at her best during largely dialogue-free scenes that showed off the comedic skills, especially the talent for mimicry, that she had perfected in the silent years.

Ironically, Swanson's inability to deliver her lines colloquially would serve her well in *Sunset Boulevard*, signaling her "pastness" throughout the film. She and Stroheim, in vivid contrast with William Holden, Nancy Olson, and the film's other younger cast members, are mummified vestiges of an earlier era. They are the equivalent of celestial stars, whose light reaches our eyes long after they have ceased to emit it.

In 1934, Erich Pommer cast Swanson in his film *Music in the Air*, a frothy operetta with dialogue cowritten by the Hollywood newcomer Billy Wilder. Prophetically, she played an aging diva who sets her sights on a handsome (song)writer a decade younger than she. The movie was a box-office disaster, leading Swanson, a woman who prided herself on her lack of illusions, to retire from movies.

CHAPTER THREE

WRITERS IN WONDERLAND

The delicate and perpetually frustrating art of writing for the screen was a subject of considerable interest to Brackett and Wilder, who had each struggled to make a name as a screenwriter—Wilder twice, first in Berlin, then in Hollywood. True professionals, they were fascinated by writing and its vicissitudes. No surprise, then, that the main characters in *Sunset Boulevard* are all writers or would-be writers. Joe Gillis, a hack who couldn't sell a screenplay during his lifetime, delivers a whopper of a tale from beyond the grave. Norma Desmond, his lover and murderer, is desperate to sell her muddled script, devising plots even more hackneyed than his, while Betty Schaefer, the woman Joe falls for, a story analyst for Paramount, is herself a fledgling screenwriter. Even Max von Mayerling, Norma's butler, is a writer of sorts, surreptitiously penning fake fan mail to post to her every day.

Norma tells Joe she rues the day that movies were taken over by "talk, talk, talk" and strangled by "a rope of words." But it is the superbly crafted script for this story of failed, naive, or incompetent writers that pulls us in with its brilliant use of language. *Sunset Boulevard* is a dazzling testament to the art of "talk, talk, talk" on the movie screen, and it resounds not only with first-rate banter and aspersive dialogue but also with an ever-present voice-over narration, a species of extended monologue.

As the film's central consciousness, through which everything is filtered, Joe appears in almost every scene. The movie, however, is not simply the story of one feckless writer but of all writers in Hollywood who endure indignity after indignity before either quitting the business (in Joe's case, that meant going back to his former job at the copy desk of the *Dayton Evening News*) or somehow managing to attach their names to a successful picture. Both Brackett and Wilder had spent years in the wilderness before making their mark, and they wove into Joe's story some of the slights and humiliations they had suffered. Even after being hired on a film, screenwriters were subject to the whims of directors, producers, and movie stars, who, having no respect for a finished script, could twist it around any way they liked.

Thinking about the would-be screenwriter Betty, Joe muses, "She was so like all us writers when we first hit Hollywood—itching with ambition, panting to get your names up there: Screenplay by. Original Story by. Hmph! Audiences don't know somebody sits down and *writes* a picture. They think the actors made it up as they go along." Or as Billy Wilder once observed, "Most people do not say clever or interesting things. That is why they have to pay clever screenwriters so much money to make up these clever things."

★ ★ ★

Unlike Billy Wilder, Charles Brackett came from a privileged background. His ancestors arrived in the New World only a few years after the *Mayflower*. One of his great-uncles invented the Corliss Steam

Engine, a powerhouse machine that was featured at the Centennial Exposition of 1876 and played a pivotal role in the industrialization of Gilded Age America. Despite Brackett's well-to-do upbringing, his childhood was marked by tragedy. When he was eight, his older brother, Edgar, accidentally shot himself in the leg with a starter's pistol. A tiny metal fragment that broke away from the barrel ripped into Edgar's flesh. The wound did not appear serious, and it caused the boy only minor discomfort. A few days later, though, while the family was at supper, he had difficulty swallowing. Charlie, too young to understand the seriousness of the moment, thought it was a joke and giggled. Their father, a prosperous lawyer, banker, and state senator from Saratoga Springs, New York, shouted in alarm for the little boy to be quiet. Two days later, Edgar died from lockjaw. Until his own death twenty years later, Charlie's father never said another word to him. He could only communicate with his father through the medium of writing. And thus, out of necessity, Brackett learned from an early age to put his feelings into words—or use them to disguise or abate those feelings. Words, he found, could provide him with an emotional shield, and for the rest of his life they served as armor against his own persistent self-doubt and chronic self-loathing, which he kept well hidden from everyone, confiding them only to his rigorously candid private diary.

After graduating from Williams, Brackett served in the diplomatic corps of the American Expeditionary Forces in France. While he was there, his mother submitted one of his short stories to the *Saturday Evening Post*, which ran it. Despite earning a law degree from Harvard and being nominally appointed vice president of the family-owned bank, he wanted nothing more than to be a creative writer. Before long he was contributing stories to the *Post* and *Vanity Fair* and publishing novels as well. In 1926, Harold Ross, the cofounder of a new magazine called *The New Yorker*, hired him as a replacement for the magazine's original drama critic, the cantankerous, heavy-drinking, and remarkably witty Herman J. Mankiewicz, who had left the drama desk to try his hand in

Hollywood. ("Mank" later cowrote, with Orson Welles, the script for *Citizen Kane*.)

Brackett's theater reviews, typical of the magazine at that time, were light and fluffy, more given to clever one-liners than serious critical assessments. The house style of *The New Yorker* depended for its existence, wrote the literary historian John W. Aldridge, "upon a view of the world as a vast cocktail party where the very best people say the most frightening things about themselves and one another in a language which the servants are not expected to understand, where the most tragic confession of personal ruin is at once diluted by the ironic twitter in the speaker's voice...."

Brackett's fussy prose exemplifies the brittle sophistication—or pseudo-sophistication—that Aldridge described. Of a musical comedy titled *Naughty Riquette*, Brackett wrote, "Its pachyderm caperings almost crushes [*sic*] me to speechlessness." Or, in a theater review from a few weeks later: "The production of *Kaja the Dancer* is a little like one of those jewel-boxes in cook's room one admired so extravagantly in childhood, but in the crumply velvet at the bottom of it lies a trinket which, though it has been trodden under heavy heels, still glitters a little and has smartness." His review of the comedy *The Play's the Thing* described it as "a comedy which a great many not sophisticated people are going to love 'because it's so sophisticated.'"

At the same time Brackett was reviewing theater for *The New Yorker*, he honed his wit at the Algonquin Hotel, located on 44th Street in Midtown Manhattan, where an informal group of New York actors, authors, producers, critics, and columnists gathered at a large round table in the Rose Room to trade barbs. Regulars included humorists Robert Benchley, George S. Kaufman, Harpo Marx, Alexander Woollcott, and Dorothy Parker, whose fame today rests mostly on her quip about leading "whores to culture" and various other linguistic somersaults ("I'd rather have a bottle in front of me than a frontal lobotomy"). In her later years, Parker offered a devastating assessment of the Algonquin wits (herself among them), contending that their reputation was undeserved. "These were no giants. Think who was writing in those days—Lardner, Fitzgerald, Faulkner, and Hemingway. Those were the real giants. The Round Table was just a lot of people telling jokes and telling each other how good they were. Just a bunch of loudmouths showing off, saving their gags for days, waiting for a chance to spring them.... There was no truth in anything they said. It was the terrible day of the wisecrack, so there didn't have to be any truth."

Parker had a point. Still, their verbal adroitness was perfectly suited to the coming of sound in the late 1920s. Wisecracking, dependent on quick wit and rapid verbal exchanges, became a necessity in audio cinema as directors sought ways to offset the sluggishness of the early sound cameras. Movie moguls, made insecure by the new, unfamiliar medium of talking pictures, grabbed for people already celebrated for their mastery of words: novelists, playwrights, theater critics, and journalists who had shown themselves adept at turning out fresh copy on tight deadlines.

Brackett, no longer *The New Yorker*'s theater critic but well published as a novelist, was summoned to Hollywood in September 1932 to do exactly what Norma Desmond would have reviled: add dialogue to a romantic tale being developed by RKO. The proposed movie was inspired by a magazine article about the real-life romance in the mid-1920s between the heavyweight boxing champion Jack Dempsey and the motion picture star Estelle Taylor. The original article had been penned by Gloria Swanson's friend Adela Rogers St. Johns. As yet untitled, the movie was to be directed by the successful Broadway theater director turned filmmaker George Cukor and produced by the dynamic young David O. Selznick, who at age thirty had become RKO's head of production.

When Brackett arrived from the East Coast, Cukor befriended him, introducing him to his largely gay inner circle of writers, actors, directors, and interior designers. Brackett's social calendar filled quickly, and everyone seemed to like him, but that was not enough to guarantee tenure in Hollywood. It was one thing to write criticism but another altogether to construct a compelling drama. Brackett did not yet grasp the rhythms of cinematic storytelling. His efforts to add plot complications to the story by Rogers St. Johns did not go over well. "I don't see it that way at all," she chided him during a story conference: "The boy loved that girl. The girl loved that boy. They loved each other." Brackett found her comment maddeningly simplistic, but he was only the writer, and he had no say in the matter. He was dropped from the project.

Perhaps his instincts were right, since the proposed film never reached the screen. That said, the team of Cukor and Selznick, working from another original idea by Rogers St. Johns, knew how to tell a good story. They had previously scored success with an inside view of the movie business titled *What Price Hollywood?* (1932). The tale of a Hollywood hopeful on her way up who is discovered by an alcoholic director (or actor or musician) on his way down was remade four times over the next nine decades under the new title *A Star Is Born* (1937, 1954, 1976, and 2018).

Brackett was hired by another RKO producer, Merian C. Cooper (who had previously produced *King Kong*), to adapt Louisa May Alcott's *Little Women*. He raced through the book and produced a treatment within weeks but again failed to please his employers. When *Little Women* appeared two years later, in 1934, it won an Academy Award for its two credited screenwriters, the married couple Sarah Y. Mason and Victor Heerman, while nine other writers, Brackett among them, received no credit at all. (Directed by Cukor, the film made a star of an ethereal young theater actor from back east named Katharine Hepburn. Dorothy Parker once sniped that Hepburn's acting skills "ran the gamut of emotions from A to B.")

RKO did not renew Brackett's contract. This mortified him. Whatever intellectual scorn he might have felt for Adela Rogers St. Johns and her ilk, he blamed himself for his inability to play the game. Before leaving Hollywood, he paid a courtesy call on Selznick. According to

Brackett's diary, the young producer apologized that the studio had not been able to make proper use of the writer "of known attainments" that he was. Characteristically self-critical, Brackett chastised himself for "the smallness of [his] accomplishments" and for daring to imagine himself "a flourishing author and a well-known one" when, in fact (or so it seemed in his dark mood), that was not the case.

When he ran into Selznick at a party in New York later that year, he was "inordinately pleased" when the producer told him that he "was the only author he had ever known to leave Hollywood like a gentleman." It was a classic case of damning someone with faint praise, however sincerely it might have been offered. Brackett confided to his diary, "As I write, I am just about passing into my 40th year, and I am as discouraged about my career as one can be who is cursed with a foolishly sanguine disposition." He concluded the entry, "I have an interesting, scattered life, and I have gotten nowhere and I am getting nowhere. I wish I knew the answer."

Two years later, he published *Entirely Surrounded* (1934), a breezy roman à clef about his friends from the Algonquin Round Table, among them the humorist Alexander Woollcott, the alluring magazine illustrator Neysa McMein, and Dorothy Parker, to whom he dedicated the book. In an undated notebook entry, F. Scott Fitzgerald, who knew Brackett from summers with their respective families on the French Riviera, remarked about one of Brackett's novels, "I finished it [in] six and a half minutes while getting a shave in the Continental Hotel. It is what we call a book written at a fine pace." He didn't identify the novel, but all five of Brackett's have the same problem: They're shallow and breezy, without offering much in the way of narrative structure, depth of characterization, or richness of language. Nonetheless, with the commercial success of *Entirely Surrounded*, Hollywood again came calling. Willing to give the film business another try, Charlie moved west with his wife, Elizabeth Barrows Fletcher Brackett, and their two young daughters.

Now on contract to Paramount instead of RKO, Brackett worked on numerous scripts concurrently, as was the custom for lesser-known writers. When he finally did receive screen credit, the film was a flop. *Rose of the Rancho* (1936) was a tepid story of adventure and romance in Old California. Critics and audiences alike shunned it. Noting that he was the last of eight writers listed in the credits, Brackett confided to his diary, "All the composure and perspective I acquired in the East collapsed like foam. Though basically in agreement with the reviews, I resent them hotly." He concluded with an entreaty: "May God give me strength never to accept a really silly project again."

Rose of the Rancho was unusual for listing eight writers in the credits. Mostly, contributing writers were not acknowledged. It was common practice in Hollywood to have writers "write behind" the work of other writers, all in the producers' hopes of turning out a box-office hit. During development and then production of *Gone with the Wind*, which reached the screen in 1939, Selznick hired eighteen writers, most of them uncredited.

Brackett was not alone in his distaste for the assembly-line approach to screenwriting. As Leo Rosten, the sociologist of Hollywood, observed in 1941, "The Hollywood writer is not writing prose or producing literature. He is feeding an enormous machine that converts words, faces, sounds, and images into some nine thousand feet of celluloid. His material is thrown into a hopper of movie making, where other men and minds, other preferences and prejudices, grind it into pieces and champ it into a pattern no one of them completely controls or envisages." The screenwriter Dalton Trumbo said it more tartly: "The system under which writers work would sap the vitality of a Shakespeare. They are intelligent enough to know they are writing trash but they are not intelligent enough to do anything about it."

Writers in Hollywood made considerably more money than they could earn in New York, but they enjoyed considerably less prestige. Unlike fiction writers and playwrights back east, Hollywood writers were workers for hire at the start of a process that churned out movies as Detroit did cars. As the crime novelist and sometime screenwriter Raymond Chandler noted from personal experience, in Hollywood the screenwriter is "an employee without power or decision over the uses of his own craft, without ownership of it, and, however extravagantly paid, almost without honor for it."

★ ★ ★

Dorothy Parker moved to Hollywood in 1933 with her second husband, a handsome stage actor turned writer named Alan Campbell, with whom she formed a writing team. Brackett was the best man at their wedding. Parker's career as a screenwriter illuminates the frustration and self-loathing later felt by Brackett and Wilder's fictional creation Joe Gillis. She, like so many of her (and Brackett's) East Coast peers, disdained the very medium by which she earned vaster sums than she could ever make as a writer at home in New York. Between 1933 and 1938, Parker and Campbell received screen credits for fifteen films, all forgotten today, apart from the first version of *A Star Is Born*, which earned them, together with Robert Carson, an Oscar nomination for best screen adaptation. The nomination only confirmed for Parker her cynical view that she and her husband were "working for cretins."

The distinguished New York playwright and much-in-demand screenwriter Sidney Howard noted in 1937, "There has existed among authors... a great snobbery against writing for pictures. The New York author has been ashamed to engage himself in it and the screen writers have been hypersensitively defiant about it." Donald Ogden Stewart, one of the most highly remunerated romantic comedy writers of the 1930s (*Holiday*, *Philadelphia Story*), recalled that "The competition was very great—you couldn't make mistakes because there were other writers waiting to step in and fix your script up the way you were fixing someone else's." Because "producers had the theory that the more writers they had to work on the scripts the better they would be," the secret to success as a screenwriter was to be hired after a script had already gone through two or three—or more—iterations, and production deadlines demanded that further rewriting cease. "It became a game to be the last one before they started shooting so that you would not be eased out of the screen credit."

According to Brackett, Campbell did more of the actual work on the Parker-Campbell screenplays than Parker did, but it was her reputation as one of the premier wits of the 1920s that got them hired. Campbell rather liked Hollywood, but Parker despised it and everything it stood for: vulgarity, vacuity, and idiocy.

★ ★ ★

Parker slyly remarked that the only "ism" adhered to in Hollywood was plagiarism. But in fact, in the politically tumultuous 1930s, the movie town was roiled by three or four major isms: capitalism, communism, trade unionism, and antifascism. During her years in Hollywood, Parker became increasingly militant about left-wing political causes, particularly the formation of the Screen Writers Guild, a trade union that she and nine other screenwriters initiated in 1933. In doing so, she was taking a stand against the studios that made her a wealthy woman, risking the displeasure of the bosses who were adamantly opposed to collective bargaining by the writers.

The movie moguls had a particularly paternalistic view of labor in all aspects of the motion picture business, but whereas they could accept the fact that the members of the various trades (electricians, carpenters, costumers, musicians, and so on) organized themselves into craft guilds, they felt that for the writers to do so was a sign of ingratitude. In the cleverly named book *Stars and Strikes*, an early (1941) historian of labor in Hollywood wrote, "Within the tall gates of each major studio are between two thousand and three thousand employees—actors, writers, directors, stenographers, architects, carpenters, painters, electricians, cameramen and sound men, to mention but a few of the 276 trade and professional groups involved in the making of a feature picture." The members of those "legitimate" unions worked with their hands, but the writers worked with their *minds*. Almost by definition, writers were individualists, each of them following the dictates of his (or, more rarely in sound-era Hollywood, her) personal imagination. What would happen if these individualists were to organize? Surely, they would lose both their individuality and their creativity.

Moreover, the system operated in such a way as to incite Darwinian competition among the writers, rather than build communal solidarity. Writers were played off against one another, competing, whether directly or indirectly, with other writers who were also brought onto the project in question. The same principle did not hold for the craft departments; it would not be efficient to set the carpenters or the painters or the focus pullers in competition with one another, but wouldn't more writers lead to a greater abundance of usable ideas?

The most outspoken opponent of the guild in its formative stage was Irving G. Thalberg, the revered head of production at MGM. "Among the producers," wrote Ian Hamilton, "Irving Thalberg was the most vehement and active opponent of the Guild, furious and puzzled that 'his' writers didn't come to him when they had problems." Veteran screenwriter Frances Marion pointed out that "We would not have blinked had L.B. [Mayer] roared out a threat to close the studio unless we gave up the guild idea, but when Irving Thalberg made his threat in chilling tones we were shocked into a dread silence, which revealed his enormous power over us."

Joining Howard and Parker in establishing the guild were Philip Dunne (later to write the pro-union *How Green Was My Valley*), Donald Ogden Stewart, and other left-wingers. The odd man out in the group was Charlie Brackett, a lifelong Republican, who had not yet made a name for himself in Hollywood. What prestige he possessed was left over from his *New Yorker* and Algonquin Round Table days, and that was running out fast.

Brackett had a sense of justice and fair play. Sometimes his largesse was private in nature, as when in the summer of 1938 he nursed Dashiell Hammett through his many drunken binges, paying his gambling debts, liquor bills, and six months' back rent at the Beverly Wilshire Hotel before putting him on a plane to New York, where Lillian Hellman was waiting to care for him. Brackett twice served as the vice president of the guild's executive board and once as its president. His stolid demeanor may have lent the radicals a certain amount of cover. "If I were casting a picture and I needed a perfect Supreme Court judge, it would be Charles Brackett," said his writing partner, Billy Wilder.

Though his political sympathies were with the left, Wilder generally avoided politics. A refugee from Hitler, he believed he was vulnerable to deportation for expressing thoughts that might be judged anti-American. With the Nazi specter looming over Europe, deportation to Austria would have amounted to a death sentence. He feared for the lives of his mother and grandmother, who still resided in Vienna, but he was slowly climbing the American ladder of prestige and fortune, enjoying the material and psychological benefits his accomplishments accrued. Why mess with success?

Other founding members of the Screen Writers Guild included Hammett, Hellman, Nathanael West, Ogden Nash, and the married team of Frances Goodrich and Albert Hackett, who during this period wrote the witty scripts for *The Thin Man* films based on Hammett's novel. Not all movie writers joined the guild or supported its mission. Herman Mankiewicz, a highly paid maverick who worked as a ghostwriter on numerous movies, *The Wizard of Oz* among them, objected to screenwriters forming a guild, seeing no purpose for it. Joe Mankiewicz, his younger brother, was an outspoken proponent for the guild, claiming that the best-paid writers in Hollywood owed it to the lowest-paid to help them earn respectable wages and not be ill-treated by the studios.

Those same studios tried many tactics, including sweet-talking and strong-arming, to prevent the writers from ratifying the guild, but they were unable to stop the train from leaving the station thanks to the National Labor Relations Act (known as the Wagner Act) passed by Congress in 1935. The act guaranteed the right of private-sector employees to organize into trade unions, engage in collective bargaining, and take collective action. In addition, it prohibited employers from threatening to fire employees who joined the union, thus depriving studio bosses of a significant lever of power.

★ ★ ★

One of the best novels about Hollywood, Budd Schulberg's *What Makes Sammy Run?* (1941), uses the creation of the Screen Writers Guild as its main subplot. Schulberg, twenty-six when he wrote the novel, had a ringside view of the troubled formation of the union. On one hand, he was a political radical who campaigned vigorously for the guild. On the other, he was the son of B. P. Schulberg, one of Hollywood's pioneer movie moguls, who had been a business partner of Louis B. Mayer before breaking off to help form Paramount Pictures in the mid-1920s. Young Schulberg had grown up knowing Mayer as Uncle Louie. After graduating from Dartmouth, he was hired by Selznick, another offspring of Hollywood royalty, as a script polisher for the *Star Is Born* screenplay written by Parker, Campbell, and Carson. Budd's low-paying, $75-a-week job was seen by his father, Uncle Louie, Irving Thalberg, Samuel Goldwyn, and others of the studio elite as a brief apprenticeship for the young prince of Hollywood before he took his rightful place among the bosses.

Told in the first person by a fictitious Hollywood screenwriter named Al Manheim, *What Makes Sammy Run?* chronicles the rags-to-riches rise of a hustler named Sammy Glick. Born to immigrant Jewish parents in the slums of the Lower East Side, Sammy works his way up the ladder of success, but not with the Horatio Alger combination of luck, pluck, and a good heart. Instead Sammy lies, cheats, flatters, cajoles, plagiarizes, and sleeps his way to the top. By the end of the novel, he is poised to run a Hollywood studio. The book mounts a strong criticism of the movie industry, but Schulberg, a member of the American Communist Party, clearly intended to go after a larger target than Hollywood: capitalism itself. Sammy represented not only Hollywood types, and not only Jewish ones at that (Schulberg, a Jew, was criticized for fueling antisemitism), but go-getter Americans in every line of work and every ethnicity who gamed the system.

Before the book appeared in print in 1941, Schulberg's "Uncle Louie" tried to block its publication, claiming, as he was later to do with *Sunset Boulevard*, that it portrayed Hollywood in a negative light. The independent producer Samuel Goldwyn offered Schulberg $1,000 not to publish it, saying it reinforced the most heinous stereotypes about Jews. Goldwyn, who had long ago changed his name from Sammy Goldfish, may also have worried that readers would assume Sammy Glick, né Glickstein, was modeled on him. Schulberg ignored the pressure. The novel quickly became a bestseller, despite publisher Bennett Cerf's warning to the young author that books about Hollywood don't sell: "The problem is that people who read novels have no interest in Hollywood, and the people who go to movies don't read books."

★　★　★

A popular refrain among Hollywood writers went like this: "They ruin your stories. They massacre your ideas. They prostitute your art. They trample on your pride. And what do you get for it? A fortune." Most writers didn't earn a fortune or anywhere near it. In his early years in Hollywood, Brackett had to rely on private income, particularly from his wife's family, while Wilder, with no private income, took refuge beside a women's lavatory at the Chateau Marmont. The four-story Paramount writers' building, jokingly referred to as the Tower of Babel, housed more than a hundred writers separated into tiny offices. On their own, neither Brackett nor Wilder achieved notice among this throng, let alone distinction. Brackett, as self-doubting as ever, contemplated leaving the movie business again and returning to New York with his family. Wilder contemplated no such thing; going back to Nazi Berlin was not an option.

All this changed when Manny Wolfe, the head of Paramount's writers' department, brought the two writers face-to-face in the summer of 1936. "Charlie Brackett," he said, "meet Billy Wilder. From now on you're a team." They'd been chosen to write a new film for Ernst Lubitsch.

CHAPTER FOUR

"THE HAPPIEST COUPLE IN HOLLYWOOD"

Late at night on August 17, 1936, Brackett recorded in his diary the most noteworthy event of the day: "I am to be teamed with Billy Wilder, a young Austrian I've seen about for a year or two and like very much. I accepted the job joyfully." Brackett, a courtly, Ivy League patrician, wrote and spoke elegant English; his new partner, a brash Central European immigrant who had left university after only a term, barely spoke English at all. Brackett, quiet and sedentary, his thick head of hair parted down the middle in an outdated style, abhorred sunshine, exercise, and vitamins but religiously observed an hour's nap every day after lunch. Wilder, with his trademark fedora that he unconventionally wore indoors to conceal a receding hairline, was incapable of sitting still.

Manny Wolfe, the story editor at Paramont, had paired them to write an adaptation of *Bluebeard's Eighth Wife*, a popular French farce that had enjoyed a long theatrical run in Paris before being adapted for a

1923 silent comedy (now lost) starring Gloria Swanson. The new adaptation, intended for Claudette Colbert and Gary Cooper, two of Paramount's biggest stars, would be directed by yet another kingpin in the Paramount lineup: Ernst Lubitsch.

The same age as Brackett, Lubitsch had grown up in Berlin, the son of a Russian-Jewish shopkeeper. Exempted from serving in the German army during the Great War because of his parentage (Germany was at war with Russia) and bored with shopkeeping, he tried his hand at acting, eventually winning a place for himself in the troupe of Max Reinhardt, Germany's most renowned and innovative theater director. With a knack for mimicry and comic impersonations of elderly Jews, young Lubitsch had no trouble shifting his talents from stage to screen. Before long, he was behind the camera, directing a rapid succession of frisky comedies interspersed with grand historical epics of surprising emotional depth, all of them exhibiting the ability of Lubitsch's camera to convey feelings that would be diminished if put into words. In the final scene of *Anna Boleyn* (1920), for example, the condemned English queen stands in a prison doorway, waiting to be led to the scaffold. When finally she is called, she proceeds calmly toward her destiny while the silent camera, as if too discreet to follow her, remains behind, still focused on the rough-hewn wall. In this brief, wordless moment, Lubitsch conveys a profound dignity and stoic acceptance of death.

Mary Pickford, America's most beloved star in the late 1910s and early 1920s, was moved by Lubitsch's subtle way with cameras and actors alike, and in 1923 she invited him to Hollywood to direct her next movie, *Rosita*, a hybrid historical film and comedy, for which he seemed perfectly suited. Alas, when she met the German maestro in person, she found him crude and vulgar, not to mention *Jewish*. She did not get along with him, and the resulting film fared poorly at the box office. Nonetheless, Lubitsch decided to stay in Hollywood rather than return to Berlin, and his career in America quickly took off. He was best known for his urbane comedies of manners, suffused with Continental sophistication.

Lubitsch transitioned smoothly to talkies, despite never gaining fluency in English. "If you think I have an accent," Wilder often quipped, "you should have heard Ernst Lubitsch." Linguistic challenges notwithstanding, Lubitsch turned out a handful of glittering musical comedies with the charming French hoofer and singer Maurice Chevalier. In these films, Chevalier's character remained always cheerful despite awkward embroilments that typically involved women with titles and wealth, leading the ever-amorous Chevalier to express himself in song.

Critics extolled Lubitsch for his inimitable "touch" as a director—his deft and often subtle mise-en-scène that propelled his story while simultaneously exploring the psychological/sexual/moral implications of a scene. He might, for example, use a prolonged focus on a closed bedroom door to indicate that the two lovers within are making love. (Wilder: "Lubitsch could do more with a closed door than most directors can do with an open fly.") Studio publicists endlessly used the term *the Lubitsch touch* to emphasize the elegance of his films. To categorize the brilliance of Lubitsch's camerawork as a sleight of hand, however, is to underestimate the genius of his work. "I've often wondered who started that phrase," he confided to a friend. "One shouldn't single out 'touches.' They're part of a whole." And a very grand whole.

While Lubitsch's early talkies were popular, by the mid-1930s, with the advent of the screwball comedy, these Old World farces started to look old-fashioned. Screwball comedies—the name derived from baseball terminology for a pitch that deviates from its flight path in unpredictable ways—relied on wild-goose-chase narratives that involved sassy humor and unlikely situations, most of them embarrassing for one, or both, of the leading characters. The classic screwball comedy starts out with a man and a woman in an adversarial relationship that intensifies and takes 90 to 105 minutes to resolve. The circuitous journey from discord to reconciliation involves lots of verbal sparring, pratfalls, and even fisticuffs when necessary. As the philosopher Stanley Cavell has pointed out, screwball comedies derive from Shakespearean comedy (for example, *Much Ado about Nothing*), in which lovers who have yet to realize their romantic interest test their wits against each other, often hiding their true identities but always coming triumphantly together at the end in rites of marriage. Among the best screwball comedies were Frank Capra's *It Happened One Night* (1934), Gregory La Cava's *My Man Godfrey* (1936), Leo McCarey's *The Awful Truth* (1937), and Howard Hawks's *Bringing Up Baby* (1938).

The producers at Paramount believed an updated version of *Bluebeard's Eighth Wife*—Swanson's silent version had been a commercial success—would be the perfect vehicle to launch Lubitsch into the new era. For starters, they needed a fast and funny script. After their first day of collaborating on the project, Brackett wrote in his diary: "Worked with Billy Wilder, who paces constantly, has over-extravagant ideas, but is stimulating.... He has humor—a kind of humor that sparks with mine."

Early in their partnership, still in the first flush of infatuation, Brackett praised the cinematic literacy of Wilder, who, he noted, "had cut the teeth of his mind on motion pictures." Brackett's new partner, despite little formal education, brought to the table an inquiring mind, a phenomenal memory, and a wealth of lived experience. Here was a man who had met Schnitzler and Freud, reported on robberies, homicides, and double suicides, written scripts for German movies, escaped from Hitler, and struggled to get by in Hollywood while teaching himself English.

Brackett also admired Wilder's determination to find *le mot juste* for every line of the script, and yet at times he couldn't help being annoyed by Wilder's "niggling passion for changing words without changing the meaning." What Brackett seemed not to grasp was that Wilder's compulsive word changing came from the relentless drive of a nonnative speaker to capture the elusive nuances of a language gleaned from taxi drivers, girlfriends, radio announcers, soap-opera stars, and the play-by-play commentary of baseball broadcasters. Wilder sought some authentic form of the vernacular that perhaps eluded the ivory-towered Brackett.

Brackett and Wilder met regularly with Lubitsch from January through March 1937 at his home on Bel Air Road. Wilder had long idolized the director and wanted desperately to please him, but Lubitsch was a tough customer, routinely rejecting the team's latest suggestions and insisting, often after emerging from the toilet, where he had had time to think in peace, that they come up with better ideas, snappier dialogue, and, as he put it in his heavily accented English, more *hilahrious* scenes.

The film starts with what we now call a meet-cute, the term itself attributed to Lubitsch during the writing of *Bluebeard*. Hollywood lore has it that in trying to explain to Brackett and Wilder that he wanted the two romantic leads to meet in a fresh and unusual way, and with his limited command of English, he simply said he wanted them to "meet cute." From then on, most of Wilder's films, first as a writer and then as a writer-director, relied on this setup, including *Sunset Boulevard* when Norma Desmond mistakes Joe for a rudely late pet undertaker who has come to bury her dead chimpanzee.

The opening scene of *Bluebeard's Eighth Wife* takes place in a department store on the French Riviera, where Gary Cooper, playing a stingy American millionaire, wants to buy the top of a pajama set without the bottom and therefore only pay half price. Both the clerk and his manager refuse Cooper's absurd proposal. The standoff is resolved when a down-on-her-luck aristocrat played by Claudette Colbert overhears Cooper's conversation and announces that she is shopping for a pair of bottoms. She and Cooper go in together on the purchase, although Colbert, determined to outsmart the brash American, insists on paying only 40 percent to his 60 because bottoms cost less to produce. Thus they bicker from the start.

Surprisingly sexual in its connotations, the scene invites viewers to imagine the leads semi-naked in their sleepwear, hinting at sex without depicting it, and that eventually the pajama top and its bottom will be reunited in bed. So far, so good, but soon the movie turns ugly. Colbert marries Cooper for his money; the marriage, Cooper's eighth, quickly sours; and to learn how to dominate a fire-breathing woman, Cooper turns to Shakespeare's *The Taming of the Shrew* (thus lending credence to Stanley Cavell's claim that Shakespeare is at the root of screwball comedy). She denies him sex and deliberately misleads him into thinking she's involved with another man. He spanks her, she slaps him, and in short order the film's original lighthearted wit devolves into mean-spirited humor.

Instead of exhibiting the delicate Lubitsch touch, the heavy-handed movie abounds in misogyny and misanthropy. It was a disaster. Even Adolf Hitler, who publicly denounced Lubitsch and labeled him "the Archetypal Jew" but was in secret a fan of Hollywood romantic comedies, was bored by it: He got up in the middle of an after-dinner screening in June 1938 to retire to his study instead and compose a tract on the building of fortresses.

The inability of *Bluebeard's Eighth Wife* to make audiences laugh taught the novice writing team an important lesson. Screwball comedy required the falling-in-love hero and heroine to fight with each other *playfully* but not viciously, to antagonize *cleverly* but not spitefully, and to discover their complementary natures as two halves of a whole, like those pajamas in the French Riviera department store. Brackett and Wilder went on to write a notable corpus of films that featured assertive and audacious women, starting with the sparkling screwball comedy *Midnight* (Leisen, 1939), starring Colbert as a penniless American showgirl who fast-talks her way into the upper echelon of Parisian society only to abandon it for an earnest and loving taxi driver. Here Colbert's character reveals a sweetness-at-the-core that her character in *Bluebeard* sorely lacked; she begins the film as an opportunist but ends by forsaking money and social status for true love.

Their next collaboration, Lubitsch's *Ninotchka* (1939), a beloved film classic, contains slight nods to the screwball genre, most of them involving a hapless trio of Soviet bureaucrats wildly overspending while on a trade mission to Paris. But it's not a screwball comedy; it reverts instead, in a thoroughly charming way, to Lubitsch's romantic comedies of the early 1930s, such as the Chevalier musicals and the effervescent nonmusicals *Trouble in Paradise* and *Design for Living*.

Greta Garbo, famed for her tragic demeanor in films such as *Anna Christie*, *Camille*, and *Anna Karenina*, played a humorless Soviet envoy, familiarly known as Ninotchka, who, on the same trade mission, falls in love with an impecunious aristocrat. The movie charts her transition from an ideology-besotted apparatchik to a sentient woman who loves and laughs and learns to value romance over politics. Advertising posters, playing off the legendary publicity campaign for Garbo's first sound film, *Anna Christie* ("Garbo talks!"), promoted *Ninotchka* with the now equally famous slogan, "Garbo laughs!"

The screenplay earned Brackett, Wilder, and their collaborator, the prolific émigré screenwriter Walter Reisch, an Oscar nomination for best screen adaptation. It competed with an impressive field of contestants: *Goodbye, Mr. Chips*; *Mr. Smith Goes to Washington*; *Wuthering Heights*; and the winner, *Gone with the Wind*.

Brackett and Wilder went on to write a string of successful pictures, starting with *Arise, My Love* (Leisen, 1940), a drama that starred Claudette Colbert as a Paris-based American fashion writer who becomes a courageous war correspondent on the eve of the Second World War. In another screwball comedy, *Ball of Fire* (Hawks, 1941), with echoes of

Pygmalion, a burlesque dancer (Barbara Stanwyck) teaches a stuffed-shirt scholar (played improbably by Gary Cooper) to let go of his inhibitions and enjoy life—something streetwise Wilder failed to teach professorial Brackett.

With a growing list of hit films to their names, Brackett and Wilder rose to the top rank of Paramount screenwriters and were recognized by their peers as an invincible duo. And yet their respect for each other was deteriorating. Even as early as 1939—the miracle year of *Ninotchka* and *Midnight*—Brackett worried that a breakup was inevitable, writing in his diary: "Violent quarrel with Billy," from whom "I fear I shall have to part company, much as the thought of working alone now terrifies me."

Brackett was troubled, among other things, by his partner's philandering ways. His diaries contain multiple entries about Wilder's persistent cheating on his wife, Judith. On one occasion, "the compleat amorist," as Brackett sarcastically called Billy, boasted about his foolproof method for seducing a woman. It entailed tricking her into thinking he wasn't after sex. He would kiss his target chastely in the doorway to her apartment and then leave, only to follow up with a call from the nearest phone booth to declare his passion for her. The rest was easy, Wilder boasted to Brackett: His prey would urge him to return immediately. After recording Billy's smug accounting of his erotic exploits, Brackett added dryly, "Today Mr. Wilder was not so successful on our story. We accomplished almost nothing." Still, the mood in the suite of offices to which their success had elevated them was not uniformly grim. Brackett described other days that were "filled with [the] pleasant insanity of a writer's life in Hollywood."

★ ★ ★

As the writing duo's successes piled up, Wilder, the more ambitious of the two, grew frustrated with script alterations imposed by "hack" directors such as Mitchell Leisen or overweening stars such as the popular

Franco-American romantic leading man Charles Boyer. Wilder never forgave Boyer for refusing to deliver a moving monologue to a cockroach that Wilder had written for him in Leisen's *Hold Back the Dawn* (1941). The arrogant and, in Wilder's view, stupid movie star objected to addressing lines to an insect. Wilder seethed with resentment every time a director, producer, or actor dared to alter even a single word of his and Brackett's scripts. To protect himself from future violations of this nature, he realized it was time to shift from writer to writer-director. The only screenwriter at Paramount to enjoy control over his own scripts was Preston Sturges, the writer-director of hits such as *Sullivan's Travels*, *The Palm Beach Story*, and *Miracle at Morgan Creek*. To get his way with Paramount, Wilder begged, cajoled, and threw temper tantrums. He threatened to take his proven script-writing talents to a rival studio. Eventually the studio chiefs gave in.

The writing duo's frolicking 1942 farce, *The Major and the Minor*, marked Wilder's first Hollywood foray into writing and directing (he had been in this position eight years earlier with the French film *Mauvaise Graine*). In this effervescent comedy, Ginger Rogers, thirty-one at the time, played a broke twenty-year-old who, to save money on a train ticket, passes herself off as a twelve-year-old. She falls in love with one of the passengers, a naive army officer (Ray Milland) who chivalrously looks after what he believes to be a sprightly preteen traveling on her own. In typical screwball fashion, an amusing series of obstacles ensues with breathtaking speed until, in the final moments of the film, Milland discovers the girl is actually a woman, they declare love for each other, and order is restored.

The film's editor, Doane Harrison, taught the almost novice director to "cut within the camera"—that is, to pre-think how shots would stitch together so that a minimum of editing would be necessary, and the resulting film would glide effortlessly from one moment to the next. Another advantage of cutting-in-camera was that much less footage was shot. This intentionally parsimonious method of filmmaking prevented intrusive studio executives from insisting on recuts, since there was nothing left to cut: "When I finish a film," said Wilder, "there's nothing on the cutting room floor but chewing gum wrappers and tears."

Looking to broaden their range, Brackett and Wilder unexpectedly chose to make the espionage thriller *Five Graves to Cairo* (1943). Like the earlier Warner Bros. hit *Casablanca* (1942), it takes place in German-occupied North Africa. The plot revolves around the infiltration of Field Marshal Erwin Rommel's headquarters by a British tank commander who, to obtain vital military secrets, impersonates a hotel waiter (a profession Wilder knew well, both as the son of a hotelier and as a dancer for hire at Berlin's grand hotels). Despite its implausible plot, the movie spoke to Americans who were beset with dread during the early days of the war, and it reassured them with a happy ending in which the Germans were thwarted and the British regained their strategic advantage on the North African front.

Rommel, "the Desert Fox," is played with panache by Erich von Stroheim who, since the *Queen Kelly* debacle fourteen years earlier, had earned his living playing heavies on stage and screen. The day Stroheim came to Paramount for a wardrobe fitting, Wilder dropped what he was doing and bounded up the steps to meet the idol of his youth. Stroheim was prickly by nature and exceedingly proud. When Wilder praised him as a filmmaker ten years ahead of his time, the maestro snapped, "Twenty, Mr. Wilder. Twenty." They remained respectful toward each other throughout the shoot but did not form an affectionate bond. Wilder always held the upper hand, even if Stroheim believed that he himself should be directing the film. Six years later, Wilder would cast Stroheim in *Sunset Boulevard* as Norma Desmond's butler. A far cry from Rommel.

* * *

In its December 11, 1944, issue, *Life* magazine ran a ten-page profile of Brackett and Wilder titled "The Happiest Couple in Hollywood." The author of the piece, Lincoln Barnett, remarked on the strange nature of their pairing: "The anomaly of their relationship is that two more antithetic personalities would be hard to find. Brackett is a courtly, somewhat rumpled, affable gentleman of 52, who looks as though he might be vice president of a bank in Sarasota Springs, N.Y.—which he is. Wilder is a loquacious, elegant, sardonic man of 38 who moves with the grace of a professional dancer—which he once was." Barnett added that Wilder "knows he is a genius—a conviction by no means exclusively his own."

The profile described what sounded like an idyllic setup: a three-room suite of offices on the ground floor of the writers' building. Their secretary-typist Helen Hernandez occupied the antechamber, which had the appearance of a fashionable dentist's waiting room. The walls of the outer office were adorned with stills from Brackett and Wilder's hits, among them *Midnight, Ninotchka, Hold Back the Dawn,* and *The Major and the Minor.* Next door was the "game room" they used for their noontime cribbage matches. It was the place where fellow writers, as well as sympatico directors, producers, and actors, were welcome to join them for games and gossip. The largest of the three rooms they called "the bedroom," which was where they worked, Wilder pacing about—hat on head, Malacca walking stick in hand—while Brackett, curled up on the couch, took pages of notes in a spidery, longhand script that only Ms. Hernandez could decipher.

What this glowing account did not hint at is that, after eight years of working together, Brackett and Wilder were no longer happy with the partnership. Only a few months after they had been teamed up, Brackett complained in his diary of Wilder's penchant for stealing his ideas and rebranding them as his own: "The thing to do was suggest an idea, have it torn apart and despised. In a few days it would be apt to turn up, slightly changed, as Wilder's idea. Once I got adjusted to that way of working, our lives were simpler." Weathering both passive-aggressive hostilities toward each other and ones that were more overt, they stuck together. Each had cause to feel dependent on the other. Wilder believed that Brackett's frequent objections to his ideas forced him to come up with even better ones. Neither was eager to rock a boat they had rowed successfully through Hollywood's perennially turbulent waters.

Looking back on his partnership with Brackett, Wilder joked that in 1936 he acquired two wives: his real wife, Judith Coppicus, and his other "wife," Brackett. As his biographer Ed Sikov deftly put it, "Wilder's marriage with Judith produced two children and a lot of acrimony. His marriage with Brackett produced a lot of acrimony and eleven of the best, most successful films Paramount Pictures ever made." In 1945, Wilder divorced his legal wife. Three years later, in the midst of writing the script for *Sunset Boulevard*, he decided to divorce Brackett, too.

CHAPTER FIVE

ADULTERY, ADDICTION, AND MASS MURDER

With the war aflame in Europe and Asia, Wilder made two feature films that reflected a darkening view of humankind: *Double Indemnity*, a story of adultery, greed, and murder, and *The Lost Weekend*, the wrenching tale of an alcoholic writer. The films were essentially tragic, but their corrosive view of the human condition was offset by their brilliant plotting, superb acting, and gemlike dialogue. Not so *The Death Mills*, Wilder's twenty-two-minute documentary made at the end of the war, an edited compilation of newsreel footage documenting Nazi rallies, Nazi atrocities, and the human refuse of the concentration camps. Together, these three movies took Wilder's filmmaking into a grim psychological space he had not previously entered.

At the end of the war and as the barbarism of the Nazi regime toward Jews became universally known, Wilder came to realize that he had placed his career ahead of his family. Too busy establishing himself as a writer, he'd ignored the plight of his mother, grandmother, and stepfather until it was too late to get them out of Austria. Noting that Wilder "was perhaps the most famous film director in the world to have lost his mother and other members of his family to the Holocaust," film critic Andrew Sarris observed that the director chose not to treat the matter explicitly in his feature films: "One could never imagine Wilder's undertaking such earnestly well-meaning projects on the Holocaust as *The Diary of Anne Frank* and *Judgment at Nuremberg*. Wilder is a humorist and an ironist, not a polemicist and a propagandist." Nonetheless, Sarris argued, Wilder's recurring theme in his most powerful films is that of selfish opportunists seeking absolution for their egocentric behavior. Walter Neff of *Double Indemnity* and Don Birnam of *The Lost Weekend* were both redemption-seeking opportunists, and so was Joe Gillis. So, too, we might imagine, was their creator, Billy Wilder.

★ ★ ★

According to James M. Cain, author of the 1943 hard-boiled novel *Double Indemnity*, the idea of adapting the pulp thriller into film first occurred to Wilder when he couldn't find his secretary. A coworker said she was in the ladies' room, reading "that story." Wilder's interest was piqued. When the secretary returned clutching the sensational thriller that she hadn't been able to put down, Wilder snatched it away from her and took it home to read. The next day Paramount offered Cain $15,000 for the screen rights to his book. Based on a lurid murder trial that occurred in the 1920s, Cain's novel tells of a seductive housewife and a cocky insurance agent who, after becoming lovers, murder her husband in such a way as to make his death appear accidental, thus triggering a double-indemnity clause in his life insurance policy. Their plans go awry, however, as an intuitive claims adjuster smells a rat and begins to work out how the crime was committed.

Brackett was not taken with the book. In keeping with his moral rectitude, he bristled at the thought of adapting a story he found tawdry and lascivious. Besides, he didn't think it stood a chance of passing muster with the draconian Motion Picture Production Code. He and Wilder agreed to a temporary split, leaving Wilder to find another collaborator to work on the screen adaptation. (Brackett, meanwhile, initiated work on a pet project of his, a haunted-house story called *The Uninvited*.)

Taken with Cain's tough-guy prose and fast-paced dialogue, Wilder proposed to the studio that he and Cain collaborate on the script, but the novelist, working on a picture for another studio, was unavailable. Paramount executive Joe Sistrom suggested Raymond Chandler, an American-born, British-educated mystery writer living outside Palm Springs. Chandler knew how to write crime fiction. His first detective novel, *The Big Sleep*, featuring a tough but honest private eye named Philip Marlowe, had been published in 1939, but he had no experience with screenwriting. When Chandler came in for a meeting with Sistrom and Wilder to arrange a contract, he demanded a fee of $1,000. Sistrom, bemused by the writer's naivete, offered him ten times that amount. Wilder was to earn $44,000 for his part of the writing.

Wilder had assumed the crime novelist would be as witty and smooth in person as Marlowe was on the page. Instead, he found himself working with a charmless fifty-five-year-old former alcoholic whom he described as "an awkward, pale, elderly man, who made a somewhat strange impression. He wore a frayed, checkered tweed jacket, with leather patches on the elbows, and gray, worn-out flannel trousers. He had a sickly complexion, like a man who's drowned himself in drink." Their relationship was abrasive from the start. Chandler took offense at Wilder's signature mannerisms, including his penchant for pacing around the office with a Malacca walking stick in his hand and a fedora on his head. Chandler thought it rude for a man to wear a hat indoors.

"He did not like me very much," Wilder recalled. "He was in Alcoholics Anonymous, and I think he had a rough time with me—I drove him back into drinking." After four weeks of putting up with what he believed to be his collaborator's boorish behavior, Chandler sent Joe Sistrom an irate memo, which the producer turned over to Wilder. As the writer-director recollected:

> It was a letter of complaint against me: he couldn't work with me anymore because I was rude; I was drinking; I was fucking; I was on the phone with four broads, with one I was on the phone— he clocked me—for twelve and a half minutes; I . . . asked him to pull down the Venetian blinds [and didn't say] "please."

Chandler did indeed start drinking again during the writing of the film. He kept a pint of whiskey hidden in his briefcase and would pull it out every time Wilder stepped outside for a smoke. After finishing work for the day, the frazzled crime writer would wander around the city frequenting his favorite bars.

Years later, Chandler called *Double Indemnity* the best film he ever worked on and took sole credit for the script, saying he wrote it *for* (not *with*) "an odd little director with a touch of genius, Billy Wilder." Working with Wilder, Chandler declared, "was an agonizing experience" and "probably shortened my life." In his 1953 Philip Marlowe novel *The Little Sister*, Chandler depicts a Hollywood big shot whose office contains a pot full of Malacca walking sticks, one of which he swings as he paces through the room. "It could only happen in Hollywood. . . ." Marlowe grunted. "That an apparently sane man could walk up and down inside the house with a Piccadilly stroll and a monkey stick in his hand."

Chandler did admit to learning a thing or two from the more experienced screenwriter. Working with Wilder taught him "the most important part is what is left out"—it was up to the camera and the actors to fill in the blanks. "The best short scene I ever wrote,"

Chandler elaborated, "was one in which a girl said 'uh-huh' three times with three different intonations." Uh-huhs aside, Chandler had an ear for dialogue and is generally credited for much of *Double Indemnity*'s sizzling repartee. Early in the film, the insurance salesman Walter Neff (Fred MacMurray) makes a cold call to a residence in suburban Glendale, where he meets Phyllis Dietrichson (Barbara Stanwyck), a bleached-blond housewife with attitude as well as a tantalizing bracelet affixed to one of her shapely ankles. The two of them fall quickly and naturally into the rapid rhythm of sexual banter. "There's a speed limit in this state," Phyllis cautions Walter when he comes on too strong. "Forty-five miles an hour."

> *How fast was I going, Officer?*
> *I'd say about ninety.*

It's a clever piece of business, particularly for a film narrative that, like the lustful insurance man, races ahead at breakneck speed.

> *Suppose you get down off your motorcycle and give me a ticket.*
> *Suppose I let you off with a warning this time.*
> *Suppose it doesn't take.*
> *Suppose I have to rap you over the knuckles.*
> *Suppose I bust out crying and have to put my head on your shoulder.*

They might as well be in bed together. While the subtext of the scene was guaranteed to set off alarms at the Hays Office, it was, one could claim, simply clever small talk about driving too fast. Indeed, here was a viable template for other filmmakers working with similarly sexual material in how to circumvent the code. Howard Hawks's 1946 adaptation of *The Big Sleep*, for example, contains an almost obscene subtext to a flirtatious banter between Humphrey Bogart and Lauren Bacall that's ostensibly about horse racing. Bacall looks him over: "Speaking of horses, I like to play them myself. But I like to see them work out a little first, see if they're front-runners or come from behind."

It wasn't *Double Indemnity*'s sparkling repartee that attracted the attention of newspaper reviewers when it opened in July 1944. Instead, they praised it as a modern-day horror film, certain to shock and thrill viewers. New York's *Daily News*, for example, described the movie as "sheer horror, so realistically conveyed by the characters of the story… with a tautness of direction that leaves the beholder breathless throughout the exhibition of the film."

Similarly impressed, the reviewer for the *New York Times* wrote that Wilder, in laying out the story of the conspiring murderers, "has detailed the stalking of their victim with the frigid thoroughness of a coroner's report, and he has pictured their psychological crackup as a sadist would pluck out a spider's legs."

When the movie appeared on Parisian screens two years later, in 1946—its foreign release having been delayed by the war—French film critics praised it as the embodiment of a new, darkly pessimistic style of filmmaking they dubbed film noir. As the art historian Erika Doss concisely described them, "Noir movies articulated the anxiety, insecurity, and pessimism of modern life in a shadowy, unglamorous style fortified by fragmented narratives (flashbacks and voice-overs) and distorted, slanting compositions." With its visual density and moral complexity, *Double Indemnity* is as dark in its outlook as in its atmospheric lighting. It's a film without a hero or heroine.

The unusual narrative structure of the film enhances its fatalism, for we see events unfold in tense, doom-laden flashbacks from the perspective of an antihero who has already been shot by his lover and is bleeding to death throughout the 107 minutes of screen time it takes him to tell his story. At the end of the decade, *Sunset Boulevard* would ratchet narrative circularity one notch higher, its story narrated not by a dying man but by one who, from the start of the film, is already dead.

★ ★ ★

Concluding his tempestuous but artistically successful dalliance with Chandler, Wilder returned to the monogamy he'd enjoyed with Brackett. "After working with somebody else," he joked, "I find out that Charlie isn't so bad." His "infidelity," Wilder came to believe, had a permanent effect on his partnership with Brackett: "He always thought I cheated on him with Raymond Chandler. He got very possessive after that." Brackett saw it differently, believing that Billy had been "despondent" without him and came running back to him for his next project.

The project that reunited Brackett and Wilder was an adaptation of Charles Jackson's bestselling novel, *The Lost Weekend*, the story of an alcoholic writer's downward spiral over the course of a four-day bender. The protagonist, Don Birnam, like so many other characters populating the universe of Wilder's cinema, suffers as much from self-delusion as he does from booze. In a bravura passage written by Brackett and Wilder (it does not appear in the source novel), Birnam delivers to a skeptical bartender an encomium to the virtues of drink, claiming that it liberates and exhilarates the artistic mind:

> *It shrinks my liver, doesn't it, Nat? It pickles my kidneys, yes. But what does it do to my mind? It tosses the sandbags overboard so the balloon can soar. Suddenly, I'm above the ordinary. I'm competent, supremely competent.*

This glorification of drink is to be taken ironically, the ravings of a self-deceiving drunk who only *thinks* he does his best work while under the influence. At the same time, the screenwriters wanted to re-create, in Brackett's words, the "strange and sometimes beautiful things" that occur inside the head of an alcoholic. Hollywood had previously shown drunks as clumsy buffoons to be laughed at or derided for their foibles, but Brackett and Wilder were eager, the latter recalled, "to make the first picture where a drunk was not something funny. In those days, an alcoholic was something you roared with laughter about." Their film, a friend of Wilder's later reminisced, is "neither a sermon nor a plea for temperance. It is simply an intense study of an individual in a too little understood dilemma, the story of a weak, unfortunate man who couldn't touch liquor without drinking to excess. They looked upon him as a sick man and treated his illness with compassion and sympathy." Four years later, they were to do the same with Norma Desmond; the movie may invite the viewer to laugh at her at the start, with her histrionic gestures, bug-eyed mannerisms, and declamatory way of speaking, but by the end, our sympathies have changed.

Wilder knew a lot about alcoholism, having witnessed Raymond Chandler's sickness while collaborating with him on *Double Indemnity*. And he knew other screenwriters, most notably F. Scott Fitzgerald, who had similarly succumbed to the bottle. But it was Brackett who harbored a more personal connection to the subject matter. His wife, Elizabeth, had suffered from alcoholism for years, as did one of their two grown daughters. Brackett's grandson Jim Moore has written of his grandfather that "his family life was awash in alcoholism, depression, and despair. He could not control the boozy, violent, ultimately fatal marriage of his elder daughter. He was helpless to arrest the sad, inexorable decline of his wife Elizabeth's mental and physical health."

★ ★ ★

When the surrender of Germany was imminent, the United States Army invited Wilder—a native German speaker who had begun his illustrious filmmaking career in Berlin—to serve overseas for six months as motion picture chief of the Psychological Warfare Division. He accepted the commission and was given the rank of colonel. Part of his job was to oversee the reconstruction and rehabilitation of the German entertainment industry, a task that involved approving or rejecting a wide variety of requests that came his way, including one seeking authorization to resume the world-famous decennial Passion Play at Oberammergau. When asked if Anton Lang, a former SS officer who had impersonated Christ in a prewar production of the play, could play the role again, Wilder promptly replied, "Certainly, if you use real nails." It's easy to imagine that Wilder's penchant for this sort of witticism in the face of disaster functioned as a psychological shield that prevented others, as well as himself, from peering too deeply within.

Wilder had fled from his beloved Berlin in 1933, leaving behind a vibrant cosmopolitan metropolis on the banks of the river Spree. The city he returned to a dozen years later was in ruins, clogged with rubble that still smoldered from the aerial bombardments, tank battles, and street-to-street combat that had marked the final days before surrender. He had buried his father in Berlin, and it was in Berlin that he now received confirmation from the International Red Cross that his mother, grandmother, and stepfather had been annihilated in the death camps.

The director's main activity during his stint in Berlin was to oversee the production of a short documentary film titled *Die Todesmühlen* (*The Death Mills*), directed by Wilder in tandem with Hanuš Burger, a Czechoslovak documentary filmmaker. Wilder also supervised the editing. Compiled from graphic footage taken by British, American, and Soviet filmmakers at the liberation of the Nazi death camps in April 1945, *The Death Mills* was intended exclusively for German and Austrian viewers. By order of the War Office, it was not to be shown elsewhere. Its purpose was to prove that the atrocities Germans and Austrians were now reading about in their newspapers were not lies promulgated by the victors. When the twenty-two-minute movie was completed, it played by decree in every cinema in Austria and Germany for an entire week. Citizens could not get their food rations without proof that they had attended a screening.

With an overlay of intense dramatic music that repeats itself relentlessly throughout the movie's duration, the documentary intentionally rubs the viewer's face in otherwise hard-to-believe horrors of torture, murder, forced starvation, degradation, and depravity. Ed Sikov described the intolerable physical realities that the Allied cameramen recorded when their troops liberated the death camps: "They filmed the crematoria and the ash piles. They filmed skeletal corpses, piles of shoes, lampshades made of human skin. They took motion pictures of mass burial pits, ovens made to burn vast numbers of people, dead babies, bones. Inhuman horror, unimaginable in scale, was photographed." Nothing like this had been seen before on movie screens.

After chronicling the brutality of the concentration camps, the film shows thousands of cheering Germans thrusting their arms forward in the Nazi salute. The narrator says: "Yesterday, while millions were burned in concentration camps, Germans jammed Nuremberg to cheer the Nazi Party and sing hymns of hate." Superimposed segments of film simultaneously show three groups of individuals: civilians rapturously applauding the Führer at Nazi rallies; villagers who swear they knew nothing of the genocide in their backyards; and emaciated death-camp survivors. With deep irony, the narrator says: "Today, these Germans who cheered the destruction of humanity in their own land...who cheered the enslavement of Europe, plead for your sympathies."

The takeaway from the movie is not only that the Nazis were monsters, but also that the German people who pled ignorance of the death mills were either lying to others or lying to themselves. The film portrays a world not simply of mass delusion, as promulgated by the fascist rallies, but also of mass *self*-delusion, where educated adults refused to face the terrible truths of their complicity. After traveling throughout postwar Germany, Wilder remarked cynically, "I never met a single Nazi. Everyone was a victim, everyone had been a resistance fighter."

★ ★ ★

In the fall of 1945, preview audiences for *The Lost Weekend* responded to it enthusiastically, although, according to Wilder, one comment card "told me it was a great movie, but I should take out all the stuff about drinking and alcoholism." The film opened in late November. The critics were overwhelmed by its brutal candor, although James Agee couldn't pass up the opportunity to take a clever shot at the liquor industry: "I undershtand that liquor interesh: innerish intereshtsh are rather worried about thish film. Thash tough." At the Academy Awards ceremony in March 1946, it won every major award for which it was nominated: Ray Milland for best actor, Brackett and Wilder for best screen adaptation, Wilder for best director, and Brackett for best picture. That night, reluctant to part with his two golden statuettes, Billy took them to bed. When he and Brackett drove onto the Paramount lot the following morning, the wall of the writers' building was festooned with whiskey bottles hanging from the windows, a reference to the movie's opening sequence, in which Don has hung a whiskey bottle from the window of his New York apartment to escape the notice of his brother and girlfriend, who would have taken it away from him had they found it. It was an especially sweet tribute to Brackett and Wilder from their fellow writers.

The film's many accolades, including the top prize at the Cannes Film Festival two months later, did not necessarily transform Wilder for the better. His biographer Maurice Zolotow wrote that the triumph of *The Lost Weekend* "vindicated Billy Wilder. In his own eyes, he had always been a genius. Now…his ego swollen beyond even the customary Hollywood megalomania, he strode the make-believe streets of Paramount like a conqueror."

Wilder's success took a ruinous toll on his partnership with Brackett. Since Manny Wolfe had paired them nearly a decade earlier, the two writers, despite their alternating affection and dislike for each other, had put the success of their team ahead of their individual requirements. But now, with the overwhelming triumph of *The Lost Weekend*, Wilder seemed to think he no longer needed Brackett. Never mind that

Brackett had cowritten the screenplay and produced the film. Wilder did not want to share his glory, even with his closest collaborator. Henceforth, whenever they came to a screenwriting impasse, Wilder refused to compromise. At times the animosity between them became physical. "They quarreled and they screamed," wrote Zolotow, "and Brackett got hysterical and threw heavy objects at Wilder's head. Wilder would always throw the last punch, however. He would threaten to break up the partnership. He would threaten to get a divorce."

The *Hollywood Reporter* ran a full-page ad celebrating the screenwriting success of Brackett and Wilder. It showed them each holding a dagger behind the other's back. Clearly it was meant to be tongue-in-cheek, but, in retrospect, it seemed a perfect encapsulation of their relationship.

They hid their discontent well. In April 1948, the *New York Times* ran a puff piece on the partnership under the headline "The Happy Union of Brackett and Wilder," apparently not aware that the union had become anything but happy.

CHAPTER SIX

"THE FOOLISHNESS OF THIS FOOLISH TOWN"

On his return from Berlin, Wilder wanted to put the horrors of war behind him. Specifically, he explained, "I was looking for a project to get the images of those camps out of my mind. I had this feeling I wanted to do a musical." Wilder's intentions meshed with those of Paramount's executives, who needed a new vehicle for Bing Crosby, America's most popular radio crooner and the studio's biggest star. Without first consulting Brackett, Wilder offered to cast Crosby in an as-yet-unwritten musical comedy. Years later, Wilder, reflecting on his dissatisfaction with the resulting film, *The Emperor Waltz*, commented, "I was not up to making a musical. I don't know, I should have gone to a hospital or something, after being in Germany and cutting [a documentary] about the concentration camps."

Set in turn-of-the-twentieth-century Vienna, *The Emperor Waltz* (1948) tells of a cocky American gramophone salesman, Virgil Smith (Crosby), who introduces to the imperial court of the Austro-Hungarian emperor Franz Josef the newfangled contraption that plays back recorded voices. A memorandum by Wilder to his production team specified that the film would take place in 1906, which, he failed to note, was the year of his birth. The project was Billy's baby all the way; "I don't suppose I ever understood it very well," said Brackett. He complained in his diaries that with Wilder taking the lead on most decisions, he was relegated to a "fifth-wheel function," which he found nerve-racking, and which led to nasty quarrels between the director and his producer.

The film seems to have been doubly nostalgic for Wilder. On the most obvious level, it was an attempt to revisit the rose-tinted past of his Austrian childhood. Franz Josef was the same emperor whose funeral procession Wilder had watched as a ten-year-old boy from the second story of the Café Einstein. At the same time, the movie showed the adult Wilder's reverence for the early-1930s musicals of Ernst Lubitsch, pictures such as *One Hour with You, The Smiling Lieutenant,* and *The Merry Widow* that exuded Old World charm and sophistication.

Riding high from the back-to-back successes of *Double Indemnity* and *The Lost Weekend,* Wilder was able to demand bigger budgets and attract costlier stars, such as Crosby. But landing the biggest star in Hollywood was not enough. He wanted more: location shooting in the Canadian Rockies, extravagant sets, elaborate dance numbers with scores of extras, trees replanted to improve the mise-en-scène, flowers painted to match the décor. It was all to be filmed in Technicolor, an expensive photochemical process typically reserved for important costume dramas such as *Gone with the Wind* and elaborate musical romances such as *Meet Me in St. Louis.* Wilder, who later called the film the worst of his career, complained that the extravagant color process gave the movie the appearance of an ice cream parlor.

The Emperor Waltz received tepid reviews, and even Lubitsch, to whom Wilder meant to pay homage, did not like it, believing that Wilder had stolen from him the meet-cute—in this case a double meet-cute, in which two dog owners and their pets get embroiled in a four-way dustup. Subsequently both dogs and owners fall in love. At a private screening in the fall of 1947, Lubitsch exclaimed with a stage whisper, "That's my story, that's my story! The son of a bitch has taken my story!" Wilder was dismayed by his mentor's reaction, but he never had a chance to patch things up. Weeks later, Lubitsch, only fifty-five years of age, suffered a fatal heart attack.

★ ★ ★

Brackett and Wilder's next film, A *Foreign Affair* (1948), fits into a small subgenre of postwar films referred to as *Trümmerfilm*, or rubble films. As the name suggests, many scenes in these films were shot on the bombed-out streets of German cities. The Germans made at least a dozen rubble films, but so did directors from other nations. Roberto Rossellini's *Germany—Year Zero*, the grim story of an orphaned child in postwar Berlin, is unrelentingly bleak; less so is Carol Reed's *The Third Man*, shot amid the ruins of Vienna, with a witty script by Graham Greene, a devilishly charismatic performance by Orson Welles as a murderous black marketeer, and an unforgettable music track played on a solo zither.

A *Foreign Affair* concerns US representative Phoebe Frost (Jean Arthur), who travels to Germany as part of a congressional delegation investigating illicit behavior by American soldiers in the army of the occupation. The film opens with a stunning sequence, no doubt inspired by Leni Riefenstahl's opening to *Triumph of the Will* (1935), in which Hitler's private airplane emerges from the clouds and descends to a Nazi rally like a chariot of the gods. Wilder's airplane carrying similarly triumphant American politicians and bureaucrats flies low over the charred ruins of Berlin. Because many of Berlin's structures had been built with steel reinforcement, these buildings were not entirely flattened by bombing. In this opening flyover, they rise from the ground like bones in a macabre graveyard. The congressional representatives scramble from their seats to nearby windows to get a better view of the shattered metropolis.

The only passenger to pay no heed is Congresswoman Frost, who, instead, methodically closes the notebook in which she was writing, puts the top back on her fountain pen, tucks the pen in its holder, places the holder in a sleeve of her briefcase, snaps the briefcase shut, removes her reading glasses, and carefully puts them in their case, all the while showing a maddening lack of interest in the appalling spectacle below. When, at last, she does look at the hellish ruins, her response is simply: "Golly!" Joseph McBride, in his audio commentary for the DVD of the film, astutely notes that Phoebe is as emotionally closed as her brief-case, a situation that will change over the course of the film. But it's also important to recognize that Phoebe exemplifies those individuals in Wilder films, including the German civilians in *The Death Mills*, who live their lives in a bubble, unable to escape their own fantasies and delusions long enough to grasp the reality of a world outside themselves.

As had *The Emperor Waltz*, *A Foreign Affair* received tepid reviews. But even before the reviews appeared, Brackett knew the film was a disaster. On May 31, 1948, only days after filming ended, he confided in his diary: "I find myself searching for another picture desperately.... Where, oh where can I find a fresh project?" He pleaded, "Subconscious powers, come to my aid!"

★　★　★

One week later, on June 7, 1948, Brackett's reclusive wife Elizabeth died at their home on Bellagio Road, cause of death not noted in her obituary, though surely her chronic alcoholism played a part. Brackett wrote, "I held my dear girl's hand and, very quietly, more quietly than drifting to sleep, the breathing stopped and I was left with a sharp sense of aloneness, of realization of how I'd depended on that wise, ill woman, how she'd meant home and refuge from the foolishness of this foolish town."

On June 23, he and Billy met with Barney Balaban, the head of Paramount Pictures. The studio's chief executive, Brackett wrote, "did nothing but talk of the parlous state of the motion picture industry, give us statistics on the dropping box office and generally depress us." Wilder took the conversation especially hard; Brackett observed that Balaban "succeeded in depressing Billy pretty severely." The industry was indeed failing, as marked by the widely noted decline in ticket sales and the advancing deterioration of the studio system, with more and more films being made independently and stars and directors no longer bound to the studios by long-term contracts. Meanwhile, a new entertainment medium, television, was looming large on the horizon, seducing American audiences into abandoning the large and luminous screen of the movie palace for the small and dim TV screen of the suburban home.

In mid-July, Wilder asked Brackett to read Evelyn Waugh's short novel *The Loved One*, a bestseller nationwide, but even more so in Los Angeles, where it takes place. The story concerns an indigent young British poet who, failing to succeed as a Hollywood screenwriter, finds work at a pet cemetery euphemistically named Happier Hunting Grounds. Waugh satirized the film business and funeral business alike for manufacturing trite illusions about life and death. Brackett despised *The Loved One*, which he described as "a strange, cruel book," and the partners agreed not to pursue the idea of adapting it for the screen. Still, the meeting with Balaban, combined with Waugh's cruel satire of their profession, left the writers with a sense of encroaching doom.

During this dismal summer, tensions between Brackett and Wilder intensified, but the two managed to maintain a professional working relationship. With the declaration of Israeli independence from Great Britain and the subsequent Arab-Israeli war much in the news that summer, Wilder wanted the team to write a thriller set in modern-day Palestine, and to have the darkly handsome British actor James Mason play an arms smuggler. But they couldn't get beyond the initial premise, and the development of the story went nowhere. Billy conceded this was because, apart from what they read every day in the papers, they knew nothing about the setting or the subject. They needed to come up with an idea closer to home, one that addressed a subject they knew something about.

★ ★ ★

As they were ruminating over the topic of their next film, they noted the passing of a cinematic giant: D. W. Griffith. Regarded by many as the man who invented the close-up, or at least first grasped its dramatic potential, and who had also pioneered modern editing techniques such as cross-cutting, Griffith had commanded admiration from filmmakers around the world. His thrilling—albeit deplorably racist—Civil War epic *The Birth of a Nation* (1915) was the most commercially successful and critically acclaimed film of the silent era.

By the late 1920s, Griffith had fallen out of step with the times. His Victorian morality, the hallmark of his earlier films, seemed faintly ridiculous to filmgoers of the Jazz Age. When he tiptoed into the sound era with two talking pictures, *Abraham Lincoln* (1930) and *The Struggle* (1931), both films struck viewers as painfully dull. By the 1940s, he was a washed-up alcoholic. The industry he helped to create abandoned him. "In his later years," the Hollywood journalist Ezra Goodman recalled, "Griffith was a familiar figure as he wandered about Hollywood, lost and passé, dropping in at bars and ogling the girls, while the men who had been his office boys and assistants and had not one iota of his ability sat in big offices in the big studios doing hack work."

On an April evening in 1948, when Billy and his fiancée Audrey Young were dining with Sam Goldwyn and his wife at the Brown Derby, a haggard, inebriated man approached their table. "Son of a bitch," the drunk declared, pointing a finger at Goldwyn. "Here *you* are, and I ought to be making pictures. I'm the one—" Before he could finish his harangue, he was ushered out of the restaurant. "That man," explained Goldwyn to his puzzled dinner companions, "was D. W. Griffith." Three months later, the filmmaker was dead, having suffered a cerebral hemorrhage in the lobby of the shabby hotel where he had lived for years in isolation and near destitution.

Few people turned up at the funeral parlor; the only famous one to do so was Cecil B. DeMille. In the 1910s, Griffith and DeMille, along with Erich von Stroheim, were the preeminent film directors in America, but while DeMille continued to work in the business throughout the 1930s and 1940s, enjoying success after success, neither Griffith nor Stroheim had any such luck.

At the subsequent funeral service held for Griffith at the Hollywood Masonic Temple, Brackett, as president of the Academy of Motion Picture Arts and Sciences, delivered the eulogy. In his diary, he congratulated himself on giving a fine and noble speech, one that reflected on how difficult it must have been for a man once so esteemed to fall into oblivion: "It was the fate of David Wark Griffith to have a success unknown in the entertainment world until this day, and to suffer the agonies which only a success of that magnitude can engender when it is past."

Brackett noted that the Academy had bestowed an honorary Oscar on Griffith a dozen years earlier, but he questioned whether it wasn't in the end a hollow gesture. "I'm afraid it didn't ease his heartache much," he admitted. "When you've had what he'd had, what you want is the chance to make more pictures, unlimited budgets to play with, complete confidence behind you. What does a man full of vitality care for the honors of the past? It's the present he wants, and the future. There was no solution for Griffith but a kind of frenzied beating on the barred doors."

A few days after the funeral, "E.F.R.," a reader of the *Los Angeles Times*, sarcastically pointed out in a letter to the editor that Hollywood's power brokers might have hired Griffith when he was alive, instead of eulogizing him when he was dead. The anonymous reader wrote: "The eulogy ends. The captains and the kings depart, purged of their collective shame and in the manner of men who have righteously performed an unpleasant but full atonement for their sins of omission." The criticism stung Brackett, but he saw the truth of it: Hollywood devours its own and has no respect for its past. This, he realized, was a subject worth pursuing.

The day after reading that hurtful but honest letter, he wrote in his diary, "Billy and I spent the morning in discussion of the Hollywood story. It's all centered around a swimming pool owned by an old silent days' star."

CHAPTER SEVEN

FINDING NORMA

It was agreed. Their next project would be "the swimming pool story" or, as they also called it, "the Hollywood story." Only later did they come up with the working title "A Can of Beans," as a subterfuge to keep their unusual topic hidden from the press and rival studios; it must also have privately referenced for Wilder his impoverished, bean-eating days at the Chateau Marmont, when he was a starving writer like the protagonist of the picture he and Brackett now had under way. The film would be a satiric exploration of the film industry. But they didn't agree on the direction it would take, or who would play the "old silent days' star." Wilder wanted it to be a comedy with Mae West "as the faded glamour item," but Brackett objected "that the Mae West story, while offering riotous possibilities, could not possibly result in a picture of distinction."

Overriding Brackett's objections, Wilder set up an interview with West. The bawdy screen star, then fifty-five, was famous for her parodies of sexual fixation and her ribald double entendres: "I used to be

Snow White, but I drifted." Wilder had been a fan of West since her peak years in the early 1930s, when she starred in censorship-baiting sex comedies such as *She Done Him Wrong* and *I'm No Angel*. ("I believe in censorship," she deadpanned. "I made a fortune out of it.") In 1948, she was still a Paramount star, though she hadn't made a film in years. She and Wilder enjoyed a chummy relationship; they occasionally lunched together in the commissary or at Lucey's, a popular watering hole near the studio, where they swapped funny stories of a decidedly sexual nature. He was drawn to her vulgarity and fleshiness, not unlike the sex workers he'd known during his younger years in Vienna and Berlin.

Billy arranged to speak with her about playing the lead in the swimming pool story, but the conversation did not go well. The semi-retired stage and screen comedian who had made a career of promoting her sexuality was insulted that her friend should even ask. Who, she insisted, would believe that a woman of her shapely figure and sexual stamina would *pay* a man to be her lover? To the contrary, she boasted, if she had a lover half her age, he would barely be able to crawl out of bed after all she put him through. Her mantra was that she would never play a woman over twenty-six. As it turned out, Wilder was relieved. After discussing the project with West, he realized her acting style would turn the production into a "kind of Laurel and Hardy picture." Years later, he looked back with astonishment: "I thought of using Mae West. It's impossible to believe that now."

It was a lost opportunity for West, wrote her biographer Maurice Leonard: "Undoubtedly, the stupidest mistake Mae ever made in her life was to turn down the role." Her refusal, he added, "was symptomatic of Mae's ever-increasing megalomania, a condition which was to undermine so much of her subsequent career and signaled her descent into a way of being that consistently, though not entirely, lost touch with reality." In other words, the real-life former star reacted exactly as Norma Desmond, the fictitious one, would have. Clearly, they needed a star with emotional distance from the role, one who was more interested in playing a character as written than in playing herself.

The next candidate was Pola Negri, a dark-eyed Polish-born silent-screen vamp whose greatest rival had been none other than Gloria Swanson. Negri, living in semi-retirement in Malibu, was, like West, insulted by Wilder's proposal, though for a different reason. She abhorred the thought of appearing to her faithful fans as a bossy and belligerent older woman.

They also tried Mary Pickford, the Canadian-born actress who was by the mid-1910s the world's most popular film star. In 1948, while still affectionately known as "America's Sweetheart," she was living in semi-seclusion with her third husband, former leading man and bandleader Buddy Rogers, twelve years her junior. Having heard she was looking for a vehicle for her return to the silver screen, Brackett and Wilder arranged to meet with her at Pickfair Manor, the grand neo-Tudor mansion she had built in the 1920s with her previous husband, Douglas Fairbanks. She greeted them wearing a dark-blue dress. Sparkles emanated from her oversize diamond clips and diamond-studded bracelet. She looked, Brackett noted, "remarkably young and quite wicked."

While listening to Wilder's narration of the plot, Mary's eyes moistened. Yes, here at last was a star vehicle. She agreed to play the tragic diva, but only if they made her the full-on lead of the film; she refused to share the spotlight with whomever would play Joe Gillis. Realizing they had a real-life diva on their hands, Wilder and Brackett were pleased when, on giving the matter further thought, she turned them down.

A year and a half later, when the film appeared, Pickford was shattered. She saw that she had given up the role of a lifetime. Her old friend and rival Gloria Swanson played the part of Norma brilliantly, but Mary believed she could have done even better. In her revisionist telling, she claimed she felt compelled to reject the role because her legions of fans would never have believed her to be cruel, needy, and mad. She also claimed it was she who suggested to Brackett and Wilder that they cast Swanson as Desmond.

Wilder remembered otherwise. He recalled that his friend George Cukor, the director of beloved literary adaptations such as *David Copperfield*, *Camille*, and *Little Women*, sophisticated romantic comedies including *Dinner at Eight* and *The Philadelphia Story*, and the first tragic film about the film business, *What Price Hollywood?*, was the one who pointed him and Brackett to Gloria Swanson. Cukor, famed as a director of women, assured them she had the requisite acting skills.

Brackett and Wilder agreed that Swanson, a retired film star who now hosted a four-day-a-week interview show on a New York television station and was still striking in appearance, could transform their Hollywood tale into something truly special, even remarkable.

* * *

In September 1948, Brackett flew to New York, where he met Swanson for lunch at La Crémaillère, a country-style French restaurant. He found her "fabulously unchanged," with "the same piquant, dramatic face" that had captivated film audience in the 1920s. He invited her to California for further discussion.

Swanson, who assumed she was being asked to make an extended cameo appearance, was ambivalent about returning to Hollywood. After the 1934 debacle of *Music in the Air*, she had moved to New York City, first to 817 Fifth Avenue and eventually to a garden apartment at 920 Fifth, a limestone-clad Italianate building between East 72nd and 73rd, across the street from Pilgrim Hill in Central Park. She also had a country estate in Croton-on-Hudson, which she had purchased in the 1920s. Starting a line of women's clothing, which sold at high-end dress shops and department-store boutiques, she also founded Multiprises, a company that bought patents from European scientists and sold them to American corporations. Through Multiprises, and with the aid of her former husband, Henri de La Falaise, the Marquis de La Coudraye, who was living in Paris, she helped several Jewish scientists escape the Third Reich. The company closed its doors in late 1941, when the United States declared war on Germany. For his bravery as a liaison officer with the British 12th Royal Lancers and his heroism during the Battle of Dunkirk, where he was taken prisoner but escaped, Henri de La Falaise was awarded his second Croix de Guerre.

About this time, Gloria was invited back to Hollywood to star in a romantic comedy titled *Father Takes a Wife* (1941), in which she played an actress courted by a middle-aged shipping magnate (Adolphe Menjou). The movie did poorly at the box office, and her hoped-for return to stardom failed to materialize. Back on the East Coast, she found work in summer stock theater and in 1948 settled in as the celebrity host of the eponymous *Gloria Swanson Hour*. From a career standpoint, it was a smart move. Between 1947 and 1948, TV sales in New York City alone jumped from seventeen thousand to three hundred thousand. She was in the forefront of the new craze for home entertainment. Still, Swanson, first and foremost, was a film star who remained dedicated to the big screen, not its puny cousin. She quickly tired of the new medium, which she found banal and idiotic: "For months I had been so busy appearing on it that I'd never sat down and watched it. Now that I did [during a stay in the hospital], it depressed me. 'That's awful,' I said about one program after another. It looked cheap and thrown together, most of it, too black-and-white, too crude."

Members of the beleaguered film industry shared her sentiments. Nevertheless, it was abundantly clear that television was eroding film audiences. In 1946, before TV was widely available, moviegoers purchased more than ninety million box-office tickets per week—an extraordinary figure for a nation of 140 million citizens. Three years later, thanks in no small part to the incursions made by television, weekly box-office sales for movies had dropped by a third, to sixty million. Television was not the only threat facing the studios; in 1948 an antitrust ruling by the Supreme Court forced Paramount and the seven other major studios to end their block-booking practices and sell off their profitable theater chains, thus further choking their flow of earnings.

Unlike movies, television sets brought celebrities into living rooms, thereby forming a bond of intimacy between them and their audiences. No one capitalized on this more effectively than "Mr. Television" himself, Milton Berle. In September 1948—the same month Brackett offered Swanson a return to Hollywood—Berle, a forty-year-old ex-vaudevillian who had enjoyed only minor success in the movies, began hosting the weekly variety show *Texaco Star Theater*. With Berle at the helm, the show became so popular that restaurants, bars, and nightclubs were said to have adjusted their hours on Tuesday evenings, when most Americans were home watching "Uncle Miltie," as the rubber-faced comedian was affectionately known. A Nielsen rating showed that on Tuesdays, 97 percent of the American households with televisions tuned in to Milton Berle.

TV offered viewers more than merely crude comedy and revamped vaudeville. It also provided serious dramas that were staged live in New York television studios with well-known Broadway actors. One of several such drama hours was the *Philco Television Playhouse*, which flourished from 1948 to 1955. News of current events, as broadcast by the likes of Edward R. Murrow and Walter Cronkite, two enormously trusted commentators, also kept viewers fixed to their screens. In 1946, Americans purchased a total of seven thousand televisions. Two years later, the figure jumped to 172,000. Americans owned a million TV sets in 1949. A year later, the number had grown tenfold.

Hollywood responded by making movies more spectacular than ever, with a much higher percentage of productions in color. The studios also experimented with wide-screen formats, such as CinemaScope—which was especially suitable for westerns, war films, and musicals—to rebuff television, with its Lilliputian dimensions. In 1949, the diagonal size of the average television screen ranged from ten to twelve inches, something Norma Desmond might have been ridiculing when she said, "It's the pictures that got small."

★　★　★

By the late 1940s, Gloria Swanson, unlike Norma Desmond, had put the glamour and fanfare of Hollywood well behind her. She claimed she accepted Charles Brackett's offer of an all-expenses-paid trip to the West Coast in order to escape the demands of live television and bask a bit in the California sunshine. The former star, who embraced a healthy, macrobiotic diet, loved exercising in the outdoors. Her friend the gossip columnist Hedda Hopper, catching wind of Gloria's visit, ran a blind item in early October 1948, observing waggishly, "Charlie Brackett and Billy Wilder's story on Hollywood may feature Gloria Swanson. It's about an aging actress who falls in love with a younger man. Heck, that's not satire. It happens every day in Hollywood." (So much for keeping the subject of "A Can of Beans" secret.)

The only hitch for Swanson was the screen test Brackett and Wilder insisted she take. As one of the most admired and highly paid film actors of the silent era, she had already starred in more than fifty films. It seemed unimaginable to her that she should have to undergo a screen test. Swanson believed that screen tests for veteran actors were used as a ploy to undermine their confidence, making them more malleable to the director's wishes when shooting began for real. She turned for advice to her old friend George Cukor: Would it be unreasonable for her to refuse the test Brackett and Wilder wanted from her? Cukor replied, "Yes, it would be unreasonable. If they ask you to do ten screen tests, do them, or I'll personally shoot you."

Sensing Swanson's ambivalence, Brackett offered to put her up at the luxurious Beverly Hills Hotel and dangled before her a possible salary of $50,000 if she were cast. "Much as I hated the idea of a screen test," she wrote years later, "at that point $50,000 was music to the ears of someone who had been creating a whole TV show for $350 a week."

Screen test and salary aside, Swanson was intrigued by the project's intended mix of reality and fiction, past and present, and real-life actors playing fictional characters eerily like themselves. The script, what little there was of it (they assured her it would be completed soon), reminded her of the Sicilian dramatist Luigi Pirandello, whose plays in the early twentieth century deliciously scrambled the lines between reality and illusion.

Before coming to Los Angeles, Swanson had to have her appendix removed. The procedure didn't go well, requiring a second operation and additional weeks for recovery. Finally, on the last day of January 1949, she embarked by train for Los Angeles, arriving three days later at Union Station. Exhausted by the journey, but warmed by the midwinter California sun, she settled comfortably into her suite in the Beverly Hills Hotel.

The next day, she met Brackett for lunch at Romanoff's Russian restaurant on Rodeo Drive, followed by a private screening of Brackett and Wilder's most recent film, *A Foreign Affair*, which featured Marlene Dietrich. (Though only two years younger than Swanson, Dietrich, still active in movies and continuing to play roles of a distinctly erotic nature, seemed ageless. Having appeared in silent German films two decades earlier, Dietrich had gained international fame in the sound era as the siren Lola Lola in *The Blue Angel*, Josef von Sternberg's 1930 tale of lust and humiliation, as produced by Erich Pommer. Von Sternberg had considered Swanson for the role because she could sing, but then he discovered Dietrich.) When the lights in the screening room came up, Billy was waiting to greet Gloria, and he did so warmly. They reminisced briefly about *Music in the Air*, which they had made for Pommer in the early 1930s, albeit with no personal contact between them, as he was "only" the writer. With that, they got down to business.

In preparation for the screen test, she met with Edith Head, who ran Paramount's costume department. Observing Swanson as she tried on various outfits, Brackett was struck by "the extraordinary, rather violent, slightly wicked beauty of her face, of her hair." That was on Friday; on Sunday, she telephoned him in a state of alarm, saying that she couldn't grasp from the handful of pages he had given her the character she was to play in the screen test. He rushed to the hotel, where he spent a couple of hours listening to Swanson pick flaws in their characterization of Norma. Outwardly calm and reassuring, Brackett was inwardly tense as he imagined what Billy's reaction would be to a star meddling with "his" script.

Brackett's fears were unfounded. On Monday morning, when Wilder met with Swanson, he could not have been more gracious, putting her at ease with his impish wit. Stop worrying about the script, he told her; we can fix the problems later. She found him thoroughly charming.

They shot the screen test on Wednesday. Swanson was prepared. Playing opposite a young man who read the Joe Gillis line, "You're Norma Desmond. You used to be big," she pinned the camera with a Gorgon's gaze and corrected his mistake: "I *am* big. It's the pictures that got small." The ferocity with which she delivered the line startled Brackett and Wilder. "She has no inhibitions," Brackett noted in his diary that night. "It's just a question of holding her back."

The screen test resulted in two changes to the film. First, Brackett and Wilder decided that Swanson looked too good on camera and needed to be aged up for audiences to accept Norma as a relic of the past. They told her they would have gray added to her hair and lines to her face so that the gulf in age between Norma and Joe would be believable. She countered that instead of making her look older, they should worry about making whoever played Joe look younger.

Second, and more significantly, they realized that Swanson, as an actor, possessed both the technical skills and emotional depth to make Norma a dramatically stunning character. The part they brought her to Hollywood to play, in its original concept, was that of a dotty but likable woman of a certain age, yet thanks to Swanson's edgy, almost demented screen test, they began to see much more depth to the role, more room for a downward spiral into madness. In Maurice Zolotow's words, the former silent star "exuded such savagery and madness from the screen that Brackett and Wilder shifted the story radically and now made Norma Desmond the central role in the film."

They grasped that Norma was a tragic figure, not a vehicle for comedy (as Mae West would have been), but comic nonetheless. The dual nature of the character they now came to develop with Swanson in mind was bound to confuse viewers who had difficulty understanding that a movie could cross genres and be *both* a comedy and a tragedy. Brackett later noted that he and Wilder deliberately avoided taking a sentimental view of Norma, which would have caused audiences to have "an audible lump" in their throats; instead, "We thought it effective to suppress the pitying sounds and let the audience find the pity for themselves."

This meant writing new scenes for Norma. Later, when the film was in production, they consulted with Swanson daily to find out what Norma would say in this or that situation, so thoroughly did the real-life former movie star inhabit the role of the fictional one. This was an extraordinary change for a director who normally rankled at dialogue suggestions from his actors. The story still belongs to Joe Gillis; after all, he's the narrator and protagonist of the film, the one who tries to take advantage of an older woman only to find himself possessed by her, both materially and psychologically. Yet in the end, Norma, as played by Swanson, *owns* the movie.

While avidly agreeing that the role of Norma needed expanding, Brackett and Wilder couldn't concur on how to write her: Is she "a rich egocentric woman" (Brackett's words) who gradually goes mad, or is she mad from the beginning? As the film scholar Steven Cohan has noted, "From the writing of the script, to the filming, to the editing, to the cycles of previews and to the many reshoots, the two men would argue about Norma's mental state—whether to keep her arrogance or add an undercurrent of vulnerability, whether to make her lose her sanity or be crazy from the start."

Thrilled that she had done so well on the screen test, Swanson relaxed and took pleasure in being "home" again. Indeed, the Beverly Hills Hotel overlooked the twenty-two-room mansion she had owned in the 1920s. She dined with old friends: the Goldwyns, Joan Fontaine, Ray Milland, Cole Porter, and Clifton Webb. Errol Flynn hosted a dinner for her, with other guests that included Mary Pickford, Raoul Walsh, and Billy Haines, a gifted comedian and popular leading man of the silent era, whose movie career crashed when he refused to embark on a studio-imposed Hollywood marriage to allay rumors that he was gay. Taking his banishment in stride, Haines became the film colony's leading interior designer.

Swanson wrote to her lifelong friend Virginia Bowker, "All I have done since I have been here is reminisce. I have seen so many old friends and spots. It has been old home week and a busman's holiday, sandwiched in with tests, interviews and business conferences." A large sign, erected outside the Paramount gate to highlight the studio's twenty-fifth anniversary, featured painted representations of its top moneymakers of the past quarter century. Swanson was in the lead position, even though she hadn't made a movie for Paramount in twenty years. Lined up behind her were depictions of the studio's current stars Bob Hope, Bing Crosby, Barbara Stanwyck, and Betty Hutton. When a casting director told her he was glad to see her prominently ranked ahead of the others, Swanson was amused. "That's when I knew I was home," she recollected, "right back in the jungle, up to my ears in the rat race."

Unlike the other former screen goddesses who had turned down the role out of vanity or fear of disappointing their fans, Swanson was intrigued by the part, especially because she regarded herself as Norma's opposite: a levelheaded realist. Clear-eyed about the career options open to her as a woman of fifty, she understood the challenges and opportunities that such a complex role could provide. Vanity was not going to hold her back. As far as she was concerned, the only true similarity she had with the character she was asked to play was that both had been stars of the silent screen; beyond that, the similarities ceased. She could *play* Norma because in real life she was nothing like her. In other words, she had to be eminently sane and technically proficient to portray a madwoman. As Richard Strauss exclaimed of Wagner's *Tristan*, "Such fire of sustained passion! It could only have been written by a man of ice!"

Gloria knew the Hollywood jungle. She knew the rat race. She knew Norma Desmond. She knew the world that had made Norma and then abandoned her. That was all Swanson needed.

★ ★ ★

In 1949, one of Hollywood's most sought-after women worked behind, not in front of, the camera. But everyone in the business knew her name. Shy and self-conscious about her own appearance (she never smiled, having been teased as a child about her protruding front teeth), Edith Head ran the wardrobe department at Paramount Pictures, a position she had held since 1938. Under her watch, Paramount's female leads were regarded as the best costumed in the business. Referred to in the industry as the dress doctor, she was courted by stars, who knew they could only look as good on screen as her creations allowed. She was similarly sought after by producers and directors who recognized that costume designs could make or break their pictures.

The first woman to run a studio costume department, Head saw her role differently from that of her predecessors, who had focused more on their elaborate designs than on the women who would wear them. She liked to have friendly conversations with stars in the early stages of production, woman-to-woman or, in some cases, woman-to-man. Putting them at ease, she learned from them—not the director or cinematographer—what *they* considered their most and least attractive physical features. It was the costume designer's job, Head believed, to design apparel that would show off the former and disguise the latter. Deception was her stock in trade. "Accentuate the positive and camouflage the rest," she was fond of saying. For *Sullivan's Travels* (1941), she even managed to disguise the advanced pregnancy of the vixenish Hollywood newcomer Veronica Lake, who, to complicate matters further, played an unemployed actress who disguises herself as a boy. Head's artful deception not only "camouflaged" Lake's pregnancy but also launched her career as one of the great sex symbols of the Second World War.

Head began her illustrious career in the mid-1920s when she was hired as a sketch artist in Paramount's wardrobe department. She was one of the low-level studio female employees who were instructed to strew rose petals at Gloria Swanson's feet on the day the studio's greatest star returned as the Marquise de La Coudraye in a limousine lined in faux leopard skin, creating an indelible impression on the young costume designer.

Head received her first screen credit for designing Mae West's skin-tight, semi-transparent gowns for *She Done Him Wrong*, a risqué comedy that, in the darkest days of the Great Depression, was one of the biggest moneymakers of 1933. West instructed Head, "Make the clothes loose enough to prove I'm a lady, but tight enough to show 'em I'm a woman." Head understood that female viewers, even the most practical ones—perhaps them most of all—went to the movies to be astonished by the fantastic, the unimaginable: costumes they could wear only in their dreams. "Make it look as tricky, as bizarre, as unusual as you possibly can," Edith said. "Be sure it doesn't look like something you can buy in a store. Be sure that people will gasp when they see it." On the other hand, Head, like the chief costume designers for the other studios, availed herself of commercial tie-ins with garment manufacturers and department-store buyers, who offered low-priced, scaled-back, off-the-rack versions of the latest screen fashions.

In early 1949, when Swanson came to Hollywood for her screen test, Head relished the opportunity to exchange costume design ideas with this most famous clothes horse of the Jazz Age, a woman adulated by other women for her unique sense of style. The two became fast friends. Head had never worked with an actress as clothes-savvy as Swanson. They gossiped about the great stars and directors that one or the other or both had worked with during their respective careers, Swanson mostly in the 1920s and Head in the 1930s and 1940s. They were approximately the same age (Head, two years older) and the same height (five feet), both were perfectionists in their respective professions, and both regarded costume design as an art.

Together they imagined what Norma Desmond would wear; how this strange, erratic, and eccentric holdover from an earlier era would apparel herself in 1949. Wilder reminded them that Norma, a fashion trendsetter in the 1920s, would have been aware of late-1940s fashions, including Christian Dior's New Look, which only a year or so earlier had swept America. Would wealthy middle-aged Norma choose the New Look or remain committed to a modified flapper style that harked back to her glory days? They opted for a blend of the two, visually reinforcing Norma's dual nature as someone who existed in both the present and the past. Head remembered it as her most challenging assignment: "Everything about her clothes, her hair, her accessories, her negligee, and her furs had to convey a feeling that they weren't exactly from the current era, despite the fact that they were obviously fine, new clothes worn by a woman of wealth and style to whom image meant a great deal." The costume designer was surprised she was not nominated for an Academy Award for *Sunset Boulevard*; instead, she was nominated for—and won—an Oscar for her other major assignment of the year, *All About Eve*, which, to her mind, required less subtlety and nuance of vision.

In the storage rooms of Paramount, Head found several pairs of high-heeled shoes, size 2½, with the name "Miss Swanson" affixed to them. Swanson had worn them in the 1920s, and she would wear them again in *Sunset Boulevard*.

★ ★ ★

On April 15, three days before principal photography was to begin on *Sunset Boulevard*, Wallace Beery died at age sixty-four. Only years later in her memoir did Swanson record her response to the news. She had never forgiven her first husband for raping her on their wedding night and subsequently slipping her, or so she believed, an under-the-counter drug that caused her to miscarry their child. Nonetheless, she occasionally saw him in social situations over the years and usually maintained her composure. One night was different. At a Hollywood dinner party in November 1919, when others at the table were congratulating her on the success of her films with DeMille, Beery said to her, "This may sound funny, but I want you to know I've always prayed you'd be a failure, Gloria, so you would come back to me." The remark stunned everyone, including Swanson, who could not hide her contempt: "He had played out his little game and stayed married to me for the duration of the war [that is, World War I], and now he was actually trying to make it sound to my old friends as if I had been an ambitious starlet who had used him briefly in my scramble to success, broken his heart, and then dropped him; and worse yet, as if he had, nevertheless, sadly kept a light burning in the window."

In a letter dated April 15, 1949, that Swanson sent to her friend and publicist Barron Polan in New York, she did not mention Beery's death, perhaps because the news hadn't reached her yet, or perhaps because she wasn't interested in revisiting distasteful memories. "Picture officially starts on Monday," she wrote. "I tested all day for clothes today. Have something like twelve changes. Edith Head and I have gone crazy creating things out of this world." To this she added, "The part is fabulous. It has somewhat changed since they saw my test and

I blinked my pretty blue eyes at them. But today while testing they crept up on me and put some gray streaks in my hair, hoping to make me a little older that way." Despite the attention suddenly lavished on her again after more than two decades away from the Hollywood spotlight, Swanson was determined to keep her feet on the ground. She ended her letter by saying she "cannot wait to get back to the cinders of New York. They agree with me much more than smog, smudge, and fog."

CHAPTER EIGHT

THE MAN YOU LOVE TO HATE

In the early 1950s, the humorist and former Marx Brothers scriptwriter S. J. Perelman published a memory piece in *The New Yorker* on a silent film actor who had had a tremendous impact on him in his youth. "He was a short man, almost squat, with a vulpine smirk that told you, the moment his image flashed upon the screen, that no wife or bank roll must be left unguarded. The clean-shaven bullethead, the glittering monocle, and the ramrod back (kept rigid by a corset, it was whispered) were as familiar and as dear to the moviegoing public as the Pickford curls.... He was the ace of cads, a man without a single redeeming feature, the embodiment of Prussian Junkerism, and the greatest heavy of the silent film, and his name, of course, was Erich von Stroheim."

Perelman recalled that in his youth he was so taken with Stroheim's erotic drama *Foolish Wives* (1922), which Stroheim wrote, directed, and starred in, that "For six months afterward," he wrote, "I exhibited a maddening tendency to click my heels and murmur '*Bitte?*' along with a twitch as though a monocle were screwed into my eye." His mannerisms finally abated when the dean of Brown University took him aside and "confided that if I wanted to transfer to Heidelberg, the faculty would not stand in my way."

About Stroheim's persona as a villain, Perelman wrote: "Whatever von Stroheim's shortcomings were as an artist, he was consistent. When he set out to limn a louse, he put his back into it. He never palliated his villainy, never helped old ladies across the street to show he was a sweet kid au fond or prated about his Oedipus complex." Recalling old Hollywood advice that the best way to designate a villain is to have him kick the nearest dog, Perelman admiringly observed, "Von Stroheim not only kicked the dog; he kicked the owner and the S.P.C.A. for good measure."

Perelman's caricature of Stroheim is delightful but one-dimensional. The real Stroheim was a complex figure. Grasping the complexity at work in *Sunset Boulevard* requires an understanding of this proud, arrogant, narcissistic genius who, against type, played a humble, self-effacing, passionately in-love servant to the film's main character, who is herself a narcissist. But whereas she is delusional, von Mayerling, as played by Stroheim, is a sad and clear-eyed realist.

Erich von Stroheim's greatest artistic achievement was not his body of work per se, but rather himself. In the annals of Hollywood, no one surpassed him as a master of self-invention. Here's his autobiographical résumé, which he apparently passed along to his first biographer, Peter Noble:

> Erich Oswald Hans Carl Marie Stroheim von Nordenwald was born on September 22nd, 1885 in Vienna, where his father was

a Colonel in the 6th Regiment of Dragoons, and his mother a lady-in-waiting to Elizabeth, Empress of Austria. The boy was educated at the Austrian Military Academy, and at the age of seventeen was commissioned—somewhat inevitably—as a Second Lieutenant in the cavalry. He remained in the Austrian army for seven years.

All sheer fabrication, except for the birth date and birthplace. Stroheim (he later added the "von") was born in Vienna to a lower middle-class family of observant Jews. His father, a hatter, was of Polish extraction; his mother came from Prague. Erich, who later claimed military glory for himself—the prominent scar on his forehead was the result, he said, of a saber wound incurred during a skirmish in Bosnia-Herzegovina—spent no more than a few months in the Austro-Hungarian army before he deserted or was expelled, it's not clear which. He emigrated to America in 1909 at age twenty-four. Immigration records show that he had fair skin and brown eyes, was five feet five inches in stature, and bore a scar on his forehead. Rather than admit to being Jewish, he declared himself a Roman Catholic—as any good Austrian aristocrat would have been. As soon as he could, he enlisted in the New York National Guard but was removed from the rolls after only two months, probably for insubordination. Insubordination appears to have been his most defining personality characteristic.

He next made his way to Oakland, California, where he found work wrangling horses and washing dishes at a dude ranch. There he met and began a love affair with Margaret Knox, an emotionally fragile woman six years his elder. After a period of living together, they married, both prevaricating on their marriage certificate: She claimed to be eighteen though she was thirty-three, and he asserted that his mother was a German baroness. Margaret supported Von, as he liked to be called, with her meager income, while he sought to earn a living as a writer. None of his stories, novels, or plays was published or produced. Frustrated and humiliated, he took to drink and, when drunk, lashed out at Margaret, threatening her with physical violence. In the spring of 1914, a year after they'd wed, she filed for divorce. Meanwhile, Von heard that Hollywood was hiring extras, particularly ones who knew their way around horses, for the filming of a Civil War epic, *The Birth of a Nation*. Von auditioned, and, within a day of starting work, he realized his vocation was not to wrangle horses but to direct motion pictures.

Stroheim proudly claimed to have been one of the hooded Klansmen who ride to the rescue in the thrilling, disturbingly racist finale of D. W. Griffith's deeply problematic masterpiece. He also asserted that his strength and bravery as a stuntman led Griffith to make him an assistant director, though neither of these claims has been verified.

By a trick of history, Stroheim happened to be the right man in the right place. The Great War had broken out in Europe, and Hollywood studios, eager to capitalize on the conflagration, began churning out anti-German propaganda melodramas, even though the United States had yet to enter the war. Appearing in no fewer than five of these movies as a barbaric "Hun," the head-shaven, bullnecked actor quickly attracted audience attention. It was then that studio publicists gave him his famous moniker, the man you love to hate.

With the coming of peace in November 1918, Americans lost interest in Prussian villains, and Stroheim was suddenly out of work. He concentrated on writing and came up with a film idea that he wanted to star in and also direct. After weeks of positioning himself outside the office of Universal Pictures' German Jewish studio chief Carl Laemmle, he finally got the opportunity to pitch it. (In an alternative version, he trekked out on foot, because he didn't drive and couldn't afford carfare, to Laemmle's home in the San Fernando Valley to make the pitch.) Laemmle, affectionately known as Uncle Carl, liked to help the careers of fellow immigrant Jews from Germany and Austria. Stroheim was an exceptionally persuasive storyteller who fixed the listener with his intense gaze and slow, august manner of speaking. Enthralled,

Laemmle agreed to the would-be director's ambitious request. The resulting film was titled *Blind Husbands* (1919).

"Until the coming of Orson Welles," wrote the film historian Richard Koszarski, "*Blind Husbands* was the most impressive and significant debut film in Hollywood history." To be sure, Stroheim's directorial debut has neither the technical brio, narrative complexity, nor socio-historical depth of *Citizen Kane*. Nonetheless, he went overnight from has-been actor to the most vaunted writer-director-actor in cinema. Audiences were absorbed by the movie's adult themes and sexual audacity. The monocled director was immediately heralded as the heir to Griffith and peer to DeMille. Such comparisons, however, missed their mark. Stroheim's worldview was uniquely and perversely his own.

Blind Husbands is a compelling tale of intended adultery in the Austrian Alps. An Austrian lieutenant, played by Stroheim, attempts to seduce an American housewife whose "blind husband" neglects her while he goes mountain climbing. What drives the film is not the plot but the animal magnetism Stroheim exudes. One restless night, the wife sees him in her dreams. His monocled face detached from his body, his cigarette holder poised between his lips, his eyes leering out at her from the darkness, he resembles a human cobra.

Variety called his next film, the now lost *Devil's Pass Key* (1920), "interminable," which was the first but not last time viewers of Stroheim films would be undone by their inordinate length. "The story is jerky and jumpy," one critic complained. This jerkiness and absence of continuity was an unfortunate characteristic of all the Stroheim pictures that followed *Blind Husbands*, thanks to their being radically truncated to fit the standardized time slots demanded by movie theater managers. An over-length feature film would prevent theaters from offering two screenings per evening and thus jeopardize box-office revenues. Stroheim, however, refused to make movies of standard length. In his view, the longer they were, the better. He envisioned for his films the expansive length of Victorian and Russian novels, which allowed authors the space needed to explore characters in depth. His final cut of his third film, *Foolish Wives,* came in at nearly eight hours. When asked how it would be possible to present a film of that length for an evening's entertainment, he replied, "That is a detail I hadn't time to bother about." *Photoplay* suggested the film be retitled "Foolish Directors."

The year *Foolish Wives* was released, 1922, was a watershed in modern culture. Ezra Pound called it Year One of a new era, for it marked the publication of two of the most influential texts of literary modernism, James Joyce's *Ulysses* and T. S. Eliot's *The Waste Land.* These were challenging works, affronts to both conventional literary aesthetics and conventional morality. *Foolish Wives,* too, can be considered modernist in its defiance of cinematic norms and its steely amorality. It offers no characters with whom to identify and refuses to placate viewers with a sentimental happy ending. It even plays a meta-textual joke: Stroheim's libertine character gives the woman he attempts to seduce a copy of *Foolish Wives,* a novel that didn't actually exist outside the world of the film, by an author whose name appears on the cover as "Erich von Stroheim."

Stroheim plays a fake aristocrat (not unlike "von" Stroheim himself) who, residing in Monte Carlo, passes counterfeit bills at the casinos, seduces the wife of an American envoy, drives his previously seduced female servant to suicide, and, in footage now lost, rapes a simpleminded teenage girl. He had no hesitation in portraying a lightly disguised version of himself as a character of the deepest depravity. French critic André Bazin neatly summed up the cinema of Erich von Stroheim: "He has one simple rule for direction. Take a close look at the world, keep on doing so, and in the end it will lay bare for you all its cruelty and its ugliness."

Universal insisted that Stroheim edit the film to a more manageable length, which he attempted to do, but not to their satisfaction: His new cut ran for more than four and a half hours. A special railroad car was added to the train transporting the film east for its New York premiere so that a team of editors could work around the clock to cut it down further. This made for good press coverage, which aroused readers' anticipation to see this already controversial production. By the time *Foolish Wives* reached its destination, it ran three and a half hours.

The movie bounded so far over budget that the publicists at Universal capitalized on the film's outrageous extravagance, setting up an electric sign in Times Square that posted the mounting costs from hour to hour. The illuminated billboard crowed, "He's going to make you hate him! Even if it takes a million dollars of our money to do it!" They spelled his name as $troheim. Audiences eagerly awaited the premiere, wanting to see for themselves the most expensive movie ever made. Desperate to shorten the film, the editors on the cross-country train scrapped some scenes altogether. Likewise, individual shots were shorn of their openings and closings. When the spectacle at last reached viewers, they were perplexed by its baffling gaps in continuity.

Nevertheless, the film played throughout the world and was heralded as an overwhelming success—or, perhaps more accurately, a succès de scandale. So much so that Louis B. Mayer, MGM's cofounder and head of the studio, bought into Stroheim's next project, which was to write and direct a feature film titled *Greed* (1924). Meanwhile, Mayer hired Irving Thalberg away from Universal and appointed him MGM's chief of production. Only twenty-six at the time, Thalberg was known as "the boy wonder" because of his unparalleled ability to pick winners and draw the best out of his personnel. He had already had a taste of Stroheim's inflexibility at Universal, where the two of them clashed over a movie called *Merry-Go-Round*. Halfway through production, Thalberg canned Stroheim and replaced him with another director. Now, two years later with the production of *Greed*, he naively believed he could control the mad genius of American film. He was mistaken. The director's cut ran for a shocking thirteen hours. When Thalberg implored the arrogant director to cut it down, Stroheim submitted an eight-hour version but refused to go further. Thalberg fired him and oversaw the editing (some would say butchering) of the film to two and a half hours.

Whereas *Foolish Wives* rubbed audience's faces in the ugly side of a single individual, *Greed* aimed more broadly to show the ugliness of the human race. Adapted from *McTeague*, Frank Norris's bleak 1899 masterpiece of American literary naturalism, *Greed* does not hold back in its unabating examination of moral weakness; nor does it offer a tidy or sentimental resolution, as was the Hollywood tradition. Like a Greek tragedy set in modern times, it took the unpopular, if not also un-American, view that individuals are victims of heredity and an indifferent, or downright hostile, universe.

Set by Stroheim in modern-day San Francisco, *Greed* tells of a dentist and his partially disabled wife whose marriage unravels when she wins a lottery and hoards her winnings rather than spend them or share them with her husband. After their growing animosity bursts into mutual hatred, he strangles her and escapes with a bag of her gold to Death Valley. A fight to the death ensues between McTeague and a dogged pursuer, who, before dying, manages to handcuff himself to McTeague. The movie ends with its greedy antihero standing alone in the middle of the desert, chained to a dead man. With its disturbing imagery, its brutal violence, and none of the glamour and eroticism of *Foolish Wives*, *Greed* was a box-office disaster.

In a profile of Stroheim that the young Billy Wilder, then living in Berlin, published in the art magazine *Der Querschnitt*, the future filmmaker reported that *Greed* ran "for exactly one day at the Ufa-Palast am Zoo. Never has there been this kind of scandal in Berlin." Wilder, himself a cynic, could see beyond the film's disturbing depiction of the human condition. He grasped Stroheim's cinematic originality: "People are aghast that he is five years ahead of us. Independent of the Russians, he uses the Russian style before they do. He foresees something along the lines of visual editing and montage." And indeed, Stroheim was revered in the Soviet Union, where his films were praised and carefully studied. When asked whom he most admired in Hollywood, Sergei Eisenstein replied, "Chaplin, von Stroheim, and Walt Disney." Similarly, Mayer called Stroheim the greatest director in the world. "That's a fact," he said. "And no one who knows pictures would dispute it." To this he added that the director was a "crazy artist" who was impossible to work with—another statement few in Hollywood would have disputed.

Accounts of Stroheim's obstinance were legendary. During a heated exchange with the boy wonder, Stroheim is said to have roared, "I am an artist. I find my inspiration everywhere. I don't go by schedules prepared by lunatics with stopwatches, dummkopfs counting words on a page. I embroider, I paint, red here, blue there, I compose, pianissimo, fortissimo. This is how I work. You cannot tell me, Erich von Stroheim! What do you know? Where do you come from? An asylum, maybe?"

Stroheim stretched the patience of studio executives again with his follow-up to *Greed*, *The Merry Widow* (1925). An adaptation faithful in name only of Franz Lehár's popular 1905 operetta, Stroheim's *Merry Widow* served primarily as a springboard for the director's erotic fantasies. The film abounds in writhing pelvises, bare breasts, naked dancers, ogling men, and prolonged close-ups of women's feet. According to legend, Thalberg, disturbed, among other things, by the length of the film, accused the director of having a foot fetish. "And you, sir," Stroheim retorted, "have a footage fetish." Stroheim insisted that the extras playing the palace guards in *The Merry Widow* wear silk underwear embroidered with the king's monogram even though the undergarments would not be seen. With its kinky eroticism and cheerful amorality, the film was an international hit, though Stroheim always spoke dismissively of it because of what he saw as its uncharacteristic concession to commercial imperatives.

Stroheim established a newly mature vocabulary for the depiction of sexuality in cinema. He took sex seriously and insisted that audiences do so as well. When a journalist baited him by saying that moralists deemed his films unfit for children, the director took umbrage. "You Americans are living on babyfood," he replied with contempt. "My ears have rung with [your] united cry: 'it is not fit for children!' Children! Children!" His movies, he impatiently explained, were made for adults, not children. He understood more clearly than anyone else that erotic attraction was the bedrock of cinema from its earliest beginnings. One of the first films in motion picture history, an eighteen-second short titled *The Kiss* (1896), consisted entirely of a prolonged smooch between a man and a woman. Like his contemporary James Joyce in literature and his older countryman Sigmund Freud in psychoanalysis, Stroheim believed that sex for purposes other than procreation was fundamental to human experience and therefore should not be suppressed or otherwise avoided—and that went for movies as well as any other medium of cultural expression.

★ ★ ★

In 1928, Stroheim was approached by Gloria Swanson, then head of Gloria Productions, and her associate Joe Kennedy. Reveling in the success of her latest film, *Sadie Thompson*, which she'd both produced and starred in, Swanson was looking for a director who would propel her production company to a new level of prestige within the industry. Stroheim, with his edgy and unbridled style as a filmmaker, seemed the man for the job, the checkered history of his films notwithstanding.

Sharing Swanson's opinion of Stroheim was Kennedy, her business partner and lover, who had come to Hollywood in 1926 to apply his entrepreneurial skills to the film business, buying and reorganizing unprofitable film studios. The pictures produced by the would-be movie mogul were disposable westerns that earned him no respect. He saw a route to respectability when Swanson invited him to coproduce a movie by the most controversial and artistically acclaimed motion picture director in America. Together he and Swanson met with von

Stroheim on scenic Catalina Island and offered him the opportunity to write and direct a romantic epic of his choosing. He accepted the offer and went away to create what he believed would be his magnus opus, a script he titled *The Swamp* before later changing it to *Queen Kelly*. Although Swanson had warned Kennedy that Stroheim was known to be uncompromising, the cocky investor brushed off her concerns. "I can handle him," he assured her in four famous last words. He should have spoken with Hollywood's boy wonder about the chances of riding Stroheim's whirlwind.

Early on, the production ran up against two obstacles. One was technological: The movie had been planned as a silent film, but by 1928, in the industrial vortex caused by the first fully synchronized sound picture, *The Jazz Singer* (1927), studios rushed to add sound to their silent films in production. The dynamic visuals Stroheim had already filmed for *Queen Kelly* would have to be reshot with cumbersome cameras and intrusive sound-recording equipment. Encased in layers of soundproofing, movie cameras could not soar with the sensuous fluidity of the silent cameras. The other obstacle was Stroheim himself. True to form, the director kept upping the costs of the production and overrunning its shooting schedule. Despite his bravado, Kennedy could not rein in his director's oversize ambitions.

Queen Kelly is the story of a sixteen-year-old convent girl, Kitty Kelly, played by Swanson, soon to turn thirty. Kitty wins the heart of a handsome prince in a fictitious Germanic kingdom. The lovers "meet cute," but for Stroheim the cute focuses on fetish. The prince and his contingent of cavalry come across a gaggle of convent girls who are on an outing in the countryside. The girls are not used to seeing men, particularly such dashing ones. Kitty trembles so furiously in her excitement that her knickers drop to her ankles. When the prince laughs at this, the indignant girl steps out of her panties, crumples them into a ball, and throws them at his face. He catches them and tucks them into his tunic. (The original plan was for him to sniff them, but Swanson, as the film's coproducer, objected, saying it was vulgar and would never pass the censors.) That night, the prince sneaks into the convent in search of the girl with the unruly underwear. So begins their forbidden romance.

Swanson exulted in the way Stroheim photographed her. In one exquisitely staged chiaroscuro scene, Kitty prays in a darkened chapel, her virginal face illuminated by flickering candles (this is the footage that would later be shown in the home projection scene in *Sunset Boulevard*). In her autobiography, Swanson wrote, "Those first rushes were breath-taking. Every scene was alive with glowing light play and palpable texture. . . . Each scene seemed richer and more dazzling than the one before."

As a director, Stroheim was like none other. "He was so painstaking and slow," Swanson wrote, "that I would lose all sense of time, hypnotized by the man's relentless perfectionism. A scene that Allan Dwan or Raoul Walsh would have wrapped up in an hour might take Stroheim all day, fondling and dawdling over the tiniest minutiae, only to announce late in the afternoon that he would like to try it once more the following day."

While the artist in Swanson admired the director's stubborn refusal to let a scene stand without trying and trying again to improve it, the producer in her did not. With so much of her personal fortune tied up in the film, she was wary of his compulsive reshooting, as well as his insistence on sexually suggestive scenes she knew the Hays Office would insist be cut. With the film's budget exhausted after only two months of filming, Kennedy refused to write another check, Swanson fired Stroheim, and the production shut down altogether. *Queen Kelly* was later completed in 1932 in a sound-added version with a new ending, directed by the Russian-Polish theater and film director Richard Boleslawski and shot by the later-to-be-famous Hollywood cinematographer Gregg Toland. It was released in Europe and South America but, because of copyright disputes, never shown in the United States during Swanson's lifetime. Film preservationists have since compiled a partial restoration of Stroheim's original, but it remains one of the most notorious unfinished films in the history of cinema.

★ ★ ★

With the abrupt end of his directing career, Stroheim returned to acting. The interwar years offered him a variety of roles, most of them boiling down to the man you love to hate. One of his performances, however, transcended the genre: that as Major von Rauffenstein, a sympathetically depicted World War I German flying ace and prison camp commandant in Jean Renoir's remarkable antiwar film *La Grande Illusion* (1937). By now Stroheim was living and working in France, where a new generation of film enthusiasts and filmmakers, Renoir among them, lionized him. When contacted by Paramount in November 1948 to ask if he would play the role of Max von Mayerling in a new film by Billy Wilder, the ex-director, now sixty-three and semi-retired, wrote to Paul Kohner, his agent, "I don't have to tell you that I would not at all mind working with 'witty-Billy.' His last endeavor with me [*Five Graves to Cairo*] had a tremendous success here in France, or was it my extraordinary popularity here that made his picture go over big? Ask him."

Nonetheless, Stroheim, with his undaunted pride, resented having to play a lackey, especially the lackey of Gloria Swanson, the woman who had summarily ended his directing career. In the scene in which Max awaits Gillis in the moonlit garage, Stroheim utters one of the most self-referential and pathos-inducing lines in the film when he says, "I directed all her earlier pictures [in reality, Stroheim directed Swanson in only one film, *Queen Kelly*]. There were three young directors who showed promise in those days: D. W. Griffith, C. B. DeMille, and

Max von Mayerling." This revelation is topped a moment later by Max's admission to Norma's present lover, "It was I who came back, humiliating as it may seem. I could have gone on with my career, only I found everything unendurable after she divorced me. You see, I was her first husband." How humiliating these lines must have been to a man whose entire life seemed to have been self-engineered to avoid humiliation, whether in public or on the screen.

Paramount offered Stroheim $35,000 for his role. He demanded $50,000: the same amount Swanson was reportedly being paid. But Paramount stood its ground, telling Wilder and Brackett that they would have to look for someone else to play the part if Stroheim didn't accept their initial offer. Stroheim caved. He needed the money: "Even geniuses have to eat at least twice a week," he said, only half joking.

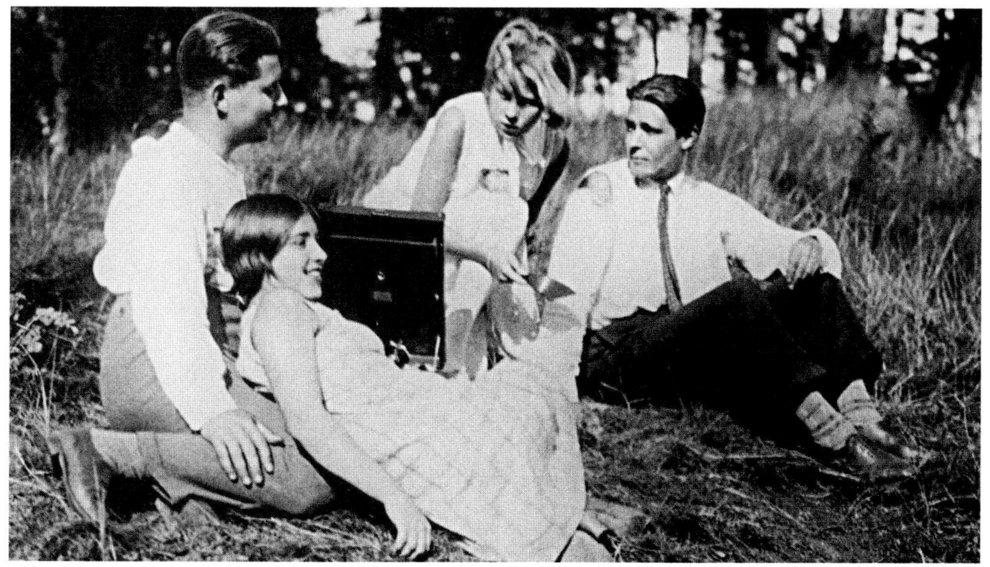

Wilder's first success as a screenwriter: *People on Sunday* (1930)

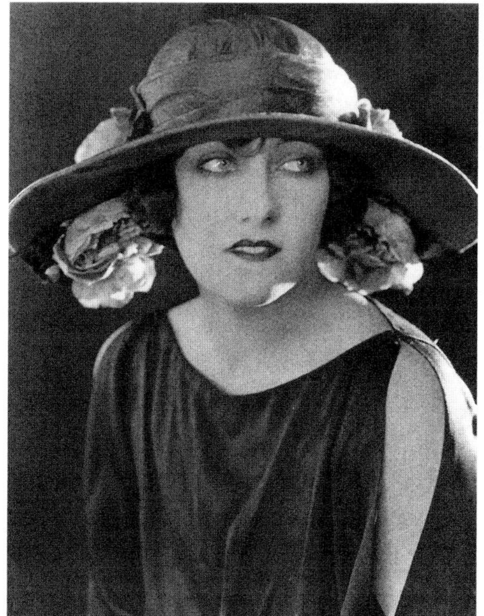

Gloria Swanson in the mid-1920s

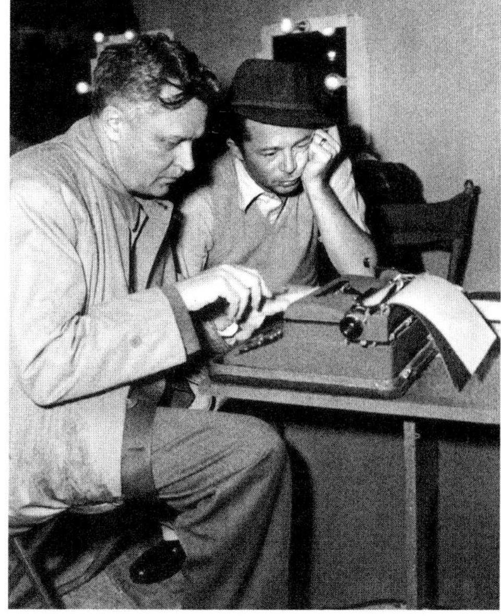

Brackett and Wilder at work on
The Major and the Minor in 1942

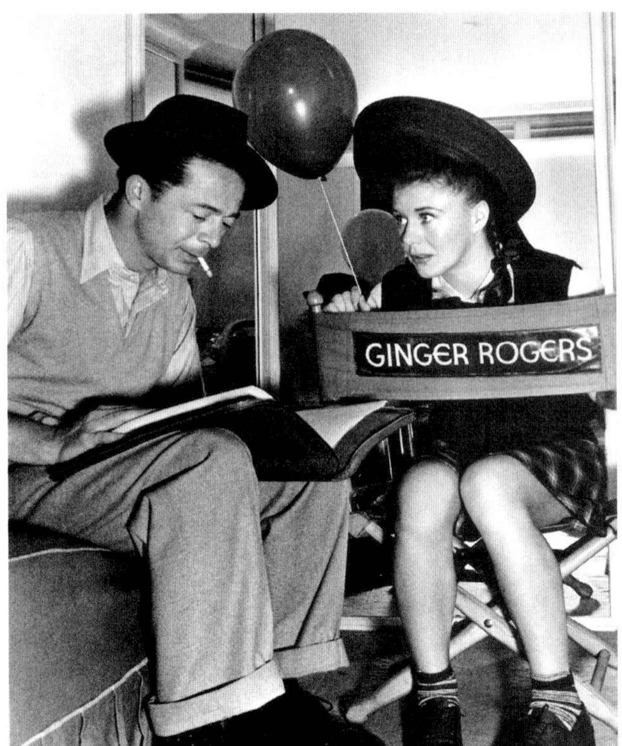

Wilder and Rogers on set:
The Major and the Minor

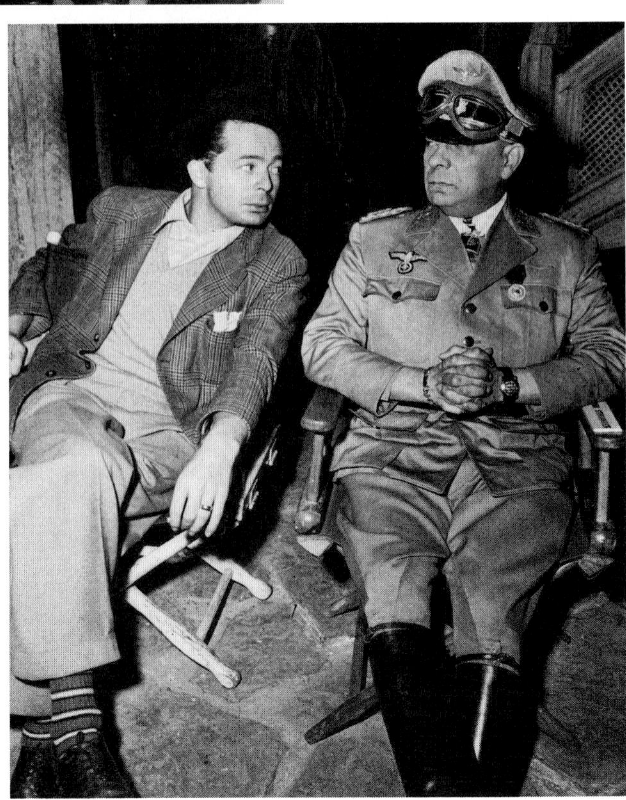

Wilder and von Stroheim
on set: *Five Graves to Cairo*

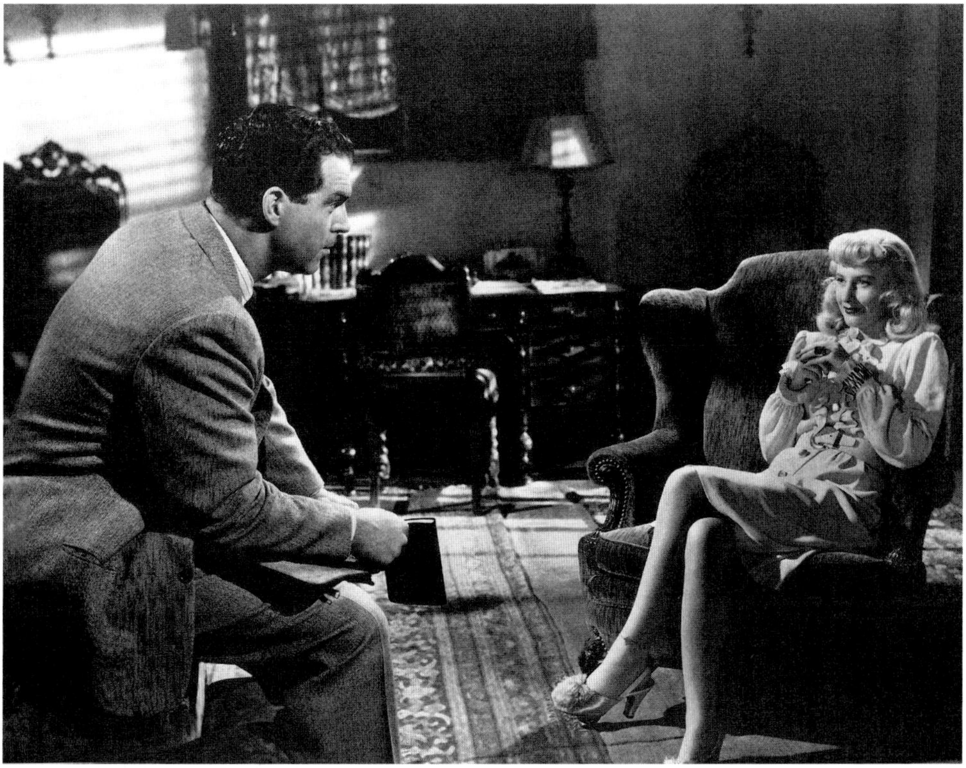

Double Indemnity: "How fast was I going, officer?"

The Lost Weekend: a bottle's eye view of a desperate drinker

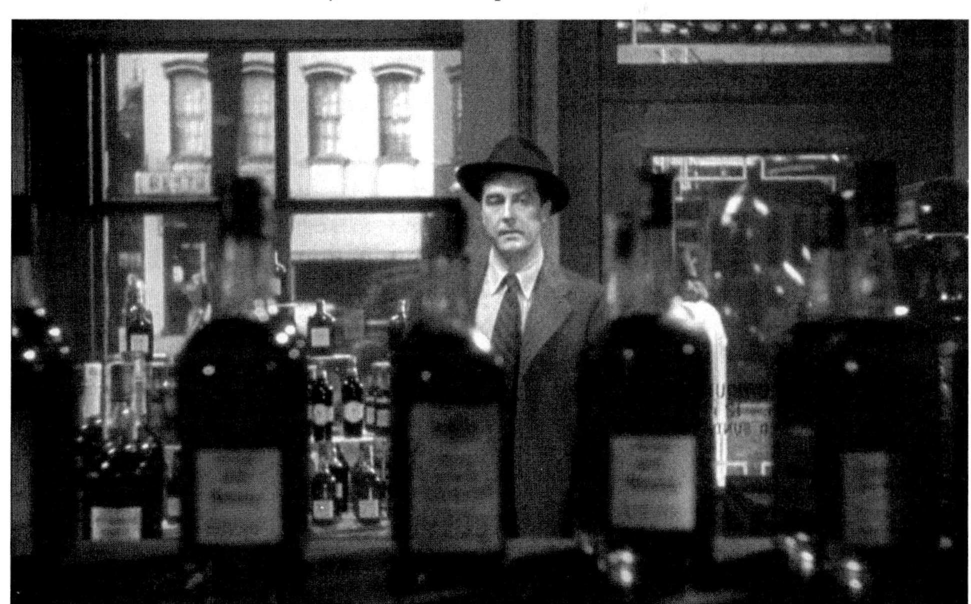

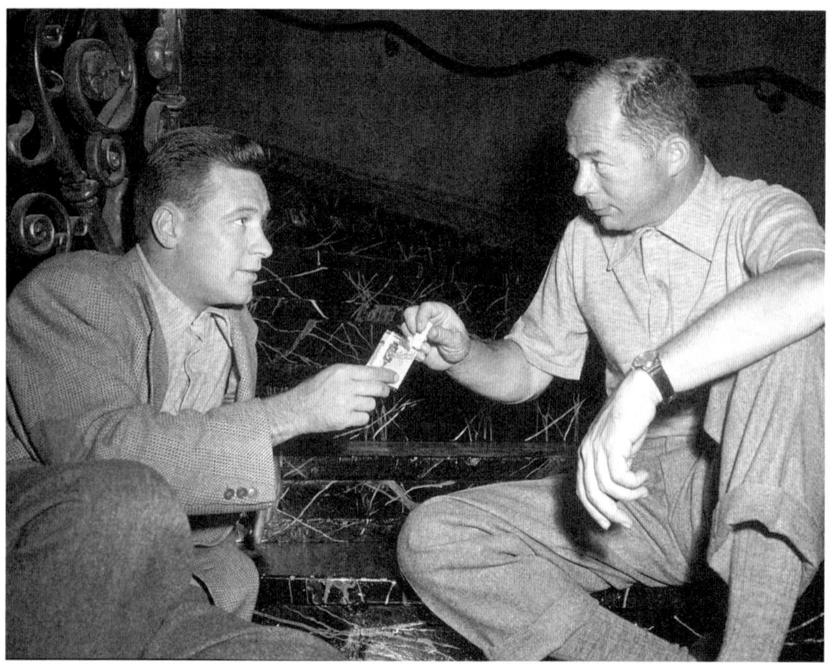

Holden offers Wilder a smoke on Norma's stairway

Gillis approaching "Miss Havisham" mansion

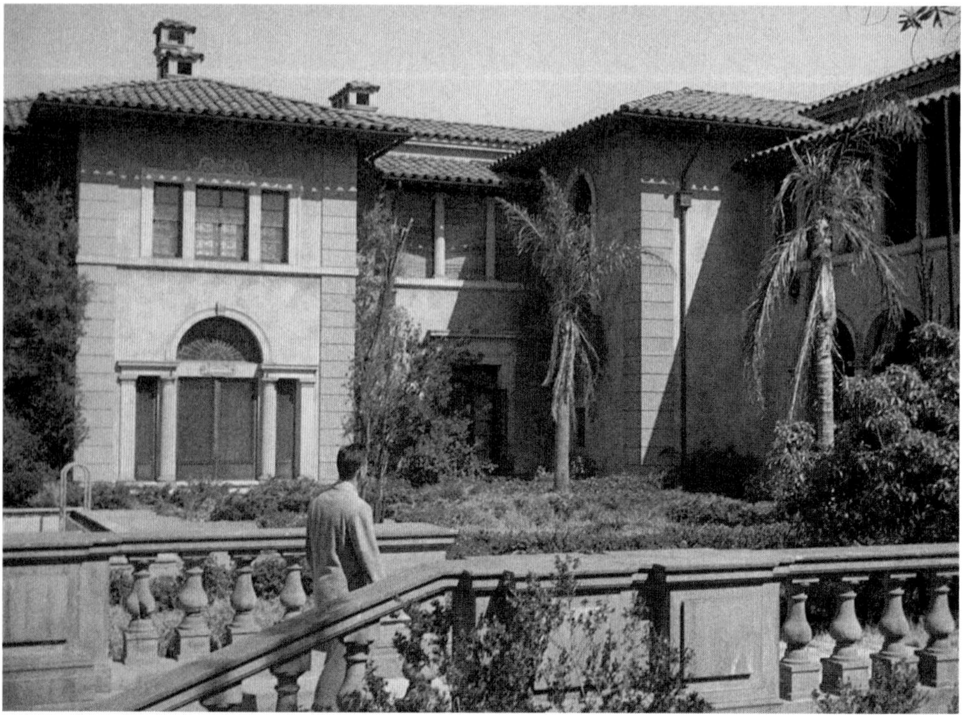

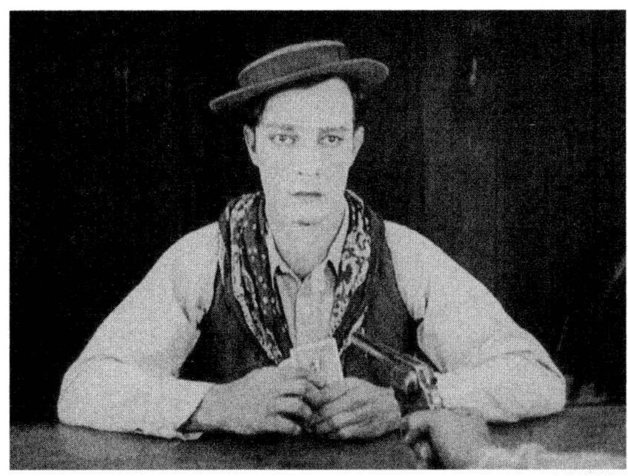

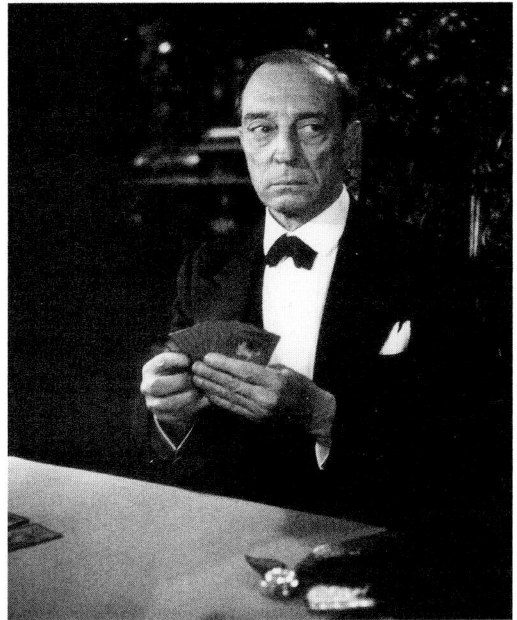

Buster Keaton: the Great Stone Face plays cards in 1925 (*Go West*) and 1950 (*Sunset Boulevard*)

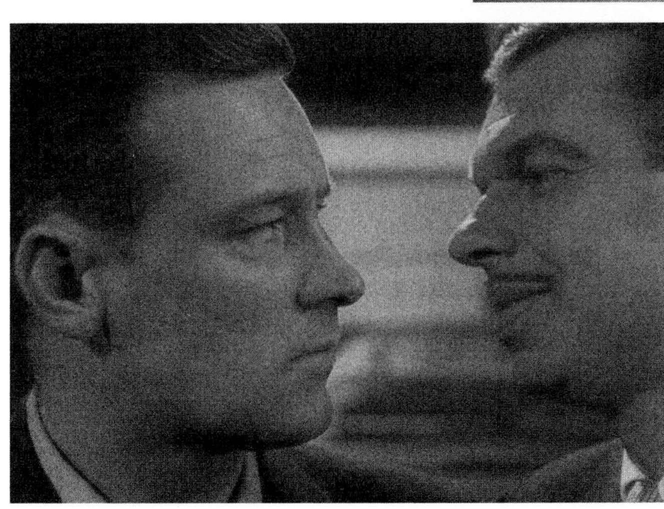

"As long as the lady is paying for it, why not take the vicuña?"

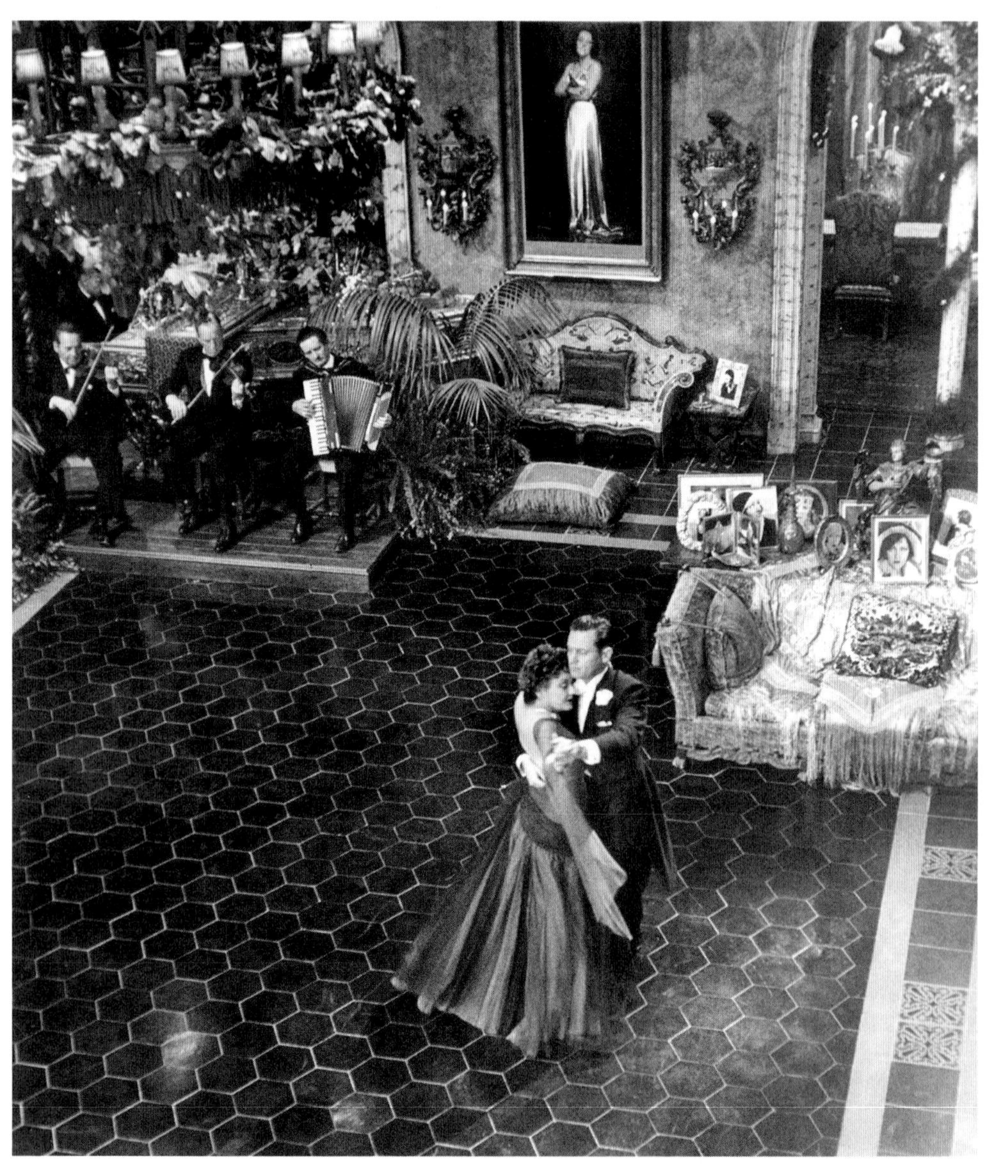

The lonely dancers

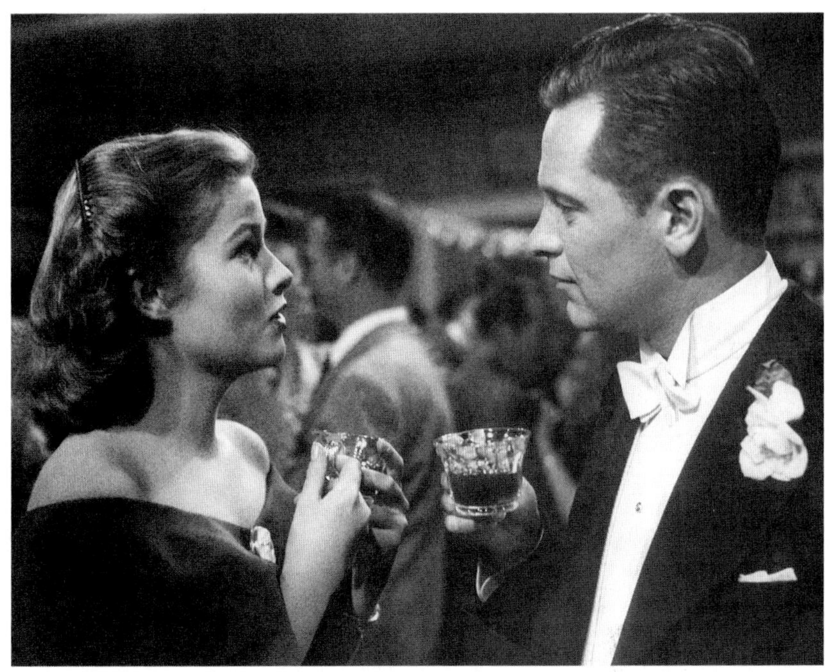

Betty and Joe banter at a livelier New Year's Eve party

Wilder sets up the boudoir embrace

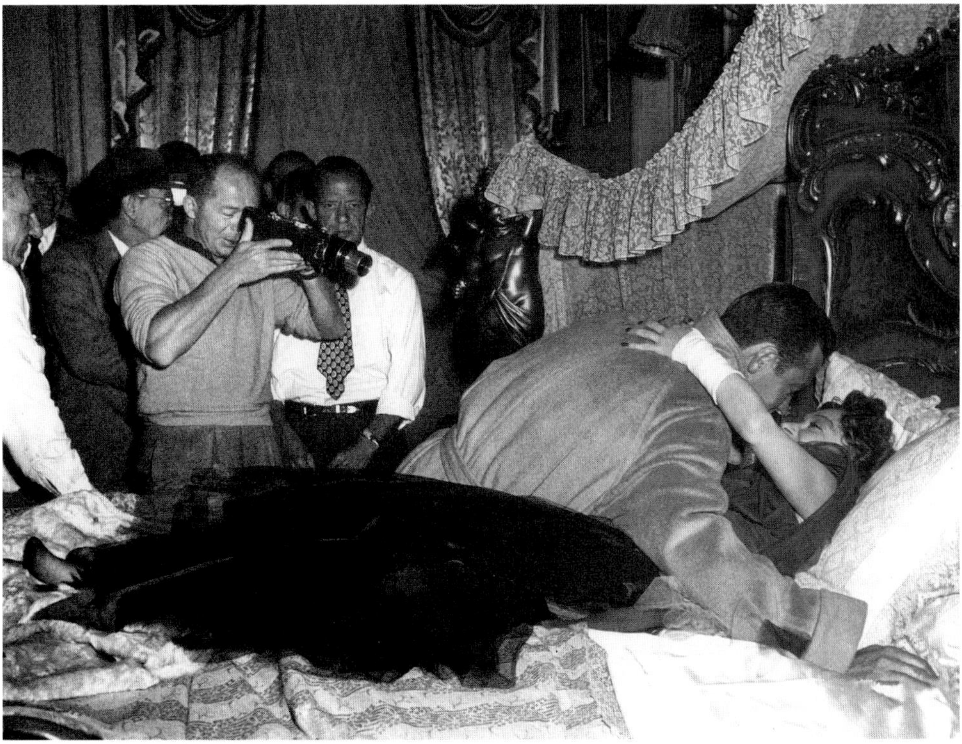

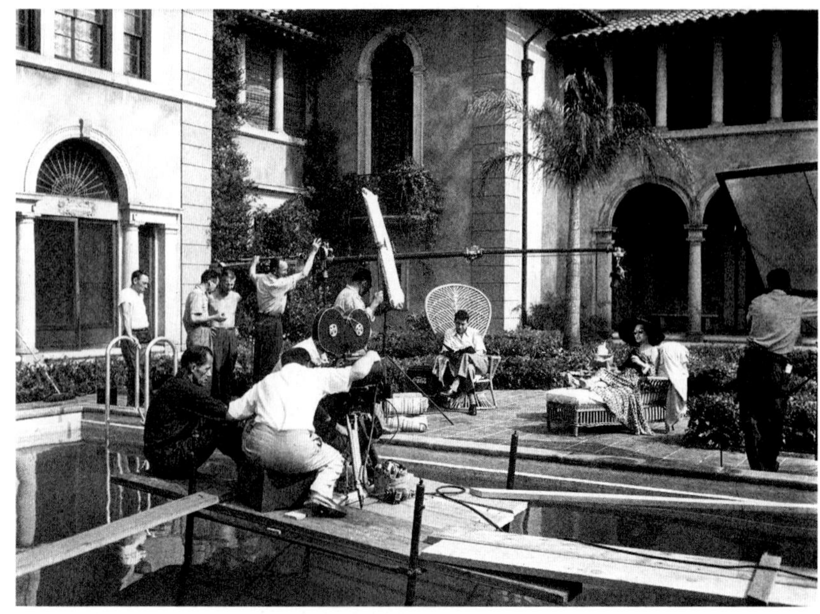

Poolside setup

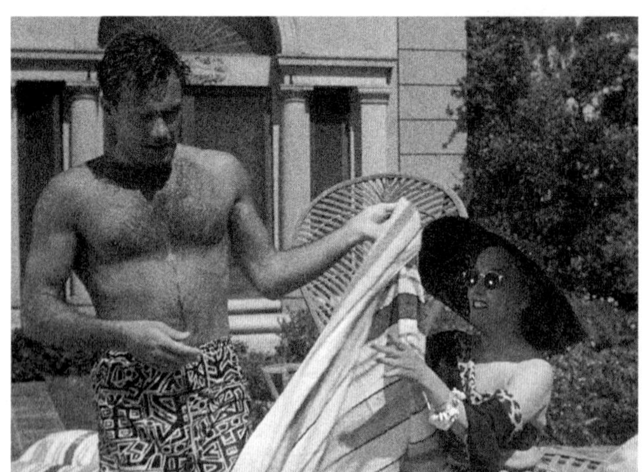

Joe emerges from Norma's swimming pool—this time alive, not dead

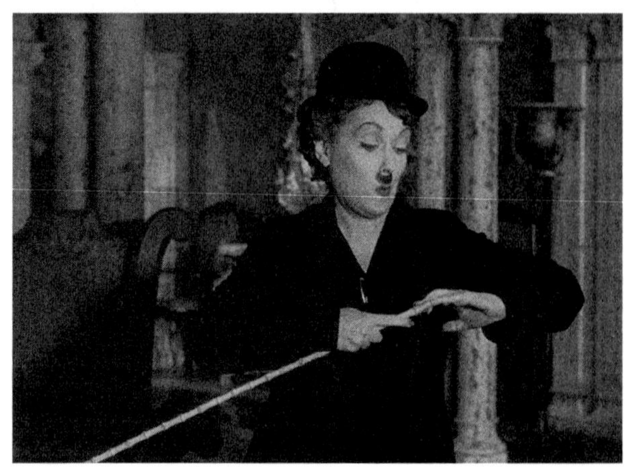

Norma as Chaplin's Little Tramp

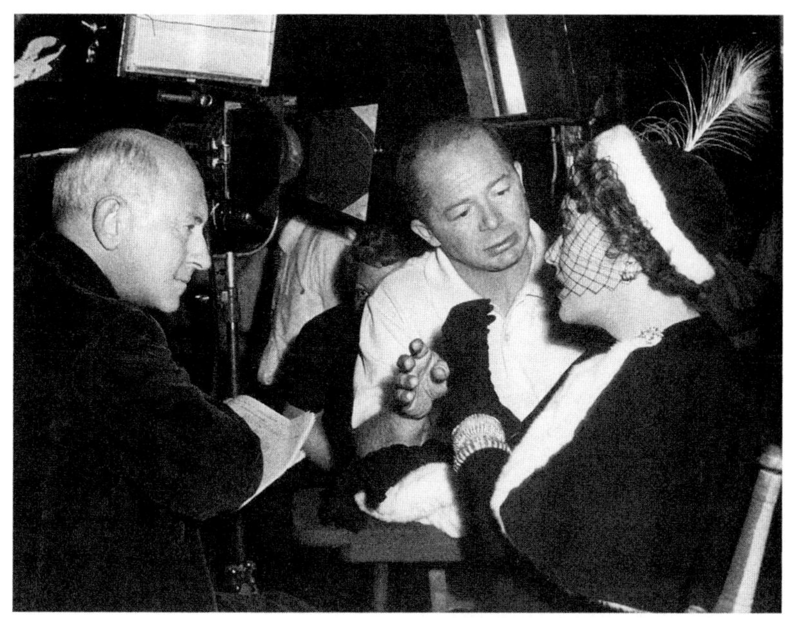

Wilder rehearses
DeMille and
Swanson

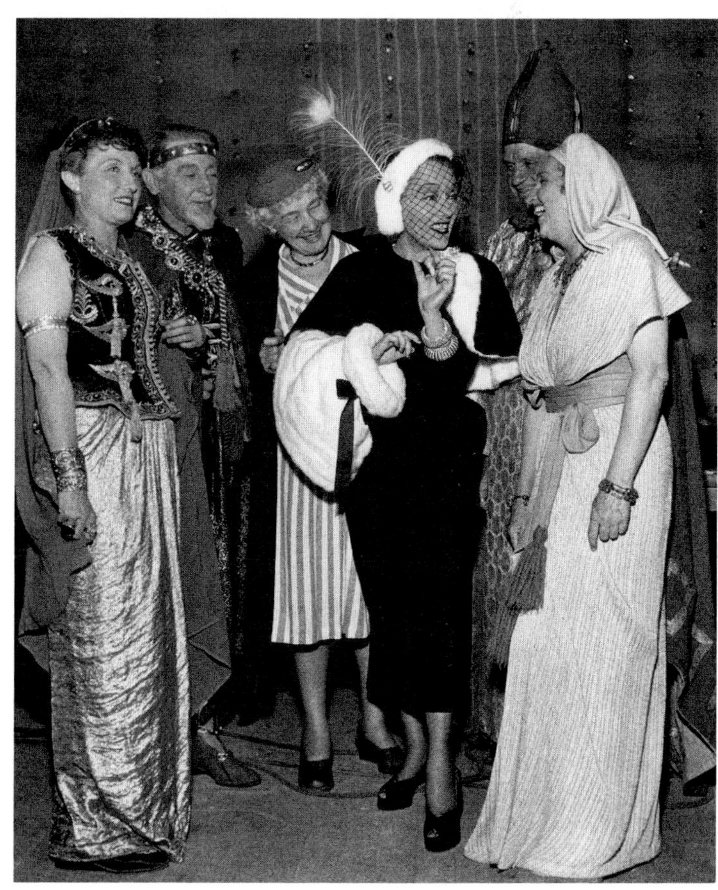

Swanson relaxes
with extras

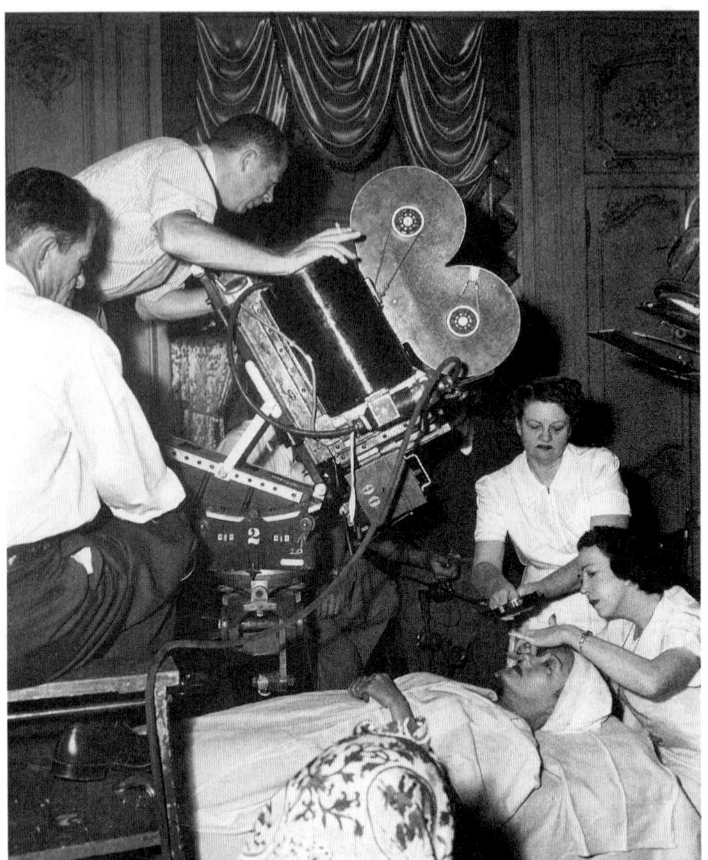

Wilder sets up a shot of beauticians working on Norma

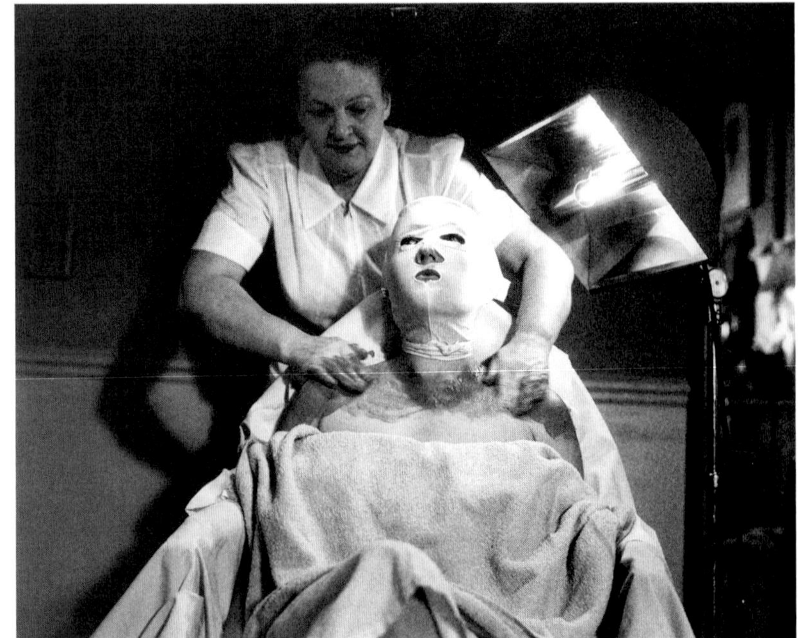

All in the name of beauty: Norma masked and massaged with mud

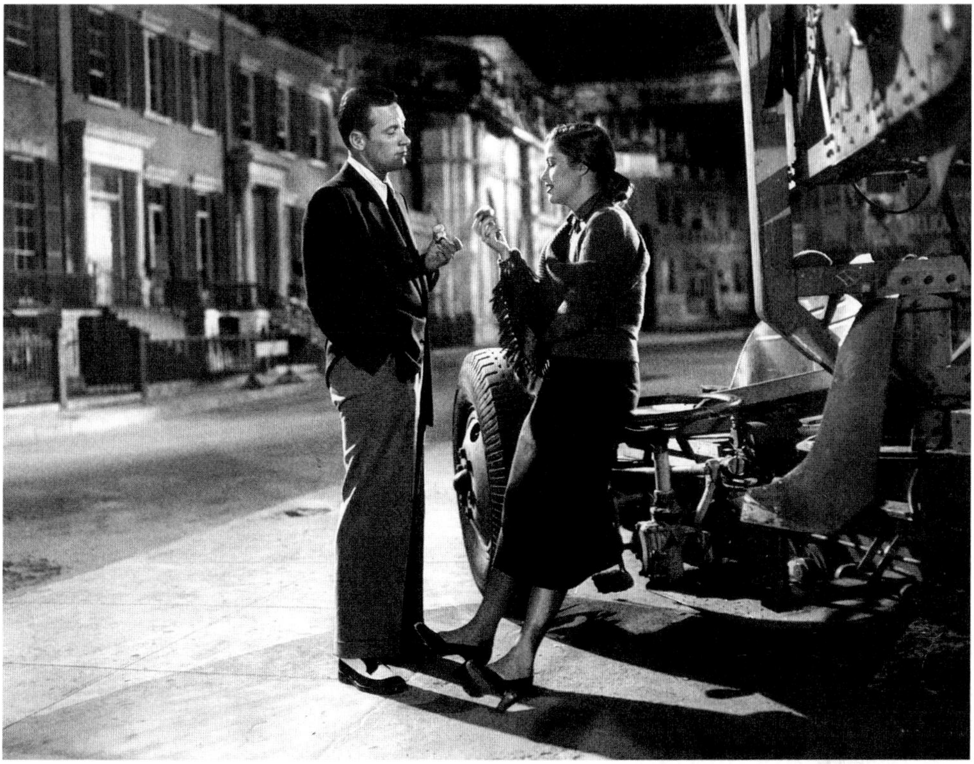

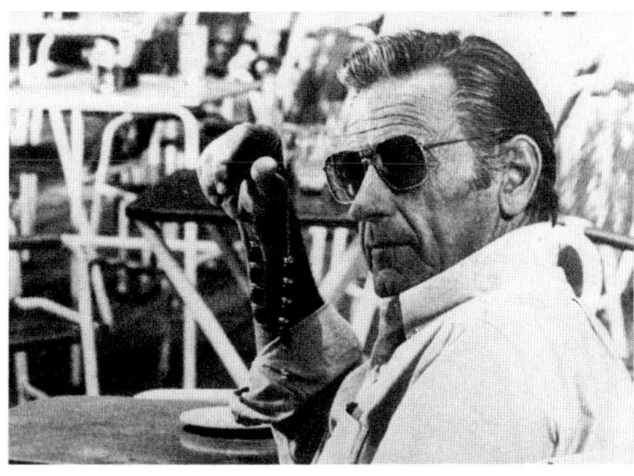

"Look at this street. All cardboard, all hollow, all phony. All done with mirrors. I like it better than any street in the world."

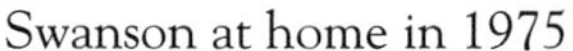

Swanson at home in 1975

Holden in Wilder's *Fedora* (1978)

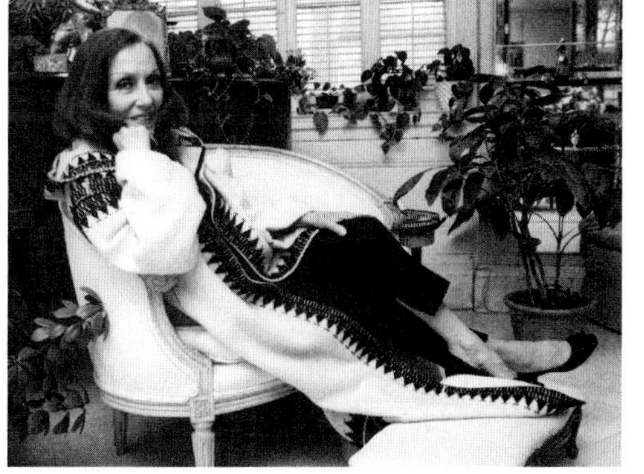

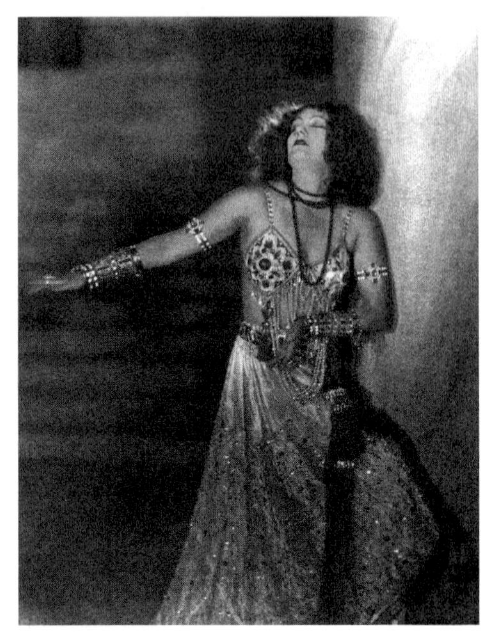

Swanson plays Salome
in *Stage Struck* (1925)

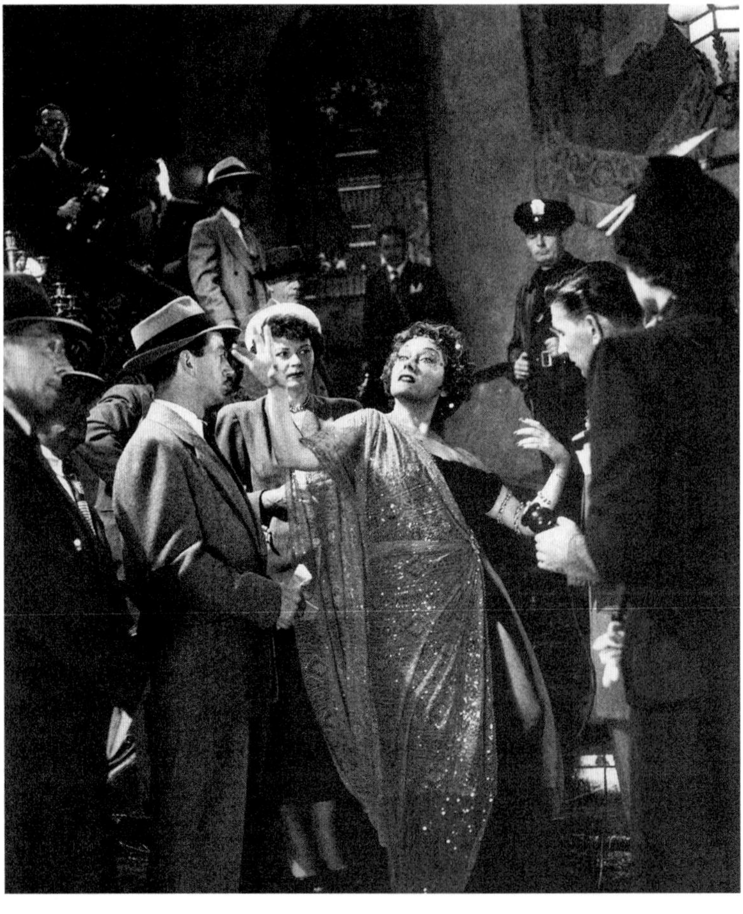

Swanson plays
Salome in her
head (1950)

CHAPTER NINE

"HELLO, YOUNG FELLOW"

Two-thirds of the way through the film, Norma, who has sent her massive Salome script to DeMille, orders Max to chauffeur her large and exotic Isotta Fraschini to the Bronson Gate of Paramount studios. A two-story arch in the style of the Spanish Baroque, the Bronson Gate was adorned with geometric medallions, two pairs of scrolled pillars, and a complexly patterned, wrought-iron grille. Constructed in 1926, it was of the same vintage as both the Isotta Fraschini (1929) and Norma's mansion (1924). To this day, the Bronson Gate remains the most recognizable studio entrance in the world. On the other side of this gate, the imposing structure seemed to declare, lies a realm of the imagination, where anything is possible: Bygone eras are brought back to life and dreams and fantasies made to seem real. In this regard, the gate is a physical embodiment of Norma's frustrated desire to escape her barren present outside the gate and regain her glorious past within it.

With her kept man seated beside her in the tonneau of the limousine, she applies her eye shadow before meeting with Paramount's most illustrious director. The screenplay described her appearance thus: "She is in full makeup, with a veil, a daring hat, a suit so stunning only she would venture to wear it."

After initially being refused entrance onto the lot, Max drives to Stage 18, where DeMille is shooting his latest biblical epic, *Samson and Delilah*. Norma mistakenly believes DeMille has invited her to the studio to discuss the untitled Salome script she has sent him. She is unaware that the head of the properties ("props") department had been trying to reach her on an entirely different matter: to rent her opulent Isotta Fraschini, with its gold-plated intercom telephone and leopard-skin upholstery, for a new Bing Crosby production. (In fact, for the making of *Sunset Boulevard*, Paramount had rented the Isotta from a rental agency for $500 a week.) When DeMille learns she is on her way, he is baffled. The assistant says of Desmond, "She must be a million years old." DeMille dryly replies, "I hate to think where that puts me. I could be her father." He suddenly realizes why Norma has come: "It must be about that appalling script of hers. What can I say to her? What can I say?"

The assistant volunteers a solution: "I can tell her you're all tied up in the projection room. I can give her the brush..."

DeMille cuts him off: "Listen, thirty million fans have given her the brush. Isn't that enough?" The assistant adds, "I hear she was a terror to work with." In a perfectly timed response, DeMille replies, "She got to be. A dozen press agents working overtime can do terrible things to the human spirit."

In this brief exchange, DeMille renders *Sunset Boulevard* its most humane moment. He transforms the viewer's opinion of Norma from an aging narcissist to a woman whom time—and the film industry—has cruelly abandoned. DeMille continues, "You didn't know Norma

Desmond as a plucky little girl of seventeen, with more courage and wit and heart than ever came together in one youngster."

He greets her at the entrance to Stage 18. "Hello, young fellow," he says. In preparing for the film, Swanson had disclosed to Brackett and Wilder that that was DeMille's term of endearment for her back in the day. Norma and DeMille embrace. She says, "Last time I saw you was someplace very gay. I remember waving to you. I was dancing on a table." DeMille smiles wryly: "Lots of people were. Lindbergh had just landed in Paris. Come on in." In the original script, Norma was to say that she recalled seeing *him* dance on a table, but DeMille insisted that Wilder change the line, as he would never in his life, he said, be caught dancing on a table.

★ ★ ★

It was not the first time that the grounds and soundstages of Paramount had featured in a Paramount picture. Eight years earlier, in *Hold Back the Dawn* (1941), written by Brackett and Wilder and directed by Mitchell Leisen, a similarly self-reflexive scene had opened the film. In that earlier film, we are taken onto Stage 5 on the Paramount lot, where a fictitious film director named Dwight Saxon, played by the film's real director, Leisen, is directing a scene from *I Wanted Wings*, the motion picture Mitchell Leisen (not "Dwight Saxon") had made before *Hold Back the Dawn*.

The self-reflexivity of *Hold Back the Dawn* occurs at the start of the movie, before it settles into its story, but in another Paramount film made that year, the sparkling screwball comedy *Sullivan's Travels*, the presence of the studio weaves its way through the tale and is indispensable to it. Written and directed by the brilliant comic filmmaker Preston Sturges, *Sullivan's Travels*—its title a nod to Swift—concerns a fictitious film director named Sullivan, based on Sturges but not played by him, who struggles to get away from Hollywood so he can plumb the depths of economic despair during the Great Depression. In the end he concludes that the best way for him to alleviate the suffering of others is to continue making funny pictures.

With *Sunset Boulevard,* the actual physical locale of Paramount Pictures would yet again appear on screen. Brackett and Wilder did not have a specific director in mind for the scene with Norma. But once they had secured Swanson for the role, they had to rethink Norma's studio visit. It was suddenly clear who would—or at least should—play the filmmaker she goes to see: the great DeMille himself, who had directed Swanson in six career-defining films in the late 1910s and early 1920s. He had been her mentor and father figure. Though nearly three decades had elapsed since they last worked together, Swanson continued to cherish memories of DeMille.

She remembered the electrifying scene in his 1919 box-office hit *Male and Female* in which she sprawled motionless on the floor of a lion's den while a real lion, his claws clipped, rested his paw on her naked back. The lion was sedated; Gloria was not. Her flesh crawled at the touch of the beast. Only twenty years old at the time, she would have done anything for Mr. DeMille. He was eighteen years older than she was and a notorious philanderer, but apparently, he never laid a hand on her. She wasn't eager to do a scene with a lion. Too much could go wrong despite safety precautions that included two lion tamers stationed off camera, a sharpshooter in the wings, and DeMille himself carrying a loaded revolver. She knew how much he wanted the scene in his film, so she gamely agreed to do what he asked of her.

When the shooting finished and Swanson was free at last to move her body, which had been instinctively frozen in fear, DeMille led her into his private office. All the tension she had been holding inside escaped in a torrent of tears. DeMille sighed with relief: "I was beginning to think that you were the perfect machine, that you could do anything.

But now I know you're much more than that. You're a real woman." He sat the diminutive actress on his knee and pulled from his desk drawer a velvet tray covered with jewelry—brooches, rings, and necklaces. He asked her to pick one for herself. She chose a small gold mesh purse with a square sapphire in the center. This quelled her tears.

DeMille, who later explained as much to his granddaughter, remembered that he was rattled by his desire to caress his young star but had restrained himself. "I sat there, I never moved," he recalled, frozen like Swanson under the lion's paw. "I kept my hands to myself. I think it was the hardest thing I ever did." A creature of an era when such behavior was apparently deemed tolerable, even normal, in Hollywood, Swanson seems to have been untroubled by the paternalism, sexism, and egregious crossing of workplace boundaries by DeMille when she described the scene in her autobiography six decades later.

In the finished film, the lion shot lasts no more than a few seconds. Nevertheless, it stunned audiences with its shocking verisimilitude and made a star of Gloria Swanson, an actress praised as much for her bravery as her beauty.

* * *

DeMille, rightfully known as "Mr. Hollywood," was intimately connected with the history of American cinema. Teaming up in the 1910s with vaudeville producer Jesse Lasky and a glove manufacturer named Samuel Goldfish (later Goldwyn), the three formed the film company Famous Players–Lasky and began cranking out fifteen- to twenty-minute silent melodramas produced in East Coast warehouses converted into studios. Recognizing the need for more interior space and more reliable weather for outdoor shooting, the trio moved cameras and crews to the West Coast, where they acquired a patch of land outside Los Angeles. In December 1913, they produced *The Squaw Man* (1914), which would go down in film history as both the first feature-length western (seventy-four minutes) and the first feature-length movie of any kind to be shot in Hollywood.

The film, a box-office hit, established DeMille as a master storyteller, and it transformed Hollywood, then a sleepy rural outpost, into the capital of America's burgeoning film industry. Famous Players–Lasky, reincorporated a decade later as Paramount Pictures, turned out a succession of hits, many of them with DeMille at the helm.

Among those hits were the marital intrigue comedies with Swanson that explored the politics of love, marriage, and desire: films that were funny but also spoke meaningfully to the millions of soldiers and sailors returning from the First World War and the women waiting for them, as they tried to pick up where they'd left off or, alternatively, embarked on new romances. These marriage comedies were meant to be provocative, even down to their titles: *Don't Change Your Husband*; *For Better, for Worse*; *Male and Female*; *Why Change Your Wife?*; *Something to Think About*; and *The Affairs of Anatol*.

With a sudden, post–World War I tidal wave of marriages and divorces, Americans turned to their local cinemas—even more, perhaps, than to their churches—for guidance in modern ways of living, looking, and behaving. It was a confusing time, with a new sexual liberalism butting up against traditional prewar and pre-Hollywood values. As John D'Emilio and Estelle Freeman have written in their history of American sexuality, "America was moving by the 1920s toward a view of erotic expression that can be defined as sexual liberalism— an overlapping set of beliefs that detached sexual activity from the instrumental goal of procreation." Affirming heterosexual pleasure as a value in itself, young people, they wrote, "defined sexual satisfaction as a critical component of personal happiness and successful marriage." Despite its conservative happy ending, in which Swanson, playing a wayward wife, returns to her mate, *Don't Change Your Husband* implicitly contended, in the words of DeMille's granddaughter, that "A woman had a right to sexual satisfaction; if denied it, she had a right to end her marriage."

Stroheim's erotic melodramas explored this new moral landscape, but with a seriousness (and length) that, for many moviegoers, made them unwatchable. Not so with DeMille's lighthearted and fast-paced comedies. With him leading the charge, Hollywood capitalized on the new sexual liberalism, showcasing it on the screen while also appearing to caution against it. DeMille was a master at having it both ways: However titillating his movies, they always ended with a sop to conventional morality.

DeMille, as we have seen, ranked alongside Griffith and Stroheim as the most lauded American directors of the silent era. Yet by 1949, when *Sunset Boulevard* was being cast, both the recently deceased Griffith and the budget-swallowing Stroheim were long forgotten. Not so DeMille. The only other film director of the day whose name on the marquee could pull in audiences was Alfred Hitchcock. But unlike Hitchcock, a British citizen who had moved to Hollywood as recently as 1939, DeMille *was* Hollywood. In a self-referential movie about the making of movies, a film that is, in essence, a history of Hollywood, who better to play the small but crucial part Brackett and Wilder had in mind than Mr. Hollywood himself? They must have been delighted with themselves when they thought to cast DeMille in the role of Norma's ally from the past. Even better was to have Cecil B. DeMille play Cecile B. DeMille, rather than a lightly disguised version of himself with a made-up name.

★ ★ ★

DeMille's films, especially in the early days, often exploited racial themes to heighten audience appeal. The original 1914 *Squaw Man* (he remade it in 1918 and 1931) featured a Native American heroine, Nat-U-Ritch, played by the Winnebago actress Lilian St. Cyr, known professionally as Red Wing. Nat-U-Ritch kills a would-be rapist and then herself so that her son can be raised by white men and thus, she believes, enjoy a better life than she could have offered him. *The Cheat* (1915) likewise plays on racist themes, its white heroine branded on the shoulder by a vengeful Asian ivory trader when she refuses to sleep with him, even though she had agreed to do so in exchange for him paying off her gambling debts.

Fellow filmmakers, including Stroheim, found DeMille lacking in both artistic vision and generosity of spirit. DeMille admitted to a fellow director that he could make better films if he desired, but he preferred to appeal to the masses. He told an audience at Harvard Business School, "I have frequently looked at my own work and wished that I myself knew the ideal formula which fuses art and efficiency in making a photoplay." For him, "efficiency" (that is, commercial success) always trumped "art."

Of medium height, trim, handsome, and bald, DeMille was a petty tyrant who strutted around his film sets with his trademark field boots, jodhpurs, and corduroy coat as if he were a lion tamer who, with one withering glance, could send a wild beast—or actor or crew member—cringing in fear. As if to reinforce the point, he carried an unconcealed revolver. "Commanding absolute loyalty from his staff," wrote Kevin Brownlow, "he directed as if chosen by God for that one task." Swanson recalled, "When Mr. DeMille came on to the set there was a great deal of AWE" because "he frightened people and if you didn't do the job demanded of you, you simply got hell, there was no question about it." Describing his vanity, Swanson noted that he "wore his baldness like an expensive hat, as if it were out of the question for him to have hair like other men."

Brackett had witnessed an episode of DeMille's wrath while visiting the set of *The Story of Dr. Wassell* (1944), a naval action picture starring Gary Cooper. When an assistant, after being bawled out by the director, tried to justify his actions, DeMille exploded in rage:

"Oh, an alibi! Please never give me an alibi. I've been in this business a long time, long enough to know all alibis." That night, Brackett recorded the incident in his diary, summing it up as, "A beastly performance before a crowd of a hundred or so people." DeMille's friend Josef von Sternberg, despite his personal fondness for DeMille, could never remain on one of the director's sets for long, so unbearable did he find the atmosphere: "The normal zeal of an actor to give his money's worth," he wrote in reference to DeMille's directorial style, "is embarrassing enough to behold, but when aided and abetted by a director [like DeMille] it becomes unbearable."

At the time Brackett and Wilder asked DeMille to play a cameo in their upcoming film, DeMille was already at work on *Samson and Delilah*, a risqué religious spectacle very loosely adapted from the Old Testament. Since the 1920s, DeMille had specialized in sexy religious costume dramas, films such as the silent *King of Kings* and *Ten Commandments* and the early talkies *The Sign of the Cross* and *The Crusades*. In the words of his biographer Simon Louvish, "The DeMille world is full of undressed and tormented women and bare-chested men heaving in some agonized lust, whether it be of power or religious fervour." These films burned up the box office with their uncanny mix of religious sanctimony and sexual suggestiveness, featuring nearly naked bodies being manacled and whipped, all to the greater glory of God.

Now, in the spring of 1949, DeMille was making a movie that would set the trend in the following decade and a half for sex-and-religion costume epics shot in glorious color on opulently constructed sets. *Samson and Delilah* starred the stunning Austro-Hungarian actress Hedy Lamarr, garbed in flesh-revealing outfits designed by Edith Head. Samson was played by a relative newcomer to the screen, a muscular young actor named Victor Mature, who had previously scored a hit as a down-on-his-luck ex-convict in the 1947 film noir thriller *Kiss of Death*. In that film, he kept his clothes on, but *Samson and Delilah* called for him to bare his arms, legs, and chest.

DeMille was dismayed when Mature first appeared in costume: The actor looked fat and flabby. He demanded that Mature lose thirty pounds and report at once to the studio gym. It wasn't only Mature's body weight that bothered DeMille. The actor, according to DeMille, was riddled with inexplicable and inexcusable phobias. He was afraid of swords, despite starring in a sword-and-sandal epic. When asked to wrestle with a wild lion that was actually toothless, well trained, and very old, Mature, terrified, demanded a stunt performer (which young Gloria Swanson had forgone thirty years earlier). For additional lion footage, Mature flailed around with a full-size lion puppet. The resulting scene is almost ludicrous in its fakery.

The final straw for the director was the actor's fear of strong winds. When large studio blowers created a violent gust of wind during the biblical battle of the jawbone, Mature suddenly fled to his dressing room. Calling him back, DeMille picked up his megaphone and, with the entire cast and crew standing at attention, boomed out his disgust: "I have met a few men in my time. Some have been afraid of heights, some have been afraid of water, some have been afraid of fire, some have been afraid of closed spaces. Some have even been afraid of open spaces—or themselves. But in all my thirty-five years of picture-making experiences, Mr. Mature, I have not until now met a man who was 100 per cent yellow."

Brackett and Wilder were put off not only by DeMille's on-set cruelty, but also by his off-set politics. However personally liberal (or libertine) DeMille may have been where sex was concerned, he was radically conservative in the political arena, advocating the blacklisting of communist sympathizers. In March 1949, two months before he shot his scene for *Sunset Boulevard*, DeMille, together with B-list actor Ronald Reagan and writer-producer Dore Schary, formed the Motion Picture Industry Council, a blacklist organization aimed at keeping Hollywood free of communists. In indignant speeches delivered to like-minded audiences, DeMille professed bitter opposition to labor unions, which he considered anti-American. Wilder, a Democrat, was appalled by the political viewpoints of his outspoken fellow director, and so was Brackett, a moderate Republican.

★ ★ ★

Brackett and Wilder wrestled with the tone of Norma's scene with DeMille. Brackett wanted it to be tender, even loving, while Wilder wanted it to be satirical. An early draft portrayed an arrogant and foolish Norma who is humiliated by her uninvited return to the studio. Subsequent drafts, prompted by Brackett's instinct to give audiences a much-needed note of humanity, softened Norma in the DeMille scene, making her seem poignantly vulnerable. A senior Paramount executive objected to the change, calling it sentimental. But Brackett stood his ground, claiming the last thing they needed was "another ice-cold scene in a chilly picture." In the end, his view prevailed, presumably because Wilder, who always held the upper hand, recognized that a warm scene would better serve the arc of the story.

Stroheim had more than once supplied Wilder with unsolicited directorial suggestions, but DeMille was too polite to do the same. When asked about this, Wilder sardonically explained, "I made a deal with him that I wouldn't make any suggestions as to how he should direct *Samson and Delilah* and he would not make any suggestions on this picture." DeMille, for his part, promised to retaliate against Wilder by casting him in *his* next film.

As the producer of a prestige picture being made at Paramount, Brackett had hoped that DeMille, as Paramount's signature director as well as a very wealthy man, would accept a token payment for his services rather than a full-fledged acting fee. Such was not the case. DeMille was not a sentimentalist, even though he featured in what was arguably the movie's only sentimental scene. He asked for and received $10,000 for one day of filming, which, in the end, Brackett conceded to have been "well worth it." When a revised line of dialogue had to be added during reshoots the following October, requiring no more than an hour or so of his time, DeMille demanded in remuneration the latest-model Cadillac (valued at $6,600), an additional payment of $3,000, and a larger, more prominent credit on the screen than any of the other cameo players. He had Brackett and Wilder over a barrel. The scene, they realized, was a highlight of their film. They anted up.

★ ★ ★

DeMille, who had confidently commanded actors from behind the camera on countless films, was nevertheless jittery about his debut in *front* of the camera, a place that was profoundly foreign to him. It took reassurances from Swanson that he only needed to relax in order to play himself convincingly. After DeMille's day of shooting had ended, Wilder patted him on the back and said, "Very good, my boy. Leave your name with my secretary. I may have a small part for you in my next picture."

CHAPTER TEN

"DO YOU KNOW BILL HOLDEN?"

When Norma tells Joe, her young "protégé," that he needs a wardrobe upgrade, he protests that he doesn't want new clothes. She insists: "Why begrudge me a little fun? I just want you to look nice, my stray little boy." She has Max drive them to an expensive men's clothing store (a studio re-creation of Bullocks men's shop on Wilshire Boulevard; seen out the window is a rear-screen projection of the storefronts across the street, which included a lunch spot named Perino's that Wilder and Brackett liked to frequent). Standing before a full-length triple mirror, Gillis is attended by two salesmen and a tailor. Norma says she wants a camel's-hair topcoat for Joe, then leaves him alone with the younger of the salesmen while going off with his colleague to look at evening clothes.

The younger salesman, played by an uncredited character actor named Archie Twitchell, shows Gillis several coats, including an expensive one made of vicuña wool—a costly fabric that made cashmere seem like a bargain. Joe curtly tells him camel's hair will be fine. The salesman whispers in his ear, "Well, as long as the lady is paying for it, why not take the vicuña?" Up until now, Joe has been able to salvage a modicum of self-respect by thinking of himself as Norma's "friend" and employee, but the salesman's insinuations force him to accept the ugly fact that he is her kept man.

Twitchell delivers his line with an insinuating sneer. Wilder's direction is flawless. He dollies the camera in tight on Gillis and the salesman. The anger in Joe's eyes melts into shame when he feels the intensity of the salesman's smug, conspiratorial grin. On the music track, a piccolo and high clarinet sound a shrill and jarring chord. This was known in the movie-music business as a "stinger" because of its venomous bite; it was the musical equivalent to an exclamation point, used to cap off a dramatic moment with an auditory shock. In this instance, the stinger acts as a harsh musical analogue to Joe's abrupt recognition of the role he's fallen into.

The scene ends before we learn if Joe accepts the more expensive topcoat. A few scenes later, however, we see him wearing the vicuña, its collar turned up in the rain. Without a car of his own, he hitches a ride to a crowded New Year's Eve party, where the host, his friend Artie Green, runs his fingers over the fabric and whistles, "What is this— mink?" Joe winces, his humiliation complete.

★ ★ ★

Brackett and Wilder's top choice for the role of Joe Gillis was Montgomery Clift, the best-known Method actor in Hollywood (Brando had yet to come west). He was twenty-eight, exquisitely handsome, and a fast-rising star. His first two films had been or were about to be released. One of these, the now classic western *Red River*, directed by Howard Hawks, climaxed with the sensitive, lean-as-a-whippet Clift standing his physical and moral ground against his monomaniacal father figure, played by John Wayne. *Red River* was the third-highest-grossing motion picture of 1948. The other film, *The Search*, was directed by Fred Zinnemann, an old friend of Billy's who had been Robert Siodmak's assistant director for *People on Sunday*, the quasi-documentary film that the three of them, along with other very talented friends, had collaboratively made in Weimar Berlin. *The Search*, which can be classified as a "rubble film," starred Clift as an American soldier in occupied postwar Germany who selflessly assumes care for a displaced child survivor of Auschwitz. Viewers were so taken in by the realism of Clift's performance that many believed Zinnemann had hired an actual soldier to play the part. "His scenes bristled with life," recalled Zinnemann. "And he filled the screen with reverberations above and beyond the movie itself."

Once those two films were in general release, Clift had his pick of projects. Among those that lay ahead in his near future were William Wyler's *The Heiress* (1949), George Stevens's *A Place in the Sun* (1951), and Zinnemann's *From Here to Eternity* (1953), all of them movies for which Clift would receive Oscar nominations. *Sunset Boulevard*, which Clift, on reading the script, excitedly called "the definitive Hollywood ghost story," could have been on this list of distinguished films. Stunningly, only a month before production was to begin, the actor broke his agreement and dropped out. He claimed he was certain no one would believe him having a romance with a much older woman: "I don't think I could be convincing making love to a woman twice my age." Wilder was furious. "Bullshit!" he yelled over the telephone at Clift's agent. "If he's any kind of an actor he could be convincing making love to *any* woman!"

Hollywood gossips contended that Clift was forced to break his contract by his longtime companion and sometime lover, Libby Holman, a "washed-up" torch singer who was sixteen years his senior. Holman may well have objected to her much younger lover playing the role of a much younger lover who romances a has-been performer. But the parallels were even closer than that. In 1932, Holman had married the scion of the R. J. Reynolds Tobacco fortune, Zachary Smith Reynolds, seven years her junior, who was an adventurer and aviator. The morning after a wild party held at Reynolda, the family estate in Winston-Salem, North Carolina, Holman's young husband was found dead with a bullet through his head. She became the prime suspect, but during a long and highly publicized murder investigation, she was cleared of charges due to a lack of evidence. The death was ruled a suicide. For Clift to have played Joe Gillis and end up shot by the older woman who had taken him as a lover—that would have stirred too many ugly memories for Holman to handle. She threatened to kill herself if he remained in the role.

★ ★ ★

At virtually the last minute, Brackett and Wilder were left without a leading man. Desperate to replace Clift, they considered Fred MacMurray, who owed his fame to Wilder for casting him in *Double Indemnity*, but MacMurray, who hadn't minded playing a sleazy, murderous insurance salesman in that earlier picture, thought it would be bad for his blossoming career to play a gigolo. Next, they tried Gene Kelly, the singer-dancer. As a former dancer himself, though not in the same league, Billy admired Kelly's athleticism. Besides, Kelly had starred in the original Broadway production of Rodgers and Hart's long-running musical *Pal Joey*, about a skunk of a nightclub entertainer who seduces an older married woman. But now Kelly was being rebranded by MGM as a good guy. Louis B. Mayer was hardly going to loan out his star hoofer for a film that would tarnish his studio's family-friendly image. They also considered John Garfield, Burt Lancaster, and even young Marlon Brando, whom they knew they couldn't get because he was steaming up Broadway as Stanley Kowalski in Tennessee Williams's hit play *A Streetcar Named Desire*. That story, too, revolves around a delusional older woman enthralled by a younger man: The age difference between the two leads, Jessica Tandy and Brando, was nearly fifteen years.

Brackett remembered a handsome but unprepossessing Paramount contract player named William Holden, whose first film, *Golden Boy* (1939), had shown great promise that he repeatedly failed to fulfill in his subsequent acting assignments over the following decade. In *Golden Boy*, based on Clifford Odets's lauded 1937 Broadway drama, Holden played a young, working-class Italian American, Joe Bonaparte, whose parents yearn for him to escape the ghetto. He's a prodigy at the violin, and they believe this will be his ticket to middle-class life. But Joe is also a gifted boxer, and he is torn between his fiddle and his fists.

⁕ ⁕ ⁕

Bill Holden understood his "golden boy" character in a profoundly personal way. Raised in a ghetto, Joe Bonaparte was forced to decide between music and boxing; raised in affluent Pasadena, Bill Holden was similarly tugged in different directions by chemistry and acting. His father, William Beedle Sr., was an industrial chemist. But at age twenty, William Beedle Jr. had caught the acting bug when playing Madame Curie's eighty-year-old father in a student production at Pasadena Junior College, where he was enrolled as a chemistry major. A Paramount talent scout who was in the audience found himself unexpectedly drawn to the young actor whose face was hidden behind an old man's beard. He went backstage afterward and handed Bill his card, asking him to come to the studio the next day for a screen test. Bill said he couldn't because he had to take a chemistry exam in the morning.

"You better come to the studio, kid," insisted the scout. "Opportunity only knocks once."

"This time it will have to knock twice," Bill replied, standing firm.

Knock twice, it did. The scout arranged for the young thespian to come another day and, when Bill made his appearance and read a few lines, he was offered a contract on the spot. He dropped out of junior college. His strict, Calvinistic parents were displeased. His mother worried that her very handsome son would be an easy target for wayward women, and his father wanted him to follow in his footsteps as an industrial chemist. Neither thought highly of acting as a profession.

The head publicist at Paramount, hesitant about the name Bill Beedle, which sounded to him like an insect, renamed the newcomer William Holden. As one contract player among many, however, Holden was passed over for numerous roles until the veteran director Rouben Mamoulian spotted him reading lines for someone else's screen test. Mamoulian had made a highly publicized national search to find a young actor who could play the demanding title role in the screen adaptation of *Golden Boy*. Of some five thousand actors who put themselves forward at open auditions, sixty-five were seriously considered, but Holden, not having auditioned, was not among them. Even so, Mamoulian was captivated by what he could see of Holden from another actor's screen test. "Here's our Golden Boy!" he cried out to his associates. After giving Holden a screen test of his own, Mamoulian cast him in the prized role.

Holden was not ecstatic at this turn of fortune. In fact, he was uncomfortable with it. Knowing his parents did not accept acting as a valid profession, he internalized their attitude and never fully relinquished it. On getting to know him a decade later, Wilder commented that "Holden is in constant revolt against authority and his family and against everything." A friend commented, "Bill's living in a strait jacket manufactured in Pasadena."

What's more, he didn't know the first thing about acting, and, college acting notwithstanding, he believed he lacked any kind of native skill, which meant he was putting himself in double jeopardy: Not only had he entered a profession of dubious value, but he was also grossly inexperienced, if not incompetent. Suddenly, he found himself jerked out of obscurity to play the lead in a major Hollywood production. In preparation for the part, the twenty-year-old had to learn the basics of both boxing and violin playing. For weeks, he started his day at six in the morning and ended it at midnight, physically exhausted from the blows he had taken in the ring and mentally exhausted from the strain of fingering the violin. Even though, at twenty, he was legally underage to consume alcohol, he began drinking heavily.

On the first day of shooting, he was so nervous he couldn't utter his lines. His costar, Barbara Stanwyck, took him aside to reassure him. She reminded him that everyone on the set that day, both behind and in front of the camera, had also once been a nervous rookie. Despite their fears of failure, they had all gotten through their first day on set, and so would he.

The rest of the cast and crew didn't see it that way. He could sense their lack of faith in him. Perhaps he was mostly projecting onto others his own self-disparagement, but the studio executives actually were worried he couldn't handle the responsibility placed on him. When Stanwyck heard about this, she marched into Harry Cohn's office. Cohn, the infamously crude and parsimonious head of Columbia Pictures—who had bought half of Holden's contract from Paramount in order to put him in the lead at Mamoulian's insistence—feared he had a disaster on his hands. "Give the boy a chance," Stanwyck demanded. "He's only had a week. Leave him alone and he'll find himself." She listed the combination of traits that made him right for the part, adding, "I don't know of any actor who could do it better." Grudgingly, Cohn agreed to back off and let "the boy" find his feet.

Stanwyck, thirty, was engaged to the actor Robert Taylor. At the end of each day's shoot, she privately coached Bill in her dressing room, helping him prepare his lines for the following day, while Taylor waited patiently outside until the sessions were over. The veteran actress helped Holden see acting as a serious profession, which was an act of generosity he never forgot. Until his death in 1981, every year on the anniversary of their first day of shooting, he sent Stanwyck a dozen roses. And until his death and beyond, she always referred to him as Golden Boy.

When the film was released and reviewers lacked enthusiasm for his performance, Holden's doubts about his abilities returned. Yet he decidedly preferred acting to chemistry, and so he remained in the business, albeit with little distinction. Usually, he was cast as the handsome friend or rival of the leading man. Few of his films attracted attention, and no Bill Holden fan clubs sprang up in his honor.

One picture that did well, however, was Mitchell Leisen's prewar aviation drama, *I Wanted Wings* (1941), the movie we see being filmed on a Paramount soundstage at the beginning of Leisen's next picture, *Hold Back the Dawn* (also 1941). The story of three young men from different sectors of society who become friends during their training as cadets in the Army Air Corps (predecessor to the US Air Force), *I Wanted Wings* features Holden as a garage mechanic who has been convinced by his former girlfriend that he isn't smart enough to amount to anything. The vixenish ex-girlfriend is played by a then-unknown nineteen-year-old actress named Veronica Lake, who sizzles on the screen. She attracted a great deal more attention for her role than Holden did for his. In his self-doubt and self-loathing, Holden's airman is similar to the character he later brought to life so memorably in *Sunset Boulevard*. Meanwhile the actor married the sultry dark-haired actress Brenda Marshall (born Ardis Ankerson), who had appeared opposite Errol Flynn in the 1940 Warner Bros. swashbuckler *The Sea Hawk*.

When the United States entered World War II, Holden enlisted in the army. Harry Cohn thought going to war would be good for him. He said to Holden, "The army'll toughen you up, put some character in that pretty face." Things weren't that simple. Self-doubt continued to plague Bill. His younger brother, Bob, a real military pilot, not a pretend one, as Bill had been in *I Wanted Wings*, perished in the South Pacific during a New Year's Day raid on Kavieng, the Japanese-held capital of a small island in Papua New Guinea.

Unlike brother Bob, Bill never saw action in the war. Instead, because of his Hollywood credentials, he was assigned to an endless round of war bond rallies, talent shows, radio programs, and training films, further eroding his sense of self-worth. When the war ended, he was twenty-seven. His career as an actor, such as it was, had grown stale. "I told you the army would do you good," bragged Harry Cohn when Bill first returned to the studio. "Now you look like a man, not just some snotty nosed kid." But Cohn didn't offer him roles by which to prove himself.

He saw himself continually cast as what he came to refer to as a "Smiling Jim." "Smiling Jim," he explained in an interview, "does not have a powerful personality. On the other hand, he isn't the killer type. If he gets into a tough spot, he smiles his way out of it. If a stranger gets mad at him in traffic and yells and curses, ole Smiling Jim just keeps smiling and before long the stranger isn't mad anymore. He's smiling too."

To this, Holden added, "Good ole Smiling Jim. I hate his guts."

★ ★ ★

When Billy Wilder contacted Holden about stepping in for Montgomery Clift, Holden was nearly thirty-one. He had been around the block, and he looked it. He had indeed earned himself a face. No longer the handsome but bland Golden Boy of yore, he was already, by 1949, showing the physical signs of too much booze, too many love affairs, too many mediocre roles, and too little self-respect. His marriage to Ardis had devolved into constant bickering and distrust; she was fed up with his compulsive philandering and dependency on alcohol.

He saw little in his future, until Billy Wilder called.

As a washed-up nobody, someone who couldn't even describe himself as a has-been, since he was essentially a never-was, Holden was perfect for the role of Gillis. At their first meeting, Wilder recognized that Bill Holden would intuitively grasp the self-loathing of the failed screenwriter. Holden was aware the part had been Clift's until he bailed out and that Brackett and Wilder considered a slew of other actors (among them MacMurray, Kelly, Lancaster, and Garfield) before the role reached him; he was the last kid in the schoolyard invited to join the team. And now he barely had time to learn his lines, let alone the character he was asked to play.

"I may not be able to understand Gillis, a gigolo, but I can sympathize with him," Holden told an interviewer. "I've found that sympathy is about all you need if you want to act a different kind of person from your real self." Holden may have seen Gillis as different from Holden's "real self," but Wilder saw otherwise, finding in the actor a desperation that would reverberate in the role of Joe Gillis. Early in the shooting, Holden confided to the director that he didn't understand the character of Joe Gillis. "Do you know Bill Holden?" Wilder asked. When Holden nodded, Wilder shrugged. "Then you know Joe Gillis."

CHAPTER ELEVEN

LOCATIONS: REAL AND IMAGINED

Evading his pursuers, Joe turns into a driveway off Sunset and pulls into the empty bay of a three-bay garage. He gets out, closes the garage door behind him, and, as shown in an ascending crane shot, mounts a stone staircase that leads to a small formal garden gone to seed. Beyond it looms what the screenplay described as a "grandiose Italianate structure, mottled by the years, gloomy, forsaken." Joe sizes it up: "It was a great big white elephant of a place. The kind crazy movie people built in the twenties. A neglected house gets an unhappy look. This one had it in spades." He continues the thought: "It was like that old woman in *Great Expectations*—that Miss Havisham in her rotting wedding dress and her torn veil, taking it out on the world because she had been given the go-by."

His reverie is interrupted by an imperious voice coming from somewhere above him, behind a bamboo blind. "You there!" an unknown woman hails him. "Why are you so late? Why have you kept me waiting so long?" Joe catches a glimpse of her through an opening in the blind; she wears dark clothes, dark glasses, and a dark wrap around her head.

Thus we meet both Norma Desmond, a woman shrouded in mystery, and her house, which, in its decayed grandeur, proves to be her perfect embodiment.

* * *

Few films have as persistent a sense of place as *Sunset Boulevard*. Location is integral to the story. The movie opens with a downward gaze at a curbstone marked "SUNSET BLVD." and then hurls the viewer, as if in a speeding car, along the thoroughfare for which the film is named. *Sunset Boulevard* is a movie, Sunset Boulevard a road. And not simply any road, but an essential artery of Los Angeles. Twenty-seven miles long, it starts downtown, slices through Hollywood, curves gently amid the exclusive communities of Beverly Hills and Bel Air, skims across the geographic edge of the UCLA campus in Westwood, and culminates in Santa Monica at the foot of the Pacific Ocean. The movie *Sunset Boulevard* similarly takes us on a journey, though a geographically more restricted one, through Hollywood, Beverly Hills, and Bel Air, though not in that order.

Aside from numerous scenes set inside or outside of Norma Desmond's mansion, fictitiously located at 10086 Sunset Boulevard (no such address exists), most of the movie takes place in Hollywood. Indeed, Brackett and Wilder originally wanted to call their tale of hubris and ambition *Hollywood Boulevard*, but *Sunset Boulevard* ended up being the more resonant title. The movie is, after all, not merely a pungent tale of the film industry centered in Hollywood, but also about individuals, and generations, that have reached their own decline or sunset.

Meta-movie that it is, provocatively blending truth and illusion, fact and fiction, real people and invented ones, *Sunset Boulevard* also juxtaposes actual places (such as the exterior of Schwab's Pharmacy at 8024 Sunset Boulevard in Hollywood) and simulacra thereof (the interior of Schwab's as meticulously re-created on a Paramount soundstage). A film about an aging Hollywood diva who experiences a mental breakdown and can no longer distinguish between fantasy and reality, *Sunset Boulevard* toys with the viewer to offer a similar, though much less intense or lethal, scrambling of planes and places of existence.

Wilder and Brackett relied heavily on location shooting to tell their story. In doing so, they were partaking of a new trend in filmmaking that had been dormant for twenty years, the so-called semi-documentary style, in which filmmakers, inspired by the hard-edged naturalism of contemporary newsreel journalism, ventured beyond studio sets to shoot scenes "on location." In the mid- to late 1940s, Hollywood filmmakers increasingly left the carefully curated confines of the studio to bring greater realism to their films. Location shooting had been common during the silent era; *People on Sunday*, for example, which Wilder and his friends had made at the end of the silent era, was filmed almost exclusively at real locations in and around Berlin. The coming of synchronized sound put an end to the semi-documentary aesthetic for nearly two decades, because sound recording mandated that movies be shot on carefully controlled soundstages with bulky, soundproofed movie cameras. In these conditions, location shooting proved costly and impractical.

Now, as lighter cameras, portable lighting systems, and compact sound-recording devices were developed and refined, location shooting was suddenly possible again. Moreover, Hollywood directors were inspired by the neorealist films coming out of postwar Italy. Directors such as Roberto Rossellini and Vittorio De Sica, working on shoestrings and not having the financial wherewithal to pay for studio time, were forced to film on location. Relying on natural lighting, jerky editing, nonprofessional actors, and actual lived-in interiors, the Italian neorealists merged a low-budget documentary style of filming with intensely dramatic narratives. In doing so, they altered movie history.

In filming *Double Indemnity*, Wilder used multiple locations in and around Los Angeles, such that, as a historian of modern California put it, the film announced "the debut of Los Angeles as *mise-en-scène*." It played out in "the homes, streets, supermarkets, train stations, and downtown office buildings of Los Angeles at the peak of its pre- and postwar fulfilment as a built environment and a state of mind."

Wilder's next film, *The Lost Weekend*, ratcheted up the use of location shooting with a celebrated scene of a down-and-out writer trudging along New York's Third Avenue while lugging his bulky typewriter, hoping to find a shop where he can pawn it. That shot, filmed with a lightweight camera hidden inside a crate in the back of a delivery truck, captured a desperate Ray Milland (a well-known actor), but also the anonymous inhabitants of New York going about their business with no idea they were being filmed. This scene was an inspiration as well as a dare to other filmmakers to venture out of their well-appointed soundstages, where every element of sound and light was carefully controlled, to shoot amid the chaos of real life.

Sunset Boulevard partakes of a semi-documentary style by shooting in real Los Angeles locations, including Paramount's Bronson Gate, soundstages, and back lots. The effect adds a heightened reality to a story that otherwise verged on gothic melodrama.

★ ★ ★

Aside from various locations in and on the grounds of Paramount Pictures, the most important location in *Sunset Boulevard* was the house that would serve as Norma Desmond's Beverly Hills mansion. In early 1949, the film's producer, Brackett, its director, Wilder, and their assistant director, Buddy Coleman, were anxious to find, as Gillis describes it, "a great big white elephant of a place" to serve as Norma's home. They could have had a fake, two-dimensional mansion constructed on the studio grounds, but Wilder, committed to location filming whenever possible, insisted they find the real thing. To this end, they scoured Los Angeles and its environs, from Pasadena to Santa Barbara, without success. Nowhere could they find an oversize and ostentatious throwback to the 1920s that would make a suitable residence for their eccentric ex-film-star.

By February 1949, less than two months before shooting was to begin, they were still looking for that perfect pile that matched the mansion in their minds' eyes. At an earlier time, there would have been scores of candidates for the preexisting structure they sought, but by the middle of the twentieth century, the aesthetics of that earlier era were under siege, and once-stately mansions were ruthlessly torn down, only to be replaced with examples of midcentury modernism. The ornate revivalist architecture of the 1920s had become as much an anachronism as Norma herself.

Linked to the shifting residential aesthetics of Los Angles were powerful changes in the city's demographics. Postwar LA was flooded with migrants lured to Southern California by its mild climate and economic promise. Real estate developers and construction companies, responding to an explosive demand for affordable housing, began mass-producing efficient and inexpensive tract homes in the so-called California ranch style. Ranch homes were horizontal, single-story structures with an open floor plan that real estate promotors equated with the wide-open spaces of the American frontier—even though the homes were densely packed together on cookie-cutter streets in sprawling suburban neighborhoods: the antithesis of the frontier.

Higher up the socioeconomic ladder, the moneyed classes also rejected the old-fashioned look embodied by Norma's mansion. Wilder's fellow Austrian émigrés Richard Neutra and Rudolph Schindler, along with Schindler's then-colleague Frank Lloyd Wright, had introduced residential modernism to the Los Angeles area in the 1920s, but, at that time, modernism was too radical for the taste of most wealthy Angelenos, who instead preferred Spanish, French, Italian, and English Renaissance revival styles. Twenty years later, tastes had swung in the opposite direction. Hollywood celebrities such as Frank Sinatra, Lucille Ball, Bob Hope, Gary Cooper, and, later, William Holden, chose midcentury modern designs for their desert homes in Palm Springs and Rancho Mirage, signaling their own up-to-date modernity and relevance. As noted in chapter 1, Wilder was likewise drawn to modernism, with its emphasis on clear functionality and minimal ornamentation. This anti-fussy style resonated with the lean visual aesthetic of his films, including *Double Indemnity*, even though that prototypical film noir abounded in slashing patterns of light and shade.

In the late 1940s, *Arts & Architecture* sponsored a widely publicized program, the "Case Study Houses" project, in which the magazine commissioned major architects, among them Wilder's friends Ray and Charles Eames, to design practical but also innovative model homes that middle-class Americans could afford. The elephantine Desmond mansion was meant by the *Sunset Boulevard* team to represent the antithesis of the new trends in midcentury architecture. But where could they find such a mangy cur?

In late February, Buddy Coleman burst into Brackett and Wilder's office with news that he had found the house they were looking for: a forlorn mansion hidden away at 641 South Irving Boulevard, only two miles from the studio. Brackett wrote in his diary, "As soon as we could, we piled into studio cars and went to the corner of Wilshire and Irving, where stands the ghost of a very great, preposterous pachyderm of a mansion in a ruined garden, with a garage in just the right relation to the house, with every detail of old box hedge, smothered in high grass, completely perfect." They were elated.

Built in 1924 by the young Los Angeles architect T. Beverley Keim for his client William O. Jenkins, the house cost a staggering quarter of a million dollars and was one of the largest homes in Los Angeles.

Shortly after it was finished, Keim committed suicide. Reporting on his death, the *Los Angeles Times* described him as having "an artistic temperament that 'clashed with the commercial world.'" Intriguingly, the characterization of Keim applies as well to the imaginary future occupant of the home, Norma Desmond, whose "artistic temperament" clashed with a film industry that, in her view, had unjustly abandoned her. Keim's patron, Jenkins, was an American robber baron from Tennessee who had installed himself in Mexico in the 1910s at the peak of the Mexican Revolution and amassed a fortune in sugar. After being kidnapped by revolutionaries and paying a large ransom, Jenkins moved to Los Angeles in the early 1920s and hired Keim to design the mansion for him, his wife, and their five daughters. They moved into the house in late 1925 but, for reasons unknown, possibly including unrecorded events that led to the architect's suicide, they lived in it less than a year before moving elsewhere. The house remained empty and unsold for over a decade. Neighbors referred to it as the Phantom House.

In 1936, the oil baron J. Paul Getty bought the house for his fourth wife, Ann Rork, as part of their divorce settlement. With multiple homes at her disposal, the former Mrs. Getty never moved into the Phantom House, only occasionally using it for entertaining. When Paramount contacted her in early 1949 about renting the house and grounds for a movie location, she consented. The house had an overgrown tennis court but, curiously, no swimming pool. Since a swimming pool was crucial to the story, the ex–Mrs. Getty allowed the studio to build one on her grounds, to be filled in after filming ended. Eager to save costs, Paramount laid in a nonfunctional pool, without proper filtering and water circulation. The pool, which was not, as planned, removed after filming ended, was used by Warner Bros. in 1955 for the James Dean and Natalie Wood teen romance melodrama *Rebel Without a Cause*. The house and pool were demolished in 1957 to make way in 1958 for the multistory headquarters of Getty's Tidewater Oil Company, an innovative hybrid of two distinct architectural styles, Corporate International and Late Moderne.

While the Phantom House gets minimal screen time, appearing in only a handful of exterior shots, it makes the ideal setting for this dark tale of a woman who is beset by phantoms and is, indeed, a phantom herself.

★ ★ ★

The home's interiors, including its grand, winding staircase, were not actually filmed in the Phantom House but were instead constructed at Paramount on Stages 5 and 9, as imagined by the head of Paramount's art department, the German émigré Hans Dreier. Trained as an engineer and architect in Munich before the First World War, Dreier found work after the armistice as an assistant designer at UFA, Berlin's preeminent film studio, where he amassed thirty credits over four years. In 1923, Lubitsch brought him to America to design sets for a historical romance-fantasy called *Forgotten Paradise* (1924). As Lubitsch had done a year earlier, Dreier chose to remain in Hollywood, where he became associated with the newly formed Paramount Pictures. Recognizing his leadership skills, Paramount executives swiftly promoted him to head of the art department, a job he held until his retirement in 1950, the year that saw the release of his masterpiece, *Sunset Boulevard*.

Orson Welles has sneered that "until the collapse of the studio system, the head of the Art Department was essentially a bureaucratic functionary and did little or none of the actual designing for which he took credit and received awards." Department heads, Welles continued, "no more designed a movie than Louis B. Mayer directed one." To a certain extent this was true of studio department heads such as Dreier, who oversaw the designs of some twenty to thirty productions a year, but the glittering elegance of the much-noted Paramount house style consistently reflected Dreier's vision. Robert Boyle, who went on to design several Hitchcock films, including *North by Northwest* and *The Birds*, fondly recalled working under Dreier, whom he described as "our presiding genius." As film historian John Baxter has written of Paramount's "look" in the 1930s, the "films had a glow. The best of them seem gilded, luminous, as rich and brocaded as a Renaissance tapestry. Décor in a Paramount production was seldom, as in Metro films, merely a background: settings, draperies, gowns insinuated themselves into the action, guiding and occasionally dictating the feel of a film."

Billy Wilder expressed much the same idea, saying, "Studios had faces then. They had their own style. They could bring you blindfolded into a movie house and you opened it and looked up and you knew. 'Hey, this is an RKO picture. This is a Paramount picture. This is an MGM picture.' They had a certain handwriting, like publishing houses."

That description of Paramount's house style in the 1930s can be applied to Dreier's interior designs for *Sunset Boulevard*, in which not only settings, draperies, and gowns, but also furniture, furnishings, and props, "insinuated" themselves into the story. The interiors of Norma's mansion are stamped with her presence, outgrowths of her relentless narcissism. As the head of production, Dreier typically entrusted the day-to-day design concepts to his assistants. But with *Sunset Boulevard* he worked closely with John Meehan, the associate art director assigned to the film. Dreier became so personally involved with the project that he used his own office on the Paramount grounds to serve as the office where by night Joe Gillis and Betty Schaefer hammer out a screenplay while also falling in love. Dreier and Meehan sharply contrasted the interiors of Norma's mausoleum with a series of non-megalomaniacal settings such as Joe's drab rented room, the comparatively commodious apartment where Artie Green hosts a thronged New Year's Eve party, Schwab's Pharmacy, and various interiors on the grounds of Paramount, specifically the spacious office of the producer Sheldrake and the industrial soundstage where DeMille shoots his latest biblical epic.

Here was an interesting challenge for any designer: to capture in the same film both the baroque Hollywood of the 1920s, as represented by Desmond's "preposterous pachyderm of a mansion," and the modern, functional workspaces, drugstores, and apartment dwellings of the new Hollywood. Dreier and Meehan's art design for *Sunset Boulevard* brought home to audiences the choice facing Joe Gillis: to pickle himself in a brine of the past or to embrace the new era of clean and efficient modernism.

Amid the clutter of Norma's huge living room—filled to excess with props that were supposedly gifts to Norma from her legions of erstwhile admirers—are some thirty or so framed photographs, drawings, and cartoon caricatures of the diva in her younger years. These were actual pictures of Swanson from her personal collection that she happily loaned to the set designers. In a film that explores cinema's ever-shifting interplay between truth and illusion, every prop mattered, and none more so than the "Desmond" picture gallery as curated by real-life Swanson.

While the camera pans across the seemingly endless array of framed images, Gillis asks in voice-over: "How could she breathe in that house, so crowded with Norma Desmonds? More Norma Desmond and still more Norma Desmond." Turning Norma's house into an echo chamber of self-absorption, Dreier and Meehan signaled the dangers of unabated egotism.

Together, Dreier and Meehan designed five interiors for the Desmond estate: the shabby, over-the-garage apartment where Max initially installs Gillis; the mansion's foyer and grand curving stairway, with its stained-glass window; Norma's bedroom, which included an antique rococo bed shaped like a wide-bodied gondola and mounted with a figurehead angel (it was said to have been built for Marie Antoinette); an alcove off the cavernous living room, where she and Joe work at separate tables adjoining a side window; and the grand living room itself, referred to in the script as "the Big Room," which resembled a baronial hall. Unlike the exterior of the house, which was Renaissance revival, the

Big Room was strictly baroque, while Norma's boudoir, like her psyche, was aswirl with rococo curlicues, cupids, and bows.

The larger-than-life "Big Room" groaned under the weight of wrought-iron railings, wooden panels of fine mahogany and bleached pine, massive tables and bureaus, rugs, tapestries, mirrors, balconies, flights of steps, a fireplace, a bar, and a large, nineteenth-century landscape painting that could be raised to reveal a movie screen for showings of Norma's old movies. Here was a last gasp of fringes and tassels, soon to be consigned to the dustbin of history.

CHAPTER TWELVE

A NEW MONKEY
FOR NORMA

Brackett and Wilder, along with "Mac" Marshman, a young film journalist they brought aboard to help hone the script, divided the *Sunset Boulevard* screenplay into five sequences or acts. The first of these acts opens with a shot straight out of Weegee (Arthur Fellig), the notorious 1940s crime photographer whose stark images, often taken at night or dawn, reported on the violent underbelly of New York City. We see a street gutter strewn with dead leaves. Stenciled on the curbstone in block letters are two words set in a modern, no-nonsense font standard for this type of road marking: "SUNSET BLVD." In visual shorthand, Wilder is telling the audience that this will be a view from below, from the lower depths; the "sunset," or decline, of a person, place, or era—even though, as we are about to learn, the action starts at sunrise.

The camera, still peering down at the pavement, slowly pulls back from the curb while the opening credits roll, the names of cast and crew appearing in the same stenciled lettering as the street-name indicator on the curb. On the music track we hear four blaring, angry strokes: brass, low clarinets, a tremolo in the strings, and a steady timpani punctuation, like that of a pounding heart. In the musical codes of the day, this insistent, edgy, attention-grabbing opening music would have signaled to audiences that a crime thriller was about to begin. The music quickly turns dark and murky, as if someone or something is submerged in water, as will immediately prove to be the case.

As the credits finish, the camera tilts and pans to catch a caravan of cars and police motorcycles speeding along Sunset. Without shifting its point of view, the camera makes us feel as though we were seated in a car that now joins the chase, keeping up with the vehicles that have hurtled past us. We are, in a sense, along for the ride. Andrew Sarris has remarked that this opening is "enough to establish *Sunset Boulevard* as one of the great movies. It's one of the most striking, stirring openings . . . ever seen in a movie."

Off camera, an unidentified man (the dead Joe Gillis, we soon learn) says in relaxed and friendly tones, "Yes, this is Sunset Boulevard, Los Angeles, California. It's about five o'clock in the morning. That's the Homicide Squad, complete with detectives and newspaper men. A murder has been reported from one of those great big houses in the ten thousand block. You'll read all about it in the late edition, I'm sure." This is the first time the dead man will directly address the audience; throughout the course of the film, he will do so another twenty-five times, not only interpreting from his limited perspective everything that happens but also creating a bond with the viewer that makes him likable and sympathetic despite his dubious morality as a kept man.

Wilder recognized an inherent problem with voice-over narration: It has a tendency "to describe what the audience already sees." Nevertheless, he liked voice-over because it provided a strong point of view and signaled the appropriate tone (comic, ironic, gothic, melancholic, what have you). Besides, it supplied necessary expository information that it would take much longer to convey by means of dialogue. Yet if not handled carefully, it could feel redundant. In *Sunset Boulevard*, Wilder made sure that the visuals accompanying the narration were not flat-footed or repetitive; they added surplus information to the narration instead of merely repeating it. For example, in a scene more than midway through the movie, Gillis matter-of-factly recounts in voice-over, "Whenever she suspected I was getting bored, she would put on a live show for me: the Norma Desmond Follies. Her first number was always the Mack Sennett Bathing Beauty." A twirling striped parasol fills the screen. The camera pulls back to reveal Norma behind the parasol, wearing a bandanna tied around her head with a rabbit's-ear bow; she has rolled her black pajama trousers above her knees and her black stockings below them to approximate a Mack Sennett bathing costume. The visuals here activate and energize Gillis's dry recitation of fact; they show us much more than his words convey by fleshing them out.

In the film's opening sequence, as Joe narrates in his convivial, offhand, guy-next-door voice, we watch the policemen and newspaper reporters jump out of their cars and rush onto the patio of a mansion. The spread-eagled corpse of a young man floats facedown in the swimming pool. An overhead view of the scene gives way to a stunning shot taken from the bottom of the pool, showing the victim's eyes frozen open, as if registering the shock of his own death. We are submerged, not quite able to make out the bloated and distorted face of the victim, his arms ghoulishly extending outward, as if at any moment he will break into a danse macabre. A crime-scene photographer detonates a flashbulb that flares blindingly over the dead man's body.

The scene is integral to Brackett and Wilder's "swimming pool story." Yet the movie did not originally open with Gillis floating dead in Norma's pool. Instead—in footage that was thought lost for half a century—it opens with an establishing shot of the Los Angeles County Morgue and quickly dissolves to the morgue's interior, a huge windowless room where three dozen shrouded extras are laid out on metal slabs arranged in orderly rows. A morgue assistant wheels in a gurney containing the latest arrival, a young white male identified by the tag on his big toe as "Joe Gillis, homicide, 5/19/49."

When the attendant turns off the light and leaves the room, the corpses sit up and began talking among themselves. A boy boasts that he and his friends were swimming off the Santa Monica Pier and took dares to see who could stay underwater the longest. He won. The corpse of a large Black man asks Joe if he caught the score of last night's ball game, but Joe answers no, he died before the morning editions appeared. Asked what has brought him here, Gillis explains he came out to Los Angeles "to catch me a swimming pool. And, by gosh, in the end I got myself one. Only there turned out to be blood in it." With that, a dissolve would transport the viewer from the morgue to a Beverly Hills swimming pool with a corpse floating on its surface.

Wilder wrote the morgue scene on his own because Brackett found the idea morbidly vulgar and washed his hands of it. To the end of his life, Wilder cited it as one of the best scenes he ever wrote and one of the best scenes he ever filmed. It didn't make it into the final cut of the movie because the preview audiences rocked with laughter when they saw it. Having formed the initial impression that they were watching a comedy with wisecracking cadavers, they were confused when things turned serious, as reflected in their mostly negative response cards.

A hard-nosed pragmatist, Wilder understood that he had to ditch the morgue and go straight to the swimming pool scene that he had already shot in June. At that time he had told John Meehan, the associate art director, that he had an offbeat shot in mind. "The shot I want is a fish's viewpoint," he explained. It would be more striking that way, more disorienting and disturbing. Meehan cleverly came up with a solution: He had a large mirror positioned at the bottom of a studio water tank and placed a camera overhead. The camera caught what the mirror showed, the underside of a body floating in the water.

As with the opening credits, which start off in the gutter, this peculiar shot indicates that the movie we are about to see will provide a bottoms-up view of Hollywood wealth and glamour. Gillis, after all, is a lowlife, a bottom feeder. The disorienting camera angle also introduces an important conceit of the film—that a corpse can talk—in a manner that seems less strange and inadvertently comic than that of chattering cadavers in a county morgue.

★ ★ ★

After its corpse-in-the-pool prologue, the movie shifts into flashback mode to give us the story of a down-and-out screenwriter who can't make his car payments. That's the narrative setup: To succeed in Hollywood, which entails traveling from meeting to meeting, Joe Gillis needs a car, and without one, he has no chance of establishing himself as a screenwriter. Hoping to scrounge up some quick cash, he has submitted to Paramount the idea for a baseball pic called *Bases Loaded*. "My agent told me it was as dead as a doornail," he recalls, "but I knew a big shot over there who always liked me, and the time had come to take a little advantage of it." This throwaway line introduces a major theme of the film: taking "a little advantage" of people. I use you to my benefit, and you use me to yours.

The "big shot" friend Joe visits is a crass producer named Sheldrake. "He was a smart producer," says Joe, "with a set of ulcers to prove it." He's ushered into Sheldrake's spacious office suite. It's a set, not a real office, but Hans Dreier and John Meehan knew what a producer's office at Paramount looked like. This one bespeaks success: mahogany tables and leather upholstery with large framed and signed photographs of Paramount stars on the wall and an Oscar statuette prominently displayed on a bookshelf.

Sheldrake is played by a character actor named Fred Clark. Appearing with great regularity in 1950s and 1960s television (*The*

George Burns and Gracie Allen Show; *The Beverly Hillbillies*; and many more), Clark came to have a familiar face—if not a familiar name. When Wilder cast him in *Sunset Boulevard*, he was not very well known. Most of his roles had been as bad guys in film noir productions of the late 1940s. Tall and baggy-eyed, with a bald, dome-shaped head, pencil-thin mustache, and resonant, low-pitched voice, Clark managed in his only scene to be both funny and intimidating. In a short feature article on him in the *Citizen-News*, a Hollywood daily, he bragged about being bald, saying that "it makes a man look more mature. Girls appreciate that." He opined that more actors should go without their toupees, claiming that his baldness got him into the movies with character roles, but still, according to the *Citizen-News*, "In every film, he says, it's a fight to keep his noggin nude."

"All right, Gillis," Sheldrake says with impatience, lighting a cigar, "you've got five minutes, what's your story about?" Gillis pitches a trite idea: "It's about a ball player, a rookie shortstop that's batting .347. Poor kid was once mixed up in a holdup but he's trying to go straight, except that there are a bunch of gamblers that won't let him!" Sheldrake, who has heard it all before, doesn't let Gillis finish his recitation. He jumps in, "So they tell the poor kid he's got to throw the World Series or else, huh?" This is an inside joke, for the clichéd plot mimics that of *Golden Boy*, the 1939 film that had given William Holden his first starring role: a talented young violinist becomes a professional prizefighter who is beholden to "a bunch of gamblers" who won't let him go straight.

Gillis ignores Sheldrake's sarcasm and continues his pitch, but Sheldrake isn't catching. The producer picks up a phone and asks for the script reader, a Miss Betty Schaefer (Nancy Olson), to come to his office and give her opinion of the Gillis submission. She does so, not knowing that Gillis, lurking behind the door, is also present. "I wouldn't bother," she reports. "It's from hunger…Just a rehash of something that wasn't very good to begin with." Gillis, making his presence known, sarcastically talks back to the attractive young woman whom viewers familiar with the rules of romantic comedy would immediately peg as his future love interest. It's a perfect Lubitsch-inspired meet-cute.

As a movie producer himself, Brackett did not approve of Fred Clark's portrayal of his profession. He had wanted another, more established character actor, Joseph Calleia, to play the part. Calleia, a Maltese-born American, typically played villains of a vaguely foreign, often Latin, origin; he had already played against Holden in *Golden Boy* as the gangster who insists that the troubled young boxer keep fighting rather than go back to his first love, the violin. But Calleia was not available, so the part went to Clark.

Brackett complained in his diary: "Saw the rushes at 4....Fred Clark, who played the producer (a Paramount producer at that) had translated the lines of what was not meant to be heavy-handed...into a scene of such nasty cruelty that I hate it violently." Wilder was upset by Brackett's criticism of the scene, but, according to Brackett, even Billy's yes-men agreed that it was misplayed. Wilder dug in his heels. "It isn't bad for our story," Brackett conceded, "but it makes our attitude towards Hollywood snide and unworthy of the [good] treatment Hollywood has given us." If Brackett, a tireless champion of good taste and evenhandedness, had succeeded in his almost daily battles with Wilder to blunt the film's sharp edges and soften its satire, it would be forgotten today.

When Betty tells Joe she found his story flat and banal, he sarcastically replies, "Exactly what kind of material do you recommend? James Joyce? Dostoevsky?" She replies, "I just think pictures should say a little something." This line is self-reflexive, challenging viewers of *Sunset Boulevard* to determine for themselves whether the picture they are watching lives up to Betty's high standard. Joe mocks her idealism: "Oh, you're one of the message kids. Just a story won't do. You'd have turned down *Gone with the Wind*." Sheldrake gets the comic response line: "No, that was me. I said, 'Who wants to see a Civil War picture?'"

After striking out with Bases Loaded and failing to persuade Sheldrake to loan him $300 to make his car payments, Gillis heads to

Schwab's Pharmacy on Sunset Boulevard. Hollywood fable had it that this was where Lana Turner was discovered by a talent scout, when in fact she was noticed by the scout at a coffee shop nearby. Nonetheless, young Hollywood hopefuls frequented Schwab's to be discovered by agents, casting directors, and gossip columnists, who also frequented the emporium for similar purposes. Gillis calls Schwab's "headquarters" for Hollywood hangers-on like him. For this scene, which was shot on a soundstage, art designers Dreier and Meehan provided Brackett and Wilder an almost perfect one-to-one re-creation of the drugstore, down to the movie magazines on the racks and toothpaste brands on the shelves.

The script called for Gillis to run into the real-life Hollywood gossip columnist Sidney Skolsky, who did use Schwab's as his unofficial office. In the scene, later cut because Wilder thought it impeded narrative flow, the columnist asks the young writer if he has "anything for the column." Joe sarcastically replies, using the names of show-business families that viewers of the day would have recognized, "Sure. Just sold an original for a hundred grand—to the King Brothers [producers of independent films], The Life of the Warner Brothers [owners of a major film studio], starring the Ritz Brothers [comedians], playing opposite the Andrews Sisters [singers]. But don't get me wrong—I love Hollywood." In the scene as it stands, Joe makes a series of calls from the Schwab's pay phone, concluding his fruitless search with the one-liner, "I talked to a couple of yes-men at Twentieth. To me they said no."

Dissolve to a sun-dappled green at the Bel-Air Golf Club, a private institution that, in its exclusivity, represents a gate, like the Bronson Gate at Paramount, that is closed to Gillis. On one of the greens, he confronts his agent, Morino, who shows no interest in advancing him the $300 he desperately needs. Morino is played by Lloyd Gough, an actor whose career had gotten off to a promising start in the late 1940s with roles in crime films that offered socially critical perspectives. In *Body and Soul* (1947), a boxing picture that's at heart a critique of capitalism, he played an unethical promoter who ruins his fighter. In the screen adaptation of Arthur Miller's *All My Sons* (1948), he portrayed an idealistic young doctor whose dreams of becoming a lifesaving medical researcher are shattered by the necessity of supporting his family.

Since the 1930s, Gough had shown a strong commitment to antifascist politics and trade-union activism. In 1952, he and his wife, the actress Karen Morley, were called to testify before the House Un-American Activities Committee (HUAC) for their former ties with the American Communist Party, and both were blacklisted. Morley never worked in the film industry again, and Gough remained professionally unemployable until the blacklist ended in the 1960s. With hindsight, knowing of Gough's commitment to progressive politics, we can surmise that he relished portraying Gillis's agent as a heartless capitalist, and Wilder probably enjoyed the irony as well.

At this point, the movie has switched genres. What started off as a gritty, Weegee-like crime story (that is, a film noir) has morphed into a satire of the film industry: a heartless, belching, rather funny film producer; a hangout for gossip columnists and Hollywood hopefuls; a posh golf course with a complacent film agent more concerned with the quality of his putts than the well-being of his clients. When Gillis, leaving the country club, turns onto Sunset Boulevard, he is spotted by the finance men looking to repossess his car. He guns his engine, and they give chase. Suddenly we are back in the world of crime, with appropriately loud, thrilling action music, but only moments later, the movie swerves to yet another genre: the horror film.

And make no mistake, as much as it's a Hollywood satire with film noir elements, it's also a horror film. As the movie critic Richard Corliss wrote in the 1970s, "*Sunset Boulevard* is the definitive Hollywood horror movie. Practically everything about this final Brackett-Wilder collaboration is ghoulish. The film is narrated by a corpse that is waiting to be fished out of a swimming pool. Most of it takes place in an old dark house that opens its doors only to the walking dead. The first time our doomed hero…enters the house, he is mistaken for an undertaker. Soon after, another corpse is buried—that of a pet monkey, in a white coffin." Corliss also mentioned the swimming pool that serves as a haven for rats, and what Gillis calls "the ghost" of a tennis court. The wind wheezes through the broken pipes of a huge old organ, on which the grim, ominously unwelcoming, white-gloved butler hammers out Bach's fearsome Toccata and Fugue in D Minor. Carrying the horror theme further, Corliss described the mistress of the haunted house as "Dracula, or perhaps the Count's older, forgotten sister, condemned to relive a former life, sucking blood from her victim (Holden)." And let's not forget that the deceased writer who narrates the film had been anonymously employed to rewrite Norma's script and is thus in both senses of the word a "ghostwriter."

Corliss is right, *Sunset Boulevard* is shot through with horror film elements—which in turn derived from nineteenth-century British gothic fiction, with haunted houses and tales of the undead, the most famous of which were Mary Shelley's *Frankenstein* (1818) and Bram Stoker's *Dracula* (1897). Yet at the same time Wilder introduces haunted house and horror film elements into his hybrid crime thriller / Hollywood satire, he also revisits the romantic comedy genre that he and Brackett played a significant role in updating with films such as Lubitsch's *Ninotchka*, Howard Hawks's *Ball of Fire*, and their own *The Major and the Minor*. When the mistress of the mystery mansion calls down to Gillis from above, "You there! Why are you so late? Why have you kept me waiting so long?" it's a twisted meet-cute moment, even if we wouldn't have understood it as such at the time.

Even an observant viewer might not realize that the large, anachronistic home that Joe has stumbled onto is the same mansion we glimpsed during the opening sequence. At that time our attention was directed not at the house but at the swimming pool beside it. Here the reverse occurs: The crane shot that follows Gillis from the garage level of the home to the garden level takes in the mansion but includes only a small portion of the pool's edge, such that we barely recognize that it's a pool.

Nearly twelve minutes of screen time have elapsed since that opening scene at the pool. In movie terms, that's a long time. Wilder and his team could safely assume that viewers, caught up in Joe's desperate situation, would fail to connect the mansion with the pool. The more the memory of the floating corpse fades from the collective awareness of the audience, the greater the shock of recognition at the end, when Joe, mortally wounded, lurches into Norma's pool. This sort of artful amnesia, of which Wilder was a master, is a theatrical technique known as Chekhov's Gun. According to the Russian playwright, a pistol that appears in the first act of a play is meant to be forgotten until it suddenly goes off in the final act.

Having trespassed onto private property, Joe is startled by the stern reprimand of the imperious woman who calls down to him from above, and he is further taken aback when a formally attired, bald butler growls at him from the doorway, "In here!" Gillis tries to explain that he has had a blowout and moved his car into an empty bay of the garage. Ignoring this, the butler reprimands Joe for not being properly dressed and orders him to wipe his feet and come inside.

And like that, *Sunset Boulevard* segues to the haunted house genre. In the Universal horror films of the early 1930s—Tod Browning's *Dracula* (1931) and James Whale's *Old Dark House* (1932), for example—a traveler on a dark and stormy night typically stumbles into a creepy castle or mansion. Part of what makes *Sunset Boulevard* such a pleasure to watch is that it's always on the verge of tipping one way or another into comedy, mystery, melodrama, social satire, or horror. This unsettling mixing of genres, which at the time rankled some of its critics, today feels playful and postmodern.

With a jerk of his bullet-shaped head, the grim butler directs the baffled visitor up the grand, winding staircase, with its marble steps, wrought-iron handrail, and stained-glass window. The butler's head, shown in profile, dominates the foreground of the shot. "If you need help with the coffin, call me," he remarks lugubriously, eliciting a well-timed double take from Joe. It's a moment stolen from Hollywood's horror comedies such as Bob Hope's *The Ghost Breakers* (1940) and *Abbott and Costello Meet Frankenstein* (1948) that put comic actors into horror film situations. Here, Holden's double take miscues the viewer that nothing truly bad is about to happen—and yet, by the end of the film, this initially harmless misunderstanding will cost Gillis his life. Ed Sikov argued that *Sunset Boulevard* is ultimately a comedy rather than a tragedy because in the end both characters' deepest wishes are, perversely, fulfilled: Norma gets her close-up and Joe, who was no good as a screenwriter in this life, has authored one hell of a story from the afterlife. He also gets the swimming pool he yearned for.

The mysterious lady at the top of the stairs leads Gillis into her boudoir, remarking, without explaining who she's talking about, that she "put him on my massage table in front of the fire. He always liked fires and poking them with a stick." This elicits another double take from Holden. Soon it becomes clear that the lady of the house has mistaken Gillis for the pet undertaker she had summoned to bury her deceased chimpanzee. She says she wants a child-size white coffin lined with red satin.

Brackett and Wilder were no doubt inspired by Evelyn Waugh's 1948 Hollywood satire *The Loved One*, which they had briefly considered adapting for the screen. Among the many follies the novel chronicles are the pet-burial habits of wealthy movie folk. Waugh, a British journalist and novelist who spent several weeks in Hollywood working on a film project that never materialized, lampooned the ostentatious send-offs that wealthy pet lovers gave to their loved ones. He mentioned, as an example, "the burial of a canary over whose tiny grave a squad of Marine buglers had sounded Taps." He mentioned, too, "the ritualistic, almost orgiastic cremation of a nonsectarian chimpanzee." California law, Waugh's narrator informs the reader, forbade certain types of burials, such as scattering the ashes of the loved one from an airplane. In this vein, Norma asks Gillis if there are "any city laws against" burying her loved one in the backyard.

At last realizing Gillis is not the pet undertaker she had summoned, Norma orders him out of her house. Her tone rankles him: "I'm sorry you lost your friend," he says without a smidgen of sorrow, "and I don't think red is the right color." Suddenly it dawns on him who he is speaking to. "Wait a minute," he says, "I know your face. You're Norma Desmond. You used to be in pictures. You used to be big."

There's something unsparingly honest and true about these simple declarative statements. They serve as a verbal springboard for Norma's own declaration, which is considerably more subjective and open to debate—a debate that, in essence, will be the driving force behind the remainder of the film:

I am big. *It's the pictures that got small.*

Learning that Gillis is a screenwriter, she immediately offers him a job editing her screenplay based on the biblical story of Salome, the seductive teenage Hebrew princess who demands the head of John the Baptist on a silver platter. He agrees, thinking smugly that he had "dropped the hook" on Norma, when in fact she has dropped it on him. At the witching hour, as eerie music plays on the soundtrack, Joe gazes out the gabled window of the dingy garage apartment where Norma has asked him to spend the night, to see her and her butler proceeding with measured steps through the overgrown garden. Max bears the white child-size coffin that the real undertaker brought that afternoon, while Norma holds aloft a candelabra, its candles flickering in the darkness. When the veteran director of photography John F. Seitz asked Wilder how to film this scene, the director replied with an insouciant shrug, "Oh, just your usual monkey funeral shot, Johnny!" Gillis, in voice-over, calls this "the last rites for that hairy old chimp, performed with the utmost seriousness—as if she were laying to rest an only child. Was her life really as empty as that?"

She is fixated on her pet monkey, Joe surmises, because she never had a child of her own. In keeping with a pre-feminist mindset, Gillis assumes that women who don't produce progeny fixate on substitutes. That misconception aside, he's onto something, since he himself, at nearly half Norma's age, can be viewed as potentially a surrogate son. As later scenes will show, he feels infantilized by Norma. If he's not her surrogate son, he's her pet monkey. In the hard-boiled lingo of the day, rather than her chimp, he's her chump.

Act 1 opens and closes with the swimming pool. The first time it appears, it's filled with water and has a corpse floating in it. At the end of the first act, we see it again, this time in flashback, only now it is empty save for a couple of rats scavenging for scraps of food. During this introductory act, the audience is encouraged to identify with Joe Gillis, when in fact, like the rodents in the pool, he, too, has become a "rat." The first act details Joe's life as bottom feeder, culminating in his meeting Norma. The second act chronicles his transformation into a surrogate for the deceased monkey.

The next morning, Gillis storms over to the main house, furious that during the night, Max transferred all his possessions from his one-room apartment in Hollywood to Norma's garage apartment. He finds Max playing Bach's majestic but also creepy Toccata and Fugue in D Minor. Written as music for the organ in the mid-1700s, the Toccata and Fugue had been a staple accompaniment to horror films of the silent era; in the early sound period, it was used in horror thrillers such as *Dr. Jekyll and Mr. Hyde* (1931) and *The Black Cat* (1934). Thus Max's playing signals to audiences that danger lies ahead while simultaneously parodying old-fashioned horror movies.

In the next sequence, Max projects one of Norma's old movies in the grand living room. The camera shows Joe and Norma seated together after dinner, their cigarette smoke caught by the projector's beam of light in shifting arabesque patterns. When Norma clasps Joe's arm, he looks down and grimaces: "Sometimes as we watched, she'd clutch my arm or my hand," Joe explains in voice-over, "forgetting she was my employer, becoming just a fan, excited about that actress up there on the screen… I guess I don't have to tell you who the star was. They were always her pictures—that's all she wanted to see."

The film they are watching is *Queen Kelly*, starring Gloria Swanson and directed by Erich von Stroheim. It was Stroheim's idea to show a clip from *Queen Kelly*, and a very good one at that. In suggesting this to Wilder, Stroheim assumed he'd be paid for the rights. Swanson, who had owned the now defunct production company that financed the film, assumed the rights were hers instead. In fact, both of them were wrong. In 1930, a Hollywood producer named Walter Futter had purchased the rights to *Queen Kelly* to supplement on-location footage for his picture *Africa Speaks* (1930), one of the first documentaries of the sound era. Now, in 1949, he sold Paramount the rights to three minutes of footage as chosen by Wilder. Wilder only needed twenty seconds.

As the brief candlelit scene from the movie-within-the-movie unfolds, showing young Norma Desmond / Gloria Swanson at the peak of her beauty, an old-fashioned intertitle appears: "Cast Out This Wicked Dream Which Has Seized My Heart." This title card did not actually appear in *Queen Kelly* but was instead created specifically for *Sunset Boulevard*. In both films, the protagonist is imprisoned by a dream: Patricia's that she had found a dashing prince to love; Norma's that she can recapture her youth and return to stardom. In actuality, the intertitle for the scene from *Queen Kelly* was much more mundane: "Holy Mother O' God…Grant That I May See the Prince Again!"

Dreams, wicked or otherwise, were the subject of *Hollywood the Dream Factory*, a study published in 1950 by the American anthropologist Hortense Powdermaker, based on a year she had spent interviewing some three hundred film industry professionals, Charles Brackett among them. The book that resulted was an unflattering ethnographic study of the movie business and its deleterious effect on the minds of moviemakers and moviegoers alike. Powdermaker explained, "Hollywood is engaged in the mass-production of prefabricated daydreams. It tries to adapt the American dream, that all men are created equal, to the view that all men's dreams should be made equal." The true American dream, in her view, originated in a public desire for a fairer and more equitable society, but it had been reduced—by Hollywood and similar popular-culture dream factories—to a matter of individual aspirations for wealth, fame, love, and success. Norma Desmond may be trapped in a wicked dream in which her only concern is for her own advancement, but as Powdermaker and other social critics of the time contended, the American dream itself had been corrupted into a matter of egocentric individualism with little thought given to the betterment of a democratic society.

Grabbing Joe's arm, and thereby taking control of him whether he likes it or not, Norma draws him (and the viewer) into her private reverie. The scene is a mini movie of her own devising, with a set (the Big Room), a handsome leading man, a supporting cast (the butler), extravagant costumes, and a dramatic climax, which arrives when Norma works herself into a frenzy of self-adoration: "Still wonderful, isn't it? And no dialogue. We didn't need dialogue. We had *faces*." She jumps to her feet, colliding with the oncoming beam of the projector as self-ardor morphs into self-righteous indignation. "Those idiot producers!" she cries, nominally to Joe but even more so to herself: "Those imbeciles! Haven't they got any eyes? Have they forgotten what a star looks like? I'll show them. I'll be up there again. So help me."

In movie history terms, this declaration of supreme determination ranks with Scarlett O'Hara's stirring vow in *Gone with the Wind*: "As God is my witness, I'll never be hungry again." Scarlett will make good on her oath in the second half of her motion picture, but Norma will not in hers. The viewer might suspect as much, for Norma is not merely trying to stave off hunger; she is trying to hold back time, an impossible ambition. Her crazy, wild-eyed assertion makes her a compelling character with whom we can't help but sympathize, so perfectly naked and headlong is her relentless desire.

In his 1965 interviews with the French filmmaker François Truffaut, Alfred Hitchcock lauded what he called "pure cinema," by which he meant filmmaking that relies more on images than words. Explaining his notion of pure cinema, Hitchcock told Truffaut, "There's no such thing as a face; it's nonexistent until the light hits it." It is the brilliance of John Seitz's lighting in this scene that monumentalizes the magnificent architecture of Swanson's face. As the film historian Jeanine Basinger put it, when Swanson rises into the flickering light and delivers the famous line about faces, "her profile stops any arguments."

Along with dialogue and lighting, the music is equally crucial. When Norma thrusts herself into the unforgiving projector beam, woodwinds strike a dissonant chord that serves as a stinger. Flutes trill, while clarinets sound a royal fanfare, appropriate for a deposed queen who insists on regaining her throne. The composer Franz Waxman, a German Jew who came to Hollywood after surviving a beating in a Berlin street by Nazi hoodlums, had received his first Hollywood assignment as an orchestrator for *Music in the Air*, the 1934 flop that starred Swanson and was cowritten by Wilder. Subsequently, Waxman wrote original music for James Whale's *The Bride of Frankenstein* (1935), a horror film that relied heavily on shocking, moody, and otherworldly strains of music that inspired many horror movie soundtracks to come.

Seitz's dramatic lighting, Head's shimmering dinner jacket for Norma, and Waxman's agitated and at times shrill musical soundscape, not to mention Norma's majestically deranged declaration of intent, as written for her by Brackett, Wilder, and Marshman and rivetingly delivered by Swanson, transform Desmond into a cinematic creature of mythic proportions. It's a reminder that moviemaking at its best is a collaborative effort.

Such stunning use of projection room chiaroscuro had marked two previous, now classic films of the 1940s, Orson Welles's *Citizen Kane* (RKO) and Preston Sturges's *Sullivan's Travels* (Paramount), both released in December 1941. In the former, a documentary newsreel introduces us to the life and death of the fictitious Charles Foster Kane. Suddenly, before the newsreel properly ends, it screeches to a halt, and we find ourselves in a darkened screening room with several faceless journalists. Gregg Toland, Welles's cinematographer, cloaks the journalists in shadow, silhouetting them against the harsh beams of light emitted from the projection booth windows.

Similarly, in an early sequence of *Sullivan's Travels*, Sturges's satiric comedy about Hollywood, a darkened screening room containing a pair of movie executives and the title character, Sullivan, is thick with shadows. These men are literally and figuratively in the dark, in Sullivan's case about how to make a socially responsible motion picture and in the case of the executives about how to humor their hotshot director without acceding to his naive insistence on making a serious (read: commercially unprofitable) work of art. The director, an idealist who believes, in line with *Sunset Boulevard*'s Betty Schaefer, that "pictures should say a little something," rises into the smoke-saturated beam of light that surges from the projection booth and waves his hand, vectoring the light into small sections, while the cynical moneymen remain unilluminated.

This shot from *Sullivan's Travels* was lit and composed by John Seitz, who eight years later shrouded Norma Desmond in a similar high-contrast, light-and-shadow apotheosis. But for *Sunset Boulevard*, to give the sequence additional volume and weight, Seitz had his assistants scatter magnesium dust into the air, creating for Norma a private, epiphanic, dreamlike atmosphere.

The intense artificial light that collides with Norma's resolute face reverberates with symbolic meanings. It accords her the limelight she so desperately desires. At the same time, it highlights her advanced age. A moment earlier, we saw young Norma in the *Queen Kelly* footage looking radiant by candlelight; now we see "old" Norma under the abrasive light of the projector, which cruelly shows her face to be a far cry from that of her on-screen avatar.

★ ★ ★

Wilder and Brackett hired three real-life silent-screen stars to join Norma for an evening of playing bridge. In voice-over, Joe recalls: "The others around the table would be actor friends—the figures you may still remember from the silent days. I used to call them her waxworks." One of them, H. B. (Henry Byron) Warner, a popular leading man in the silent era, had played Christ in DeMille's *King of Kings* (1927) and starred opposite Swanson herself in a romantic melodrama titled *Zaza* (1923). In the bridge scene, the actor appears gaunt and drawn, a ghost of a man, although in truth he was enjoying a relatively successful career as a character actor. He had found steady work in the 1930s and 1940s in various Frank Capra pictures, including *Mr. Deeds Goes to Town*, *The Lost Horizon*, *You Can't Take It with You*, *Mr. Smith Goes to Washington*, and, most recently and memorably, *It's a Wonderful Life* (1946), where he appears as a drunken druggist who nearly poisons a child by misreading a label. Another of Norma's bridge foursome was played by Anna Q. Nilsson, a Swedish-born actress and model who had starred in many silent films and continued to work in talking pictures, usually when a Scandinavian nurse, mother, or aunt was called for by the script.

The third member of Norma's entourage was one of the true giants of the silent screen, Buster Keaton. Film critic Roger Ebert has called Keaton "arguably, the greatest actor-director in the history of the movies." Keaton's heyday was from 1920 to 1929. After that, his remarkable physical plasticity started to fail, as did his marriage. He began drinking heavily and never fully recovered from his alcoholism. Holding his cards close to his chest, the Great Stone Face, as he was known, has but one word of dialogue, which he utters twice: "Pass." Replete with the pathos that had made him famous, Keaton's "pass" is a sad reminder that by midcentury, he was no longer a player, passed over by Hollywood.

Wilder had several reasons for including Keaton as a waxwork. As a youth in Vienna, the future filmmaker had adored Keaton's movies, watching them repeatedly, often in the company of his mother. Moreover, as an adult, Wilder was a dedicated bridge player and had heard that Keaton was a world-class amateur. For that reason alone, he was eager to meet him. But the ultimate reason Wilder wanted Keaton in his movie was for his unforgettable face. That face was as much an icon of the silent cinema as Chaplin's postage-stamp mustache, bowler hat, and funny way of walking, or the convergence in young Gloria Swanson's face of flashing eyes, protruding teeth, ski-jump nose, and peppery beauty mark.

Wilder filmed the bridge scene on May 3, 1949. Nilsson was called for makeup at 7:00 a.m. and Warner and Keaton at 9:00. That night, Brackett noted their appearances in his diary: Nilsson "looked well… the ghost of a beauty. H. B. Warner and Buster Keaton were somber relics of the past. And Gloria, looking absolutely sparkling, full of the sense that she had beaten the years far better than they, made a great fourth."

In her memoir, Swanson recalled shooting the waxworks scene: "Anna [Nilsson] had recently returned to the screen as a character actress and looked splendid, but H. B. Warner appeared brittle, almost transparent, when he showed up. Buster Keaton, the fourth member of the bridge party, looked ravaged, as indeed he had been, by alcohol." When the four of them assembled for the scene, Keaton looked around and muttered in deadpan, "Waxworks is right." At this, wrote Swanson, "We all howled in laughter."

Keaton received $1,000 for his appearance, whereas Nilsson, less well known (and a woman), garnered only $250. Warner, still relatively active in movies, earned as much as the other two together, $1,250.

Brackett and Wilder believed this was money well spent: These actors were screen legends, among the best-known stars of the silent era, and moviegoers of 1950 were old enough to remember them. Yet according to film historian Robert Ray, the effect on audiences was not entirely positive: "*Sunset Boulevard* used Swanson, von Stroheim, and Buster Keaton disturbingly. For the members of the audience who had grown up with these stars, seeing them aged and outmoded provided a sudden intimation of mortality." This was hardly surprising. Audiences were unused to seeing former film stars as antiques and uncomfortable with the realization that movie stars, no different from the rest of us, decay over time. "For many in the audience," recalled Jeanine Basinger, *Sunset Boulevard* "was an extraordinary blurring of fact and fiction, since for them it had been less than twenty-five years since it had all been real. When Norma's bridge group meets . . . older people in the audience gasped. I know, I was there, ushering, watching it numerous times."

★ ★ ★

Deciding that Joe's wardrobe needs an upgrade, Norma has Max wheel out the Isotta Fraschini and drive them to the exclusive men's shop where Joe first confronts his status as a kept man. (With Stroheim not knowing how to drive, the car had to be towed whenever Max is seen behind the wheel.) *Sunset Boulevard* is remembered today as a sardonic attack on Hollywood, but it's an attack on much more than that. Unscrupulous salespeople are everywhere, and they in turn reflect a culture-wide ethos that teaches us to "take a little advantage" of others when we can. Wilder delineates a social malaise that extends beyond Hollywood to the broader society of postwar America. *Time* magazine noted as much in its review of the film: "The picture itself may strike some as a disturbing symptom of a jungle mentality that flourishes in the U.S. far beyond the boundaries of Hollywood." Opportunism infects all the principal characters of *Sunset Boulevard*, as well as minor ones such as the unctuous salesman Joe encounters. Seeing himself through the salesman's eyes, Joe is forced to face the ugly truth that he has become Norma's gigolo.

Joe's epiphany in the men's shop, accompanied by the shrill blast of a piccolo and clarinet, draws act 2 of *Sunset Boulevard* to a disturbing close.

★ ★ ★

The third act opens with Max transferring Joe's belongings from the leaky garage apartment to the mansion's "room of the husbands," which is adjacent to Norma's boudoir and provides unimpeded access to it. Under Joe's needling, Max reveals that he writes all the fan mail that Norma receives, thus deluding her into believing she still has an adoring public, when in fact it abandoned her long ago. The idea for this surprise revelation came from Stroheim himself, as well as the idea of using *Queen Kelly* as the after-dinner film Max projects for Norma and Joe.

Wilder happily accepted both of these suggestions but rejected a third by Stroheim: that the butler be seen experiencing a fetishistic thrill as he hand-washes his employer's brassiere, panties, and stockings. In his personal life, Stroheim fancied himself a libertine and was proud of it. Wilder observed that Stroheim's "obsession with foot fetishism, underwear fetishism, other sexual perversions which his pictures are filled with, was the *real* Stroheim." The French filmmaker Jean Renoir, who got to know Stroheim during the shooting of *La Grande Illusion*, similarly observed that Stroheim "wanted to resemble the Marquise de Sade. He had dreams of boundless luxury, perverse women, flagellation, sexual exploits, bacchanalia and drinking bouts." It was in this context of needing to flaunt his virility that Stroheim, sixty-three, remarked to Wilder that Gloria Swanson was too young and desirable to play the role of Norma Desmond: "Look at her," he said, "I would like to fuck her now."

Wilder's response to Stroheim's obscene comment was to say, "I would rather fuck you," to which Stroheim, annoyed that he didn't get as much screen time as he believed he deserved, retorted, "You have." When the director did show him on screen, it was mostly from the rear. Erich told a makeup man he was wasting his time on his face: "Are you going to make up my ass," he inquired, "because that's all that's being photographed." It was obvious the older filmmaker thought *he* should be directing *Sunset Boulevard*. Nancy Olson Livingston has recalled that each day when scenes were being set up and shot, Stroheim moved his chair as close as possible to the cameras, as if he were more than ready to step in as director on a moment's notice.

While Max is moving Joe into the so-called room of the husbands, the writer peers into Norma's bedroom, which is "all satin and ruffles," and says of her in voice-over: "Poor devil, still waving proudly to a parade which had long since passed her by." The scene dissolves to Gillis descending the grand staircase garbed in the full-dress evening suit that Norma purchased for him. Reaching the bottom, he nervously adjusts his white tie and loosens his collar, obviously ill at ease in such formal attire or perhaps uncertain as to what awaits him. Before he enters the cavernous living room, he stops and looks around. In voice-over, he says, "It was at her New Year's party that I found out how she felt about me. Maybe I'd been an idiot not to have sensed it was coming—that sad, embarrassing revelation."

The vast room where they watch her old movies has been reconfigured into a ballroom. Furniture has been moved and rugs pulled up to make way for a waxed and polished dance floor. Max, in formal attire, stands behind a buffet table laden with buckets of champagne and silver platters of caviar. The room has been decorated with laurel garlands, and dozens of candles blaze in sconces and candelabras. On a small platform banked with palm fronds, a four-piece salon orchestra plays "La Cumparsita," a popular Latin American tango from the 1920s. *La cumparsita* translates as "the little parade," which subtly dovetails with Joe's pitying comment about Norma in the previous scene that she is still waving proudly to a parade that had long since passed her by.

At the far end of the room, Norma, wearing a veiled headpiece and a floor-length, jewel-spangled evening dress that bares one shoulder, moves rhythmically to the music, as if dancing her own private tango. Looking up from her reverie—perhaps, we might imagine, a memory of dancing here with Valentino long ago—she sees Joe and crosses over to him. While doing so, she continues her tango movements, conspicuously displaying her sensuality. This is one of the most piercing moments in *Sunset Boulevard*, thanks both to Wilder's staging (she comes to Joe, not he to her) and Swanson's acting, where she seems to be two people at once: a sensual woman living fully in the moment and a self-obsessed woman who, as if constantly in front of a camera that records her every move, habitually lives outside the moment, needing to make a display of herself.

Once famous as a Hollywood "vamp" (as Gloria Swanson had been), Norma seems here to be trying too hard to recapture the sizzling sensuality for which she had been renowned. In an earlier scene, Max tells Joe that "men would bribe manicurists to get clippings from her fingernails. There was a Maharajah who came all the way from Hyderabad to get one of her stockings. Later, he strangled himself with it." Norma's assumption of the vamp role that once became her (according to the conventional rules of age and gender) now seems inappropriate, pathetic.

In love relationships, it has been said, control belongs to the person who cares less. But in this scene, the two characters dance an emotional pas de deux: He is the stronger in one regard, because, as she confesses, "I'm in love with you. Don't you know that? I've been in love with you all along." But she is dominant in a different way: When he asks, later in the scene, "What right do you have to take me for granted?" she replies with a firm sense of ownership, "What right? Do you want me to tell you?" He lets the question go unanswered.

When they tango, Norma takes the lead ("Just follow me")—a position traditionally accorded by the logic of the erotic Latin American dance to the male partner in an assertion of his masculine authority. When Joe leans away from her, she reproves him: "Don't bend back like that." He points to her headwear: "It's that thing," he says. "It tickles." "Oh, that!" she laughs gaily. In a sweeping gesture, she removes the jaunty veiled cap from her head and flings it to the dance floor while straightening her hair and then continuing to whirl Joe in her arms.

Viewing the scene through the dead Joe's eyes, we find Norma "sad, embarrassing," and faintly ridiculous. That is Wilder's view as well. He does not make Norma into a gargoyle, a monster, a vicious man-eater. Rather, he depicts her as human and vulnerable, a perpetrator but also a victim. Swanson turns in an impressive multifaceted performance that allows the viewer to understand Desmond as both a voracious vamp (vampire) and, beneath the surface, an older woman with a reasonable desire to be *seen* and appreciated by a younger man. Norma fights mightily, one might even say heroically, against her social, sexual, and professional invisibility.

To capture the intimacy of their dance, John Seitz used a homemade contraption that he had invented for Valentino's famous tango number in *The Four Horseman of the Apocalypse* three decades earlier. It consisted of a swiveling wooden platform mounted on top of a dolly, so that the camera could come in close on the dancers and move fluidly across the dance floor with them, maintaining an intimate distance throughout. We are brought in on Norma's "wicked dream" of merging physically and spiritually with this strong and handsome younger man—a dream he does not share. Incidentally, Seitz had a strange quirk: He could not abide watching actors act. He would devise a shot such as this, set it up, fine-tune it, and then, as the final stage in the process, have his assistants execute it while he averted his eyes from the performers as they performed.

Cinematographer Ted Tetzlaff had achieved an even more impressive traveling close-up three years earlier in Hitchcock's *Notorious* (1946) for a scene described by the RKO publicity department as "the longest kiss in screen history." Tetzlaff managed to keep his camera astonishingly close to Cary Grant and Ingrid Bergman as they move through her apartment while continuously kissing and embracing. As Hitchcock later told François Truffaut, he made the viewer "the third party to this embrace. The public was being given the great privilege of embracing Cary Grant and Ingrid Bergman together. It was a kind of temporary *ménage à trois*." Whereas Hitchcock stimulated and seduced viewers of *Notorious* by bringing them into an imagined physical intimacy with Grant and Bergman, Wilder used his camera's intimacy with the dancers to discomfort, if not disturb, us.

Wilder shot the tango from a high angle looking down at the dance floor. The solitary dancers, made small by the camera's height, are trapped within the garishly overstuffed room with its surfeit of furniture, photographs, and bric-a-brac. This, too, like the uncomfortably close dance shots, engenders in the viewer a claustrophobia similar to what Joe must be feeling. It continues the motif of suffocation that presents itself at the start of the sequence when he attempts to loosen his constrictive shirt collar. In clichéd film noir terms, Joe is caught in Norma's spiderweb, but it is important to remember that she, too, is imprisoned in a web, spun of her delusional obsession with past grandeur and her unvoiced dread of an empty future.

The first New Year's Eve scene ends with Norma drunk and enraged at Joe's rejection of her advances: "What you're trying to say," she slurs, "is that you don't want me to love you. Is that it?" She slaps his face and rushes from the room. The grand staircase is off screen, but we see her ascending it by means of her reflection in an ornately decorated mirror that hangs from the wall. In reducing the size of Norma to a glimpse within the mirror, Wilder shows us her own sudden reduction from one who has imagined herself to be in command to one who feels belittled and betrayed.

The scene has captured her fluctuating strength and weakness and reshapes our understanding of her not as a caricature but rather as an explosive mixture of power and pathos. Norma doesn't want to be discarded; she doesn't want to be superannuated. Instead of mocking her as a vain old woman who foolishly yearns for the impossible, *Sunset Boulevard* increasingly reveals her to be a tragic figure who suffers from a gnawing existential ache that is profoundly human.

Two small but telling details follow. When Norma, now on the second story of the house, rushes into her bedroom and slams the door behind her, the camera closes in on the gaping hole where a lock once was. Max had earlier explained to Joe that all the door locks had been removed for Madame's safety, as she had previously attempted suicide. This camera movement, which is not from Joe's point of view and without his voice-over commentary, reminds us of Max's comment and makes clear that we might now expect her to try again. As a side note, this suggestive use of a closed door to advance the narrative is an instance of Wilder paying homage to Lubitsch, but for dramatic, rather than comedic, purposes. Downstairs, Joe takes his vicuña coat from the closet and starts to leave the mansion. As he does so, the fine-mesh chain of a gold watch Norma has given him catches on the iron grille adorning the entrance, reminding audiences that Joe is "chained" to Norma. Moreover, though we may only recognize this in retrospect, time is running out for the year, but also for both Joe and Norma and, by extension, for all of us in this sad world of finitude.

CHAPTER THIRTEEN

OUT WITH THE OLD, IN WITH THE NEW

Joe thumbs a ride to Artie Green's New Year's Eve party, which is the antithesis of Norma's. But the contrast is not simply lonely decrepitude versus youthful vivacity. Yes, we are made to feel that Artie's world is the more desirable of the two, and yet it is also shown to be superficial, lacking in the haunting purity of Norma's world, to which Gillis, who has already rejected the heartless Hollywood that rejected him, finds himself irresistibly drawn. To be sure, he enjoys the wealthy accoutrements of life with Norma, but perhaps also, as all good vampire stories attest, he is emotionally captivated by her, even mesmerized.

The revelers at Artie's party were played by young hopefuls in Paramount's deep reserve of contract actors, the very ranks out of which William Holden had emerged some ten years earlier. There are, however, two ringers at the party, nonactors that Wilder included in the scene. These were his friends Jay Livingston and Ray Evans, songwriters who worked in Paramount's music department. Three weeks before shooting began on *Sunset Boulevard*, their "Buttons and Bows" won the Academy Award for best original song of 1948. Bob Hope sang it in *The Paleface* (1948), a comedy about a nineteenth-century dentist who goes out west to make his fortune but quickly regrets his decision. On a bumpy road in the wilderness, he sings:

> *East is east and west is west*
> *And the wrong one I have chose*
> *Let's go where they keep on wearin'*
> *Those frills and flowers and buttons and bows.*

Though written for a different film—*The Paleface*, not *Sunset Boulevard*—the lyrics capture Joe Gillis's situation of having to decide where he belongs, in Norma's world or Artie's. Seemingly, being at a party thronged with his contemporaries confirms for him that he has made the wrong choice in staying with Norma in her lonely mausoleum when he could have gone instead to a place full of life and energy. In voice-over, Joe describes the partygoers as "a bunch of kids who didn't give a hoot...just so long as they had a yuk to share." These are his contemporaries, not Norma and her "waxworks" and her death-warmed-over butler. Joe wants to be among them, the young hopefuls, rather than the old has-beens. And yet the choice is not so black or white. The wrong choice, in fact, might be to return voluntarily to a state of poverty after having become accustomed to the male equivalent of buttons and bows: tailored suits, expensive watches, and golden cigarette cases.

The song's exact lyrics were not used in *Sunset Boulevard*. Instead, Wilder had Evans write new lyrics for the snippet from "Buttons and Bows" that he and Livingston perform at the party scene. They are seated at the piano with six or seven fellow revelers gathered around and singing merrily:

Hollywood for us ain't been so good
Got no swimming pool, very few clothes
All we earn are buttons and bows.

Gillis does have plenty of clothes, since we have seen Norma buy them for him. But that only reinforces the point: He has "very few clothes" of his own. The swimming pool reference is even more apt. A couple of scenes hence, we will see Joe emerging healthy and buff from a swim in Norma's now filled pool (as Nancy Olson Livingston has recalled, "The day he shot the pool scene with Gloria Swanson, I saw his beautiful architecture. . . . He had a long, toned torso with wonderfully shaped legs"). The pool also appeared much earlier in the film, when Joe looks out at night from his room above the garage to see rats scrambling in the empty shell, vying for a scrap of food. As Raymond Chandler observed in another context, "Nothing ever looks emptier than an empty swimming pool," and at that point in the narrative, Joe is empty, both of cash and of hope.

A *filled* swimming pool was for Gillis and so many other failed or failing Hollywood aspirants the enviable symbol of success. But it was not only people in Hollywood who yearned to have a pool; in postwar America, the desire was widespread. The first private swimming pools in Los Angeles were built in the 1920s and 1930s as status symbols for movie stars and other film-industry elites. Costing upward of $10,000 to $15,000, pools were beyond the reach of most Angelenos, even the affluent ones. This changed after World War II, when private residential pools began appearing in large numbers, thanks to postwar prosperity, mass migration to Southern California, and new hybrid or synthetic materials such as steel-reinforced concrete, fiberglass, and vinyl that made pool construction more affordable. Pools were touted for their recreational and health benefits and as a type of home improvement that would increase the value of private property.

The total number of swimming pools installed throughout the United States rose from 10,000 in 1949, the year *Sunset Boulevard* was filmed, to 250,000 a decade later.

Joan Didion, who grew up in parched Southern California in the 1930s and 1940s, wrote in *The White Album* that "a pool is, for many of us in the West, a symbol not of affluence but of order, of control over the uncontrollable. A pool is water, made available and useful, and is, as such, infinitely soothing to the western eye." One suspects that Didion's insight holds true for Joe Gillis: To have a pool of his own would be to demonstrate to others and, more important, himself that he had successfully corralled the chaos of his life. As his ghost points out at the beginning of the film, he finally did get his pool, but at a high price.

Artie Green's party is an embodiment of disorder, but of a friendly sort. It's manageable. When Artie greets Joe at the door of his overcrowded apartment and reaches for the vicuña coat, he is surprised and impressed by his impoverished friend's apparent good fortune. He introduces Joe to the gathered partyers: "Fans, you all know Joe Gillis: the well-known screenwriter, uranium smuggler, and Black Dahlia suspect!" Here Brackett, Wilder, and Marshman slip in not one but two contemporary references, both comic in this context but ultimately violent in nature. Uranium was the essential mineral ingredient of the atom bomb, and the Black Dahlia was the exotic nickname given by the tabloid press to a dark-haired model and would-be actress named Elizabeth Short, who, in a well-publicized and never-solved crime, was gruesomely murdered and mutilated in Los Angeles in 1947. Ignoring Artie's humor, Joe asks if he can sleep on his sofa for a week or two, and Artie happily consents.

For the role of Artie, Wilder cast a then-unknown actor named Jack Webb, who months after completing his role in *Sunset Boulevard* gained fame as the creator and star of a popular syndicated radio, and later television, police procedural series called *Dragnet*. As Sergeant Joe Friday in *Dragnet*, Webb was monotonously stone-faced with his oft-repeated investigatory catchline, "Just the facts, ma'am," yet as wisecracking Artie Green—in contrast with Gillis—he is boyish, even adolescent, with his ingratiating grin and inability to take matters seriously. Wisecracks can only get you so far in life. Betty Schaefer ultimately leaves Artie for Joe, in whom, apparently, she sees the potential for a more meaningful relationship.

As Betty, Nancy Olson exuded a wholesomeness that suited Brackett and Wilder. In the screenplay, they referred to the yet-to-be-determined actress who would play Betty as "a new face," which Olson's certainly was. Brackett did not find her particularly pretty, but that was fine. Her job as Norma's rival for Joe's love was to provide a sharp contrast between the two women. Wilder, as Olson recollected, "was extremely precise in casting me in that role. I was to be an obvious juxtaposition to Gloria, to Norma Desmond—I was to be a *complete* contrast. That's what he wanted in my tone of voice, in the way I looked, in my manner, in the fact that I was a student at UCLA, which therefore gave me a credibility that I could be a writer."

When Betty reencounters Gillis at the party, she says that she has read some of his early stories and asks if they could find a quiet place to talk. He proposes the bathroom, which Artie has jokingly dubbed "the Rainbow Room," in reference to the famed restaurant on the top floor of New York's Rockefeller Center. Seeing them leave the crowded living room, Artie quips to Gillis, "I said you could have my couch. I didn't say you could have my girl." Joe then proceeds to steal his girl. As the role is written, he doesn't yet know he will fall in love with Betty, although, thanks to movie conventions, we do. He merely flirts with her, as he would, presumably, with any other attractive *young* woman.

In the bathroom, they sit side by side on the edge of the bathtub, Joe in his white tie and tails and Betty in a party dress with bare shoulders and a modestly scooped-out back. Wilder, who hadn't liked Edith Head's designs for Betty, asked Olson to wear her own clothes throughout the film. The aspiring screenwriter shares her thoughts with Joe for turning one of his short stories into a movie script. When he deflects these, she says, "I'm serious. I've got a few ideas." He eschews seriousness: "I've got some ideas myself. One of them being this is New Year's Eve. How about living it up a little?" Betty drops the seriousness, and they banter instead, spontaneously making up the roles of "Phillip," a colonial British officer or homesteader, and his lover, "Lady Agatha."

Just as Joe, aping a stereotypical British aristocrat, moves in for the much-anticipated kiss between the fictitious Phillip and Lady Agatha (but also between the real Joe and Betty), a partygoer interrupts their flirtation to inform him that the phone he has been waiting to use is now free. The scene, however, has made it clear that something genuine has occurred between the pair. As his fiancée, Betty "belongs" to Artie, who has generously offered his best friend a place to stay. As an aspiring screenwriter, however, she is inexorably drawn to Joe, whom she may already have fallen in love with thanks to reading his touching short stories after their initial meet-cute in Sheldrake's office.

As Joe leaves to use the phone, continuing in his guise of "Phillip," he stands erect and says gravely, "Life...can be beautiful." He is mimicking the opening line of the popular soap opera *Life Can Be Beautiful*, which ran on the radio for sixteen years, from 1938 to 1954. Each episode began with a disembodied voice reminding us, "Life...can be beautiful." Joe's clever mimicry, down to the deliberate pause after "Life," highlights the difference between the lively contemporary world of popular culture and the moribund era of the waxworks.

★ ★ ★

Wilder claimed to eschew filmmaking that called attention to fancy camerawork, preferring "invisible" editing, where the transition from one shot to another was so seamless as to go unnoticed by the viewer. In this, he was aided by the proficiency of veteran film editor Doane Harrison, who worked with Wilder on his first film for Paramount, *The Major and the Minor*, and every other Wilder picture up to and beyond *Sunset Boulevard*. Wilder claimed he learned more from Harrison than he did from any of his cinematographers. As Sam Staggs has noted, "Harrison taught Wilder how to preplan each shot as part of a total editing scheme." In other words, Wilder learned from Harrison to connect a shot in one scene with that in another.

Wilder makes good use of this blind editing in the New Year's Eve sequences. We see Joe, who finally gains use of the telephone, learning from Max that Norma, fearing she has lost Joe, has sliced her wrists. Recognizing his obligation to Norma, he threads his way through the dozens of revelers in Artie's apartment and leaves from a door in the upper left-hand corner of the screen. Several beats later, we see him enter Norman's bedroom from a door similarly placed in the upper left-hand corner of the screen. It's a visual match—out one door, in another—that furthers the contrast between Artie's apartment, which pulsates with energy and life, and Norma's solitary, cloyingly baroque bedroom.

"Go away," Norma tells Joe, despondent and ashamed. "What kind of silly thing was that to do?" he asks. She responds: "To fall in love with you—that was the idiotic thing." When he replies, self-effacingly, "It sure would have made attractive headlines, Great Star Kills Herself for Unknown Writer," she answers imperiously, "Great stars have great pride." The painful honesty of this dialogue makes Joe and Betty's flirtation in the Rainbow Room seem all the more banal.

At midnight the musical ensemble downstairs launches into "Auld Lang Syne," and Joe, feeling for Norma neither love nor lust but some sort of sympathy, even empathy, approaches her. "Happy New Year, Norma," he says. She looks at him, tears in her eyes. "Happy New Year, darling." With her bandaged arms and talon-like fingers, she reaches up and pulls him down for a kiss. The Dracula's castle motif from earlier in the film—the scene in which Joe first surveys Norma's decaying property and then encounters Max—has returned in full force, and yet it's too easy to leave it at that. Norma is so much more than a female vampire or black widow spider. True, she has caught him in a carefully orchestrated trap of elegant clothes, solid-gold cigarette cases, and now guilt. But she's also a pitiable human being, an abandoned woman, a forsaken star, and, yes, a narcissist. In weaving together these separate strands of Norma's history and personality, Gloria Swanson produced a character of unforgettable resonance, well beyond anything initially provided for that character by Brackett, Wilder, and Marshman's screenplay.

When Seitz asked what kind of camera setup he wanted for the scene, Wilder shrugged. "Johnny, it's the usual slashed-wrist shot."

CHAPTER FOURTEEN

GETTING READY FOR HER CLOSE-UP

The first three acts of *Sunset Boulevard* center on Joe, and everything we see and hear is filtered through him. In act 4, however, Norma takes center stage. Quite literally so, as we see in a scene where, fearing that Joe is tiring of her, she performs for him in the Big Room: first by mimicking a Sennett bathing beauty and then with an impressive impersonation of Charlie Chaplin in his iconic role as the Little Tramp. It's a star turn for Swanson, who in the silent era was famous for her comic timing and wit. For the Chaplin sequence, Wilder, ever the jokester, had asked the wardrobe department to bring over fifty derbies for Swanson to choose from. "The next day," Swanson wrote in her memoir, "when I walked onto the set wearing the one I had picked, Billy Wilder and the whole crew were wearing the forty-nine that were left over." Two days later, "when we shot a scene of Norma and Max burying Norma's pet chimpanzee, Mr. Wilder directed me to remove the Spanish shawl covering the chimp in the white coffin, and when I did so, the stuffed monkey was also wearing a derby."

The nod to Mack Sennett is apt since he was Gloria Swanson's first employer in Hollywood, though she was never one of his Bathing Beauties. The reference to Chaplin also makes sense, for Swanson had known the actor since their days at Essanay Studios in Chicago when she was starting out; they had subsequently become friends in Hollywood when they were both internationally famous. Here she reprises a pitch-perfect imitation of him that she had performed in her 1924 comedy *Manhandled*.

Twenty-five years later, however, the invocation of Chaplin by way of an avatar constituted an act of political bravery on Wilder's part. The real Chaplin had become reviled in America because of an ugly paternity suit brought against him and because of his scandalous fourth marriage, at age fifty-four, to the eighteen-year-old daughter of Eugene O'Neill, but even more so because of his outspoken commitment to antiwar and anti-capitalist principles, which Cold War moviegoers deemed un-American. J. Edgar Hoover, the ultraconservative director of the FBI, personally detested Chaplin and instituted a smear campaign against the once-beloved silent comedian, feeding damning revelations about him to right-wing gossip columnist Hedda Hopper.

In the film's next set piece, Norma, who mistakenly believes that DeMille is interested in her comeback script, pays an unsolicited call on him at Paramount, where he is filming his latest picture, *Samson and Delilah*, although the film is not identified as such in *Sunset Boulevard*. DeMille greets Norma at the door of Stage 18, but, because the sound-stage itself was already in use, the interior of Stage 18 was re-created on Stage 5.

Meanwhile Joe dashes off to the readers' department to speak with Betty. Art director Hans Dreier used a corner of his own office to serve as Betty's cubicle, an inside joke that viewers could not have discerned, but that is yet another instance of *Sunset Boulevard* blurring the lines between fact and fiction. In the fictional world of Brackett and Wilder's film, DeMille had directed Norma Desmond in a dozen pictures more than a quarter of a century earlier, as the real DeMille had directed Gloria Swanson in six. Brackett proudly explained to Swanson early on in the shooting, "We're really going to mix up Hollywood then and now, real and imaginary."

DeMille having excused himself for leaving her momentarily alone, Norma sits in his director's chair, unnoticed by the costumed extras and crew members on the set. As she waits, a microphone mounted on a boom swings by, catching the tip of the long peacock feather that trims her hat. Annoyed, she brushes it away. It's an understated bit of comic business, relying on a clash between two props—the peacock feather and the microphone—to remind us that we are now in the era of sound cinema. But it also reminds us, by entirely visual means, free of dialogue, how expressive silent cinema could be.

"Hey, Miss Desmond! Miss Desmond!" comes a voice out of nowhere, breaking the silence. She looks about but sees no one. "Up here!" directs the voice. Norma turns her gaze upward, where she sees an electrician standing on the catwalk beside his high-powered light. "It's me! It's Hog-eye!" he calls out. There really was a man called Hog-eye at Paramount, a retired juicer (industry slang for electrician) named John Hetman. His part was played in the movie by a character actor named John "Skins" Miller, who did not receive credit for his moment on screen. Skins Miller had a warm, benevolent face. He appeared in dozens of Paramount movies, often without credit. Around the time of *Sunset Boulevard*, his uncredited parts included a bellhop in *The Paleface*, a Tyrolean farmer in Wilder's *The Emperor Waltz*, "Idiot #1" in *A Connecticut Yankee in King Arthur's Court*, and a man with a burro in *Samson and Delilah*. Apparently, he was good at imitating drunks: He played them, again without credit, in *All the King's Men*, *The Lemon Drop Kid*, *Night into Morning*, *Here Comes the Groom*, *Valley of Fire*, and several other Paramount productions.

Oddly, in the celestial heights above Norma, Hog-eye resembles an archangel in a Renaissance Annunciation painting, announcing the coming of a glorious birth, or, as she mistakenly sees it, her own rebirth. When Hog-eye's bright incandescent light beams at Norma, making her the center of attention, she beams back. This small, lovely scene is a counterpart to the earlier "we had faces" scene, in which Norma leaps up into the harsh beam of the movie projector in her living room. There, light was her enemy, a revelation of her incipient madness. Here, it's adoring, even beatific.

In her autobiography, Swanson says it was her idea to affix a single white peacock feather to Norma's hat in reference to the dazzling peacock-feathered headdress the young star wore three decades earlier in the lion's den sequence of DeMille's *Male and Female*. In Christian iconography, the peacock is a symbol of Christ's resurrection or, more generally, of eternal life, inasmuch as in the Middle Ages peacock meat was thought to have a longer shelf life than other meats. The base of the hat, a band of white cloth that encircles Norma's head, forms a secular halo. If there's any whiff of spiritual redemption in this relentlessly secular, almost nihilistic movie, this would be it.

Putting the logic of the film ahead of their dislike of DeMille, Brackett and Wilder gave the notoriously difficult director the film's sweetest and most benevolent moments. Though on screen only briefly, the semi-fictionalized DeMille shows a compassion that sets him apart from everyone else in the movie's cutthroat world of filmmaking. In the film's game of "fact or fiction," the real-life director, by means of his on-screen avatar, comes away looking like the kind and benevolent figure that many in Hollywood believed him not to be. As one cultural historian has noted, "DeMille, though a ready target for ridicule, was treated with respect by Norma Desmond and *Sunset Boulevard* both."

This is the scene in which DeMille responds to an underling who wants to give Norma the brush with the trenchant lines "Thirty million viewers have given her the brush" and "A dozen press agents working overtime can do terrible things to the human spirit." Here is a surprising grace-note of warmth wrapped up with a stinging rebuke of Hollywood for its ruthless aversion to aging.

It's worth noting, however, that this rebuke of Hollywood comes from the mouth of Mr. Hollywood himself, so it's possible to see DeMille not as a warm and caring figure but as a hypocrite who doesn't own up to his complicity in the system that spits out Norma and her ilk. From this perspective, he treats her with kid gloves not to protect her feelings but rather to get rid of her in the most expeditious manner possible.

In the 1970s, the feminist filmmaker and film critic Brandon French pointed out that while DeMille blames "a dozen press agents working overtime" for Norma's megalomania, he never acknowledges his own. He nostalgically recalls the teenage star's talent and grit when she was "a lovely little girl of seventeen," but he fails to consider the economic system by which her value to the film industry (unlike his own) was almost entirely a function of her youth. Because of that male-dominant system, wrote French, Norma "has never grown up and is obsessed with her appearance." Her former protector takes neither personal nor professional responsibility for her "arrested development, her ludicrous existence as a middle-aged child who is still dependent on her director-daddies."

Reading in Brackett's diary about the disputes he and Wilder had over the tone of various scenes, we can surmise that in this one Brackett's desire to keep the film from becoming remorselessly cold prevailed over Wilder's inveterate preference for mockery. The film is actually better for keeping both of their divergent sensibilities—the sentimental and the cynical—actively in tension.

* * *

The next and final act begins with a dissolve onto Norma's face. Joe says in voice-over, "An army of beauty experts invaded her house on Sunset Boulevard." Norma wrongly believes that DeMille is going to turn her massive Salome script into an epic movie, with her in the lead. We see a rapid-fire montage of Norma, in preparation for her come-back, attempting to rejuvenate herself by means of steam cabinets, mud masks, electric massage, creams and ointments, rubdowns, and adhesive skin-tightening patches. On the soundtrack a solo violin fiddles freneti-cally, mirroring the frantic pace of the beauty regimen to which Norma submits herself.

An oddly similar sequence, though much gentler in its spoof of the beauty industry, had appeared ten years earlier in *The Wizard of Oz* when Dorothy and her entourage visit a beauty parlor in the Emerald City for much-needed rejuvenation. The beauticians, wearing high-heeled shoes and short green skirts, stuff the Scarecrow with fresh straw, polish and buff the Tin Man, clip the Cowardly Lion's beard and claws, and give Dorothy, who hardly needs it, an application of makeup and offer to change her eye color, all while joyfully singing, "That's how we keep you young and fair in the Merry Old Land of Oz."

In the *Wizard of Oz*, the beauty sequence is disarmingly "merry," whereas in *Sunset Boulevard* it seems more like a scene from a 1930s Universal Pictures monster movie, such as *Bride of Frankenstein*, in which a mad scientist defies nature in the pursuit of a Promethean ideal. Indeed, it took no less courage on Gloria Swanson's part in 1949 to play a foolish, self-deluded, aging actress subjecting herself to an army of beauticians than it had for her in 1919 to lie down with a lion. She was willing to be shown as a modern-day Bride of Frankenstein—a weird amalgamation of body parts bolted together by technicians in lab coats.

★ ★ ★

Since its beginnings—even before D. W. Griffith's close-ups fetishized the unblemished visages of teenagers Dorothy and Lillian Gish and other paragons of female innocence—cinema has cherished and venerated the ephemeral faces of youth. Nothing surpasses the close-up in its ability to elicit adoration and instill in viewers a psychological if not also physical desire for the actress or actor portrayed. From the start of the motion picture business, movies have focused on young stars for the benefit of young viewers, as well as those viewers who are older but wish—in the dark, cloistered space of the cinema—to relive the romance and glory of youth.

The accelerated obsolescence of the female film star is baked into the Hollywood system, an uncomfortable fact that *Sunset Boulevard* brutally acknowledges. The major studios, including Paramount and its top competitor MGM, excelled at manufacturing facial beauty through lighting, makeup, and furtive plastic surgery. Even MGM's greatest star, Greta Garbo, regarded by many as the most beautiful woman in the world, resorted to surgical interventions and dental implants, a secret MGM jealously guarded. Only years later, when he was out of the business, did Mayer boast: "We hired geniuses at make-up, hair dressing, surgeons to slice away a bulge here and there, rubbers to rub away the blubber. . . . We made silk purses out of sows' ears every day of the week."

It's difficult for today's viewers to understand how shocking and crude this invasion of beauty technicians would have seemed to audiences of the time. Brackett found it vulgar and offensive. As the producer of the film, he was well within his rights to demand that it be cut. Wilder, "only" the director, insisted that it stay. He conceded that it was ugly, but, he explained, he wanted to show the torment an older woman would go through to keep a young lover. One of Wilder's cronies, William Schorr, who was there the morning of the creative clash, agreed with Billy. Incensed not only by the sequence itself but also by Wilder's impertinence, Brackett cursed both men and stomped out of the screening room. According to Schorr, Wilder confided that "this was the last film he would ever make with Charlie Brackett."

★ ★ ★

Soon after the sequence where Joe reencounters Betty at Paramount, he begins collaborating with her on a spec script, secretly and after hours. A new segment of the film begins here, which shows Joe cautiously taking steps to regain his professional and personal self-esteem. The scenes of Betty's down-to-earth pragmatism provide a sharp contrast with Norma's neo-Romantic view of the world, in which the creation of art depends on the supreme will-to-power of the individual artist.

Late one evening, Joe and Betty stroll along Paramount's back-lot streets, accompanied by Waxman's music, which is light and jazzy, conveying a sense of youthfulness and camaraderie, taking us into a world of magic and benevolent illusion. The scene furthers *Sunset Boulevard*'s overarching goal of blurring the line between real life and reel life. We see them walking on an empty "western" street, where two painters, high on a scaffolding, paint clouds on the exterior wall of a soundstage. They turn a corner onto a street lined with fake brownstones; it was Paramount's McFadden Street, part of a complex of back-lot sets that also included Boston Street and New York Street. This standing urban exterior without an actual interior was used in *The Heiress* (1949), William Wyler's adaptation of a hit Broadway play that was in turn based on Henry James's 1880 novel *Washington Square*, set in mid-nineteenth-century New York. The melodramatic plot concerns a handsome young man (Montgomery Clift) who woos a plain and not-so-young unmarried woman (Olivia de Havilland) for pecuniary gain. Its narrative dovetails nicely with *Sunset Boulevard*, a fact Clift gave as an additional reason for backing out of his contract to play Joe Gillis—he asserted that the roles were too similar.

The stroll along the New York street was simultaneously shot "on location" and "in studio," because the street is at once an actual place on the back lot, demarcated on studio maps, and a fictitious one, existing solely for purposes of artifice. Norma Desmond grows increasingly incapable of distinguishing between truth and illusion, but in this instance so do we, the film intentionally confounding our ability to sort out the real from the fake.

Betty is enraptured with the spot where their nocturnal prowl has led them. She extolls it: "All cardboard, all hollow, all phony. All done with mirrors. I like it better than any street in the world." Born two blocks from the studio to a film industry family, she claims to have played here as a kid: Her father, she tells Joe, was a studio electrician, her mother worked in the wardrobe department, and her grandmother had been a stuntwoman for the silent era damsel-in-distress Pearl White. Betty's family history was loosely based on that of Wilder's fiancée, Audrey Young, a former jazz singer, who similarly came from show-business roots: Her father, a studio carpenter, helped build film sets and erect false edifices.

Betty recalls that she tried and failed to become an actress. She shrugs off her loss of a potential career as a film star. When Gillis says, "Come clean, Betty. At night you weep for those lost close-ups, those gala openings," she replies, "Not once. What's wrong with being on the other side of the camera?" Here once again we see Betty in direct contrast with Norma. A pragmatist, Betty has settled for less that she'd dreamed of. And for this, she is a secondary character, while Norma, readying herself for a close-up that will never come, is the throbbing heart of this cautionary tale about dwelling in a world of illusions.

To be sure, Betty's role is more than simply that of a bright young thing, for she, too, has complex motivations. Nancy Olson Livingston said she "realized that the story of the characters in *Sunset Boulevard* and the tragedy for them all was that they were opportunists—even Betty Schaefer, who also wanted to be a writer and used Joe Gillis to help her, but then found herself in love with a broken and desperate man who had sold his soul for his survival."

After filming the scene, Holden asked Olson to drop by his dressing room before leaving the studio. He explained he wanted to go over the next day's shoot. She arrived to find him waiting for her in a small living room with a selection of drinks, including vodka, scotch, and an open bottle of very cold white wine. "Wholesome Olson" quickly discerned what he had in mind, and it had nothing to do with the next day's shoot. Shocked but trying not to show it, she quickly excused herself and left. She had learned an unwritten rule of Hollywood: "It was standard procedure for the leading man to make a play for his leading lady, off-screen as well as on."

In the climactic scene set on the balcony of the readers' department, Joe sees Betty silently weeping and asks what's wrong, what happened? She replies simply, "You did," and, after a moment's hesitation, they kiss with palpable desire, an inevitable action that has been delayed since their pretend-romance in the Rainbow Room. The scene was filmed late at night, with a large entourage of spectators gathered to watch, among them Holden's wife, Ardis. Wilder, ever the practical joker, had informed Holden and Olson not to stop kissing until he said cut. But he didn't say cut, and they continued kissing, until a female voice rang out from the crowd, "Cut, God damn it, cut!" It was Mrs. Holden.

★ ★ ★

Sunset Boulevard is remembered as a scathing attack on Hollywood, but that only tells part of the story. Yes, there's plenty of harsh satire in the film, particularly in the first two acts, but the movie is also a love letter to Hollywood, a place Billy fell in love with at first sight. A friend of his recalled: "Despite the snubs, the poverty, and the grubby accommodations, [Billy] cherished the place. It is a love affair that exists to this day [1970], and he is the first to defend it from its many detractors, who regard it as a cultural wasteland, or temporary watering hole for amoral opportunists, intellectual midgets, and artistic prostitutes."

Similarly, even though she acknowledged that Hollywood was rife with gossip, envy, and invidious comparison, Gloria Swanson couldn't have been happier than to find herself back in the movies: "As the weeks went by, I hated to have the picture end. None had ever challenged or engrossed me more." As an actress supposedly long past her prime, she was now at the peak of her powers, and she knew it. She might have been playing a character whose mind and emotions were addled, but she herself was radiantly in control.

When Norma shoots Joe for walking out on her, and he tumbles dead into her lighted swimming pool, we finally circle back to the opening moments of the film, with the cops fishing Joe's body out of the pool he had always wanted. A throng of policemen, reporters, and photographers has filled the vestibule of Norma's mansion. The hubbub calls to mind a passage near the end of *The Great Gatsby* (1925), a book Brackett and Wilder certainly knew, as they did its author, especially during his stint in Hollywood in the late 1930s. Brackett, who with his family had summered on the Riviera with the Fitzgeralds in the 1920s, occasionally had tea with the novelist-screenwriter now that both of them worked in Hollywood. Wilder, who made Fitzgerald's acquaintance in 1939 when they were working on separate screenplays for MGM, said of him, "It seemed to me as though he could never get beyond page 3 of a script." Wilder likened the novelist to "a great sculptor who is hired to do a plumbing job." Gloria Swanson herself had known Fitzgerald and his wife, Zelda, in the early 1920s at the zenith of his career. In the spring of 1923, she invited Scott and Zelda for dinner and dancing at the Ritz-Carlton, and that summer she attended pool parties with them on Long Island.

Recalling the day Gatsby was gunned down in his swimming pool by a jealous husband who mistakenly believed Gatsby had seduced his wife, the book's narrator, Nick Carraway, writes: "After two years I remember the rest of that day, and that night and the next day, only as the endless drill of police and photographers and newspaper men in and out of Gatsby's front door."

Perhaps the crime-scene chaos in *Gatsby* inspired the equivalent in *Sunset Boulevard*. A lieutenant from the homicide division pushes his way to a telephone and attempts to call the coroner's office, only to find the line already in use. "Who's on this phone?" he snarls into the receiver. Cut to Norma's bedroom, where, amid police officers and homicide detectives, she sits at her dressing table, gazing into the mirror while applying her makeup. Nearby, an attractive, stylishly dressed, middle-aged woman, seated on the edge of the bed, barks into the phone: "Times City Desk? Hedda Hopper speaking. I'm talking from the bedroom of Norma Desmond. Don't bother with a rewrite man, take this direct. Ready?" With that, Hopper launches into a perfectly pitched tabloid account of the scene before her: "As day breaks over the murder house, Norma Desmond, famed star of yesteryear, is in a state of complete mental shock...."

Playing herself and wearing what looks like a flying saucer on her head, exotic hats being her trademark, Hedda Hopper was the most famous gossip columnist of her day. Before becoming a columnist, she had had a solid, if undistinguished acting career on stage and screen. Starting off as a chorus line dancer on Broadway, she began acting in silent pictures in 1915—the same year as Gloria Swanson—but, unlike Swanson, she never became a star. Instead, she played supporting roles in dozens of movies in the 1920s through the 1940s. In 1938, she started a syndicated gossip column for the *Los Angeles Times* titled Hedda Hopper's Hollywood (also known as Inside Hollywood). Her power-brokering proclivities were feared in the film community. Given that she had thirty-five million readers, one crossed Hedda Hopper at one's peril. Resolutely right-wing in her politics, she routinely denounced writers, actors, and directors whom she believed had communist affiliations, or merely sympathies, and she was one of the most high-profile advocates of Hollywood blacklisting.

Hopper's greatest rival, with whom she had a long-standing feud, was Louella Parsons, the movie gossip columnist for the William Randolph Hearst media empire. Through Hearst's syndicate, Parsons enjoyed a readership of more than twenty million. Wilder wanted *both* columnists to appear in the movie's final scene. It's hard to imagine what he was thinking, for surely this sideshow would have distracted from the pathos of the climax. Years later, the director told an interviewer: "I wanted two gossip columnists—Hedda Hopper and Louella Parsons—each on the phone, one upstairs, one down, neither of them giving up the phone and saying 'Get off the line, you bitch! I was here first!'" Brackett and Wilder obtained Hopper easily, but, in Wilder's words, "Louella knew quite well she would lose that duel because Hedda was a former actress, and she would wipe the floor with her."

Hopper does indeed put her acting ability to good use when she forlornly watches Norma descend the grand staircase. Insulted by the invitation to share the screen with Hopper, Parsons gave Brackett—not, it is worth noting, his more powerful partner, Wilder—a piece of her mind. Ever the courtly euphemist, Brackett described Parsons's words to him as "scurrility" and "washerwoman abuse." Marveling in his diary at the self-control he showed in facing Parsons's "storm of abuse," he chalks this up to having reached an age (fifty-seven) where he had come to find such outbursts amusing.

★ ★ ★

Principal photography for *Sunset Boulevard* began on April 18, 1949, and ended two months later, June 18. Most of the reshooting took place in July, with yet another round occurring in October. By early January, everything was in the can except for one scene, the most important in the film: Norma's final descent of the staircase. Brackett and Wilder agreed that the previous takes of this scene, shot in June, were not working. They lacked an indefinable something that would close the picture in a powerful and provocative way. The mood was off, the tone not right. They summoned Swanson, who had returned to New York months earlier, for one last day of shooting.

Back in her Norma Desmond makeup and the loose-fitting shift that Head had designed for this climactic scene, Swanson practiced going down the faux staircase that had not yet been struck from Stage 5. She found it difficult to negotiate the curving steps while wearing high heels, especially because, with her arms gesticulating, she could not use the banister for support. Wilder suggested she remove her shoes and come down barefoot—a small change that suited the way Norma Desmond might have viewed herself at that final stage of the story: as a barefoot dancing maiden.

As if they were shooting a silent film, Wilder called for music to be played during the filming of the descent in order to help Swanson and the array of extras maintain the mood he wanted. The music chosen, appropriately, was the famous "Dance of the Seven Veils" from Richard Strauss's 1905 modernist opera *Salomé*. In postproduction, Franz Waxman adapted this concert favorite by the late romantic composer, who, coincidentally, died while Waxman was composing the movie's score. For copyright reasons, he kept the sustained trills in the flutes and violins—these are referred to in music history as *Salomé* trills—but dispensed with Strauss's recognizable melody. Instead, he takes the Norma theme he has used as a leitmotif throughout but transforms the restrained melody into a mad, sweeping, syncopated tango or habanera, a danse macabre for full orchestra that is at once stirring and bizarre. It stops abruptly when Norma reaches the bottom of the staircase.

The reshoot that day required ten takes. Sikov described them in detail: "Take two, for instance, features a wild, demented look on her face as she descended, after which she raised her arms at the foot of the steps. For take four, she was asked to effect a relaxed, pleasant look and to raise her arms at the end." He noted that the first six takes were in medium shot, after which Wilder pulled the camera back for a long shot of the descent. Again, Swanson alternated facial expressions—pleasant, wild, pleasant. For the tenth and final take, which is the one they used, Wilder directed her to let out all the stops. She more than complied. Madness flashes in her eyes, while her raised arms snake through space, her hands sensually caressing invisible silken veils.

At the bottom of the stairs, Swanson says her lines: "I can't go on with the scene. I'm too happy.... You see, this is my life. It always will be. There's nothing else—just us and the cameras and those wonderful people out there in the dark." Her eyes now brimming, she gathers her inner forces and makes a statement of resolve that is stunning in its combination of compliance and dementia: "All right, Mr. DeMille. I'm ready for my close-up." With that, Norma advances to the camera until her face—and her mind—dissolves in a blur.

Wilder waited a few beats before calling, "Cut." Swanson wrote about that moment: "When Mr. Wilder called 'Print it!' I burst into tears." At the same time, the cast and crew burst into applause. They had taken part in what they sensed would long be regarded as one of the greatest final scenes in the history of Hollywood.

Film scholars have often pointed out that Alfred Hitchcock implicates his viewers in the illicit or immoral behavior of his protagonists in movies such as *Rear Window*, *Vertigo*, and *Psycho*: He makes us desire what they desire, even though we know it's morally wrong. *Sunset Boulevard* similarly implicates its audience, especially during this closing moment. When Norma, peering straight into the camera, hails "those wonderful people out there in the dark," she's talking about *us*. We are those wonderful people, literally in the dark, who enable the Hollywood dream machine to do what it does, chewing up the lives of the Norma Desmonds, the Joe Gillises, the Max von Mayerlings, and even the

Betty Schaefers, spewing them out when the head office deems them no longer commercially viable.

Norma shatters the fourth wall at the end of the movie and enters (some might say invades) our space, coming too close for comfort. If she is delusional, living in a dream state, so are we, the viewers in the dark, for that's exactly why we go to the movies: to depart from our day-to-day reality and unite with the idealized characters on the screen. Movies, especially the best of them, take us out of ourselves, if only for the duration of the film. We reemerge from the darkness restored to our stable selves, but with a point of view broadened by the experience. Norma does not similarly return to sanity. Nor does she gain self-knowledge. *Sunset Boulevard* ends without a ray of hope or salvation: The protagonist is dead, and his killer has lost her mind. In movies from Hollywood in the succeeding decade, only Hitchcock's two sulfurous masterpieces, *Vertigo* and *Psycho*, would dare an ending as bleak as this, with an antagonist-protagonist who similarly lacks any hope of redemption.

While Hollywood of that era did not generally countenance unhappy endings, another medium did: nineteenth-century grand opera, where unhappy endings were almost de rigueur. When a decade after the film's release, Stephen Sondheim had the idea of turning *Sunset Boulevard* into a Broadway musical, Wilder advised against it, saying it could only truly be written as an opera, because it's about a deposed queen. Not unlike the title character of Vincenzo Bellini's masterpiece *Norma*, composed at the height of the Romantic era in 1831, *Sunset Boulevard*'s Norma, 120 years later, pays mightily for her transgressions. Bellini's Norma, a high priestess in ancient Gaul who is thrown over by her lover for a younger woman, is condemned to death by immolation for violating her vow of chastity. Wilder's Norma, a high priestess of silent cinema who is similarly spurned for a younger woman, sentences *herself* to immolation, consumed as she is by the flames of narcissism, jealousy, and madness.

CHAPTER FIFTEEN

REACTIONS TO *SUNSET*

They laughed hard in Evanston. But it wasn't the laughter that Brackett and Wilder wanted. It was the kind of laughter that portended catastrophe.

Hollywood studios typically previewed their A-list films at movie theaters in or around Los Angeles, but Paramount's executives chose not to preview *Sunset Boulevard* in one of their regular venues. It was a movie about Hollywood, and they needed to know how it would play to audiences that were not intimately, or at least geographically, connected to Tinseltown. They wanted to preview it instead in the American heartlands, but they grasped that an appreciation of the film demanded at least some level of sophistication that they presumed those audiences lacked. So rather than Peoria, they chose the leafy college town of Evanston, Illinois, a northern suburb of Chicago and home to Northwestern University.

The print the Evanston audience saw on a cold night in January 1950 began with the county morgue scene that Wilder had insisted on shooting, overruling Brackett's vehement objection. Brackett was right, judging from the gales of inadvertent laughter it elicited from the audience. Wilder, seated in a back row of the cinema, knew something was wrong. The scene was not intended as broad comedy. Worse, the audience greeted subsequent scenes with the same uproarious laughter. Midway through the screening, Wilder left the auditorium: "I went down some steps, leading to the toilets, and I looked up and there was a lady with a spring hat on, in her sixties, and she turned to me, and she said, 'Have you ever seen such shit in all your life?'" To this, the dejected director replied, "Frankly, no."

Preview audiences didn't know what to make of *Sunset Boulevard*; it morphed too quickly from crime thriller to social satire to haunted house spooker to Hollywood exposé to tragic melodrama—and back again. In this regard, *Sunset Boulevard* anticipated the modernist, genre-blurring, convention-snubbing masterpieces of the French New Wave at the start of the 1960s (*Breathless, Jules and Jim*) and the New Hollywood in the latter stages of that turbulent decade (*Bonnie and Clyde, The Graduate*). In its self-reflexive and self-critical examination of both the business and the art of filmmaking, *Sunset Boulevard* also led the way for the meta-cinema of the European film artists Ingmar Bergman (*Persona*), Federico Fellini (8½), Jean-Luc Godard (*Contempt*), and François Truffaut (*Day for Night*). It anticipated by fifteen to twenty years the edgy black comedy of movies such as Stanley Kubrick's *Dr. Strangelove, or How I Learned to Stop Worrying and Love the Bomb* (1964), Robert Altman's *M*A*S*H* (1970), and Hal Ashby's *Harold and Maude* (1971).

A second preview in Great Neck, New York, generated the same responses. The morgue scene had to go, forcing Wilder to open with the sequence of Joe being fished out of the water by the Homicide Squad. He and Brackett rewrote Joe's voice-over narration, with the dead man speaking directly to the viewer ("you") rather than to a small assemblage of fellow cadavers. The film previewed next in Poughkeepsie, another college town, this time with the new opening, and the audience was hooked from the start. The new cut kicked things off with a level of drama and intrigue that made it seem like a hard-boiled homicide thriller—what we now call film noir.

Wilder had pioneered the use of wall-to-wall, voice-over, first-person narration with *Double Indemnity*, and it quickly became a mainstay of film noir. By 1949, however, the first-person narration technique had become a cliché. Wilder simultaneously parodied and resurrected it by having the story told in the first person by a protagonist who is already dead.

In April 1950, Paramount invited some of the biggest names in the film industry to a VIP screening in their auditorium. Gloria Swanson wrote of the event, "These affairs are known for being morbidly restrained, devoid of the slightest overt reaction, but that night the whole audience stood up and cheered." Swanson recalled that Barbara Stanwyck, rapturous with admiration, knelt before her and kissed the hem of her dress. In her syndicated column the next day, Hedda Hopper reported that at the heart-wrenching close of the picture, many industry bigwigs "sat there and wept. Each saw in it a bit of his own life."

Not everyone was so taken with the film. According to Hollywood lore (which is to say, according to Wilder, who told the story often, with multiple variations), Louis B. Mayer, the head of rival studio MGM, found the film appalling. Standing outside the auditorium afterward, he berated Wilder for making such a viciously anti-Hollywood film: "You should be tarred and feathered and run out of town," he said, accusing the émigré filmmaker of disgracing the industry that fed him. Mayer was not one to hold back his outrage; in the 1920s, the neo-Victorian patriarch had punched a startled Erich von Stroheim—his leading director, no less—in the face for daring to proclaim in his presence, "All women are whores."

At an uncharacteristic loss for words, Wilder simply riposted, "Fuck you"—or, in another telling by Wilder, "Go shit in your hat." He couldn't understand why Mayer was so upset. Wilder always maintained that Mayer had no grounds for his reaction: "I don't say anything derogatory about pictures. There's no filth, no dirt, no *National Enquirer* gossip—nothing." That's disingenuous. While the film does indeed blow occasional kisses at the industry (DeMille's decency toward Norma; Betty's love of cinematic illusionism), it flings acid as well.

Since its founding in the early 1910s, Hollywood has made movies about itself, but usually in a lighthearted, rags-to-riches comical mode, in which the protagonist, typically female, begins in obscurity and ends in stardom. Most of these films underperformed at the box office, probably because the rest of America was not as infatuated with Hollywood's idealized view of itself as Hollywood was. Producer David O. Selznick's *A Star Is Born* (1937), which reworked his earlier show-business saga *What Price Hollywood?* (1932), became the first movie to examine the tragic side of movie stardom. It does not, however, cast a critical light on the film industry itself; the fault, the story assures us, lies not in the studios but in the stars.

Quite to the contrary, Wilder's new movie treated movie glamour as an illness, a social sickness, an addiction. It implied that we might look inside any mansion on Sunset Boulevard and find similarly troubled beneficiaries and victims of the fame game. The problems *Sunset Boulevard* depicts are not eccentric or atypical but instead fundamental to the system. No wonder Mayer objected.

But even without its jaundiced view of the film industry, *Sunset Boulevard* would have offended Mayer, who despised the new tendency in Hollywood to make sordid love stories and sleazy thrillers. He complained to an associate on another occasion, "I don't know what it is, the picture business. Everyone wants to see this," at which he clutched his crotch. "Men with dirty faces, women with messed-up hair. Who wants to look at garbage?" Billy Wilder did. He wanted not only to "look at garbage" but also sift through it for what it might reveal about a system that abandoned stars (not to mention writers and directors) when they no longer served an economic function; the narcissism of the stars themselves; and, more generally, a postwar society full of greed, hypocrisy, and delusion. *Sunset Boulevard* begins in the gutter and ends with murder and madness.

Unlike many others in the preview audience that night who vigorously applauded the film, Mayer correctly perceived it to be subversive, undermining everything he stood for. He had worked hard over the past quarter of a century to make MGM the most cherished—and lucrative—studio in Hollywood. No one had a greater hand in creating and maintaining the star system. MGM's publicists boasted the studio had "more stars than in the heavens." *Sunset Boulevard* suggested that many, if not most, Hollywood stars were not so heavenly; that they were incorrigible narcissists who grew increasingly out of touch with reality and had little ability to adapt to life when their stardom waned, as inevitably it would. The film depicted a former mega-star as a homicidal maniac, a once-powerful director as her slavish servant, and antediluvian actor friends as her "waxworks." It also showed the star system to be dependent on self-absorbed producers, exploitative agents, heartless gossip columnists, legions of hack screenwriters, and armies of cosmetologists, plastic surgeons, masseuses, dietitians, and physical trainers.

Mayer believed in making films that warmly and reassuringly celebrated the nuclear family, such as the sixteen films in his studio's beloved Andy Hardy series, in which Andy, a rambunctious teenage boy, learns important life lessons through the guidance of his kindly father, the wise Judge Hardy. *Sunset Boulevard* showed a dysfunctional, nonnuclear family with a mad mother (Norma), a long-suffering, masochistic father (Max), and a surrogate son-lover (Joe). Mayer accurately perceived that Wilder's movie attacked everything that he, Mayer, believed in and wanted to convey to the public through idealized movies about the all-American family.

Ironically, when Mayer ranted against *Sunset Boulevard*'s portrayal of a damaging star system that abandoned those who had the audacity to cross an age threshold and still expect leading roles, he himself was under attack for being too old and out of touch with the times. Mayer, more than anyone, was held accountable by MGM's parent company, Loews, Inc., for the studio's steep decline at the box office. In 1948, MGM was expected to end the fiscal year with $5 million in profits, but it posted losses of $6.5 million instead. A biographer later noted, "The blame was placed squarely on Mayer's shoulders. At age sixty-three, he was no longer staying in pace with the tastes of contemporary filmgoers. M-G-M kept spinning out sugary family pictures while audiences had started to show a preference for the American brand of neorealism, the gritty *film noirs*, and documentary-flavored melodramas." When asked if such films could legitimately be called artistic, he snorted in response (referring to an infamously violent scene in the 1947 film noir *Kiss of Death*), "Art! Kick an old lady down the stairs and then stomp on her face. That's art?"

When Mayer attended *Sunset Boulevard*'s VIP screening in April 1950, he was sixty-five years old—fourteen years older than the newly triumphant Gloria Swanson and fifteen years older than the washed-up actress she portrayed. The chief executive of Loews, Nicholas Schenck Jr., had forced Mayer to share studio leadership with Dore Schary, a producer twenty years Mayer's junior. The mogul who had cofounded the giant studio that bore his name, Metro-Goldwyn-*Mayer*, was being pushed out of his perch as the king of Hollywood. It didn't happen right away, but soon enough. On August 31, 1951, Mayer resentfully submitted to Schenck a letter of resignation. Finding retirement odious, he attempted to reinvent himself as an independent producer, though little came of it. The film industry's most powerful man had become a ghost of his former self. He spent most of his time in his mansion in Coldwater Canyon watching daytime television for as long as he could stomach it and then pacing aimlessly from room to room.

★　★　★

Before shooting closed on *Sunset Boulevard*, Swanson signed a $1,000-a-week contract to serve as Paramount's "Good Will Ambassador" from October 1949 to August 1950, when the film would release. Her job was to present a healthy and wholesome image of the motion picture industry to offset the disparaging view provided by the film in which she costarred (she received second billing for her role; Holden's name appears before hers). The studio launched her on a twenty-six-city tour in which she participated at an array of civic functions, gave newspaper interviews, appeared on local radio and television, eagerly took part in charity fundraisers, and spoke at women's clubs, where she was hailed as much for her clothing, which she had designed, as for her wit, charm, and celebrity stature. She logged more than twenty thousand miles on the tour. The purpose of her junket was to promote her own soon-to-be-released film as well as Paramount's *The Heiress*, which was already in release.

During the summer of 1950, before *Sunset Boulevard* premiered, Swanson was profiled in a flattering two-part *Saturday Evening Post* article that ran over successive issues. This was followed by a starstruck cover story in *Newsweek*. On August 10, 1950, *Sunset Boulevard* premiered in New York's largest cinema, Radio City Music Hall, to sell-out crowds. In its first four weeks, the picture took in $651,700 and was seen by 615,000 viewers. It grossed $1,020,000 in its seven-week run, which was, to date, the sixth-largest take for the Music Hall. As predicted by Paramount executives, it didn't do nearly as well in small towns and rural locations. In the end, the film, which cost $1.75 million to make, sold $2.35 million in tickets, earning a modest profit of $600,000.

During the summer of 1950, Americans had much on their minds besides movies. The Cold War was well under way, and a hot war on the Korean Peninsula had begun in late June when North Korea crossed the 38th parallel into South Korea. This action, it was feared, would lead to head-to-head military conflict between the United States and China, which had become a communist state the previous autumn. Earlier, in late summer of 1949, the Soviet Union had shocked the western world by testing an atomic bomb, ending the American monopoly on nuclear weapons. In response Harry S. Truman authorized the development of the hydrogen bomb. Meanwhile, a high-ranking State Department official, Alger Hiss, was found guilty of passing state secrets to the Soviets, which stoked the anti-communist campaigns of Senator Joseph McCarthy and FBI director J. Edgar Hoover. The latter announced that America was infiltrated by fifty-five thousand Communist Party members and five hundred thousand communist sympathizers. The North Atlantic Treaty Organization (NATO) was born as a bulwark against Soviet aggression into Western Europe.

Norma Desmond's reclusive (or, if you will, past-oriented and isolationist) paranoia may have struck some viewers as particularly suited to those troubled times. Mostly, though, reviewers fixated on the inside-Hollywood nature of the film and had little to say about it in terms of the broader paranoia sweeping the nation.

Time gushed, "It is a story of Hollywood at its worst told by Hollywood at its best." Writing in *Sight and Sound*, James Agee observed, "There are plenty of good reasons why *Sunset Boulevard* (a beautiful title) is, I think, [Brackett and Wilder's] best movie yet. It is Hollywood craftsmanship at its smartest and just about its best, and it is hard to find better craftsmanship than that, in any art or country." Turning his attention to Swanson, Agee added, "Miss Swanson, required to play a hundred percent grotesque, plays it not just to the hilt but right up to the armpits, by which I mean magnificently." The *New York Times* was full of admiration for the film, calling it "a clever compound of truth and legend," and describing it as "richly redolent of the past, yet so contemporaneous." The reviewer, Thomas M. Pryor, continued, "It is a rare blend of pungent writing, expert acting, masterly direction and unobtrusively artistic photography which quickly casts a spell over the audience and holds it enthralled for a shattering climax." At the same time, though,

Pryor faulted the writers for giving away too much of the mystery at the beginning, thus allegedly ruining the audience's sense of suspense.

The *Los Angeles Times* columnist Neill Beek noted that the film "is heavy with laughable incongruities and scenes that would be side-splitting if they were not so real, so human and hence so sad." Darr Smith, a reporter for the *Los Angeles Daily News*, wrote, "It took a lot of guts for Swanson to come back to the screen to portray a woman who could be—but is not, by any means—Swanson." As for Stroheim, Smith observed, "He is the one who brings things down to shocking reality. It might be said that he is the Greek chorus of the piece." Calling *Sunset Boulevard* one of the most intelligent—and exciting—movies ever to come out of Hollywood, Dilys Powell, the film critic for London's *Sunday Times*, wrote that, "by setting side by side the present and the past, the cynical young writer with his wisecracking friends and the middle-aged passionate woman with her theatrical poses, the film conveys a criticism of both worlds: of today's flimsy vulgarity and the ostentation of yesterday."

Not all reviews were so enthusiastic, but those were the exception. Echoing the complaint by the *New York Times* reviewer, Lowell E. Redelings of the *Hollywood Citizen-News* faulted the film's structure: "The narration is overdone. It gets a bit monotonous about midway. And the flashback technique used to tell the story is most unfortunate. You know from the start what happens to the screen writer and who did the deed...and consequently much of the film's suspense is lost." Redelings may have overestimated the ability of first-time viewers to connect the corpse seen at the beginning of the film with the screenwriter whose story becomes its narrative focus; for many if not most viewers, the return to the pool at the end comes with a shock of sudden recognition, thanks to diversionary tactics employed by Wilder to make audiences forget about it until its callback in act 5. Redelings apparently failed to see that the suspense in *Sunset Boulevard* comes not from discovering *who* killed Joe Gillis but discovering *why*. The power of the movie resides in its characters, not its plot.

In a review tinged with the dismissive sexism of the era, Terry Ramsaye, a pioneering film historian, disdained *Sunset Boulevard* as "an elaborately presented simple tale of feminine vanity developing into mania against a decidedly mildly revealing Hollywood background, the whole wrapped up and scented in genuine soap opera mood." Today some viewers of the film inadvertently echo these reductive sentiments when they call Billy Wilder a misogynist for depicting Norma as a monster, vampire, or human gargoyle driven by feminine vanity, as if that's all there is to her. In fact, the film goes well beyond the neurosis of a single individual to examine the *systemic* production of vanity, feminine or otherwise, in a youth-and-beauty-obsessed consumer culture. Wilder does not belittle Norma for being an unsatisfied woman but instead shows her tragically trying and failing to resist the unwritten law of modern society that makes women beyond childbearing age invisible, irrelevant, mockable, and devoid of economic value, apart from their spending power.

Swanson won the best actress award at the Golden Globes ceremony held in February 1951. This was an accolade she was expected to receive again during the annual Academy Awards ceremony a month later. She was the early favorite, until another contender got in her way.

★ ★ ★

Not everyone thought highly of the Oscars. Ever since the golden statuettes were first presented by Louis B. Mayer and his fellow film moguls in 1929 for movies released in 1927 and 1928, the Academy Awards ceremony had its critics. In the early 1940s, for example, Raymond Chandler submitted a commentary to a Los Angeles paper that the editors dared not publish; it later appeared in *The Atlantic*. Wrote the dyspeptic Chandler in a sentence of Jamesian length:

If you can go past those awful idiot faces on the bleachers outside the theater without a sense of the collapse of human intelligence; and if you can go out into the night and see half the police force of Los Angeles gathered to protect the golden ones from the mob in the free seats, but not from the awful moaning sound they give out, like destiny whistling through a hollow shell; if you can do these things and still feel the next morning that the picture business is worth the attention of one single, intelligent, artistic mind, then in the picture business you certainly belong, because this sort of vulgarity, the very vulgarity from which the Oscars are made, is the inevitable price Hollywood extracts from each of its serfs.

Despite such withering disdain, the Oscars were a boon to the film industry. The organization that bestowed them, the Academy of Motion Picture Arts and Sciences, was established to claim legitimacy for what many observers regarded as the bastard child of theater and the fine arts. If fine artists could have their national or royal academies, why not filmmakers? The Academy was created as a way of lending prestige to a scorned industry. Moreover, it was conceived by Louis B. Mayer and his cronies as an encompassing company union that would obviate the need for individual guilds and unions—a ruse that did little to persuade actors, writers, and others to allow the Academy to do their collective bargaining for them.

Another benefit the studios gained from creating an annual awards ceremony was that it fueled box-office attendance. The Oscars, as the awards came to be known (reputedly because Bette Davis joked that the golden statuette reminded her of her uncle Oscar), served two purposes: They made filmgoers eager to know which movies they should be sure not to miss, and they sparked even more consumer interest by setting up a suspenseful competition among movie folk within their various guilds. Who doesn't love a horse race?

A third benefit Mayer and his confreres derived from this handing out of awards was the gratitude of their employees. In retirement, the former mogul boasted, "I found that the best way to handle [moviemakers] was to hang medals all over them." He continued, "If I got them cups and awards they'd kill themselves to produce what I wanted. That's why the Academy Award was created."

At the 1951 ceremonies, Mayer received a golden statuette for his "distinguished service" to the motion picture industry. They might as well have given him the Oscar for his distinguished service "in the past." More than an act of appreciation, the award was the signal that Mayer was on his way out. As Wilder tartly remarked decades later in reference to himself, once you start receiving Lifetime Achievement Awards, you know your career is over. Every one of them, he bitterly informed a friend, was "simply another marker to the grave."

★ ★ ★

Sunset Boulevard came into the 1951 Academy Awards ceremony with eleven nominations, including one for Erich von Stroheim as best supporting actor. True to form, Stroheim had threatened to sue Paramount for not promoting him for the best actor award instead. The movie's main competition that year, including for best actress, best director, and best picture, was *All About Eve*, a deliciously witty backstage comedy about backbiting in the theatrical realm. Written and directed by Joseph Mankiewicz, it surpassed *Sunset Boulevard*'s eleven nominations with a record fourteen of its own.

All About Eve concerns an aging Broadway diva (Bette Davis) who finds she must choose between her professional career and her love for a younger man, a much-in-demand stage and screen director she wishes to marry. This sounds bleak, but with its exceptionally clever dialogue, the movie speeds along from one zinger to the next. (Film critic Manny Farber, as contrarian as ever, derided it as "a story of the bright lights, dim wits, and dark schemes of Broadway.") Davis was forty-one when she starred in *Eve* and at a low point in her career, having appeared in a succession of lackluster films over the previous five years. She and Swanson both gave superb performances as aging actresses facing the indifferent hand of time when they were in fact aging actress facing a socially imposed expiration date. And the award for best actress went to…Judy Holliday.

Holliday, a newcomer to Hollywood, was twenty-nine when she reprised for movie audiences her leading role in Garson Kanin's hit Broadway comedy *Born Yesterday*. She played Billie Dawn, the "dumb blonde" girlfriend of an uneducated and uncouth gangster (Broderick Crawford) who wants her to display more ladylike charm when she accompanies him to Washington, DC, where he intends to conduct illegal business with corrupt congressmen. To this end, he hires an idealistic young journalist (William Holden) to give Billie a smattering of education so she will become a classy dame. The idealist chooses to teach Billie to think by instructing her in the fundamental principles of democracy. Blossoming under his tutelage, Billie breaks free of her gangster boyfriend's domination.

Holliday's charming performance lacked the raw nerve laid bare by Swanson's and Davis's respective performances. Perhaps the members of the Academy of Motion Picture Arts and Sciences were not comfortable giving their top acting award, in either Swanson's case or Davis's, to a middle-aged woman whose very presence on screen called into question the moral legitimacy of the entertainment industry. Holliday's character, too, challenged traditional gender roles, but in a reassuring way, not in the unsettling manner of the aging-out or aged-out characters played Davis and Swanson. Besides, *Born Yesterday* exuded pride in America, celebrating the triumph of democratic ideals (Billie sees the light and in pursuit of truth and liberty dumps her autocratic boyfriend), whereas neither the vehicle for Swanson nor that for Davis ended triumphantly.

Additional reasons may have caused both Swanson and Davis to lose out to Holliday. For one, their respective performances of a lifetime split votes, opening a lane for a third nominee. Moreover, Anne Baxter, who played the title, though secondary, role of Eve, should have been nominated in the supporting actress category, but she, like Stroheim, obstreperously objected to being nominated for a lesser award; she prevailed in her quest for a more prestigious nomination, while he did not. As a result, Baxter went head-to-head with her costar Davis. In effect, all three performances canceled out one another. Swanson herself believed she lost the Oscar that year because viewers mistakenly assumed she was only playing herself and was therefore not really acting. A similar curse had robbed John Barrymore and Greta Garbo of the Oscars they deserved: Audiences were convinced, wrote Swanson, that "Barrymore *is* Hamlet. Garbo *is* Camille. Swanson *is* Norma Desmond."

The fifth actress to be nominated that year, Eleanor Parker, gave a riveting performance in *Caged* as a tormented young inmate in a woman's prison, where she was incarcerated for driving the getaway car for her husband, a small-time crook. Over the course of the film, she goes from being a naive accomplice to a childbearing convict to a hardened criminal. Part woman's picture and part prison film, *Caged* was too raw and realistic to win any of the major awards that year.

For best picture, the race was clearly down to Paramount's *Sunset Boulevard* and Twentieth Century Fox's *All About Eve*. The other three nominees that year lacked the brilliance and gravity of the other two. Made concurrently with the rise to power of Senator Joseph McCarthy (whom Broderick Crawford uncannily resembled), Columbia's *Born Yesterday* may have offered audiences both a comic primer in the nature of democracy and a jab at political thuggery, but it was also simplistic and didactic. MGM's family comedy *Father of the Bride* starred Spencer Tracy as a lovable curmudgeon who balks at the imminent marriage of his only daughter, played by the winsome eighteen-year-old Elizabeth Taylor. The fifth film under consideration was MGM's lavishly colored and shot-on-location adventure film *King Solomon's Mines*, based on H. Rider Haggard's 1885 colonialist adventure novel about a demure Victorian woman (Deborah Kerr) who engages the services of a "Great White Hunter" (Stewart Granger) to find her husband, who has gone missing while in search of treasure in the unexplored African interior.

As always when it comes to considering why a certain movie beat out its competitors for best picture, we can only speculate. Despite its caustic dialogue, *All About Eve* must have reassured audiences by offering a considerably milder, less astringent view of female aging in the entertainment business than *Sunset Boulevard* did. At the end of the film, Margo Channing, the forty-year-old actress played by Davis, stops fighting the advance of age and concedes that marrying her younger lover is ample reward for retiring from the stage. At the same time, the film roundly attacks Margo's obsequious acolyte, Eve Harrington (Baxter), a duplicitous scoundrel who worms her way into Margo's world in order to usurp her as Broadway's grande dame. This dual, hand-in-glove message about the proper role of women (female domesticity good, female ambition bad) would have been infinitely more tolerable for 1950s audiences than a tawdry tale of a relentlessly ambitious and sexually voracious middle-aged woman who refuses to go gently into the night.

By the end of the evening, *Sunset Boulevard* had garnered Oscars for art design (Hans Dreier and John Meehan), original musical score (Franz Waxman), and original screenplay (Brackett, Wilder, and Marshman Jr.). Whatever her true feelings were about her loss to Judy Holliday, Swanson congratulated the winner with a grace and warmth that would have been impossible for Norma Desmond to muster.

★　★　★

The blacklisted screenwriter Maurice Rapf, looking back on American films of the 1950s, wrote, "Social problems [that had preoccupied filmmakers in the 1930s and 1940s] simply disappeared from the screen.

Unwed mothers, tramps, prisoners who want to go straight, the plight of tenant farmers, injustices of all kinds were ignored. The films of the fifties projected the national image—ours was a splendid society and we were urged to cooperate with it, not to criticize." The problem with this, added Rapf, was that it was "hard to make films without any problems at all—where's the conflict that makes a story?" He noted that Hollywood loved musicals, which generally eschewed social problems: "Three of the ten Academy Award-winners of the fifties were musicals or closely related thereto—*An American in Paris*, *Around the World in Eighty Days*, and *Gigi*. Two [other winners] were closely related to show business—*All About Eve* and *The Greatest Show on Earth*."

Rapf wasn't being entirely fair, for he did not mention best picture winners of the 1950s such as *From Here to Eternity* (1953), *On the Waterfront* (1954), *Marty* (1955), and *The Bridge on the River Kwai* (1957), or the best-picture-nominated anti-McCarthy allegory *High Noon* (1952), which lost out to DeMille's spectacular big-top movie *The Greatest Show on Earth*. These were popular films that seriously addressed contemporary social, moral, or psychological problems. Nonetheless, Rapf's observation rings true: In general, Hollywood in the 1950s steered clear of pressing social issues, especially controversial ones.

In 1953, *Variety* summed up the new Hollywood protocol of message avoidance in characteristically concise terms: "H'wood Nix on Message Pix." Made slightly before this anti-message, anti-critical way of thinking took control of Hollywood, *Sunset Boulevard* put audiences through a dark and essentially social-critical experience that called into question the harsh nature of the dream factory and the greed it encouraged in its luminaries at the top, mediocrities in the middle, and losers at the bottom. Betty Schaefer, who believed motion pictures should say "a little something," might have found herself increasingly frustrated as the 1950s went along.

CHAPTER SIXTEEN

WHAT BECAME OF . . . ?

What became of the makers of *Sunset Boulevard* after the cameras stopped rolling, the sets were struck, the movie was previewed and re-previewed, the tickets were sold, and the awards ceremonies were forgotten? Taking part in the creation of a cinematic masterpiece was a career-defining, even life-changing, experience for many of the principal participants. This was not the case, however, with the unheralded members of the cast and crew, among them a bit player with the Dickensian name Archie Twitchell.

Twitchell is remembered today for two things, neither of which made his name widely known. One of these, of course, is his very brief appearance in *Sunset Boulevard* as the men's shop salesman, a scene marked by his unctuous voice and reptilian grin as the camera slowly and almost rudely moves in on him and Joe Gillis. Even though he got to deliver one of the most notorious lines in the film ("As long as the lady is paying for it, why not take the vicuña?"), he was not listed in the credits.

Twitchell's other brush with history occurred in the sky. Having played minor roles in minor films for nearly a decade, especially low-budget westerns, using the screen name "Michael Brandon" or "Michael Branden," Twitchell retired from movies in 1955 to take up his first love, flying. He had piloted military supply planes during the war. Now, on a crystal-clear January morning in 1957, he served as the copilot on a Douglas DC-7B commercial transport plane that was taking a test run over the San Fernando Valley. An air force fighter jet, its flight path not registered with civilian air control, streaked out of nowhere and clipped a wing of Twitchell's plane. While his pilot struggled to control his plummeting aircraft, Twitchell cried into his radio transmitter, "Uncontrollable, uncontrollable…midair collision…We are going in…We've had it, boys. I told you we should have had chutes." His last words: "Say goodbye to everybody."

The pilot of the fighter jet ejected to safety, but not so Twitchell and his three fellow members of the DC-7B crew, all of whom perished when the transport crashed through the roof of a church auditorium in the small San Fernando Valley town of Pacoima. Debris from the impact hurtled like shrapnel onto the playground of the junior high school next door to the church. The playground was thronged with boys and girls enjoying recess. Many were injured and three were killed. The Pacoima crash is famous in aeronautic history, but Twitchell is not—he remained a bit player to the end of his life.

* * *

Buster Keaton spoke fewer words in *Sunset Boulevard* than Archie Twitchell—only two ("Pass," said once and then repeated) versus Twitchell's fourteen—but at least Keaton received screen credit. Though largely forgotten by 1949, having been out of the limelight for decades, his "stone face" visage was nonetheless unforgettable to those old enough to have seen his remarkable comedies during the 1920s. In September 1949, four months after Keaton and his fellow "waxworks" appeared before Billy Wilder's camera, *Life* published a widely read and much-commented-on article by James Agee. Titled "Comedy's Greatest Era," the article set out to praise American silent comedy, particularly the four silent era comedians Agee regarded as transcendent geniuses: Charlie Chaplin, Harold Lloyd, Harry Landon, and Keaton. About Keaton, he wrote that his "face ranked almost with Lincoln's as an early American archetype; it was haunting, handsome, almost beautiful, yet it was irreducibly funny; he improved matters by topping it off with a deadly horizontal hat, as flat and thin as a phonograph record." Agee continued, "No other comedian could do as much with the dead pan. . . . Everything that he was and did bore out this rigid face and played laughs against it. When he moved his eyes, it was like seeing them move in a statue."

Keaton's cameo appearance in *Sunset Boulevard* helped revive interest in the all-but-forgotten silent comedian. Thanks to the visibility that came from the bridge scene in Wilder's picture and the encomiums of Agee's *Life* profile, he was suddenly honored by old-timers and new-timers alike for the brilliant physical plasticity of his body in a decade's worth of movies he had written, starred in, and directed. In 1952, Keaton's friend and former rival Charlie Chaplin cast him in *Limelight* as the friend and former rival of an aging vaudeville comedian played by Chaplin. Even though the film failed at the box office, not only because of its mawkishness but also because Chaplin was reputed to be a communist sympathizer, the Keaton revival of the 1950s was under way. Between 1950 and 1964, the comedian appeared at least seventy times on TV variety shows and even briefly had a program of his own, which he quit when he couldn't keep up with the demands of weekly television. He was also featured in a wide range of droll TV commercials, in which he peddled products as diverse as Colgate toothpaste, Mars candy bars, Pure Oil, Shamrock Oil, Ford Motors, Northwest Orient Airlines, RCA Victor, U.S. Steel, and Alka-Seltzer effervescent pain reliever.

In 1957, Hollywood made a dull biopic about him called *The Buster Keaton Story*, starring the pliable comedian Donald O'Connor. Meanwhile local TV stations began to broadcast Keaton's many classic films from his peak years in the 1920s. In the early 1960s, the Great Stone Face returned to the movies in a series of moneymaking teenage comedies from American International Pictures. These bore intentionally provocative titles such as *Pajama Party*, *Beach Blanket Bingo*, and *How to Stuff a Wild Bikini*. Keaton had little to do in these low-budget movies ("exploitation films," they were called) beyond appearing as a lovable, if eccentric, relic of the past whom youthful California surfers befriend. In 1965, he played the lead in a short avant-garde film by Samuel Beckett titled *Film*—a far cry from *How to Stuff a Wild Bikini*. Keaton died in 1966, soon after appearing in the Hollywood adaptation of Stephen Sondheim's *A Funny Thing Happened on the Way to the Forum*. His character in that farce bore the perfect name for a sad-sack comedian who had made a lifelong career of playing losers: Erronius.

★ ★ ★

Cecil B. DeMille's cameo in *Sunset Boulevard* augmented his reputation as the most important veteran director still turning out hit movies (John Ford, another survivor of the silent era, didn't have the same level of box-office cachet). DeMille's avuncular presence in the film made audiences love him; they were unaware of the discrepancy between the compassionate character he played in his cameo and the irascible tyrant he was in real life. *Samson and Delilah* was not only the top-grossing movie of 1950 but also, at that time, the third-highest-grossing motion picture in Hollywood history, after *Gone with the Wind* (1939) and *The Best Years of Our Lives* (1946).

DeMille's right-wing politics clashed directly with Billy Wilder's left orientation in October 1950, only two months after the premiere of *Sunset Boulevard*. DeMille, who served on the board of the

Directors Guild of America (DGA), proposed that every member of the organization—some six hundred in all—sign a loyalty oath to the United States of America. He explained to the DGA president, Joseph Mankiewicz, "Now is the time for good Americans to stand up and be counted." "Very true," replied Mankiewicz, "but who appointed you to do the counting?" He cautioned DeMille that his plans to provide the studios with the names of DGA guild members who refused to comply was effectively creating a blacklist, which was unlawful and, he added tartly, un-American. Incensed, DeMille called for Mankiewicz to step down.

Fourteen guild members, including Billy Wilder and John Huston, dared to risk DeMille's ire by signing a petition to keep Mankiewicz in place as the titular head of the DGA. Signing a petition was unusual for Wilder, who generally steered clear of politics. Perhaps not surprisingly for a survivor of the Holocaust, he kept his head down and his political views to himself. In 1947, for example, when HUAC summoned ten so-called unfriendly witnesses to Washington to testify about their current or former involvement with the Communist Party, a number of Hollywood luminaries, including Humphrey Bogart, Lauren Bacall, and Gary Cooper, flew to Washington to protest. Wilder chose not to join them, saying he was too busy shooting a film. Referring to the infamous witnesses, he acerbically commented, "Of the Unfriendly Ten, only two have talent—the other eight are just unfriendly." He jokingly referred to the blacklist, ruining the lives of scores of his fellow Hollywood actors, writers, and directors, as the "Blacklist, schmacklist." It was therefore a big step for him to sign a freedom-of-speech petition.

At a heated late-night meeting of the full membership of the guild, DeMille mocked the signers of the petition in support of Mankiewicz by exaggerating the "foreign" pronunciation of their names: "Mr. Villiam Vyler, Mr. Fred Ssinnemann, Mr. Billy Vilder." He was booed by those who took his mockery to be not only xenophobic but also antisemitic. William Wyler stood up and said, "I am sick and tired of being called a

Communist... The next person who calls me a Communist," he added, pointing at DeMille, "no matter how famous he is, how old he is, I am going to kick the shit out of him." The guild membership voted almost unanimously to keep Mankiewicz in place.

DeMille's career was not diminished by the debacle at the directors guild. The movie he made after *Samson and Delilah*, a circus drama titled *The Greatest Show on Earth*, was the biggest moneymaker of 1952 and won that year's Academy Award for best picture. It introduced a new film star named Charlton Heston, who went on to play Moses in DeMille's greatest success, *The Ten Commandments* (1956), which turned out to be the last film of his storied career. Today, adjusted for inflation, it ranks as the eighth-highest-grossing film of all time. DeMille would have been pleased to know it. He died in 1959, proud of his integral role in the commercial, if not artistic, history of Hollywood.

★ ★ ★

Nancy Olson made three more films with William Holden between 1950 and 1951: *Union Station*, a modest crime thriller set in a big-city train station; *Force of Arms*, the story of a love affair between a US infantryman and a Women's Army Corps (WAC) officer during his five-day leave from combat in the Battle of San Pietro; and *Submarine Command*, where Olson played the wife of a traumatized submarine captain (Holden again) during the Korean War.

Despite the promise she showed in *Sunset Boulevard*, she never attained movie-star status. She lacked both the animal magnetism to be a 1950s sex star and the dramatic range to be an emotionally compelling actor. Her career as a leading lady fizzled by the mid-1950s. In 1960, she appeared as Hayley Mills's governess in the nostalgic Disney comedy *Pollyanna* and then as Fred MacMurray's girlfriend in *The Absent-Minded Professor* (1961) and his wife in the sequel, *Son of Flubber* (1963), both films also made for Disney.

In 1950, Olson married the songwriter Alan Jay Lerner, whom she met while he was working on the screenplay for *An American in Paris* (1951). She was his third wife. One wintry night in Connecticut, she was woken by her husband and his composer partner, Frederick "Fritz" Loewe, who asked her to come downstairs to listen to the new song they had just written for their Broadway musical *My Fair Lady* (1956). On hearing the infectious number that they named "The Rain in Spain," Nancy cautioned the duo that the audience would be so taken with it that they'd momentarily lose touch with the story. She was right; it was a song you couldn't get out of your head. With Nancy in mind, Lerner wrote the lyrics to Loewe's haunting ballad "I've Grown Accustomed to Your Face." Ironically, the title proved prophetic, as Lerner tired of Nancy and soon moved onto his fourth wife (followed by a fifth and a sixth).

Olson's second husband, Alan Livingston, was also in the music business, but very much behind the scenes. He was a longtime Capitol Records executive who signed Frank Sinatra, Judy Garland, and other celebrated singers to the label. His greatest coup, however, was being the Capitol executive who had the good sense to sign an obscure rock band from Liverpool, the Beatles.

Nancy Olson Livingston has said that she might have made it as a movie star, but only if she were willing to sacrifice her family for her career, an option she rejected. Norma Desmond, though only a fictional character, had made clear to Olson what she did not want to be, a woman "who allowed herself to be exploited by an industry that casually threw her away when it was done with her." Looking back on her life, she has "often wondered if I was not deeply affected by the truth of this movie. I knew even then that I did not want to be a movie star who would someday be thrown away."

At ninety-four, with the assistance of Hollywood historian Cari Beauchamp and others, Nancy Olson Livingston published a sharp and witty autobiography. The title, *A Front Row Seat*, acknowledged that she was more of a bystander to Hollywood and Broadway history than a maker. Yet she prided herself in having played an integral role in one of the great classics of American cinema. *Sunset Boulevard*, she has said, "haunts my entire life."

★ ★ ★

After completing his part in *Sunset Boulevard*, Stroheim and his long-time companion Denise Vernac returned to their home in a small chateau some twenty-five miles southwest of Paris. Already greatly admired by the French, Stroheim was extolled for his moving performance in the film whose title they translated as *Boulevard du Crépuscule*. French audiences adored his work, both as a director and an actor, whereas the Americans, Stroheim grumbled, were too insular and narrow-minded to grasp his world-historical significance.

In 1952, the Belgian Museum of Fine Arts polled one hundred leading filmmakers on what they considered the ten greatest films of all time. When the results were tabulated, Stroheim's *Greed* ranked number seven. Directors Luchino Visconti, Orson Welles, and Billy Wilder each assigned their second-place choice to *Greed*; *La Grande Illusion* was first for Visconti, *City Lights* for Welles, and *Battleship Potemkin* for Wilder. In response to the Belgian referendum, the British publication *Sight and Sound* put the same question to eighty-five film critics from around the world. They, too, collectively ranked *Greed* as the seventh-greatest film in cinema history. When the *Sight and Sound* poll was repeated ten years later, in 1962, *Greed* had moved up three places to number four.

In January 1954, Britain's National Film Theatre, running a series of Stroheim films, invited him to London for a press conference. Stroheim was suspicious; after reading a selection of newspaper articles publicizing the film series, he said, "The morons! Not a word about the films, not an intelligent word. It's all the old stuff about The Bullet-headed Prussian. I'm not a Prussian, I'm Austrian. It's like calling an Englishman Irish.

And my head isn't bullet-shaped. I've seen bullets." Denise persuaded him to go to London despite his reservations. The press conference was a disaster, because Stroheim responded with hostility to the journalists who posed loaded questions that he found degrading. The day after the conference, one headline read, "And Here Girls, Is the Man Your Mother Loved to Hate." The final insult of the press conference was when the photographers gathered around him insisted that he put on his monocle. When he replied that he did not have one, someone called out, "Fake it with a coin." According to London's *Daily Herald*, he shot back that he did not "fake" things and proceeded to tell the photographers what they could do with their coins.

Not long after the release of *Sunset Boulevard*, Swanson conceived the idea of turning the drama into a stage musical. She wrote a warm letter to Stroheim, asking him to reprise the role of Max but this time sing his lines instead of saying them. He politely replied, "Whether I would like to play my little part?... What a superfluous question!" When it came to carrying a tune, however, he was less confident in his abilities, writing (the emphasis his), "With a *very loud orchestra* I could manage." This was his way of saying he couldn't do it. Half a year later, Erich asked Denise to write Gloria a letter thanking her for "the wonderful article you wrote about him" in Swanson's syndicated column for United Press International. Denise ended the note by saying, "We cherish you Gloria because you are one, even amongst the few who count. Love, Denise." Whatever animosities Stroheim might have harbored toward Swanson for the *Queen Kelly* debacle three decades earlier, or she toward him, had long vanished.

In 1956, Stroheim began to experience severe pain in his back. A diagnosis pointed to prostate cancer. Soon he was unable to walk. He remained in bed, suffering acutely. In March 1957, he was carried down to his drawing room to meet with a delegation that had come to bestow the Legion of Honour. Barely able to speak, he could not voice his gratitude, but—master of silent cinema that he was—he did so instead with a physical gesture, raising his arm in a feeble salute. The moment was recorded in a photograph reproduced in *Life* with the explanatory caption, "A Famous Film Villain Touched by an Award. At his villa near Paris the stricken man lifted his arm and acknowledged a tribute to his career with a pathetic but proud gesture. He was Erich von Stroheim, 71, one of the most famous of all actors and movie directors, who for the past six months had been paralyzed." After the ceremony, wrote *Life*, "the movie villain did something he would almost never have done on screen. He wept."

As a thwarted film director, he grieved that he had not been allowed to continue his directorial career. With death approaching, he bitterly told a friend, "This isn't the worst. The worst is that they stole twenty-five years of my life."

★ ★ ★

Sunset Boulevard set William Holden on the path to becoming one of the top three domestic box-office leaders of the 1950s (James Stewart and Charlton Heston placed slightly ahead of him in the rankings). He played an idealistic, democracy-loving journalist in *Born Yesterday*, a guilt-ridden ship captain in *Submarine Command*, and a wily prisoner of war in Billy Wilder's *Stalag 17*, for which Holden won the Oscar for best actor. Following that success, he played a rich playboy who falls in love with Audrey Hepburn in Wilder's *Sabrina* (Holden and Hepburn had an off-screen romance as well). In *Executive Suite*, he played a corporate product designer whose idealistic visions for a company in turmoil persuade the warring factions of the executive board to come together in electing him CEO. In *Love Is a Many-Splendored Thing*, he played an American journalist in Hong Kong who falls in love with a doctor of Euro-Asian parentage; in *Picnic*, he was a bare-chested drifter who stirs up the desires and yearnings of various repressed women in a small Kansas town.

The capstone to Holden's career in the 1950s was David Lean's epic World War II adventure *Bridge on the River Kwai*, in which he played a cynical American commando who, sent to blow up a Japanese bridge deep in the jungles of Burma, forgoes his cynicism and instead sacrifices his life for the success of the mission. Holden's allure, first put on full display in *Sunset Boulevard*, was that within his handsome face, athletic body, and ironic demeanor, there lurked a sensitive, soulful, self-torturing idealist.

Throughout these years, Holden was afflicted with alcoholism. Every morning before leaving his house for the studio, he would telephone his secretary to tell her it was time to "warm up the ice cubes." His marriage finally fell apart after years of mutual hostility and distrust; he and Ardis developed a better personal relationship after their divorce than before. Nonetheless he retained his chronically low opinion of himself.

By the late 1950s, Holden's film career was in decline, thanks in no small part to a series of poorly chosen roles. Meanwhile, seemingly overnight, he lost his beautiful face; it became leathery and ravaged, a product, no doubt, of his excessive drinking and dissolute living. As Pauline Kael was to describe Holden in the mid-1970s, "His sunken-cheeked, lined, craggy face takes the camera marvelously." David Thomson was blunter, calling Holden's face in his late career an instance of "early embalming" and Holden himself "the Marlboro Man at menopause." Another writer cruelly likened the crisscrossing lines of Holden's face to "a map of the United States." As a young pretty-boy, Holden had yearned for a more rugged face. Like Joe Gillis, he got what he asked for, but the price was a little high.

Holden's decline as a leading man continued into the 1960s. Personal troubles beset him as well, most notably in a drunken-driving incident on the night of July 26, 1966, when, pushing his Ferrari to excessive speeds on the Italian autostrada, he came up too suddenly on a little Fiat. The impact hurled the Fiat into the oncoming lane of traffic, killing the driver. An Italian court found Holden guilty of manslaughter, which carried a mandatory five-year sentence, but his lawyers got him off with an eight-month sentence, which was suspended after their client settled with the victim's widow for $80,000.

In a short piece on *Sunset Boulevard* published in 1968, Kael wrote of the actor, "When, in a mixture of pity and guilt, he makes love to [Norma], he expresses a nausea so acute that we can almost forgive Holden his career during the last decade: this man knows the full self-disgust of prostitution." His plummet as a screen star was briefly arrested in 1969 when the director Sam Peckinpah, who specialized in revisionist westerns, gave him the lead in *The Wild Bunch*, a film of shocking graphic brutality, with a surfeit of violent death in slow motion. Holden played a washed-up desperado leading a gang of similarly washed-up outlaws on the Mexican border in 1915.

He was good at washed-up: He played a washed-up cowboy in *Wild Rovers* (1971), a washed-up television executive in *Network* (1976), for which he received an Academy Award nomination, and a washed-up film producer in Billy Wilder's next-to-last film, *Fedora* (1978), where Holden's character unsuccessfully attempts to lure back to the screen an aging, reclusive, and self-exiled film star who is a cross between Greta Garbo and Norma Desmond. In *Breezy* (1973), Clint Eastwood's third outing as a director, Holden played an emotionally washed-up businessman in Los Angeles who is tired of life until revivified by his love affair with a flower child thirty years his junior. The film was a flop, but in some ways, it came closer to depicting the real Bill Holden than any of his more famous roles.

Africa, which he cherished for its remoteness from the corrupt world he knew too well, became Holden's personal obsession, leading him to establish a game reserve in Kenya. He dedicated himself to wildlife preservation. He also loved the California desert and in 1968 commissioned the midcentury-modern architect Hugh Kaptur to design a glass-box home for him on a hillside in Palm Springs with a panoramic view of the valley. Its minimalist aesthetic, noted the architectural historians Michael Stern and Alan Hess, "shows that the economy and elegance of his acting were part of the man himself." For his sojourns in Los Angeles, Holden stayed in a distinctive thirteen-story modern apartment building that he partially owned. Known then as the Shorecliff Tower Apartments (later renamed the Oceanaire), it was built in 1963 by the modern architectural innovator A. Quincy Jones with the spare lines and graceful disposition of space that appealed to the actor. Poised on the bluffs of Santa Monica, surrounded by palm trees at its base, it afforded its residents magnificent views of the Pacific.

Gloria Swanson was once visiting a friend in Palm Springs, and, on a lark, they went over to Holden's house to pay a call. He was in Africa, but the staff invited Swanson and her friend to have a look around. When Holden returned, the staff informed him that Miss Swanson had left him a message on the toilet seat in his bathroom. It read: "Dear Joe, I'm leaving this note where I know you'll find it. Where is Max? Where is DeMille? Where is Hedda? Where has everybody gone? Love, Norma Desmond."

In mid-November 1981, Holden was found dead in his getaway apartment in Santa Monica. It was where he liked to be alone with his bottles. He had been so inebriated that he keeled over in his bedroom, cracking his head on the edge of a night table. His body was discovered four days later. The coroner detected high levels of beer and vodka in his blood. Unable to crawl to the phone and call for help, Hollywood's Golden Boy died drunk and alone.

In mourning for his longtime friend, Billy Wilder told the *New York Times*: "If somebody had said to me, 'Holden's dead,' I would have assumed that he had been gored by a water buffalo in Kenya, that he had died in a plane crash approaching Hong Kong, that a crazed jealous woman had shot him and he drowned in a swimming pool. But to be killed by a bottle of vodka and a night table—what a lousy fadeout for a great guy."

The actor who'd brought Joe Gillis to life three decades earlier went out even more ignominiously than the character he played. Gillis died for taking a stand against his own inauthenticity, whereas Holden died for one more drink.

★ ★ ★

After Brackett and Wilder ended their acclaimed partnership, Brackett left Paramount and began producing films for Twentieth Century Fox. He was very successful, especially with movies that he also cowrote. One of these was the film noir *Niagara* (1953), which was atypically shot in Technicolor instead of black and white. As the movie's producer, Brackett gave Marilyn Monroe her first leading role, and it made a star of her. She played a newlywed who schemes with her lover to murder her husband, a traumatized World War II veteran—while on her honeymoon, no less! Brackett's *Titanic* (also 1953), a movie he cowrote with Walter Reisch (who some fifteen years earlier had collaborated with Brackett and Wilder on the script for *Ninotchka*), won the Oscar for best original screenplay.

Brackett's greatest hit as a producer was the film adaptation of the Rodgers and Hammerstein blockbuster Broadway musical *The King and I*. The movie ranked as the fourth-highest-grossing film of 1956, though not anywhere near DeMille's *Ten Commandments* in terms of revenue. It was nominated for nine Academy Awards and won five. No film Brackett had made with Wilder was remotely as successful at the box office as *The King and I*.

Brackett led the staid, conservative, banker-like life that made him such a stalwart of the film community, where he served as the president of the Academy of Motion Picture Arts and Sciences from 1949 to 1955. The raciest thing he ever did was marry Lillian "Buff" Fletcher, the younger sister of his late wife, Elizabeth, some five years after her death in 1948. On the day after Christmas in 1953, Brackett and Buff Fletcher exchanged vows in an historic Episcopal church in Tucson, Arizona, with no family in attendance.

In 1958, the Academy honored Brackett with a lifetime achievement award. He continued writing and producing movies. One of these was a popular screen adaptation of Jules Verne's 1864 fantasy novel *Journey to the Center of the Earth* (1959). It starred the number one pop singer of the era—the clean-scrubbed, all-American boy next door, Pat Boone. Brackett cast Boone again in *State Fair* (1962), a remake of an earlier film with music by Rodgers and Hammerstein, but it fared poorly at the box office, perhaps because, among its other failings, it starred a singer who by that point had been eclipsed by Elvis Presley and other bad-boy rock-and-rollers of the pre-Beatles era.

In public, Brackett and Wilder always spoke well of each other, coming to each other's defense. In 1952, for example, a German-émigré journalist, film editor, and TV producer named Herbert G. Luft, who had survived internment in Dachau before fleeing to the United States, published an article in a film journal accusing Wilder of being overly critical of the country he called home—in other words, anti-American. Luft decried Wilder's alleged callousness to human suffering and his snide skepticism: "He treats his characters with an obscene, obnoxious witticism," and his doing so reveals "the luxurious cynicism of a sophisticate who has acclimatized himself to the ivory tower of Beverly Hills."

Brackett led off his refutation in that same edition of the journal by dismissively claiming that Luft's takedown of Wilder was like "reading an essay about Van Gogh by someone who is color blind." The critic's problem, Brackett contended, was that he was too deficient in a sense of humor to appreciate Wilder's, which, according to Brackett, had deep roots in American culture: "Predominant among Billy Wilder's qualities is humor—a fantastically American sense of humor. . . . It was the outstanding trait of the young man with whom I started to work some seventeen years ago. He was sassy and brash and often unwise, but he had a fine, salutary laugh. Also, he was in love with America as I have seen few people in love with it."

In 1962, Wilder returned the favor when Twentieth Century Fox, in a cost-saving effort, canceled Brackett's contract when it still had two years left to go. Billy called a press conference and flayed the studio, saying, "I cannot imagine any self-respecting artist, whether director, writer, actor, producer or musician going to work for 20th Century Fox under its present administration." Wilder's shaming of the studio embarrassed Fox, which backed down and bought out the remaining two years of Brackett's contract.

Brackett suffered a debilitating stroke in 1967, at age seventy-four. His old friend Garson Kanin visited him from time to time. Kanin was the playwright and screenwriter whose Broadway hit *Born Yesterday* had created the role that enabled Judy Holliday to beat out Bette Davis and Gloria Swanson for the best actress Oscar in 1951. Kanin was also friends with Billy Wilder. In his memoir, titled *Hollywood*, Kanin detailed a melancholy visit he paid to the critically ailing Brackett at his Bel Air home on a rainy Sunday afternoon.

During their conversation, Kanin asked Brackett what had caused the split with Wilder. Brackett confided he was at a loss to explain: "I never knew what happened, never understood it, we were doing so well. I always thought we brought out the best in each other, didn't you?...It was such a blow, such an unexpected blow, I thought I'd never recover from it. And in fact, I don't think I ever have."

The conversation ended with the normally stoic Brackett sighing, "I'm sick. I'm so sick." Kanin tried to comfort him. "You'll get better, Charlie. You're a hell of a lot better this Sunday than you were last." Kanin ended his account by tersely informing the reader, "He never did."

Charlie died at home in 1969 with Buff at his side. He was seventy-six. The house on luxurious Bellagio Road, in which he had lived for decades, was around the corner from Sunset Boulevard, the thoroughfare he and Wilder had enshrined in popular culture. Few people today have heard of Charles Brackett, let alone know of his crucial role in making one of Hollywood's darkest, but also brightest, contributions to world cinema.

*   *   *

As classic Hollywood would have it, newspapermen are the most cynical people around. They are skeptical, hard-drinking, and hard-boiled. Wilder's first film post-Brackett, *Ace in the Hole* (aka *The Big Carnival*, 1951), is the ultimate cynical-reporter movie. Surely the loathsome main character in *Ace in the Hole*, a heartless and self-centered journalist played by Kirk Douglas, was based by Wilder on fellow reporters he had known in his youth—and no doubt on his own personal experiences as a hungry freelance journalist in post–World War I Vienna and Berlin. The story, drawing on the infamous Floyd Collins mining disaster of the 1920s, is about an unscrupulous reporter who gets an exclusive story from a man trapped in a cave-in; in order to prolong his headline-grabbing coverage, the reporter delays the victim's rescue until it's too late to save him.

The picture was a critical and commercial disaster—the sorriest in Wilder's career up until then (there were more to follow in the 1960s and 1970s). This was the movie that inflamed Herbert G. Luft's rancor toward Wilder's alleged cold-heartedness, an accusation that has stuck over the decades. Wilder, who had produced, directed, and cowritten *Ace in the Hole*, was stung by the outrage against his film. It was a turning point in his career, maybe even a moral turning point. For most of the decade that followed, he prioritized commercial success over any sort of "message"—in other words, he consciously or subconsciously fell out of line with his own dictum that a "picture should say a little something."

In 1956, when an interviewer for the British film magazine *Sight and Sound* asked Wilder if he had deliberately changed course "since the bitterness and protest of *Sunset Boulevard* and *Ace in the Hole*," the maestro shrugged off the question, saying, "No, I don't think so. You see, I'm a director who prefers not to have a particular style, unlike Hitchcock or Ford. If I get a story I like or subject that appeals to me, I make it." On another occasion, he said, "My pictures are not intended to inform people." Instead their job was "to make them forget the popcorn."

Between *Ace in the Hole* in 1951 and *Some Like It Hot* in 1959, Wilder bought the rights to bestselling novels and hit Broadway plays and turned them into (mostly) surefire, crowd-pleasing pictures. These movies include *Stalag 17*, set in a World War II German prisoner-of-war camp; *Sabrina*, a romantic comedy in which Holden and Humphrey Bogart are wealthy brothers who vie for the love of the ingenue played by Audrey Hepburn; *The Seven Year Itch*, a bedroom farce in which Marilyn Monroe, standing over a Manhattan subway grate, appears as giddy as a child at an amusement park when a sudden updraft hoists her dress above her waist; *Love in the Afternoon*, in which young Hepburn finds romance in the arms of a much older man played by a woefully overaged Gary Cooper; and the courtroom drama *Witness for the Prosecution*, based on the hit Agatha Christie play, in which Wilder's old friend Marlene Dietrich takes the lead as a woman whose husband stands trial for murder in London's Old Bailey.

A major change occurred in Wilder's career, and his life, when he found the best writing partner he had had since his breakup with Brackett, a Romanian Jewish immigrant named I. A. L. ("Izzy") Diamond. Together they loosely adapted a 1935 French farce and its 1951 German remake, calling it *Some Like It Hot*. This brilliant, hilarious, and poignant romantic comedy, set in the 1920s, starred Tony Curtis and Jack Lemmon as two male Prohibition-era jazz musicians who impersonate female musicians to evade Chicago mobsters who are after them. After they're hired as members of an all-woman band, they are taken under the wing of a voluptuous but emotionally vulnerable jazz singer played by Marilyn Monroe. Working with Diamond, Wilder followed up this huge box-office success with another, *The Apartment*, starring Jack Lemmon as a corporate schlemiel who bravely defends the honor of his boss's suicidal mistress, played by Shirley MacLaine (Monroe is rumored to have sought the role, but Wilder had found working with her on their previous film too challenging and was not interested). Both films, Betty Schaefer might have agreed, had plenty to say about love, gender, sexuality, and sexual predation.

One of Wilder's follow-up films, *Irma la Douce* (1963), about a sweetheart of a Parisian prostitute (MacLaine) and the gendarme who falls in love with her (Lemmon), was another box-office success, while *Kiss Me, Stupid* (1964) was the director's greatest critical and commercial failure since *Ace in the Hole*. Some of Wilder's movies in the later 1960s and the 1970s made money but added nothing to his reputation. His next-to-last film, *Fedora* (1978), was a sad, clumsy film and a devastating flop, although from today's perspective it seems very much to be about its fedora-wearing director as he himself faced old age.

His final film was *Buddy Buddy* (1981), a comedy starring his two favorite actors, Jack Lemmon and Walter Matthau, but no one liked it, including Wilder, and his career as a filmmaker hastened to an end. After *Fedora* and *Buddy Buddy*, he could never again obtain financial backing for his story ideas. He was now seventy-five, considered by most contemporary viewers to be a relic of Old Hollywood, whose work looked stunningly prosaic compared with that of the new generation of directors that included Francis Ford Coppola, George Lucas, Martin Scorsese, and Steven Spielberg. He contemptuously called them "the bearded horde."

The honors began rolling in, but Wilder shrugged them off, saying they're what you get when you've been around too long, and no one wants to hire you ("I get offered all these prizes and they say how great my pictures are, but they don't offer me anything to do"). Ironically, the bearded horde that he did not admire idolized him. Cineastes all, they considered Wilder one of the true Hollywood greats, even though they debated among themselves how high to rank him in the pantheon. The prestigious young Broadway director Mike Nichols looked to him and his movies for guidance. Coming to Hollywood in 1965 to make his first film, *Who's Afraid of Virginia Woolf?*, Nichols sought Wilder's advice, and Wilder generously gave it, urging the novice filmmaker to space out the best scenes in his movie rather than crowd them together: "Don't forget to leave string for the pearls," he said. Nichols never forgot this advice, saying, "It was the most useful thing anyone ever said to me." When Wilder entered his nineties, Cameron Crowe, a former journalist for *Rolling Stone* and now a successful director of romantic comedies such as *Jerry Maguire*, conducted a series of wide-ranging interviews with him that appeared in 1999 as *Conversations with Wilder*. It showed the nonagenarian to be as witty and biting as ever.

Wilder's films were screened at film festivals and revival houses and on late-night television, while videotapes and then DVDs made them accessible to the wider public. He continued to go daily into his small office on Little Santa Monica Boulevard and type out scripts and scenarios that would never be produced. He was brokenhearted when Izzy Diamond, his closest associate over the past thirty years, and with whom he shared his office, died in 1988 of multiple myeloma at the young age of sixty-seven.

In 1970, when he was sixty-four, Wilder had told one of his biographers, "I'll never retire. They'll have to take my camera away from me before I'll stop making pictures. Renoir [the impressionist] painted even when they had to tie a brush to his arthritic fingers." But in the end they did take his camera away from him.

Billy, who had begun buying modern art in Berlin in the early 1930s after finding his initial success as a screenwriter, continued to augment his private collection until there was no space left for it in either his home or his office. He knew he had to cull it. In 1989, Christie's in Beverly Hills held an auction of the choicest pieces from his collection, works by the likes of Picasso, Braque, Matisse, Balthus, and Kirchner. The sale fetched $32.6 million.

The satirist who for over four decades had made film audiences around the world experience laughter, sorrow, suspense, titillation, and shock, died of pneumonia in 2002. He was ninety-five. His last years were marked by bitterness and frustration but also by his famously coruscating sense of humor. Accepting an award from the American Film Institute in 1986, he spelled out his life philosophy: "You got to take the bitter with the sour." Writing three years before Wilder's death, Ed Sikov, his biographer, called him "the fastest, funniest, meanest mind in Hollywood," a gadfly who had been "ridiculing friends and enemies in three languages for most of his ninety-two years." There will never be another filmmaker like him.

★ ★ ★

After her great success in *Sunset Boulevard*, Gloria Swanson received a multitude of leading-lady offers. Unfortunately, all of them were essentially the same role: a former film star who cannot adjust to the loss of her glory. Swanson recalled in her autobiography, "I had a huge specter in the spotlight with me. She was just about ten feet tall, and her name was Norma Desmond."

Surely, had one of these scripts been top-flight, Swanson would have been interested, but no such opportunities came her way. She did make one film shortly after *Sunset*, the instantly forgettable comedy *Three for Bedroom C* (1952), because, as she explained to an interviewer years later, "nobody offered me anything else. My agent said it would be a chance to do comedy, get away from the *Sunset Boulevard* image." In the mid-1950s, while based in Europe as a roving columnist for United Press

International (UPI), Swanson accepted the role of Agrippina, Emperor Nero's evil mother, in a low-budget Italian costume drama titled *Mio Figlio Nerone* (*My Son Nero*, aka *Nero's Big Weekend*), where she played opposite the neorealist filmmaker and actor Vittorio De Sica; Italy's favorite postwar comedian, Alberto Sordi; and the reigning French sexpot, Brigitte Bardot. Even this high-powered cast could not salvage the film, which was a mess. It did nothing to burnish Swanson's reputation or anyone else's.

In 1952, she hired the newly minted songwriting team of Dickson Hughes and Richard Stapley to create a musical version of *Sunset Boulevard* with grand lyrical songs. It would be called *Boulevard!* Swanson, of course, would play the lead. This was when Stroheim turned down her invitation to reprise his role as Max, shortly before he became ill with the cancer that would kill him. After she had invested considerable time, money, and effort into the project, it fell through in 1957 when Paramount Pictures, which owned the rights to the film, denied her permission to adapt it for the stage, saying that the adaptation could be damaging to the integrity of the original version. A few years later, after finishing *A Funny Thing Happened on the Way to the Forum*, Stephen Sondheim briefly entertained the idea of making his own adaptation, if Paramount would grant the rights, but his chance encounter with Billy Wilder at a cocktail party changed his mind. In the early 1990s, *Sunset Boulevard* finally appeared as a lavish musical scored by the prolific hitmaker Andrew Lloyd Webber. When he saw it, Wilder commented dismissively, "It's like my movie in a permanent long shot."

Swanson's film career, revived briefly by *Sunset Boulevard*, became moribund again, and she staked a claim on the public's attention by reconstituting herself as a celebrity—someone who is famous for being famous. She leveraged her reputation for having once been someone of great acclaim to sell her fashion designs and trigger audience applause when she walked onstage in roadshow versions of Broadway plays and as a replacement for Eileen Heckart in the well-received Broadway comedy *Butterflies Are Free* (1969). She appeared as either herself or a lightly veiled version of herself in TV dramas such as *Ben Casey* and *Dr. Kildare* and comedies such as *The Beverly Hillbillies*. She was a special guest on the popular programs *What's My Line* and *This Is Your Life* and frequented television talk shows—a genre she had helped to create in the late 1940s. She bantered on air with hosts Jack Paar, Merv Griffin, Johnny Carson, and Dave Garroway, along with many others. She sang, she danced, she traded quips. As a passionate advocate of organic, locally grown foods, macrobiotic diets, and mindful eating, she often had it written into her contract that she would be allowed time to proselytize for what many considered fad diets, but which she believed in wholeheartedly. Showing off her remarkably "well-preserved" face and figure could be chalked up to vanity, but she justified doing so as a means of advertising the benefits of healthful living.

Even as early as the 1930s, Swanson was a favorite of drag queens and female impersonators, including the Black nightclub entertainer George Winston, who called himself "the Sepia Gloria Swanson." By the late 1960s, Swanson had become something of a Swanson impersonator herself. Along with other larger-than-life entertainers such as Carol Channing and Liza Minnelli, she was regarded as a queen of camp. Her public persona was that of a self-assured, sexually robust older woman who seemingly defied age. In a 1974 episode of *The Carol Burnett Show*, for example, she comes onstage clinging to the arm of her tall, handsome, tuxedoed escort (*Burnett Show* regular Lyle Waggoner) and refuses to let go. She comically fondles him before the live audience and asks him if he has plans for after the show. In an overly long musical number, she dances the tango with six tall men in evening jackets who have their jet-black hair brilliantined like Rudolph Valentino, all the while singing an insipid song. Taping a segment for the nationally syndicated *Good Day* show in 1976, the seventy-seven-year-old entertainer told a reporter from *Time*, "Of course, my sex life is very healthy." When the reporter teasingly asked if a grandmother should be talking so lustily, "the unsilent screen star" replied, "'I'm a matriarch now, and I can say anything I want to.'"

In an August 1970 episode of *The Dick Cavett Show*, Swanson, seventy-one, shares the spotlight with Janis Joplin, twenty-seven. The singer, with no makeup, a mop of unruly, multicolored hair, and tie-dyed clothes, looks likes she barely rolled out of bed, while the heavily made-up former movie diva wears a slinky black-and-white, drop-shouldered designer dress and a flapper-style headband. Joplin speaks with a casual, low-emphasis Texas twang, while Swanson carefully enunciates every word, as she did in her early talking pictures. The generation gap could not have been more pronounced.

Swanson, though, was indefatigable. In a 1974 made-for-television horror film called *Killer Bees*, her role called for her to lie inert on the floor while swarms of real-life worker bees crawl or buzz up and down her body. Her film career had come full circle—once again she put her safety on the line as she had done half a century earlier in the lion scene from DeMille's *Male and Female*. Anything for her art.

She remained active and engaged to the very end of her life. After a brief illness in April 1983, she died from heart failure. She was eighty-four.

THE LEGACY OF *SUNSET BOULEVARD*

V anity of vanities," the book of Ecclesiastes reminds us, "All is vanity." It's a theme that has been around for millennia: Everyone and everything ultimately crumbles into dust; there's no holding back time or escaping death. Dutch painters of the Baroque era were justly renowned for their still-life paintings of flowers shedding their petals and fruit beginning to rot. These works, called *vanitas* paintings for their symbolic depiction of the futility and finality of human existence, were at once dazzling in their attention to detail and melancholy in their reminder of what awaits all of us. *Sic transit gloria mundi.* Thus passes worldly glory.

While some viewers have looked down on Norma Desmond as a vain and foolish creature, pathetically refusing to "grow up" and act her age, she is nonetheless an archetypal figure that embodies our compulsive search for fame and acceptance (how many "friends," how many "likes"), our obsession with youth and beauty, our dread of old age, and our fear of becoming irrelevant. *Sunset Boulevard* examines the pathology of fame: what maladies it breeds in those who have it, those who lose it, and those who, like most of us, never attain it.

Looking back from the vantage point of half a century, Roger Ebert wrote, "*Sunset Boulevard* remains the best drama ever made about the movies because it sees through the illusions, even if Norma doesn't." The movie's treatment of America's most significant industrial manufacturer of fame, Hollywood, as seen from the perspective of those who toil at its margins, feels germane today, when social media, reality TV, and other technologies for imaginary intimacy with strangers have created a public that is more intrigued than ever by fame and its discontents. Yet as this book has argued, *Sunset Boulevard* is more than simply an acerbic critique of the movie business, more even than "the best drama ever made about the movies." That it certainly is, but the film transcends its specialized niche to explore matters of greater existential concern.

★ ★ ★

The movie's contemporary relevance appears in the political realm as well. A week after Joe Biden clinched the 2020 presidential election, Maureen Dowd published a *New York Times* opinion piece that compared the delusional thinking of outgoing president Donald J. Trump, who refused to accept his defeat, to Norma Desmond descending her staircase in the final scene of *Sunset Boulevard*. Dowd noted that Trump has frequently identified *Sunset Boulevard* as his favorite film. His obsession with it was confirmed a year later in a memoir by former White House press secretary Stephanie Grisham, who described seeing the movie for the first time at Camp David:

> The boss was excited all through dinner beforehand and couldn't believe I had never seen it. I must admit, I loved it and

was shocked at all of the similarities between President Trump and Norma Desmond, the lead character of the movie, who was a former silent-film star obsessed with her looks and with making a triumphant return to the screen. Here was a woman who was convinced that everyone loved her and lived in a fantasy world of her own making. I'm sure that Trump had no clue—like none—how similar to him she was. Still, the president was thrilled that I enjoyed the movie so much, and it would be a frequent topic of conversation between us over the next few years.

In 2022, the business reporter Timothy O'Brien recalled watching *Sunset Boulevard* with Trump on the latter's private jet some twenty years earlier. During the projection scene in which Norma bemoans her loss of stature and seethes, "Those idiot producers. Those imbeciles! Haven't they got any eyes? Have they forgotten what a star looks like? I'll show them. I'll be up there again, so help me!" Trump leaned over and whispered, "Is this an incredible scene or what? Just incredible." With Trump aiming for a "comeback" of his own, wrote O'Brien, he "plans to show any doubters what he's made of. He'll be up there in the White House again, so help him."

Trump is not alone in admiring Norma's indomitable spirit. In a book on women, aging, and sexuality, the distinguished cultural historian Lois Banner argued that *Sunset Boulevard* was proto-feminist in offering a criticism of a system that requires women to adhere to gendered beauty norms. The film does not criticize Norma's "female vanity" (as some of its original viewers contended) so much as it sheds an incriminating light on a society that separates women from an early age into rigidly differentiated beauty castes. In this, her tale has a universal appeal. After viewing the movie on its release in Britain, a young fan wrote to Swanson, "I have just seen *Sunset Boulevard* and I do want to tell you how much I enjoyed it. Even at 25, life can be very cruel—and although half her age, I think I understand the fictitious Miss Desmond's story."

Despite its delicious wisecracks, deft satire, and ironic mindset, *Sunset Boulevard* is in essence a tragedy. It tells a cautionary tale of a narcissist who recklessly assails reality in a vain—in both senses of the word: conceited and futile—attempt to regain *les temps perdu*. She is a victim of her own hubris, but also of a society that scorns or otherwise discredits individuals, especially women, who have the audacity to act other than their age, as conventionally defined.

Comedy, crime film, horror story, Hollywood exposé, romantic melodrama, and psychological thriller, *Sunset Boulevard* is above all an unsentimental examination of our innate unwillingness to accept the inevitability of decline, decay, and death. The seventeenth-century French aphorist La Rochefoucauld wisely observed that it is impossible to stare directly at either the sun or death. Norma's game is to avoid looking death, or its earthly emissary, old age, in the face.

In a poem of great poignancy, the nineteenth-century poet and Jesuit priest Gerard Manley Hopkins lamented the unwanted signs of aging and the inevitable decline of beauty: "No waving off of those most mournful messengers... sad and stealing messengers of grey... Nor can you long be, what you now are, called fair."

Norma may be eccentric and deviant, but her compulsion to wave off those "sad and stealing messengers of grey" is the most human of stories, and she is its embodiment. Thus, while the rest of us must age and die, Norma Desmond will remain immortal.

ACKNOWLEDGMENTS

I would like to thank my agent, Elias Altman, for helping me every step of the way to convert a vague idea into what became a book that I found remarkably fun to research and write.

Thanks, too, to my editor, Colin Dickerman, for his faith in this project and his astute critical comments. Colin's assistant, Ian Dorset, ably guided me through the many details involved in preparing a book for publication, as did Jeff Holt, my production editor.

James Harper and Kylie Bradley in Wake Forest University's inter-library loan department were fast and thorough in helping me track down hard-to-find books and newspaper and magazine articles. Peter Romanov and Patrick Ferrell at the circulation desk kept me plentifully supplied with old movies that were germane to my research and others that were peripheral yet still provided valuable context.

In the Art Department, audio-visual librarian Kendra Battle was extraordinarily helpful in making clips and screen grabs. I couldn't have done this without you, Kendra. I wish to thank all my departmental colleagues, especially Jay Curley. Wake Forest has generously supported my research and writing over the years. In particular, I wish to thank Provost Rogan Kersh and his successor, Provost Michele Gillespie, for their continuing enthusiasm.

The head of the Paramount Pictures Archive, Andrea Kallas, and her team, in particular Larry McAllister, who licensed images for the book, were helpful and always gracious. My go-to person in Special Collections at the Margaret Herrick Library in Beverly Hills was Genevieve Maxwell; at the Harry Ransom Center in Austin, Steve Wilson, the director of the center's vast Gloria Swanson papers, was also knowledgeable and welcoming. I want to thank Gloria Swanson's granddaughter Brooke Anderson for sharing with me her intimate memories of her grandmother.

The following friends and colleagues gave me feedback on various chapters of the book or otherwise supplied fresh insights and pertinent information: Phil Archer, Heidi Dawidoff, Peter Dreyer, Joel Drucker, Bryan Gilliam, Alan Hess, David Korn, Gus Lubin, Angus MacLachlan, Barry Maine, Paul Marley, Angela Miller, Alex Nemerov, Joel Pfister, Tom Phillips, Dale Pollock, Dick Schneider, Anthony Slide, Phil Smith, Peter Werner, and Jonathan Wiener. My students over the decades have also sharpened my understanding of *Sunset Boulevard* by vigorously debating its ambiguities from their twenty-first-century perspectives.

In 2022, the National Endowment for the Humanities awarded me a Public Scholar grant, intended to bring academic research to a broad-based readership. I hope I have achieved this goal.

For being my own personal, live-in editor—and much more than that—I thank Libby Lubin.

NOTES

Prologue: The Early Hours

x   **In his diary, he wrote:** Charles Brackett, *"It's the Pictures That Got Small": Charles Brackett on Billy Wilder and Hollywood's Golden Age,* ed. Anthony Slide (New York: Columbia University Press, 2014), 355 (entry for November 7, 1948).

xi   **Twenty-two years later:** Gloria Swanson, *Swanson on Swanson* (New York: Random House, 1980), 477, says she earned $350 a week on WPIX.

xi   **Holden, too, worried:** Michelangelo Capua, *William Holden: A Biography* (Jefferson, NC: McFarland, 2010), 51. See also Bob Thomas, *Golden Boy: The Untold Story of William Holden* (New York: St. Martin's Press, 1983), 59–60.

xii   **Innocent and girl-next-door-ish:** Nancy Olson Livingston, *A Front Row Seat: An Intimate Look at Broadway, Hollywood, and the Age of Glamour* (Lexington: University Press of Kentucky, 2022), 41.

xii   **Thrilled to be cast:** Interview with Nancy Olson Livingston in the 2008 special feature documentary, *"Sunset Boulevard: A Beginning,"* included in various DVD and Blu-ray editions of the film, approximately fifteen minutes into the documentary.

xii   **Her mother had to explain to her:** Livingston, *A Front Row Seat,* 38.

Chapter 1: The Man in the Pool

1   **The man who owned the pool:** The anecdote is told in various iterations; see, for example, Maurice Zolotow, *Billy Wilder in Hollywood* (New York: Putnam, 1977), 59, and Otto Friedrich, *City of Nets: A Portrait of Hollywood in the 1940's* (New York: Harper and Row, 1986), 44.

2   **Whether or not they are true:** The following sections on Wilder's early life draw on all the standard biographies, most notably Charlotte Chandler, *Nobody's Perfect: Billy Wilder, A Personal Biography* (New York: Simon and Schuster, 2002); Cameron Crowe, *Conversations with Wilder* (New York: Knopf, 1999); Kevin Lally, *Wilder Times: The Life of Billy Wilder* (New York: Henry Holt, 1996); Axel Madsen, *Billy Wilder* (Bloomington: Indiana University Press, 1969); Joseph McBride, *Billy Wilder: Dancing on the Edge* (New York: Columbia University Press, 2021); Gene D. Phillips, *Some Like It Wilder: The Life and Controversial Films of Billy Wilder* (Lexington: University Press of Kentucky, 2010); Ed Sikov, *On Sunset Boulevard: The Life and Times of Billy Wilder* (New York: Hyperion, 1998); and Zolotow, *Billy Wilder in Hollywood*. The first book devoted to detailed analyses of Wilder's individual films was Neil Sinyard and Adrian Turner, *Journey Down "Sunset Boulevard": The Films of Billy Wilder* (Ryde, Isle of Wight: BCW Publishing, 1979). For a sampling of Wilder's many interviews and reminiscences, see *Billy Wilder: Interviews*, ed. Robert Horton (Jackson: University Press of Mississippi, 2001).

2   **As Wilder liked to say:** Charles Brackett, *"It's the Pictures That Got Small": Charles Brackett on Billy Wilder and Hollywood's Golden Age*, ed. Anthony Slide (New York: Columbia University Press, 2014), 87 (entry for August 18, 1936).

3   **Pointing to the boy in white:** Chandler, *Nobody's Perfect*, 26. See also Lally, *Wilder Times*, 3, drawing on a personal communication from Wilder; Sikov, *On Sunset Boulevard*, 9–10, citing Hellmuth Karasek, *Billy Wilder: Eine Nahaufnahme* [*Billy Wilder: A Close-Up*] (Hamburg: Hoffman und Campe, 1992), 23–24; and Zolotow, *Billy Wilder in Hollywood*, 20.

4   **In his posthumously published memoir:** Stefan Zweig, *The World of Yesterday: An Autobiography* (New York: Viking, 1943), 83 and 87.

4   **Alternating between the sentimental and the rudely obscene:** Salka Viertel, *The Kindness of Strangers* (New York: Holt, Rinehart and Winston, 1969), 35. For Viertel's recent biography, see Donna Rifkind, *The Sun and Her Stars: Salka Viertel and Hitler's Exiles in the Golden Age of Hollywood* (New York: Other Press, 2020).

5   **Unable to afford the luxury:** Madsen, *Billy Wilder*, 13.

5   **Years later, perhaps to save face:** Lally, *Wilder Times*, 9, in response to Zolotow, *Billy Wilder in Hollywood*, 26 and 339–44. Sikov, *On Sunset*

Boulevard, 16–17, similarly dismisses the Ilse story. See also Joseph McBride and Todd McCarthy's 1979 interview, in which Wilder denounces Zolotow's "primer level" Freudian analysis of the Ilse incident as "Bullshit. Total bullshit." McBride and McCarthy, "Going for Extra Innings," *Film Comment* 15:1 (January–February 1979): 40–48; discussion of the Ilse story on 43.

6   **The encounter corrupted his faith:** Lally, *Wilder Times*, 4–5.

6   **The film historian Charles Higham:** Charles Higham, *The Art of the American Film* (Garden City, NY: Anchor Press / Doubleday, 1973), 241.

6   **On finishing high school:** See Billy Wilder, *Billy Wilder on Assignment: Dispatches from Weimar Berlin and Interwar Vienna*, ed. Noah William Isenberg, trans. Shelley Laura Frisch (Princeton, NJ: Princeton University Press, 2021).

7   **Annoyed by the interruption:** Wilder told the story to novelist Richard Gehman in "Charming Billy," *Playboy* (December 1960): 9, reprinted in Robert Horton, ed., *Billy Wilder: Interviews* (Jackson: University Press of Mississippi, 2001), 27. Zolotow, *Billy Wilder in Hollywood*, 28–29, recounts it, as does Sikov, *On Sunset Boulevard*, 23, noting that "the tale appears in nearly every profile of Wilder ever written," but he does not establish its veracity. Noah Isenberg, who has edited an authoritative edition of Wilder's journalism from Vienna and Berlin, summons it in his introduction to *Billy Wilder on Assignment*, 7, observing that there are "no extant articles to corroborate such audacious claims."

7   **While Wilder came of age:** Hilde Spiel, *Vienna's Golden Autumn, 1866–1938* (New York: Weidenfeld and Nicolson, 1987).

7   **He accused psychoanalysts:** Karl Kraus, *Half-Truths & One-and-a-Half Truths: Selected Aphorisms*, ed. and trans. Harry Zohn (New York: Carcanet Press, 1986), 78 (psychoanalysts); 74 (education); and 105 (dresses).

8   **In defense of his controversial aesthetic:** Adolf Loos, "Ornament and Crime" (1908), in *Ornament and Crime: Selected Essays* (New York: Penguin Classics, 2019).

8   **Furthering the point, he added:** Quotation from Wilder's June 1963 *Playboy* interview with an unidentified interviewer: 64. For another statement by Wilder of his disdain for "arty" camera angles, see Gehman, "Charming Billy," reprinted in Horton, ed., *Billy Wilder: Interviews*, 32–33.

9   **The fourteen-story tower:** Alan Hess, email to DML, September 26, 2022, on Victor Gruen. On Wilder's taste in art and architecture,

see Gerald Clarke, "Portrait: Billy Wilder: *Sunset Boulevard*'s Creator Talks of the Town," *Architectural Digest* (April 1994): 22 and 26. In the early 1950s, Victor Gruen pioneered the shopping mall, which he later renounced for its disruption of residential neighborhoods and non-commercial public spaces. See M. Jeffrey Hardwick, *Mall Maker: Victor Gruen, Architect of an American Dream* (Philadelphia: University of Pennsylvania Press, 2000).

10   **In Weimar Berlin:** Peter Gay, *Weimar Culture: The Outsider as Insider* (New York: Harper and Row, 1968).

10   **"Above all," wrote the journalist:** See Otto Friedrich's richly detailed account of Weimar Berlin, *Before the Deluge: A Portrait of Berlin in the 1920's* (New York: Harper and Row, 1972), quotation from page 8. On Wilder in Berlin, see Helene Stapinski and Bonnie Siegler, *The American Way: A True Story of Nazi Escape, Superman, and Marilyn Monroe* (New York: Simon and Schuster, 2023), 26–32; also 49–50.

10   **He likened it to a "hugely desirable woman":** Alexandra Richie, *Faust's Metropolis: A History of Berlin* (New York: Carroll and Graf, 1998), 331–32.

10   **Eric Weitz, the distinguished historian of Weimar Germany:** Eric D. Weitz, *Weimar Germany: Promise and Tragedy* (Princeton, NJ: Princeton University Press, 2013), 11.

11   **In 1927, when he was still twenty:** Isenberg, ed., *Billy Wilder on Assignment*, 23–41.

12   **They talk, swim, picnic:** Noah Isenberg, "Young People Like Us," essay in the booklet accompanying the Criterion Collection's DVD edition of *People on Sunday*, 2011. See also Lutz Koepnick, "The Bearable Lightness of Being: *People on Sunday*" (1930), in Noah William Isenberg, ed., *Weimar Cinema: An Essential Guide to Classic Films of the Era* (New York: Columbia University Press, 2009), 237–53.

14   **Their new hire couldn't speak proper English:** Zolotow, *Billy Wilder in Hollywood*, 55.

15   **Or so Wilder recounted:** Sikov, *On Sunset Boulevard*, 580. For the text of Wilder's acceptance speech on the Academy Awards broadcast of April 11, 1988, see http://aaspeechesdb.oscars.org/link/060-23/.

15   **Or so he said:** See Madsen, *Billy Wilder*, 18, for a variation on this anecdote.

15   **Displaying a fanatical desire:** Madsen, *Billy Wilder*, 18.

16   **For the rest of his life:** Armand Deutsch, *Me and Bogie: And Other Friends and Acquaintances from a Life in Hollywood and Beyond* (New York: Putnam, 1991), 160.

16   **Wilder was rankled:** The resonant term *culture industry* is from Max Horkheimer and Theodor W. Adorno, "The Culture Industry" (1944), in *Dialectic of Enlightenment: Philosophical Fragments*, ed. Gunzelin Schmid Noerr, trans. Edmund Jephcott (Stanford, CA: Stanford University Press, 2002). See David Jenemann, *Adorno in America* (Minneapolis: University of Minnesota Press, 2007), 128–47, on Horkheimer and Adorno's failed attempt to make a sociologically oriented Hollywood film.

17   **Perhaps his motivation was to help:** Zolotow, *Billy Wilder in Hollywood*, 59.

Chapter 2: Glorious Gloria

19   **Unlike her peers, however:** Gloria Swanson, obituary, *New York Times*, April 3, 1983.

20   **A reciprocal relationship evolved:** See Anthony Slide, *Inside the Hollywood Fan Magazine: A History of Star Makers, Fabricators, and Gossip Mongers* (Jackson: University Press of Mississippi, 2010).

20   **Studio publicity departments:** See Robert Dance and Bruce Robertson, *Ruth Harriet Louise and Hollywood Glamour Photography* (Berkeley: University of California Press, 2002); and John Kobal, *The Art of the Great Hollywood Portrait Photographers, 1925–1940* (New York: Knopf, 1980).

20   **Her mind works swiftly:** Edward Steichen, *A Life in Photography*, np; the quotation comes three pages after plate 112.

21   **Cecil B. DeMille, who knew all about glamour:** Annette Tapert, *The Power of Glamour: The Women Who Defined the Magic of Stardom* (New York: Crown, 1998), 15–16.

21   **The star system itself:** Richard deCordova, *Picture Personalities: The Emergence of the Star System in America* (Urbana: University of Illinois Press, 1990).

21   **The movie star's sensational memoir:** Gloria Swanson, *Swanson on Swanson* (New York: Random House, 1980).

22   **Impressed with her spirit:** Stephen Michael Shearer, *Gloria Swanson: The Ultimate Star* (New York: Thomas Dunne Books / St. Martin's Press, 2013), 40–41; also Lawrence Quirk, *The Films of Gloria Swanson* (Secaucus, NJ: Citadel Press, 1984), 17 and 20.

22   **She thought the movie:** Swanson, *Swanson on Swanson*, 26.

23   **"No girl ever got on the lot":** Alan Selwyn, screenwriter, as quoted in Tony Bilbow and John Gau, *Lights! Camera! Action! A Century of Cinema* (Berkeley: University of California Press, 1995), 142.

23   **He recalled being struck:** Mack Sennett, *King of Comedy*, as told to Cameron Shipp (Garden City, NY: Doubleday, 1954), 171–72.

23   **Nevertheless, she was determined:** Swanson, *Swanson on Swanson*, 61 and 63.

25   **A modern girl:** For the international appeal of "the modern girl," see The Modern Girl Around the World Research Group, *The Modern Girl around the World: Consumption, Modernity, and Globalization*, ed. Alys Eve Weinbaum et al. (Durham, NC: Duke University Press, 2008).

26   **Typically, she played a timid housewife:** For a detailed analysis of *Why Change Your Wife?* see Mark Garrett Cooper, *Love Rules: Silent Hollywood and the Rise of the Managerial Class* (Minneapolis: University of Minnesota Press, 2003), 122–34. See also Sumiko Higashi, "The New Woman and Consumer Culture: Cecil B. DeMille's Sex Comedies," in Jennifer M. Bean and Diane Negra, eds., *A Feminist Reader in Early Cinema* (Durham, NC: Duke University Press, 2002), 298–332; and Charles Musser, "Divorce, DeMille and the Comedy of Remarriage," in Kristine Brunovska Karnick and Henry Jenkins, eds., *Classical Hollywood Comedy* (New York: Routledge, 1995), 282–313.

26   **The United States led:** Roderick Phillips, *Untying the Knot: A Short History of Divorce* (New York: Cambridge University Press, 1991); and Lenore J. Weitzman, *The Divorce Revolution: The Unexpected Social and Economic Consequences for Women and Children in America* (New York: Free Press, 1985). See also Stephanie Coontz, *Marriage, A History: From Obedience to Intimacy, or How Love Conquered Marriage* (New York: Viking, 2005).

26   **Fears of abandoning their children:** On the history of abortion in premodern America, see Janet Farrell Brodie, *Contraception and Abortion in Nineteenth-Century America* (Ithaca, NY: Cornell University Press, 1994); James C. Mohr, *Abortion in America: The Origins and Evolution of National Policy, 1800–1900* (New York: Oxford University Press, 1978); Eva R. Rubin, *The Abortion Controversy: A Documentary History* (Westport, CT: Greenwood Press, 1994); and Carroll Smith-Rosenberg, "The Abortion Movement and the AMA, 1850–1880," in her *Disorderly*

Conduct: Visions of Gender in Victorian America (New York: Knopf, 1985), 217–44.

27   **To this she added:** Quoted in *Theater Magazine*, 1919, from untitled, unpaginated, and undated clipping in the Gloria Swanson files (MWE2+W.C. 28,069) at the New York Public Library for the Performing Arts.

28   **Photoplay reported:** Figures from an unidentified issue of *Photoplay*, as given in Meher Tatna, "Forgotten Hollywood: Gloria Swanson," Golden Globe Awards, April 5, 2022: https://goldenglobes.com/articles /forgotten-hollywood-gloria-swanson/.

28   **The IRS dropped:** Tricia Welsch, *Gloria Swanson: Ready for Her Close-Up* (Jackson: University Press of Mississippi, 2013), 187.

28   **According to Photoplay:** Adela Rogers St. Johns, "Gloria! An Impression," *Photoplay* (September 1923); this and the following quotation are from 105.

28   **Movie-star historian:** Larry Carr, *Four Fabulous Faces: The Evolution and Metamorphosis of Garbo, Swanson, Crawford, Dietrich* (New Rochelle, NY: Arlington House, 1970), 4.

29   **Cosmetic surgery:** See David M. Lubin, *Grand Illusions: American Art and the First World War* (New York: Oxford University Press, 2016), chapter 8, "Behind the Mask," 211–41.

29   **She did indulge herself:** Anonymous, *Hollywood Undressed: Observations of Sylvia [Ulback], as Noted by Her Secretary* (New York: Brentano's, 1931).

29   **As late as 1915:** Kathy Lee Peiss, *Hope in a Jar: The Making of America's Beauty Culture* (New York: Metropolitan Books, 1998), 55.

30   **In 1920, only 1 percent:** Statistics from James D. Lutz, "Lest We Forget, A Short History of Housing in America" (unpublished paper, Energy Analysis Department, Lawrence Berkeley National Laboratory, August 2004), 189–90; Lutz in turn cites US Department of Commerce, National Bureau of Standards, *Plumbing Manual: Building Materials and Structures, Report* BMS66 (Washington, DC: US Government Printing Office, 1940).

31   **At the premiere:** Swanson, *Swanson on Swanson*, 9.

31   **This highly sexualized costume:** On Leisen's career, see David Chierichetti, *Mitchell Leisen, Hollywood Director* (Los Angeles: Photoventures Press, 1995).

31   **"One could mount a survey":** John Kobal, *People Will Talk* (New York: Knopf, 1985), 10; pages 3–21 reprint Kobal's 1964 profile of Swanson.

32   **Theater owners called her:** Swanson, *Swanson on Swanson*, 7–8.

32   **The word *glamour*:** Tapert, *The Power of Glamour*, 10; Carr, *Four Fabulous Faces*, 21.

32   **She feared that if it was discovered:** Swanson, *Swanson on Swanson*, 4 and 230.

33   **For weeks, she wrote:** Swanson, *Swanson on Swanson*, 5.

34   **This made a lasting impression:** Edith Head, with Jane Kesner Ardmore, *The Dress Doctor* (Boston: Little, Brown, 1959), 42; and Head, with Paddy Calistro, *Edith Head's Hollywood* (New York: Dutton, 1983), 89–90.

34   **She ruminated:** Swanson, *Swanson on Swanson*, 11.

35   **True to form, she arrived:** Peter H. Brown and Jim Pinkston, *Oscar Dearest: Six Decades of Scandal, Politics and Greed behind Hollywood's Academy Awards 1927–1986* (New York: Harper and Row, 1987), 88.

35   **Kennedy was not only:** On Kennedy's Hollywood career, see Cari Beauchamp, *Joseph P. Kennedy Presents: His Hollywood Years* (New York: Knopf, 2009).

36   **In a reminiscence:** Adela Rogers St. Johns, *My Hollywood Story: Love, Laughter, and Tears* (Garden City, NY: Doubleday, 1978), 156.

36   **The historian of early sound cinema:** Richard Barrios, *A Song in the Dark: The Birth of the Musical Film* (New York: Oxford University Press, 1995), 140; see also 319–20.

Chapter 3: Writers in Wonderland

39   **Or as Billy Wilder once observed:** Maurice Zolotow, *Billy Wilder in Hollywood* (New York: Putnam, 1977), 48. Wilder did not, however, idealize screenwriting, observing that anyone who claimed to love writing was clearly not a writer. This dovetails with Thomas Mann's well-known remark that "a writer is someone for whom writing is more difficult than it is for other people."

40   **Words, he found, could provide:** Telephone conversation with Brackett's grandson Jim Moore on September 17, 2020. On Brackett's chronic unhappiness and sense of dislocation in Hollywood, see Anthony Slide, "Introduction," Charles Brackett, *"It's the Pictures that Got Small": Charles Brackett on Billy Wilder and Hollywood's Golden Age*, ed. Slide (New York: Columbia University Press, 2014), 12.

41   **The house style of *The New Yorker*:** John W. Aldridge, *After the Lost Generation: A Critical Study of the Writers of Two Wars* (New York: McGraw Hill, 1951), 146–47.

41   **Of a musical comedy titled:** Charles Brackett, *New Yorker* reviews, in sequence: "Two Painful Episodes and a Wow," September 25, 1926: 29; "Some Charm, Some Smartness, Some Pity," October 30, 1926: 31; and "A Midlander, Molnar, and a Morality," November 13, 1926: 33.

41   **In her later years, Parker offered:** Parker quoted in Margaret Case Harriman, *The Vicious Circle: The Story of the Algonquin Round Table* (New York: Rhinehart, 1951), 78.

43   **His efforts to add plot complications:** Brackett, as quoted in Lincoln Barnett, "The Happiest Couple in Hollywood," *Life* (December 11, 1944): 106, reprinted in Robert Horton, ed., *Billy Wilder: Interviews* (Jackson: University Press of Mississippi, 2001), 8–9.

44   **Characteristically self-critical:** Brackett, "*It's the Pictures*," 41 (October 27, 1932).

45   **Brackett confided to his diary:** Brackett, "*It's the Pictures*," 43 (November 25, 1932).

44   **In an undated notebook entry:** F. Scott Fitzgerald, *The Notebooks of F. Scott Fitzgerald*, ed. Matthew J. Bruccoli (New York: Harcourt Brace Jovanovich, 1978), 157.

45   **Noting that he was the last:** Brackett, "*It's the Pictures*," 68 (January 7, 1936).

45   **As Leo Rosten, the sociologist of Hollywood:** Leo C. Rosten, *Hollywood: The Movie Colony, The Movie Makers* (New York: Harcourt, Brace, 1941), 308–09.

45   **The screenwriter Dalton Trumbo:** Trumbo, as quoted in Rosten, *Hollywood*, 309.

46   **As the crime novelist:** Raymond Chandler, "Writers in Hollywood," *Atlantic Monthly* (November 1945): 50, reprinted in Raymond Chandler, *Later Novels and Other Writings* (New York: Library of America, 1995), 993–1003, quotation on 994.

46   **The nomination only confirmed:** John Keats, *You Might as Well Live: The Life and Times of Dorothy Parker* (New York: Simon and Schuster, 1970), 178.

46   **The distinguished New York playwright:** Sidney Howard, "The Story Gets a Treatment," in *We Make the Movies*, ed. Nancy Naumburg (New York: Norton, 1937), 47.

46   **Donald Ogden Stewart:** Donald Ogden Stewart, "Writing for the Movies," *Focus on Film* 5 (November–December 1970): 52.

47   **According to Brackett:** Arthur F. Kinney, *Dorothy Parker, Revised* (New York: Twayne, 1998), 33.

47   **Parker slyly remarked:** Parker, as given by Rosten, *Hollywood*, 133.

47   **In the cleverly named book:** Murray Ross, *Stars and Strikes: Unionization of Hollywood* (New York: Columbia University Press, 1941), 4.

48   **"Among the producers":** Ian Hamilton, *Writers in Hollywood, 1915–1951* (New York: Harper and Row, 1990), 95.

48   **Veteran screenwriter Frances Marion:** Marion quoted in Hamilton, *Writers in Hollywood, 1915–1951*, 95.

49   **Sometimes his largesse:** Slide, "Introduction," Brackett, *"It's the Pictures,"* 12; Hamilton, *Writers in Hollywood, 1915–1951*, 253–55; William F. Nolan, *Hammett: A Life at the Edge* (New York: Congdon and Weed, 1983), 165–66.

49   **"If I were casting a picture":** Wilder as quoted in Nancy Lynn Schwartz, *The Hollywood Writers' Wars* (New York: Knopf, 1982), 109. Schwartz, who died before completing her book, does not provide her source for this remark.

49   **Herman Mankiewicz:** On Herman's objection to a guild for writers, see Kenneth L. Geist, *Pictures Will Talk: The Life and Films of Joseph L. Mankiewicz* (New York: Scribner's Sons, 1978), 174; and Sydney Ladensohn Stern, *The Brothers Mankiewicz: Hope, Heartbreak, and Hollywood Classics* (Jackson: University Press of Mississippi, 2019), 117–18.

50   **After graduating from Dartmouth:** See Budd Schulberg, "Afterword" (1989), in *What Makes Sammy Run?* (1941) (New York: Random House, 1990), 319–22. Chip Rhodes analyzes the novel in terms of Hollywood labor practices in *Desire and the Hollywood Novel* (Iowa City: University of Iowa Press, 2008), 49–72.

51   **The novel quickly became a bestseller:** Bennett Cerf, as quoted in Schulberg, "Afterword," *What Makes Sammy Run?*, 321.

51   **A popular refrain:** Rosten, *Hollywood*, 310.

52   **All this changed:** Barnett, "The Happiest Couple in Hollywood," 106, reprinted in Horton, ed., *Billy Wilder: Interviews*, 9.

Chapter 4: "The Happiest Couple in Hollywood"

53   **Late at night on August 17:** Charles Brackett, *"It's the Pictures That Got Small": Charles Brackett on Billy Wilder and Hollywood's Golden Age,*

ed. Anthony Slide (New York: Columbia University Press, 2014), 86 (August 17, 1936).

54 **Alas, when she met the German maestro:** Joseph McBride, *How Did Lubitsch Do It?* (New York: Columbia University Press, 2018), 153.

55 **"If you think I have an accent":** An often-quoted line; see for example Ed Sikov, *On Sunset Boulevard: The Life and Times of Billy Wilder* (New York: Hyperion, 1998), 107.

55 **"Lubitsch could do more with a closed door":** Another oft-repeated witticism; see David Freeman, "Annals of Hollywood: *Sunset Boulevard* Revisited," *New Yorker* (June 21, 1993): 74.

55 **"I've often wondered":** McBride, *How Did Lubitsch Do It?*, 141. For more on the origins of the "touch" rubric, see Herman G. Weinberg, *The Lubitsch Touch: A Critical Study*, 3rd ed. (New York: Dover, 1977); also Kristin Thompson, *Herr Lubitsch Goes to Hollywood: German and American Film After World War I* (Amsterdam: Amsterdam University Press, 2005).

56 **As the philosopher Stanley Cavell:** Stanley Cavell, *Pursuits of Happiness: The Hollywood Comedy of Remarriage* (Cambridge, MA: Harvard University Press, 1981).

56 **After their first day of collaborating:** Brackett, "*It's the Pictures*," 87 (August 18, 1936).

56 **Early in their partnership:** Brackett, "*It's the Pictures*," 87 (undated addendum to August 18, 1936).

56 **Brackett also admired:** Brackett, "*It's the Pictures*," 89 (September 11, 1936).

57 **Wilder had long idolized the director:** See Charles Brackett and Billy Wilder, "Ernst Lubitsch: A Symposium," *Screen Writer* no. 3 (January 1948): 15–16, quotation on 15. See also McBride, *How Did Lubitsch Do It?*, 356.

58 **Even Adolf Hitler:** Bill Niven, *Hitler and Film: The Führer's Hidden Passion* (New Haven, CT: Yale University Press, 2018), 226–27. See also Ben Urwand, *The Collaboration: Hollywood's Pact with Hitler* (Cambridge, MA: Belknap Press of Harvard University Press, 2013), 12. Hitler was particularly partial to *King Kong*, Disney cartoons, and romances starring Greta Garbo (Urwand, 6–7 and 12–13). On the Nazi demonization of Lubitsch, see McBride, *How Did Lubitsch Do It?*, 19–20.

60   **Even as early as 1939:** Brackett, *"It's the Pictures,"* 134 (July 27, 1939).

60   **On one occasion:** Brackett, *"It's the Pictures,"* 93 (November 23, 1936).

60   **Still, the mood in the suite:** Brackett, *"It's the Pictures,"* 93–94 (November 24, 1936).

62   **"When I finish a film":** Charlotte Chandler, *Nobody's Perfect: Billy Wilder, a Personal Biography* (New York: Simon and Schuster, 2002), 105–06; see also Sam Staggs, *Close-Up on* Sunset Boulevard: *Billy Wilder, Norma Desmond, and the Dark Hollywood Dream* (New York: St. Martin's Press, 2002), 145–47.

62   **Despite its implausible plot:** Dale M. Pollock gives the film an extended analysis in "An Unconventional War Film: Death, Disguise and Deception in *Five Graves to Cairo*," in *Billy Wilder, Movie-Maker: Critical Essays on the Films*, ed. Karen McNally (Jefferson, NC: McFarland, 2011), 26–40.

62   **When Wilder praised him:** See Ezra Goodman, *The Fifty-Year Decline and Fall of Hollywood* (New York: Simon and Schuster, 1961), 360; and Zolotow, *Billy Wilder in Hollywood*, 108.

62   **The author of the piece:** Lincoln Barnett, "The Happiest Couple in Hollywood," *Life* (December 11, 1944), 102, reprinted in Robert Horton, ed., *Billy Wilder: Interviews* (Jackson: University of Mississippi Press, 2001), 4–5.

63   **Only a few months after:** Brackett, *"It's the Pictures,"* 95 (November 7, 1936).

64   **As Ed Sikov deftly put it:** Sikov, *On Sunset Boulevard*, 116.

Chapter 5: Adultery, Addiction, and Mass Murder

65   **Too busy establishing himself:** See, for example, Ed Sikov, *On Sunset Boulevard: The Life and Times of Billy Wilder* (New York: Hyperion, 1998), 237 and 240.

66   **Andrew Sarris observed:** Andrew Sarris, *"You Ain't Heard Nothin' Yet": The American Talking Film in History & Memory* (New York: Oxford University Press, 1998), 333.

66   **According to James M. Cain:** Peter Brunette and Gerald Peary, interviewers, "James M. Cain: Tough Guy," in *Backstory: Interviews with Screenwriters of Hollywood's Golden Age*, ed. Patrick McGilligan (Berkeley and Los Angeles: University of California Press, 1986), 128. See also Otto Friedrich, *City of Nets: A Portrait of Hollywood in the 1940's* (New York: Harper and Row, 1986), 162.

67   **Instead, he found himself working:** Jeffrey Meyers, "Introduction," Billy Wilder [and Raymond Chandler], *Double Indemnity: The Complete Screenplay* (Berkeley and Los Angeles: University of California Press, 2000), x, quoting from Hellmuth Karasek, *Billy Wilder: Eine Nahaufnahme* [*Billy Wilder: A Close-Up*] (Hamburg: Hoffman und Campe, 1992), 259.

68   **"He did not like me very much":** Billy Wilder to Kevin Lally, April 12, 1995, quoted in Kevin Lally, *Wilder Times: The Life of Billy Wilder* (New York: Henry Holt, 1996), 129.

68   **After four weeks:** Wilder in Ivan Moffat, "On the Fourth Floor of Paramount: Interview with Billy Wilder," in *The World of Raymond Chandler*, ed. Miriam Gross (New York: A & W, 1977), 46.

68   **Chandler did indeed start drinking again:** Maurice Zolotow, *Billy Wilder in Hollywood* (New York: Putnam, 1977), 114–15; see also Zolotow, "Through a Shot Glass Darkly: How Raymond Chandler Screwed Hollywood," *Action* (January–February 1978), reprinted in *Los Angeles Herald Examiner* (July 20, 1980).

68   **Years later, Chandler called *Double Indemnity*:** Chandler quoted in Meyers, "Introduction," *Double Indemnity*, xi.

68   **In his 1953 Philip Marlowe novel:** Raymond Chandler, *The Little Sister* (1949), in Chandler, *Later Novels and Other Writings* (New York: Library of America, 1995), chapter 18, 299.

68   **Working with Wilder taught him:** Zolotow, *Billy Wilder in Hollywood*, 122.

70   **New York's *Daily News*:** Kate Cameron, "'Double Indemnity': A Tense Melodrama," review in *New York Daily News* (September 7, 1944): 35.

70   **Similarly impressed:** Bosley Crowther, *Double Indemnity* review, *New York Times* (September 7, 1944). Also see Mark Jancovich, "Realistic Horror: Film Noir and the 1940s Horror Cycle," in Karen McNally, ed., *Billy Wilder, Movie-Maker: Critical Essays on the Films* (Jefferson, NC: McFarland, 2011), 56–69.

70   **As the art historian Erika Doss:** Erika Doss, "Hopper's Cool: Modernism and Emotional Restraint," *American Art* 29, no. 3 (Fall 2015): 22.

71   **"After working with somebody else":** Joseph Wechberg, "Idea-a-Minute Men," *Liberty* 23, no. 18 (May 4, 1945): 59.

71   **His "infidelity," Wilder came to believe:** Garson Kanin, *Hollywood: Stars and Starlets, Tycoons and Flesh Peddlers, Movie-Makers and Money-makers, Frauds and Geniuses, Hopefuls and Has-Beens, Great Lovers and Sex Symbols* (New York: Viking Press, 1974), 178.

71　　**Brackett saw it differently:** Wechberg, "Idea-a-Minute Men": 19.

71　　**"It shrinks my liver, doesn't it, Nat?":** Billy Wilder [and Charles Brackett], *The Lost Weekend*, screenplay with introduction by Jeffrey Meyers (Berkeley and Los Angeles: University of California Press, 2000), 27.

71　　**At the same time:** Eileen Creelman, "Charles Brackett and Billy Wilder Discuss the Filming of 'The Lost Weekend,'" *New York Sun* (October 14, 1944), quoted in Lally, *Wilder Times*, 145.

71　　**Hollywood had previously shown drunks:** Wilder quoted in Charles Higham and Joel Greenberg, *The Celluloid Muse: Hollywood Directors Speak* (Chicago: Regnery, 1969), 249.

72　　**Their film, a friend of Wilder's later reminisced:** Tom Wood, *The Bright Side of Billy Wilder, Primarily* (Garden City, NY: Doubleday, 1970), 88.

72　　**And he knew other screenwriters:** Meyers, "Introduction," Wilder [and Brackett], *The Lost Weekend*), ix–x; see also Gene D. Phillips, *Some Like It Wilder: The Life and Controversial Films of Billy Wilder* (Lexington: University Press of Kentucky, 2010), 72–73.

72　　**"He was helpless to arrest":** Moore, "Foreword," Brackett, "*It's the Pictures*," xiv.

73　　**When asked if Anton Lang:** Wood, *The Bright Side*, 2. This quip is ubiquitous, appearing in multiple variations. See, for example, Richard Lemon, "The Message in Billy Wilder's Fortune Cookie: 'Well, Nobody's Perfect…'" *Saturday Evening Post* (December 17, 1966): 30–42; anecdote on 36; reprinted in Robert Horton, ed., *Billy Wilder: Interviews* (Jackson: University Press of Mississippi, 2001), 49.

73　　**The director's main activity:** For details on the making of *The Death Mills*, see David Bathrick, "Billy Wilder's Cold War Berlin," *New German Critique* 110 (Summer 2010): 31–47, especially 32–34.

74　　**Ed Sikov described the barbaric physical realities:** Sikov, *On Sunset Boulevard*, 237.

74　　**After traveling throughout postwar Germany:** Kevin Lally, *Wilder Times: The Life of Billy Wilder* (New York: Henry Holt, 1996), 155, quoting from Karasek, *Billy Wilder*, 313.

75　　**Preview audiences for *The Lost Weekend*:** Wilder quoted in Christopher Hitchens, "It Happened on Sunset," *Vanity Fair* (April 1995): 217.

75　　**The critics were overwhelmed:** James Agee, review of *The Lost Weekend* in *The Nation*, December 22, 1945, reprinted in *James Agee: Film Writing and Selected Journalism* (New York: Library of America, 2005), 215.

75   **It was an especially sweet tribute:** Wilder sleeping with his Oscars is from Brackett, "*It's the Pictures*," 286 (March 9, 1946); the writers' building garlanded with whiskey bottles is from Brackett, "*It's the Pictures*," 285 (March 8, 1946).

75   **His biographer Maurice Zolotow:** Zolotow, *Billy Wilder in Hollywood*, 149.

76   **"They quarreled and they screamed":** Zolotow, *Billy Wilder in Hollywood*, 149.

76   **The *Hollywood Reporter*:** The ad is described by John Weber, a lifelong Marxist who was also a Hollywood story editor and later a representative for the William Morris Agency, in Patrick McGilligan and Paul Buhle, *Tender Comrades: A Backstory of the Hollywood Blacklist* (New York: St. Martin's Press, 1997), 689. Weber doesn't give a date for the *Hollywood Reporter* ad, and I have not located it.

76   **In April 1948, the *New York Times*:** Phil Koury, "The Happy Union of Brackett and Wilder," *New York Times* (April 18, 1948).

Chapter 6: "The Foolishness of This Foolish Town"

77   **Specifically, he explained:** Charlotte Chandler, *Nobody's Perfect: Billy Wilder, A Personal Biography* (New York: Simon and Schuster, 2002), 133.

77   **Years later, Wilder:** Cameron Crowe, *Conversations with Wilder* (New York: Knopf, 1999), 70.

78   **A memorandum by Wilder:** Billy Wilder and Charles Brackett, memorandum to all concerned with the production, May 31, 1946, Paramount Collection, Margaret Herrick Library, as cited in Gene D. Phillips, *Some Like It Wilder: The Life and Controversial Films of Billy Wilder* (Lexington: University Press of Kentucky, 2010), 91.

78   **The project was Billy's baby:** Kanin, *Hollywood*, 153; see also Phillips, *Some Like It Wilder*, 88–90.

78   **He complained in his diaries:** Charles Brackett, "*It's the Pictures That Got Small*": *Charles Brackett on Billy Wilder and Hollywood's Golden Age*, ed. Anthony Slide (New York: Columbia University Press, 2014), 287 (April 18, 1946).

78   **Wilder, who later called the film:** Phillips, *Some Like It Wilder*, 91, quoting from Hellmuth Karasek, *Billy Wilder: Eine Nahaufnahme* [*Billy Wilder: A Close-Up*] (Hamburg: Hoffman und Campe, 1992), 340.

79   **At a private screening:** Scott Eyman, *Ernst Lubitsch: Laughter in Paradise* (Baltimore: Johns Hopkins University Press, 2000), 350.

79   **Brackett and Wilder's next film:** On *Trümmerfilm*, see Eric Rentschler, "The Place of Rubble in the 'Trümmerfilm,'" *New German Critique* 110 (Summer 2010): 9–30; on *A Foreign Affair*, see David Bathrick, "Billy Wilder's Cold War Berlin," *New German Critique* 110 (Summer 2010), 34–41. On the photography of Berlin in ruins by another Jewish émigré artist who temporarily returned to his homeland after the war, see Vivien Green Fryd, "Walking with *The Murderers Are Among Us*: Henry Ries's Post-WWII Berlin Rubble Photographs," *Arts* 9, no. 3 (2020): 1–25.

79   **The film opens:** Rentschler, "The Place of Rubble in the 'Trümmerfilm,'" 15.

80   **Joseph McBride, in his audio commentary:** Joseph McBride, audio commentary on *A Foreign Affair* (1948), Blu-ray disc from Kino Lorber, 2019. See also McBride's *Billy Wilder*, 344.

80   **On May 31, 1948:** Brackett, "*It's the Pictures*," 343 (May 31, 1948).

80   **One week later:** "Wife of Producer Brackett Dies," *Los Angeles Times* (June 8, 1948): 13.

81   **Brackett wrote:** Brackett, "*It's the Pictures*," 343 (June 7, 1948).

81   **Wilder took the conversation:** Brackett, "*It's the Pictures*," 343 (June 23, 1948).

81   **In mid-July:** *Los Angeles Times* (August 1, 1948), section 3: 4.

81   **Brackett despised *The Loved One*:** Brackett, "*It's the Pictures*," 345 (July 12, 1948).

82   **They needed to come up with an idea:** Brackett, "*It's the Pictures*," 346 (July 23, 1948).

82   **"In his later years":** Ezra Goodman, *The Fifty-Year Decline and Fall of Hollywood* (New York: Simon and Schuster, 1961), 3.

83   **"That man," explained Goldwyn:** A. Scott Berg, *Goldwyn: A Biography* (New York: Knopf, 1989), 447. See Sam Staggs, *Close-Up on Sunset Boulevard: Billy Wilder, Norma Desmond, and the Dark Hollywood Dream* (New York: St. Martin's Press, 2002), 2–5, for a vivid description of this awkward encounter.

83   **Few people turned up:** Richard Schickel, *D. W. Griffith: An American Life* (New York: Simon and Schuster, 1984), 604.

83   **In his diary, he congratulated himself:** A draft of Brackett's eulogy for Griffith is in the Charles Brackett papers, Margaret Herrick Library, Academy of Motion Picture Arts and Sciences, folder 986. The avant-garde filmmaker and film historian Jay Leyda attended Griffith's funeral;

for his withering account of Hollywood hypocrisy, see Leyda, "The Art and Death of D. W. Griffith," *Sewanee Review* (Fall 1948): 350–56. Richard Schickel, Griffith's biographer, finds Brackett's eulogy for Griffith melodramatic, banal, and self-congratulatory. See Schickel, *D. W. Griffith*, 604.

83 **"I'm afraid it didn't ease his heartache":** Goodman, *The Fifty-Year Decline*, 14; see also Kevin Brownlow, *The Parade's Gone By . . . : A Vivid, Nostalgic, Immediate Portrait of an Art in the Making* (New York: Knopf, 1968), 96–97.

84 **The anonymous reader wrote:** E.F.R., "Sic Transit Gloria—D.W.G.," *Los Angeles Times* (August 2, 1948), section 2: 4.

84 **The day after reading that hurtful but honest letter:** Brackett, "It's the Pictures," 348 (August 3, 1948).

Chapter 7: Finding Norma

85 **Wilder wanted it to be a comedy:** Charles Brackett, *"It's the Pictures That Got Small": Charles Brackett on Billy Wilder and Hollywood's Golden Age*, ed. Anthony Slide (New York: Columbia University Press, 2014), 348–49 (August 11 and August 12, 1948). See Kevin Lally, *Wilder Times: The Life of Billy Wilder* (New York: Henry Holt, 1996), 186, for a differing view of Brackett's and Wilder's respective intentions.

86 **"I believe in censorship":** Karen Weekes, *Women Know Everything!: 3,241 Quips, Quotes, & Brilliant Remarks* (New York: Quirk Books, 2011), 86. On West, sexual transgression, and camp, see Pamela Robertson, *Guilty Pleasures: Feminist Camp from Mae West to Madonna* (Durham, NC: Duke University Press, 1996), 23–53; on West and censorship, 46–48. See also Ramona Curry, "*Goin' to Town* and Beyond: Mae West, Film Censorship and the Comedy of Unmarriage," in Kristine Brunovska Karnick and Henry Jenkins, eds., *Classical Hollywood Comedy* (New York: Routledge, 1995), 211–37.

86 **He was drawn to her vulgarity:** Maurice Zolotow, *Billy Wilder in Hollywood* (New York: Putnam, 1977), 157.

86 **Her mantra was:** Simon Louvish, *Mae West: It Ain't No Sin* (New York: St. Martin's Press, 2005), 368.

86 **After discussing the project:** Emily Wortis Leider, *Becoming Mae West* (New York: Farrar, Straus and Giroux, 1997), 350, referencing Gerald Clarke, "Portrait: Billy Wilder: *Sunset Boulevard*'s Creator Talks of the Town," *Architectural Digest* 406.

86   **Years later, he looked back:** Charlotte Chandler, *Nobody's Perfect: Billy Wilder, A Personal Biography* (New York: Simon and Schuster, 2002), 145.

86   **It was a lost opportunity:** Maurice Leonard, *Mae West: Empress of Sex* (Secaucus, NJ: Carol Publishing Group, 1992), 275–76.

87   **She looked, Brackett noted:** Brackett, *"It's the Pictures,"* 357 (December 7, 1948).

87   **A year and a half later:** See Eileen Whitfield, *Pickford: The Woman Who Made Hollywood* (Lexington: University Press of Kentucky, 1997), 337–38.

88   **Brackett and Wilder agreed:** Gloria Swanson, *Swanson on Swanson* (New York: Random House, 1980), 374–77, on her work in early television.

88   **He found her "fabulously unchanged":** Brackett, *"It's the Pictures,"* 350 (September 4, 1948).

88   **After the 1934 debacle:** Stephen Michael Shearer, *Gloria Swanson: The Ultimate Star* (New York: Thomas Dunne Books / St. Martin's Press, 2013), 291.

89   **For his bravery:** Shearer, *Gloria Swanson*, 293.

89   **Between 1947 and 1948:** Swanson, *Swanson on Swanson*, 475.

89   **She quickly tired:** Swanson, *Swanson on Swanson*, 476.

90   **Americans owned a million TV sets:** See, among a number of statistical and anecdotal sources, Erik Barnouw, *Tube of Plenty: The Evolution of American Television* (New York: Oxford University Press, 1982), 114–17; and Richard Butsch, *The Making of American Audiences: From Stage to Television, 1750–1990* (New York: Cambridge University Press, 2000), 235–36.

91   **Her friend the gossip columnist:** Shearer, *Gloria Swanson*, 311, quoting Hedda Hopper, "Old Glory," *Los Angeles Times* (October 8, 1948).

91   **Cukor replied:** Swanson, *Swanson on Swanson*, 479.

91   **"Much as I hated the idea":** Swanson, *Swanson on Swanson*, 477.

92   **The script, what little there was of it:** Swanson, *Swanson on Swanson*, 482.

93   **Observing Swanson:** Brackett, 362 (February 4, 1949).

93   **Outwardly calm and reassuring:** Brackett, 362 (February 6, 1949).

93   **"She has no inhibitions":** Brackett, 363 (February 9, 1949). Swanson's marked-up copy of her pages for the screen test is in the Gloria Swanson Papers, Harry Ransom Center, University of Texas at Austin.

93   **The part they brought her:** Richard Armstrong, *Billy Wilder, American Film Realist* (Jefferson, NC: McFarland, 2000), 46.

94   **In Maurice Zolotow's words:** Maurice Zolotow, *Billy Wilder in Hollywood* (New York, Putnam, 1977), 163.

94   **Brackett later noted:** Charles Brackett, "A Matter of Humor," *Quarterly of Film, Radio and Television* 7, no. 1 (Autumn 1952): 69.

94   **While avidly agreeing:** Brackett, "*It's the Pictures*," 367 (March 19, 1949).

94   **As the film scholar Steven Cohan has noted:** Steven Cohan, *Sunset Boulevard* (New York: Bloomsbury / British Film Institute, 2022), 23.

95   **Swanson wrote to her lifelong friend:** Swanson to Virginia Bowker (Stubbs), February 25, 1949 (original in the Swanson papers at the Harry Ransom Center), quoted in Tricia Welsch, *Gloria Swanson: Ready for Her Close-Up* (Jackson: University Press of Mississippi, 2013), 319.

95   **"That's when I knew":** Stanley Frank, "Grandma Gloria Swanson Comes Back, Part Two," *Saturday Evening Post* (July 29, 1950): 56.

96   **In other words, she had to be:** Wilder, in his 1963 *Playboy* interview, said that Swanson put on no airs while shooting *Sunset Boulevard* but instead "worked like a dog." *Playboy* (June 1963), 65.

96   **As Richard Strauss exclaimed:** Quoted in Raymond Weaver, "Introduction," *The Shorter Novels of Herman Melville* (New York: Fawcett World Library, 1970), 30, but without providing a source. Weaver was probably referring to a brief essay from 1914, in which Strauss remarked, "The head that composed *Tristan* must have been as cold as marble." See Ernest Newman, "Heart and Head in Music," *Musical Times* 55, no. 857 (July 1, 1914): 440. My thanks to the Strauss expert Bryan Gilliam for his help in tracking down this passage.

96   **Shy and self-conscious:** This section on Edith Head derives from her autobiography, written with Jane Kesner Ardmore, *The Dress Doctor* (Boston: Little, Brown, 1959); her second, posthumously completed autobiography with Paddy Calistro, *Edith Head's Hollywood* (New York: Dutton, 1983); David Chierichetti, *Edith Head: The Life and Times of Hollywood's Celebrated Designer* (New York: HarperCollins, 2003); Chierichetti, *Hollywood Costume Design* (New York: Harmony, 1976); Jay Jorgensen, *Edith Head: The Fifty-Year Career of Hollywood's Greatest Costume Designer* (Philadelphia: Running Press, 2010); and Jorgensen

and Donald L. Scroggins, *Creating the Illusion: A Fashionable History of Hollywood Costume Designers* (Philadelphia: Running Press, 2015).

97 **"Accentuate the positive":** Head varied her adage. In *How to Dress for Success*, written with Joe Hyams (Random House: New York, 1967), x, she stated the principle as "accentuate the positive and camouflage the negative." Less saucily in *The Dress Doctor*, 207, she phrased it as "accentuate the positive; eliminate the negative." She devoted chapters of *How to Dress for Success* to topics such as "How to Dress to Get a Man…and Keep Him" (17–41) and "Success in Fashion Camouflage" (145–52).

97 **She was one of the low-level:** Head and Ardmore, *The Dress Doctor*, 42.

97 **West instructed Head:** Jorgensen and Scroggins, *Creating the Illusion*, 229.

97 **"Make it look as tricky":** Quoted in Jorgensen, *Edith Head*, 35.

97 **On the other hand:** Jorgensen, *Edith Head*, 37–38, and Head and Calistro, *Edith Head's Hollywood*, 40.

98 **Head remembered it:** Head and Calistro, *Edith Head's Hollywood*, 89.

99 **Swanson had worn them:** On Swanson's size 2½ shoes, see Head and Ardmore, *The Dress Doctor*, 98, and Head and Calistro, *Edith Head's Hollywood*, 90. On Swanson and the New Look, see Chierichetti, *Edith Head*, 103–06, and Chierichetti, *Hollywood Costume Design*, 69. On the advent of high heels in the Jazz Age and their moral and sexual symbolism, see Summer Brennan, *High Heel* (New York: Bloomsbury Academic, 2019), 92–93; on the injunctions against them by female fashion editors, home economists, and physical educationalists in the interest of women's health and well-being, see Linda Przybyszewski, *The Lost Art of Dress: The Women Who Once Made America Stylish* (New York: Basic Books, 2014), 25–27.

99 **On April 15:** "Wally Beery, Veteran Film Actor, Dies" [obituary], *Los Angeles Times* (April 17, 1949).

99 **At a Hollywood dinner party:** This and the following quotation are from Swanson, *Swanson on Swanson*, 141.

99 **"Picture officially starts:** Gloria Swanson to Barron Polan in Rocky Lang and Barbara Hall, eds., *Letters from Hollywood: Inside the Private World of Classic American Moviemaking* (New York: Abrams, 2019), 155, reproducing a typewritten letter in the Gloria Swanson Papers, Harry Ransom Center, University of Texas at Austin.

Chapter 8: The Man You Love to Hate

101   **In the early 1950s:** S. J. Perelman, "Cloudland Revisited: Vintage Swine," in *The Most of S. J. Perelman* (New York: Simon and Schuster, 1958), 594, reprinted from *The New Yorker* (September 20, 1952): 34.

101   **Perelman recalled:** Perelman, "Cloudland Revisited," 595.

102   **About Stroheim's persona:** Perelman, "Cloudland Revisited," 598.

102   **Here's his autobiographical résumé:** Peter Noble, *Hollywood Scapegoat: The Biography of Erich von Stroheim* (1950, reprinted New York: Arno Press and the *New York Times*, 1972), 4. Noble drew heavily on his subject's autobiographical notes, this falsified biographical sketch a case in point. See Denis Marion, "Erich von Stroheim: The Legend and the Fact," *Sight and Sound* 31, no. 1 (Winter 1961): 22, 23, and 51. See also Don Whittemore and Philip Alan Cecchettini, *Passport to Hollywood: Film Immigrants Anthology* (New York: McGraw Hill, 1998), 88–145.

105   **"Until the coming of Orson Welles":** Richard Koszarski, *The Man You Love to Hate: Erich von Stroheim and Hollywood* (New York: Oxford University Press, 1983), 32, revised and expanded edition, Koszarski, *Von: The Life and Films of Erich von Stroheim* (New York: Limelight Editions, 2004), 41.

105   ***Variety* called his next film:** *Variety* (August 20, 1920); *New York Times* (August 9, 1920); both quoted in Arthur Lennig, *Stroheim* (Lexington: University Press of Kentucky, 2000), 125 and 126.

106   **When asked how it would be possible:** *Variety*, January 20, 1922; *Photoplay*, February 1922, as quoted in Lennig, *Stroheim*, 136.

106   **The year *Foolish Wives* was released:** Kevin Jackson, *Constellation of Genius: 1922: Modernism Year One* (New York: Farrar, Straus and Giroux, 2013), 3.

106   **French critic André Bazin:** André Bazin, "The Evolution of the Language of Cinema," in *What Is Cinema?* vol. 1, trans. Hugh Gray (Berkeley: University of California Press, 1967), 27.

107   **The movie bounded so far over budget:** Jean Renoir, *My Life and My Films* (New York: Atheneum, 1974), 167; and Tricia Welsch, *Gloria Swanson: Ready for Her Close-Up* (Jackson: University Press of Mississippi, 2013), 211.

107   **They spelled his name:** Stroheim, quoted in Herman G. Weinberg, "Coffee, Brandy & Cigars," in *Homage to Stroheim: A Compilation of Selected Articles and a Filmography*, ed. Charlotte Gobeil (Ottawa:

Canadian Film Institute, 1966), 43. Koszarski, *The Man You Love to Hate*, 75 (and *Von*, 89), disputes this as myth, noting that a photograph of the sign in *Motion Picture Weekly* (August 13, 1921): 16 indicates that it did not even include Stroheim's name.

107   **Nevertheless, the film played:** See Koszarski, *The Man You Love to Hate*, 79–80 (and, slightly revised, *Von*, 93).

108   **In a profile of Stroheim:** Billie Wilder, "Stroheim, The Man We Love to Hate" (1929), in Billy Wilder, *Billy Wilder on Assignment: Dispatches from Weimar Berlin and Interwar Vienna*, ed. Noah William Isenberg and trans. Shelley Laura Frisch (Princeton, NJ: Princeton University Press, 2021), 150.

108   **He grasped Stroheim's cinematic originality:** Isenberg, ed., *Billy Wilder on Assignment*, 150. See also Wilder's brief note on *Greed* in the *B. Z. am Mittag* on July 10, 1928, in Isenberg, ed., *Billy Wilder on Assignment*, 176.

109   **When asked whom he most:** Herman G. Weinberg "Erich von Stroheim," *Film Art* 4, no. 10 (Spring 1937): 8, reprinted in Weinberg, *Saint Cinema: Writing on the Film, 1929–1970*, 2nd rev. ed. (New York: Dover, 1973), 39, and adapted, with slight variations, as "Stroheim's Place in Film History" in Noble, *Hollywood Scapegoat*, 196–201, quotation on 196.

109   **Similarly, Mayer called Stroheim:** Thomas Quinn Curtiss, *Von Stroheim* (New York: Random House, 1971), xvii.

109   **During a heated exchange:** Samuel Marx, *Mayer and Thalberg: The Make-Believe Saint* (New York: Random House, 1975), 39.

109   **According to legend:** Marx, *Mayer and Thalberg*, 74.

109   **When a journalist baited him:** As quoted in Lennig, *Stroheim*, 147, from interview with Stroheim by Willis Goldbeck, "Von Stroheim, Man and Superman," in *Motion Picture Classic* (September 1922).

110   **Like his contemporary James Joyce:** Noble, *Hollywood Scapegoat*, 82; see also Lennig, *Stroheim*, 477, n. 3.

110   **Sharing Swanson's opinion of Stroheim:** See Cari Beauchamp, *Joseph P. Kennedy Presents: His Hollywood Years* (New York: Knopf, 2009).

110   **Together he and Swanson:** Doris Kearns Goodwin vividly described this encounter in *The Fitzgeralds and the Kennedys* (New York: Simon and Schuster, 1987), 398–401.

111   **"I can handle him":** Gloria Swanson, *Swanson on Swanson* (New York: Random House, 1980), 347. The story of the *Queen Kelly* debacle is told

in Bret Wood, "Introduction," *Queen Kelly: The Complete Screenplay by Erich von Stroheim*, ed. Bret Wood (Langham, MD: Scarecrow Press, 2002), 1–25.

112   **In her autobiography, Swanson wrote:** Swanson, *Swanson on Swanson*, 368.

112   **A scene that Allan Dwan:** Swanson, 368–69.

113   **When contacted by Paramount:** Ed Sikov, *On Sunset Boulevard: The Life and Times of Billy Wilder* (New York: Hyperion, 1998), 287, quoting letter from Erich von Stroheim to Paul Kohner, November 21, 1948.

114   **He needed the money:** Herman G. Weinberg, quoting from his undated conversation with Stroheim, in "A Note on the Wedding March," in Gobeil, ed., *Homage to Stroheim*, 3.

Chapter 9: "Hello, Young Fellow"

115   **To this day, the Bronson Gate:** On the Bronson Gate, see Steven Bingen, with Marc Wanamaker, *Paramount: City of Dreams* (Guilford, CT: Taylor Trade Publishing, 2017), 68–73.

116   **The screenplay described her appearance thus:** Billy Wilder [and Charles Brackett], *"Sunset Boulevard": The Complete Screenplay*, "Introduction," Jeffrey Meyers (Berkeley and Los Angeles: University of California Press, 1999), 82.

116   **In fact, for the making of *Sunset Boulevard*:** See Maurice Zolotow, *Billy Wilder in Hollywood* (New York, Putnam, 1977), 165, and Meyers, "Introduction," *Sunset Boulevard*, xii. The Isotta-Fraschini now belongs to the Museo dell'Automobile Carlo Biscaretti di Ruffia in Turin. See Charles McEwen, "Driving Miss Desmond: The Car's a Scene-Stealer," *New York Times* (March 19, 1995), section 11: 1.

117   **"Hello, young fellow":** Gloria Swanson, *Swanson on Swanson* (New York: Random House, 1980), 482.

118   **He was eighteen years older:** See Swanson, *Swanson on Swanson*, 108–09, on DeMille's notorious "harem" and rumors that she had become its newest member.

118   **DeMille sighed with relief:** Swanson, *Swanson on Swanson*, 123.

119   **"I sat there, I never moved":** Cecilia de Mille Presley and Mark A. Vieira, *Cecil B. DeMille: The Art of the Hollywood Epic* (Philadelphia: Running Press, 2014), 84. This large-format book abounds with sumptuously printed archival stills, illustrating nearly all of DeMille's movies, from *The Squaw Man* (1914) to his final film, *The Ten*

Commandments (1956). See also John Kobal's posthumously published *The Lost World of DeMille* (Jackson: University Press of Mississippi, 2019).

119   **A creature of an era:** Anne Edwards, *The DeMilles: An American Family* (New York: Harry Abrams, 1988), 86; Scott Eyman, *Empire of Dreams: The Epic Life of Cecil B. DeMille* (New York: Simon and Schuster, 2010), 167–68.

120   **Affirming heterosexual pleasure:** John D'Emilio and Estelle Freedman, *Intimate Matters: A History of Sexuality in America*, 2nd ed. (Chicago: University of Chicago Press, 1997), 241.

120   **Despite its conservative happy ending:** Presley and Vieira, *Cecil B. DeMille*, 79.

122   **DeMille admitted to a fellow director:** Josef von Sternberg, *Fun in a Chinese Laundry* (New York: Macmillan, 1965), 37–38.

122   **He told an audience:** Joseph P. Kennedy, ed., *The Story of the Films* (1927, reprinted New York: Jerome S. Ozer, 1971), 124.

122   **Of medium height:** For examples of DeMille's autocratic on-set discipline, see Simon Louvish, *Cecil B. DeMille: A Life in Art* (New York: St. Martin's Press, 2007), 246 and 362.

122   **"Commanding absolute loyalty:** Kevin Brownlow, *The Parade's Gone By . . . : A Vivid, Nostalgic, Immediate Portrait of an Art in the Making* (New York: Knopf, 1968), 206.

122   **Swanson recalled:** Transcript of Gloria Swanson oral history, Harry Ransom Center, Gloria Swanson Papers (269.11), from reel 5, p. 7.

122   **Describing his vanity:** Swanson, *Swanson on Swanson*, 93.

122   **When an assistant, after being bawled out:** Charles Brackett, *"It's the Pictures That Got Small": Charles Brackett on Billy Wilder and Hollywood's Golden Age*, ed. Anthony Slide (New York: Columbia University Press, 2014), 224 (July 21, 1943).

123   **DeMille's friend Josef von Sternberg:** Sternberg, *Fun in a Chinese Laundry*, 37–38.

123   **In the words of his biographer:** Louvish, *Cecil B. DeMille*, 436.

124   **He demanded that Mature lose:** Charles Higham, *Cecil B. DeMille* (New York: Charles Scribner's Sons, 1973), 286–87.

124   **Calling him back:** Higham, *Cecil B. DeMille*, 287.

125   **But Brackett stood his ground:** Brackett, *"It's the Pictures,"* 371 (April 14, 1949).

125   **When asked about this, Wilder sardonically explained:** Ezra Goodman, *The Fifty-Year Decline and Fall of Hollywood* (New York: Simon and Schuster, 1961), 201.

125   **He asked for and received:** Brackett, "*It's the Pictures*," 370–71 (April 12, 1949).

126   **After DeMille's day of shooting had ended:** Ed Sikov, *On Sunset Boulevard: The Life and Times of Billy Wilder* (New York: Hyperion, 1998), 296.

Chapter 10: "Do You Know Bill Holden?"

129   **Viewers were so taken in:** Patricia Bosworth, *Montgomery Clift: A Biography* (New York: Harcourt Brace Jovanovich, 1978), 138.

129   **"His scenes bristled with life":** Bosworth, *Montgomery Clift*, 130.

129   ***Sunset Boulevard,* which Clift:** Bosworth, *Montgomery Clift*, 158.

129   **He claimed he was certain:** Bob Thomas, *Golden Boy: The Untold Story of William Holden* (New York: St. Martin's Press, 1983), 59.

130   **She threatened to kill herself:** Maurice Zolotow, Billy *Wilder in Hollywood* (New York, Putnam, 1977), 161–62. Bosworth, *Montgomery Clift*, 216–24, provides a succinct account of Clift and Holman's tortured relationship. Holman's involvement in the Smith imbroglio is fictionalized in Jean Harlow's 1935 comedy-drama *Reckless* and Douglas Sirk's classic 1950s melodrama *Written on the Wind* (1956). Holman went on to become a civil rights activist and a close friend and financial supporter of Martin Luther King Jr. I learned much about the never-solved mystery of Smith's death from Phil Archer, deputy director of Reynolda House Museum of American Art and curator of the gripping 2023 Reynolda House exhibition *Smith & Libby: Two Rings, Seven Months, One Bullet.*

132   **Even so, Mamoulian was captivated:** Thompson, *Herr Lubitsch Goes to Hollywood*, 25; Capua, *William Holden*, 16.

132   **A friend commented:** Both quotations are from Ezra Goodman, *The Fifty-Year Decline and Fall of Hollywood* (New York: Simon and Schuster, 1961), 254.

132   **In preparation for the part:** Pete Martin, "Hollywood's Most Improbable Star," *Saturday Evening Post* (September 4, 1954).

133   **On the first day of shooting:** Victoria Wilson, *A Life of Barbara Stanwyck: Steel-True, 1907–1940* (New York: Simon and Schuster, 2013), 776–81.

133   **At the end of each day's shoot:** It's been intimated that Stanwyck and Holden were more than friends during the shooting of *Golden Boy*: see Dan Callahan, *Barbara Stanwyck: The Miracle Woman* (Jackson: University Press of Mississippi, 2012), 103.

134   **One picture that did well:** Thanks to Alex Nemerov, author of *Wartime Kiss: Visions of the Moment in the 1940s* (Princeton, NJ: Princeton University Press, 2013), for making this film available to me and sharing his ideas about it.

134   **He said to Holden:** Thomas, *Golden Boy*, 44.

135   **"I told you the army would do you good":** Thomas, *Golden Boy*, 48–50.

135   **To this, Holden added:** Thomas, *Golden Boy*, 58.

136   **"I may not be able to understand Gillis":** Holden from a 1962 interview as quoted in Jay Leyda, ed., *Voices of Film Experience: 1894 to the Present* (New York: Macmillan, 1977), 209.

136   **"Do you know Bill Holden?":** Thomas, *Golden Boy*, 61.

Chapter 11: Locations: Real and Imagined

140   **In filming *Double Indemnity*:** Kevin Starr, *Embattled Dreams: California in War and Peace, 1940–1950* (New York: Oxford University Press, 2002), 239.

142   **Twenty years later:** See Michael Stern and Alan Hess, *Hollywood Modern: Houses of the Stars* (New York: Rizzoli International Publications, 2018), especially 164–69. See also Alan Hess, with photographs by Alan Weintraub, *Forgotten Modern: California Houses, 1940–1970* (Layton, UT: Gibbs Smith, 2007); and Cristina Montes, *Los Angeles Houses* (New York: teNeues, 2002). The most acclaimed photographer of midcentury architectural modernism in Southern California was Julius Shulman, himself a modernist whose work is collected at the Getty Museum. See, for example, Christopher James Alexander, *Julius Shulman's Los Angeles* (Los Angeles: J. Paul Getty Museum, 2011); and Sam Lubell and Douglas Woods, *Julius Shulman Los Angeles: The Birth of a Modern Metropolis* (New York: Rizzoli, 2016); also Michael Stern and Alan Hess, *Julius Shulman: Palm Springs* (New York: Rizzoli, 2008).

142   **In late February:** Charles Brackett, *"It's the Pictures That Got Small": Charles Brackett on Billy Wilder and Hollywood's Golden Age*, ed. Anthony Slide (New York: Columbia University Press, 2014), 364 (February 21, 1949).

143   **Reporting on his death:** See "Architect Ends Life at Office," *Los Angeles Times* (October 24, 1926): 3, and "Funeral for Keim Planned for Today," *Los Angeles Times* (October 25, 1926). See also the brief entry on Keim in Henry F. Whithey and Elsa Whithey, *The Biographical Dictionary of American Architects (Deceased)* (Los Angeles: New Age Publishing, 1956), 334; and the page on Keim in the Pacific Coast Architectural Database (PCAD): https://pcad.lib.washington.edu/person/1965/. For more on the history of the house, see Historic Los Angeles: Wiltshire Boulevard When It was Residential: https://wilshireboulevardhouses .blogspot.com/2013/02/641-south-irving-boulevard-please-see.html.

143   **The house and pool were demolished:** The building, now known as the Harbor Building, was designed by the LA modern architect Claud W. Beelman. David R. Ginsburg defends it aesthetically in a blog post of February 19, 2021, on the Martin Turnbull website: https://martinturnbull .com/2021/02/19/the-norma-desmond-mansion-from-sunset -boulevard-being-demolished-641-s-irving-blvd-los-angeles-1957-2/. See also the Los Angeles Conservancy description at https://www .laconservancy.org/learn/historic-places/harbor-building/. My thanks to Alan Hess for taking me to see the building in person.

144   **Recognizing his leadership skills:** On Dreier's professional biography, see Beverly Heisner, *Hollywood Art: Art Direction in the Days of the Great Studios* (Jefferson, NC: McFarland, 1990), 165–85, especially 180–83; and John Hambley and Patrick Downing, *The Art of Hollywood: Fifty Years of Art Direction* [catalog to a 1979 exhibition by that name at the Victoria and Albert Museum] (London: Thames Television, 1979), 36–43. Dreier summarized his thoughts on set design in Hans Dreier, "Designing the Sets," in Nancy Naumburg, ed., *We Make the Movies* (New York: Norton, 1937), 80–89. See also Léon Barsacq, *Caligari's Cabinet and Other Grand Illusions: A History of Film Design*, rev. and ed. Elliott Stein (Boston: New York Graphic Society, 1976), 62–63. On the symbolic significance of décor in *Sunset Boulevard*, see Charles Affron and Mirella Jona Affron, *Sets in Motion: Art Direction and Film Narrative* (New Brunswick, NJ: Rutgers University Press, 1995), 152–56; and Virginia Wright Wexman, *Creating the Couple: Love, Marriage, and Hollywood Performance* (Princeton, NJ: Princeton University Press, 1993), 149–50.

144   **Orson Welles has sneered:** Undated letter from Orson Welles to John Hambley, as reproduced in Hambley and Downing, *The Art of Hollywood*, 3.

144   **Robert Boyle, who went on to design:** Hambley and Downing, *The Art of Hollywood*, 43.

145   **As film historian John Baxter:** John Baxter, *Hollywood in the Thirties* (New York: A. S. Barnes, 1968), 33–34.

145   **Billy Wilder expressed much the same idea:** Wilder quoted in Neal Gabler, *An Empire of Their Own: How the Jews Invented Hollywood* (New York: Crown, 1988), 187.

Chapter 12: A New Monkey for Norma

148   **Brackett and Wilder, along with "Mac" Marshman:** See Anthony Slide's essay on D. M. "Mac" Marshman Jr., "The Man Behind 'Sunset Boulevard,'" appearing in Leonard Maltin's blog for January 22, 2017: https://leonardmaltin.com/the-man-behind-sunset-blvd/. Marshman was a film reporter for *Life* and *Time* magazines. See, for example, his *Life* profile on Robert Siodmak, Wilder's old friend from Berlin: Donald Marshman, "Close-Up: A Bald Tennessean with a Katzenjammer Accent Is the Newest Top-Flight Director in Hollywood," *Life* (August 25, 1947): 100ff. Sikov writes, "After an early screening of *The Emperor Waltz*, Marshman critiqued the film so extensively and so intelligently that Brackett and Wilder told him they'd ask him to collaborate on something in the future" (Ed Sikov, *On Sunset Boulevard: The Life and Times of Billy Wilder* [New York: Hyperion, 1998], 288). Marshman's subsequent and much less critical review of *The Emperor Waltz* appeared in *Life* on June 21,1948: 72.

148   **The first of these acts:** See Weegee [Arthur Fellig], *Naked City* (New York: Essential Books, 1945).

149   **On the music track:** The musicologist Bryan Gilliam helped me understand the musical instrumentation and key signature for the credit sequence. Waxman borrows the thundering opening chords of the third movement of César Franck's Symphony in D Minor to set the film in motion.

149   **Without shifting its point of view:** For a detailed analysis of this opening sequence, see Nikolaj Feifer, "And So the Story Begins: An Analysis of Selected Opening Shots and Scenes," *P.O.V.*, issue 18 (December 2004): https://pov.imv.au.dk/Issue_18/section_1/artc5A.html. See also Claudia Sternberg, *Written for the Screen: The American Motion-Picture Screenplay as Text* (Tübingen, Germany: Stauffenburg Verlag, 1997), 221.

149   **Andrew Sarris has remarked:** Andrew Sarris in *Sunset Boulevard: A Look Back*, a twenty-five-minute short that is also known as *The Making of* Sunset Boulevard. DVD, Paramount Pictures, 2002.

149   **This is the first time:** Sternberg, *Written for the Screen*, 138–39.

149   **Wilder recognized an inherent problem:** From "Wilder's Tips for Writers," in Cameron Crowe, *Conversations with Wilder* (New York: Knopf, 1999), 357.

150   **The visuals here activate and energize:** In contrast, the literary critic W. J. T. Mitchell contends that Wilder was not successful in avoiding redundancy between the visuals and the voice-over: "The visual narrative seems invariably to illustrate Joe's voice in the most straightforward ways: when he describes something, we see it on the screen; when he narrates an action, it is performed for us; when he recalls a memory or a dream, it is projected in full." Mitchell, *Picture Theory: Essays on Verbal and Visual Representation* (Chicago: University of Chicago Press, 1994), 101–02. Thanks to David Steinberg for bringing this passage to my attention.

151   **"The shot I want":** John Meehan, "Death…Goes to a Party: A Shot from *Sunset Boulevard*," *Society of Art Directors Bulletin* 1, no. 5 (May–June 1951), 6, 7, and 18. See also Herb Lightman, "Old Master, New Tricks," *American Cinematographer* 31, no. 9 (September 1950): 318; and Sikov, *On Sunset Boulevard*, 298–99. As reported by Hedda Hopper in her syndicated column, the underwater tank was on the grounds of Universal-International Pictures. Hopper, Inside Hollywood, dateline June 17, 1949.

153   **In a short feature article:** Aline Mosby, "Down with Toupees! Being Bald O.K., Says Fred Clark," *Hollywood Citizen-News* (December 10, 1949): 13.

154   **Brackett complained in his diary:** Charles Brackett, *"It's the Pictures That Got Small": Charles Brackett on Billy Wilder and Hollywood's Golden Age*, ed. Anthony Slide (New York: Columbia University Press, 2014), 374 (May 9, 1949).

155   **In the scene, later cut:** Sikov, *On Sunset Boulevard*, 290, citing Sidney Skolsky, "Hollywood Is My Beat," *Hollywood Citizen-News* (August 29, 1949).

156   **As the movie critic Richard Corliss:** Richard Corliss, *Talking Pictures: Screenwriters in the American Cinema* (New York: Penguin, 197), 147–48.

157　**And let's not forget:** Brandon French calls the double meaning of *ghost-writer* the film's extended pun: see French, *On the Verge of Revolt: Women in American Film of the Fifties* (New York: Frederick Unger, 1978), 2.

157　**Corliss is right:** On the blending of the modern and the gothic in *Sunset Boulevard*, see Julian Wolfreys, "Hollywood Gothic/Gothic Hollywood: The Example of *Sunset Boulevard*," in Andrew Smith and Jeff Wallace, eds., *Gothic Modernisms* (New York: Palgrave, 2001), 207–24.

159　**Ed Sikov argued:** Ed Sikov, *Laughing Hysterically: American Screen Comedy of the 1950s* (New York: Columbia University Press, 1994), 113; for Sikov's full reading of *Sunset Boulevard* as a comedy, see 88–113.

159　**He mentioned, as an example:** Evelyn Waugh, *The Loved One: An Anglo-American Tragedy* (Boston: Little, Brown, 1948), 24.

160　**When the veteran director of photography:** Maurice Zolotow, *Billy Wilder in Hollywood* (New York, Putnam, 1977), 166.

161　**Written as music for the organ:** On the use of the Toccata and Fugue in horror movies, see Julie Brown, "*Carnival of Souls* and the Organs of Horror," in Neil Lerner, ed., *Music in the Horror Film: Listening to Fear* (New York: Routledge, 2010), 8. On its parodic use in *Sunset Boulevard*, see David P. Neumeyer, *Meaning and Interpretation of Music in Cinema* (Bloomington: University of Indiana Press, 2015), 186. For a succinct history of the piece and its place in popular culture, see Megan Sarno, "How Bach's Toccata and Fugue in D Minor Became Halloween's Theme Song," *The Conversation* (October 30, 2023): https://theconversation.com/how-bachs-toccata-and-fugue-in-d-minor-became-halloweens-theme-song-216523.

162　**Now, in 1949:** Copy of contract between Walter Futter and Paramount Pictures, dated August 25, 1949, in Paramount Pictures production records, Margaret Herrick Library, Academy of Motion Picture Arts and Sciences, folder 4823.

162　**In actuality, the intertitle:** Erich von Stroheim, *Queen Kelly: The Complete Screenplay by Erich von Stroheim*, ed. Bret Wood (Langham, MD: Scarecrow Press, 2002), 57–58.

162　**Dreams, wicked or otherwise:** See Hortense Powdermaker, *Hollywood the Dream Factory: An Anthropologist Looks at the Movie-Makers* (Boston: Little, Brown, 1950), 3–5 and 39. In his diary entry for December 3, 1946, Brackett wrote, "A long talk with Dr. Hortense Powdermaker, who is working on a study of Hollywood from a purely anthropological point of view." Brackett, "*It's the Pictures*," 296. Around this time, in *Magic and Myth of the Movies* (New York: Holt, 1947), xxi, the film critic Parker Tyler, writing on the same theme as Powdermaker but from a different angle, noted that "movies are dreamlike and fantastic."

164 **In his 1965 interviews:** As spoken by Hitchcock in the 2015 documentary *Hitchcock Truffaut* [starting at eight minutes, twenty-eight seconds]; appearing somewhat differently in François Truffaut, with the collaboration of Helen G. Scott, *Hitchcock* (1967; rev. ed. New York: Simon and Schuster, 1984), 183.

164 **It is the brilliance of John Seitz's lighting:** On lighting in *Sunset Boulevard*, see Robert Miklitsch, "Hollywood Noir: Scripting the Death of Romance in *Sunset Boulevard* (1950) and *In a Lonely Place* (1951)," in Alain Silver and James Ursini, eds., *Film Noir: Light and Shadow* (New York: Applause, 2017), 152–59. For Seitz's earlier work on *Double Indemnity*, see Sheri Chinen Biesen, "*Double Indemnity*: A Shadowy Exemplar of Film Noir Visual Style," in Silver and Urbini, 210–17.

164 **As the film historian Jeanine Basinger:** Jeanine Basinger, *Silent Stars* (New York: Knopf, 1999), 235.

164 **Subsequently, Waxman wrote:** Tony Thomas, ed., *Film Score: The View from the Podium* (South Brunswick, NJ: Barnes, 1979), 51–52; see 57 for Waxman's comments on his score for the film. On Waxman, see also William Darby and Jack Du Bois, *American Film Music: Major Composers, Techniques, Trends, 1915–1990* (Jefferson, NC: McFarland, 1990), 116–156, especially 137–41; and Christopher Palmer, *The Composer in Hollywood* (London: Marion Boyers, 1990), 94–117, especially 104–110. Specifically focused on music in *Sunset Boulevard* is Christina Gier, "Music and Mimicry in *Sunset Boulevard* (1950)," in *Anxiety Muted: American Film Music in a Suburban Age*, ed. Stanley C. Pelky II and Anthony Bushard (New York: Oxford University Press, 2015), 31–48. A full-length compact disc recording of the original motion picture score is available from Varese Sarabande on *Franz Waxman: Sunset Boulevard*, Royal Scottish National Orchestra, cond. Joel McNeely, with a booklet containing a 1989 reminiscence about Waxman by Wilder and an analytical essay by film music historian Christopher Husted, who notes that the jazzy sound of *Sunset* shows the influence of Kurt Weil's cabaret music on Waxman.

166 **Film critic Roger Ebert:** Roger Ebert, "The Films of Buster Keaton,"

November 10, 2002: https://www.rogerebert.com/reviews/great-movie -the-films-of-buster-keaton.

167 **As a youth in Vienna:** Kevin Lally, *Wilder Times: The Life of Billy Wilder* (New York: Henry Holt, 1996), 5–6.

167 **That night, Brackett noted:** Brackett, *"It's the Pictures,"* 373 (May 3, 1949).

167 **In her memoir, Swanson recalled:** Gloria Swanson, *Swanson on Swanson* (New York: Random House, 1980), 483.

167 **Keaton received $1,000:** Sam Staggs, *Close-Up on* Sunset Boulevard: *Billy Wilder, Norma Desmond, and the Dark Hollywood Dream* (New York: St. Martin's Press, 2002), 72.

168 **Yet according to film historian Robert Ray:** Robert B. Ray, *A Certain Tendency of the Hollywood Cinema, 1930–1980* (Princeton, NJ: Princeton University Press, 1985), 148.

168 **"For many in the audience":** Jeanine Basinger, *Silent Stars* (New York: Knopf, 1999), 234; Staggs, *Close-Up on* Sunset Boulevard, 153.

168 *Time* **magazine noted as much:** "Cinema: The New Pictures," *Time* 56, no. 7 (August 14, 1950): 82–84; quotation on 83.

169 **Wilder happily accepted:** Zolotow, *Billy Wilder in Hollywood*, 169.

169 **In his personal life, Stroheim:** Zolotow, *Billy Wilder in Hollywood*, 109.

169 **The French filmmaker Jean Renoir:** Renoir, *My Life and My Films*, 165–66.

169 **It was in this context:** Brackett, *"It's the Pictures,"* 374 (May 4, 1949).

170 **Erich told a makeup man:** Brackett, *"It's the Pictures,"* 373 (April 29, 1949).

170 **Nancy Olson Livingston:** Interview with Livingston in the 2008 special feature documentary, *"Sunset Boulevard:* A Beginning," included in various DVD and Blu-ray editions of the film.

170 **On a small platform:** Ten years later, Wilder used "La Cumparsita" for comic purposes in *Some Like It Hot* (1959), when Jack Lemmon's character, dressed in drag and calling himself Daphne, tangos to it with the millionaire he/she hopes to snag; the Latin band is blindfolded, a nod to Stroheim's *The Merry Widow*. Thanks to David Korn for calling "La Cumparsita" to my attention.

172 **Incidentally, Seitz had a strange quirk:** Billy Wilder in 1976 taped interview with Rudy Behlmer, as quoted in Staggs, *Close-Up on* Sunset Boulevard, 120.

173 **As Hitchcock later told:** Truffaut and Scott, *Hitchcock*, 261–62.

Chapter 13: Out with Old, In with the New

177 **"All we earn":** A satiric second song written and performed by Livingston and Evans was cut from the New Year's Eve sequence but was published at the film's release in sheet music form as "The Paramount-Don't-Want-Me Blues." It opens with the lyrics, "I got those Paramount don't want me / Warner Brothers only taunt me / And the others seem to flaunt me blues." The plaintive singer continues, "Though I'm terrific, my talent is immense, / Guess I'll only get in pictures / By paying eighty cents [the then-current price of a ticket]. / Producers' souls are on their shoes." The deleted scene is now included on Paramount's 2012 Blu-ray rerelease of the film. Thanks to Charles Stepczck, Paramount archivist, for showing me the original sheet music.

177 **A couple of scenes hence:** Nancy Olson Livingston, *A Front Row Seat: An Intimate Look at Hollywood, Broadway, and the Age of Glamour* (Lexington: University Press of Kentucky, 2022), 39.

177 **As Raymond Chandler observed:** From chapter 16 of Raymond Chandler, *The Long Goodbye* (Boston: Houghton Mifflin, 1954), 82, reprinted in *Raymond Chandler: Later Novels and Other Writings* (New York: Library of America, 1995), 515.

178 **The total number of swimming pools:** Dorothy Janet Lefevre, "Geographic Aspects of the Private Swimming Pool Industry in Los Angeles," unpublished thesis, master of arts in geography, University of California at Los Angeles (1961): 9–15. See also John L. Springer et al., "The Big Boom in Pools," in *All About Swimming Pools* (New York: Fawcett, 1960), 4-7. On the underlying political meanings of private and public swimming pools, see Jeff Wiltse, *Contested Waters: A Social History of Swimming Pools in America* (Chapel Hill: University of North Carolina Press, 2007).

178 **Joan Didion, who grew up:** Joan Didion, "Holy Water," in *The White Album: Essays* (New York: Farrar, Straus and Giroux, 1979), 64. For a much less optimistic take, see John Cheever's haunting short story "The Swimmer" (1964), in which suburban swimming pools signify spiritual and existential voids. Reprinted in *The Stories of John Cheever* (New York: Vintage International, 2000), 603–12. For a third modern view of swimming pools, see David Hockney's cool, elegant, and vibrant pop-art paintings of residential pools in Los Angeles.

178 **As his ghost points out:** For more on the significance and symbolism of

the Southern California swimming pool, see Christopher Ames, *Movies about the Movies: Hollywood Reflected* (Lexington: University Press of Kentucky, 1997), 194–96.

178   **Here Brackett, Wilder, and Marshman:** See Mark Nelson and Sarah Hudson Bayliss, *Exquisite Corpse: Surrealism and the Black Dahlia Murder* (New York: Bulfinch Press, 2001), for a provocative account of the crime in terms of American surrealism in the 1940s. The American novelist James Ellroy invented a background to the ghastly murder in *The Black Dahlia* (New York: Mysterious Press, 1987).

178   **For the role of Artie:** On Jack Webb, see Sam Staggs, *Close-Up on* Sunset Boulevard: *Billy Wilder, Norma Desmond, and the Dark Hollywood Dream* (New York: St. Martin's Press, 2002), 267–69 and 271–73. See also Gene Sculatti, ed., *The Catalog of Cool* (New York: Warner Books, 1982), 167.

179   **Brackett did not find her:** Charles Brackett, *"It's the Pictures That Got Small": Charles Brackett on Billy Wilder and Hollywood's Golden Age,* ed. Anthony Slide (New York: Columbia University Press, 2014), 364 (March 4, 1949).

179   **Wilder, as Olson recollected:** See Kevin Lally, *Wilder Times: The Life of Billy Wilder* (New York: Henry Holt, 1996), 191; and Livingston, *A Front Row Seat,* 38.

179   **Wilder, who hadn't liked:** Livingston, *A Front Row Seat,* 41.

181   **As Sam Staggs has noted:** Staggs, *Close-Up on* Sunset Boulevard, 46.

181   **Norma is so much more:** On Norma Desmond's depiction as a vampire, see Lucy Fischer, *"Sunset Boulevard: Fading Stars," in Women and Film,* ed. Janet Todd (New York: Holmes, 1988), 97–113, especially 103–04.

182   **When Seitz asked:** Ezra Goodman, *The Fifty-Year Decline and Fall of Hollywood* (New York: Simon and Schuster, 1961), 202.

Chapter 14: Getting Ready for Her Close-Up

183   **"The next day":** Gloria Swanson, *Swanson on Swanson* (New York: Random House, 1980), 483–84.

184   **J. Edgar Hoover:** On the FBI using the gossip columnist to besmirch Chaplin's reputation in the late 1940s, see Charles Maland, *Chaplin and American Culture: The Evolution of a Star Image* (Princeton, NJ: Princeton University Press, 1989), 268 and 273. See also Jennifer Frost, *Hedda Hopper's Hollywood: Celebrity Gossip and American Conservativism* (New York: New York University Press, 2011), 84–88. The animus of both

Hoover and Hopper against Chaplin is well documented in Scott Eyman, *Charlie Chaplin vs. America: When Art, Sex, and Politics Collided* (New York: Simon and Schuster, 2023).

184 **DeMille greets Norma at the door of Stage 18:** See Steven Bingen, with Marc Wanamaker, *Paramount: City of Dreams* (Guilford, CT: Taylor Trade Publishing, 2017), 148.

184 **Art director Hans Dreier:** Bingen, *Paramount*, 138–39.

185 **Brackett proudly explained:** Swanson, *Swanson on Swanson*, 481.

185 **There really was a man:** Ed Sikov, *On Sunset Boulevard: The Life and Times of Billy Wilder* (New York: Hyperion, 1998), 290.

185 **Apparently, he was good at imitating drunks:** Internet Movie Database (IMDb) entry on John "Skins" Miller.

186 **In her autobiography:** Swanson, *Swanson on Swanson*, 482.

186 **As one cultural historian has noted:** Joseph Horowitz, *Artists in Exile: How Refugees from Twentieth-Century War and Revolution Transformed the American Performing Arts* (New York: HarperCollins, 2008), 303.

187 **In the 1970s:** Brandon French, *On the Verge of Revolt: Women in American Film of the Fifties* (New York: Frederick Unger, 1978), 6.

189 **Even MGM's greatest star:** Michaela Krützen, *The Most Beautiful Face on the Screen: The Fabrication of the Star Greta Garbo* (New York: Peter Lang, 1992), 69.

189 **Only years later:** Louis B. Mayer, interview with Gitta Parker and William Woodfield, "What Makes a Star?" in *American Weekly* [a syndicated Sunday supplement magazine] (June 8, 1958): 26. The interview is available on page 42 of a Mayer clippings file on microfiche in the Core Biography Collection of the Academy of Motion Picture Arts and Sciences. My thanks to Genevieve Maxwell, senior reference librarian at the academy's Margaret Herrick Library in Beverly Hills, for locating this difficult-to-find article.

190 **According to Schorr:** Schorr, as quoted by Maurice Zolotow, *Billy Wilder in Hollywood* (New York, Putnam, 1977), 163–64.

190 **They turn a corner:** See Bingen, *Paramount*, 185–87 and 193.

191 **Betty's family history:** Zolotow, *Billy Wilder in Hollywood*, 162, first made the connection to Audrey and her family. Nancy Olson Livingston supported this view; see Nancy Olson Livingston, *A Front Row Seat: An Intimate Look at Hollywood, Broadway, and the Age of Glamour* (Lexington: University Press of Kentucky, 2022), 41.

191   **Nancy Olson Livingston:** Livingston, *A Front Row Seat*, 44.

192   **She had learned an unwritten rule:** Livingston, *A Front Row Seat*, 40.

192   **Wilder, ever the practical joker:** Livingston, *A Front Row Seat*, 42.

192   **A friend of his recalled:** Tom Wood, *The Bright Side of Billy Wilder, Primarily* (Garden City, NY: Doubleday, 1970), 177.

193   **Similarly, even though she acknowledged:** Swanson, *Swanson on Swanson*, 484.

193   **Wilder, who made Fitzgerald's acquaintance:** Gene D. Phillips, *Some Like It Wilder: The Life and Controversial Films of Billy Wilder* (Lexington: University Press of Kentucky, 2010), 16, from an interview Phillips conducted with Howard Hawks in 1973.

193   **Gloria Swanson herself had known Fitzgerald:** Sarah Churchwell, *Careless People: Murder, Mayhem, and the Invention of "The Great Gatsby"* (New York: Penguin, 2014), 103.

193   **Recalling the day Gatsby:** F. Scott Fitzgerald, *The Great Gatsby* (New York: Scribner, 2004), 163. Thanks to Elias Altman for pointing out to me (email July 9, 2020) that Brackett and Wilder "filched the pool-death from *Gatsby*."; see Jeffrey Meyers, "Introduction," Billy Wilder [and Charles Brackett], *"Sunset Boulevard": The Complete Screenplay* (Berkeley and Los Angeles: University of California Press, 1999), xiv–xv; Maureen Corrigan also drew the connection in *So We Read On: How "The Great Gatsby" Came to Be and Why It Endures* (New York: Little, Brown, 2014), 139–40, 150.

195   **Hopper's greatest rival:** George Eells, *Hedda and Louella* (New York: Putnam, 1972).

195   **Years later, the director told an interviewer:** Sikov, *On Sunset Boulevard*, 291. Hopper reported on her cameo appearance in *Sunset Boulevard* in her syndicated column for June 17, 1949.

195   **Marveling in his diary:** Charles Brackett, *"It's the Pictures That Got Small": Charles Brackett on Billy Wilder and Hollywood's Golden Age*, ed. Anthony Slide (New York: Columbia University Press, 2014), 377 (June 14, 1949).

196   **For copyright reasons:** Email from Bryan Gilliam, May 5, 2021.

196   **The reshoot that day:** Sikov, *On Sunset Boulevard*, 300–01.

197   **Wilder waited a few beats:** Swanson, *Swanson on Swanson*, 484.

198   **When a decade after:** Meryle Secrest, *Stephen Sondheim: A Life* (New York: Knopf, 1998), 219. Note that Wilder is also on record calling

opera "an idiotic art form." See Lemon, "The Message in Billy Wilder's Fortune Cookie," 37; reprinted in Robert Horton, ed., *Billy Wilder: Interviews* (Jackson: University Press of Mississippi, 2001), 50.

198   **Wilder's Norma, a high priestess:** On women and madness in grand opera, see Catherine Clément, *Opera, or the Undoing of Women*, trans. Betsy Wang (Minneapolis: University of Minnesota Press, 1988). The feminist musicologist Susan McClary discussed madwomen in opera in "Excess and Frame: The Musical Representation of Madwomen," in her *Feminine Endings: Music, Gender, and Sexuality* (Minneapolis: University of Minnesota Press, 1991), 80–111.

Chapter 15: Reactions to *Sunset*

200   **Midway through the screening:** Wilder loved to tell this story; for one of its many iterations, see Cameron Crowe, *Conversations with Wilder* (New York: Knopf, 1999), 254–55.

201   **Gloria Swanson wrote:** Gloria Swanson, *Swanson on Swanson* (New York: Random House, 1980), 484.

201   **In her syndicated column:** Hedda Hopper, Hedda Hopper's Hollywood, *Los Angeles Times* (April 16, 1950): C1, as quoted in Jennifer Frost, *Hedda Hopper's Hollywood: Celebrity Gossip and American Conservatism* (New York: New York University Press, 2011), 220.

201   **Mayer was not one to hold back:** Bosley Crowther, *Hollywood Rajah: The Life and Times of Louis B. Mayer* (New York: Holt, Rinehart and Winston, 1960), 117.

201   **At an uncharacteristic loss for words:** Otto Friedrich, *City of Nets: A Portrait of Hollywood in the 1940's* (New York: Harper and Row, 1986), 421.

202   **Wilder always maintained:** Kevin Lally, *Wilder Times: The Life of Billy Wilder* (New York: Henry Holt, 1996), 202.

202   **Since its founding:** For a broad array of such films, see Christopher Ames, *Movies about the Movies: Hollywood Reflected* (Lexington: University Press of Kentucky, 1997); Patrick Donald Anderson, *In Its Own Image: The Cinematic Vision of Hollywood* (New York: Arno Press, 1978); Alex Barris, *Hollywood According to Hollywood: How the Cinema World Has Seen Itself in Its Films* (South Brunswick, NJ: Barnes, 1978); Rudy Behlmer and Tony Thomas, *Hollywood's Hollywood: The Movies about the Movies* (Secaucus, NJ: Citadel Press, 1975); Steven Cohan,

Hollywood by Hollywood: The Backstudio Picture and the Mystique of Making Movies (New York: Oxford University Press, 2018); and Richard Meyers, *Movies on Movies: How Hollywood Sees Itself* (New York: Drake Publishers, 1978).

202   **Most of these films underperformed:** According to Behlmer and Thomas, *Hollywood's Hollywood,* 76, when Selznick set out to produce the 1937 version of *A Star Is Born,* he believed that "no movies about the place [Hollywood] had been successful."

202   **He complained to an associate:** Scott Eyman, *Lion of Hollywood: The Life and Legend of Louis B. Mayer* (New York: Simon and Schuster, 2005), 432, citing Dore Schary interview in the Bosley Crowther papers at Brigham Young University.

204   **A biographer later noted:** This and the next quotation are from Gary Carey, *All the Stars in Heaven: Louis B. Mayer's MGM* (New York: Dutton, 1981), 281.

204   **The film industry's most powerful man:** B. P. Schulberg, formerly production head of Paramount and, like Mayer, one of the founders of the movie business, also found himself unemployable because of his age (fifty-seven). In 1949, Schulberg (father of the novelist and screenwriter Budd Schulberg) took out a full-page ad in the trade papers asking for work: "Seems I can't get a job," he wrote. Referencing D. W. Griffith, he wondered, "Must we always wait until a productive pioneer is found dead in some 'obscure Hollywood hotel room' to feel sympathetic?" Quoted in Gene Brown, *Movie Time: A Chronology of Hollywood and the Movie Industry from Its Beginnings to the Present* (New York: Macmillan, 1995), 199.

204   **He spent most of his time:** Eyman, *Lion of Hollywood,* 478; and Neal Gabler, *An Empire of Their Own: How the Jews Invented Hollywood* (New York: Crown, 1988), 413.

205   **The studio launched her:** Stephen Michael Shearer, *Gloria Swanson: The Ultimate Star* (New York: Thomas Dunne Books / St. Martin's Press, 2013), 324.

206   **Mostly, though, reviewers:** On another Hollywood movie about Hollywood that exhibits Cold War paranoia, see Dana B. Polan's monograph on *In a Lonely Place* (London: BFI Publishing, 1993).

206   ***Time* gushed:** "Cinema: The New Pictures," *Time* 56, no. 7 (August 14, 1950): 82–84; quotation on 82.

206 **Writing in *Sight and Sound*:** James Agee, "Comedy's Greatest Era," *Sight and Sound* (November 1950): 283–85; quotations on 283 and 284; reprinted in *James Agee: Film Writing and Selected Journalism* (New York: Library of America, 2005); the review appears on 467–71, the first quotation is on 467, and the next on 469.

206 **The *New York Times*:** Thomas M. Pryor ("TMP"), *New York Times* (August 11, 1950).

207 **The *Los Angeles Times*:** *Los Angeles Times* (August 26, 1950).

207 **Darr Smith, a reporter:** Clipping for August 25, 1950, in Academy of Motion Picture Arts and Sciences, Margaret Herrick Library, *Sunset Boulevard* files, microfiche 1.

207 **Calling *Sunset Boulevard*:** See Dilys Powell, *The Golden Screen: Fifty Years of Films*, ed. George Perry (London: Pavilion Books, 1989), 91, for her August 1950 review of *Sunset Boulevard*.

207 **Echoing the complaint:** Lowell E. Redelings, *Hollywood Citizen-News*, August 29, 1950.

208 **In a review tinged with:** Terry Ramsaye, *Motion Picture Herald*, October 27, 1950, in Margaret Herrick Library, *Sunset Boulevard* Collection, microfiche 2.

208 **Wrote the dyspeptic Chandler:** Raymond Chandler, "Oscar Night in Hollywood," *Atlantic* (March 1948), 26, quoted in Peter H. Brown, *The Real Oscar: The Story Behind the Academy Awards* (Westport, CT: Arlington House, 1981), 20–21. For a more sociological study of the Oscars, see Emanuel Levy, *And the Winner Is . . . : The History and Politics of the Oscar® Awards* (New York: Ungar, 1987). For a recent take on the Academy Awards, see Michael Shulman, *Oscar Wars: A History of Hollywood in Gold, Sweat, and Tears* (New York: Harper, 2023).

209 **Moreover, it was conceived:** Brown, *Real Oscar*, 40.

210 **In retirement, the former mogul boasted:** Eyman, *Lion of Hollywood*, 117, quoting from Academy of Motion Picture Arts and Sciences, Margaret Herrick Library, Core Biography Collection, Louis B. Mayer file, "What Makes a Star?" *American Weekly*, June 8, 1958: 28 [p. 44 of AMPAS microfiche].

210 **As Wilder tartly remarked:** Armand Deutsch, *Me and Bogie: And Other Friends and Acquaintances from a Life in Hollywood and Beyond* (New York: Putnam, 1991), 158.

210 **Film critic Manny Farber:** Manny Farber, "Ugly Spotting" (1950), in *Negative Space: Manny Farber on the Movies* (New York: Praeger, 1971), 61.

212   **A similar curse:** Swanson, *Swanson on Swanson*, 259.

213   **The blacklisted screenwriter Maurice Rapf:** Maurice Rapf, *Back Lot: Growing Up with the Movies* (Lanham, MD: Scarecrow Press, 1999), 155.

214   **In 1953, *Variety* summed up:** Quoted in Barry Norman, *The Story of Hollywood* (New York: New American Library, 1987), 214.

Chapter 16: Whatever Became of . . . ?

216   **The Pacoima crash is famous:** See the front-page, top-of-the-fold account by Gladwin Hill, "7 Die as Planes Collide and One Falls in Schoolyard," *New York Times* (February 1, 1957): 1. See also Cecilia Rasmussen, "The Day Fiery Disaster Fell from the Sky," *Los Angeles Times* (January 28, 2007). The future Chicano rock guitarist and singer Ritchie Valens, author of the 1958 hit song "La Bamba," was a fifteen-year-old student at Pacoima Junior High but was absent that day because he was attending his grandfather's funeral. He developed a severe fear of flying that was not unfounded. Two years after the deadly Pacoima incident, Valens died in a plane crash with fellow rock performers Buddy Holly and The Big Bopper (J. P. Richardson); this was the event immortalized in Don McLean's 1971 hit song "American Pie" about "the day the music died."

217   **In September 1949:** James Agee, "Comedy's Greatest Era," *Life* (September 3, 1949), reprinted in *James Agee: Film Writing and Selected Journalism* (New York: Library of America, 2005), 9–33; quotations from 26–27.

218   **Meanwhile local TV stations:** On Keaton's revived career, see two recent biographies, James Curtis, *Buster Keaton: A Filmmaker's Life* (New York: Knopf, 2022); and Dana Stevens, *Camera Man: Buster Keaton, the Dawn of Cinema, and the Invention of the Twentieth Century* (New York: Atria Books, 2022).

218   **DeMille's right-wing politics:** Scott Eyman, *Empire of Dreams: The Epic Life of Cecil B. DeMille* (New York: Simon and Schuster, 2010), 402, and Sydney Ladensohn Stern, *The Brothers Mankiewicz: Hope, Heartbreak, and Hollywood Classics* (Jackson: University Press of Mississippi, 2019), 230–35. For a thorough account of the DeMille debacle, see the chapter wittily titled "The Night They Drove Old C. B. Down" in Kenneth L. Geist, *Pictures Will Talk: The Life and Films of Joseph L. Mankiewicz* (New York: Scribner's Sons, 1978), 173–206. Victor S. Navasky succinctly

recounted the episode in *Naming Names* (New York: Penguin, 1980), 179–81.

219   **Signing a petition was unusual:** On Wilder's avoidance of political commitment, see, for example, Fred Lawrence Guiles, *Hanging On in Paradise* (New York: McGraw Hill, 1975), 265–66; McBride, *Billy Wilder*, 426; and Ed Sikov, *On Sunset Boulevard: The Life and Times of Billy Wilder* (New York: Hyperion, 1998), 131–32.

219   **Referring to the infamous witnesses:** This is one of Wilder's most widely quoted quips, appearing, with variations, in many books, starting with Ezra Goodman, *The Fifty-Year Decline and Fall of Hollywood* (New York: Simon and Schuster, 1961), 419. See also Tom Wood, *The Bright Side of Billy Wilder, Primarily* (Garden City, NY: Doubleday, 1970), 4; Navasky, *Naming Names*, 79; and Otto Friedrich, *City of Nets: A Portrait of Hollywood in the 1940's* (New York: Harper and Row, 1986), 304.

219   **He jokingly referred to the blacklist:** Goodman, *The Fifty-Year Decline*, 419.

219   **At a heated late-night meeting:** Eyman, *Empire of Dreams*, 235.

219   **William Wyler stood up:** Barry Norman, *The Story of Hollywood* (New York: New American Library, 1987), 218; also Eyman, *Empire of Dreams*, 406.

220   **The movie he made:** In interviews over the years, Steven Spielberg has remarked that witnessing the impressive train wreck in *The Greatest Show on Earth* as a child inspired him to make movies. See, for example, Joseph McBride, *Steven Spielberg: A Biography*, 3rd ed. (London: Faber and Faber, 2012), 60. See also Manohla Dargis, "'The Fabelmans' Review: Steven Spielberg Phones Home," *New York Times* (November 10, 2022); and Susan King, "Steven Spielberg's Lifelong Love Affair with Oscar-Winning 'The Greatest Show on Earth,'" *GoldDerby* (January 18, 2023): https://www.goldderby.com/article/2023/steven-spielbergs-lifelong-love-affair-with-oscar-winning-the-greatest-show-on-earth/.

221   **Nancy Olson Livingston has said:** Nancy Olson Livingston, *A Front Row Seat: An Intimate Look at Hollywood, Broadway, and the Age of Glamour* (Lexington: University Press of Kentucky, 2022), 44.

222   **Yet she prided herself:** Scott Feinberg, "'Sunset Blvd.' Turns 70: Nancy Olson on Wilder, Holden and Why She Walked Away from Stardom," *Hollywood Reporter* (April 19, 2020).

222   **In January 1954, Britain's National Film Theatre:** Karel Reisz, quoted in Arthur Lennig, *Stroheim* (Lexington: University Press of Kentucky, 2000), 459.

223   **The press conference was a disaster:** Lennig, *Stroheim*, 460; *Daily Herald* [London] (January 6, 1954). Nonetheless, he did pose with a coin in his eye, as seen in a photo in the clippings file for Stroheim at the Billy Rose Collection of the New York Public Library of the Performing Arts.

223   **He politely replied:** Harry Ransom Center (HRC), University of Texas at Austin, Gloria Swanson Papers, von Stroheim box 61, folder 1, letter dated December 13, 1955.

223   **Half a year later:** The article in question, undated and untitled but appearing between September and December 1955, was number 36 of a total of 118 pieces that Swanson wrote for UPI. The typescript for the article is in the Harry Ransom Center's Gloria Swanson Papers, box 226, folder 4, article 36. Thanks to Steve Wilson and his staff at the HRC for locating it for me.

223   **Barely able to speak:** *Life* (April 8, 1957): 49.

224   **With death approaching:** Thomas Quinn Curtiss, *Von Stroheim* (New York: Farrar, Straus and Girioux, 1971), 334.

225   **Every morning before leaving his house:** Bob Thomas, *Golden Boy: The Untold Story of William* Holden (New York: St. Martin's Press, 1983), 88.

225   **As Pauline Kael was to describe Holden:** Pauline Kael, "Hot Air," review of *Network, New Yorker* (December 6, 1976): 182; reprinted in Kael, *When the Lights Go Down* (New York: Holt, Rinehart and Winston, 1980), 221–24.

225   **David Thomson was blunter:** David Thomson, *A Biographical Dictionary of Film*, 3rd ed. (New York: Knopf, 1995), 344–45.

225   **Another writer cruelly likened:** Unidentified critic quoted in IMDb mini biography of Holden by I. S. Mowis.

225   **As a young pretty-boy:** Thomas, 44.

225   **Personal troubles beset him:** Thomas, 158–59.

226   **In a short piece on *Sunset Boulevard*:** Pauline Kael, mini review of *Sunset Boulevard* in *Kiss Kiss Bang Bang* (Boston: Little, Brown, 1968), 446–47; quotation on 447.

226   **He also loved the California desert:** Michael Stern and Alan Hess, *Hollywood Modern: Houses of the Stars* (New York: Rizzoli International Publications, 2018), 164–69, quotation on 166.

227   **For his sojourns in Los Angeles:** See Cory Buckner, *A. Quincy Jones* (New York: Phaidon, 2002), 140–45.

227   **Gloria Swanson was once visiting:** Thomas, *Golden Boy*, 210.

227   **In mid-November 1981:** For views of Holden's suite after it was remodeled in 2001, see Kaya Morgan, "William Holden's Santa Monica Penthouse," *Island Connections* (2002): http://www.islandconnections.com/edit/william_holden.htm.

227   **In mourning for his longtime friend:** Quoted in Stephen Farber, "Wilder: A Cynic Ahead of His Time," *New York Times* (December 6, 1981), section 2: 1.

229   **On the day after Christmas:** Hedda Hopper, Hedda Hopper's Hollywood, *Los Angeles Times*, December 27, 1953.

229   **In 1952, for example:** Herbert G. Luft, "A Matter of Decadence," *Quarterly of Film, Radio and Television* 7, no. 1 (Autumn 1952): 58–66; first quotation from 63, second from 62.

229   **Brackett led off his refutation:** Charles Brackett, "A Matter of Humor," *Quarterly of Film, Radio and Television* 7, no. 1 (Autumn 1952): 66–69; quotations from 66–67.

230   **In 1962, Wilder returned the favor:** Kevin Lally, *Wilder Times: The Life of Billy Wilder* (New York: Henry Holt, 1996), 206–07.

230   **Brackett suffered a debilitating stroke:** Sikov, *On Sunset Boulevard*, 513.

230   **During their conversation:** Garson Kanin, *Hollywood: Stars and Starlets, Tycoons and Flesh Peddlers, Movie-Makers and Moneymakers, Frauds and Geniuses, Hopefuls and Has-Beens, Great Lovers and Sex Symbols* (New York: Viking Press, 1974), 178.

230   **The conversation ended:** Kanin, *Hollywood*, 180.

231   **In 1956, when an interviewer:** John Gillett, "Wilder in Paris," *Sight and Sound* 26, no. 3 (Winter 1956): 143.

232   **On another occasion, he said:** Wilder quoted in André Balazs, ed., *Hollywood Handbook* (New York: Universe Publishing / Rizzoli, 1996), 45.

233   **It was a sad, clumsy film:** On the pairing of *Sunset Boulevard* and *Fedora*, see Gerd Gemünden, *A Foreign Affair: Billy Wilder's American Films* (New York: Berghahn, 2008), 76–99. The British novelist Jonathan Coe imagined the filming of *Fedora* through the eyes of a footloose young woman in *Mr. Wilder and Me* (New York: Viking/Penguin, 2020).

233   **The honors began rolling in:** Wilder in conversation with producer David Brown, as quoted in Charlotte Chandler, *Nobody's Perfect: Billy*

Wilder, a Personal Biography (New York: Simon and Schuster, 2002), 301; see also 303.

234   **Cineastes all, they considered Wilder:** See, for example, Andrew Sarris, *The American Cinema: Directors and Directions, 1929–1968* (New York: Dutton, 1968).

234   **The prestigious young Broadway director Mike Nichols:** Mark Harris, *Mike Nichols: A Life* (New York: Penguin Press, 2021), 156.

234   **When Wilder entered his nineties:** Cameron Crowe, *Conversations with Wilder* (New York: Knopf, 1999).

234   **In 1970, when he was sixty-four:** Maurice Zolotow, *Billy Wilder in Hollywood* (New York, Putnam, 1977), 17.

234   **Billy, who had begun buying modern art:** Sikov, *On Sunset Boulevard*, 582–84; see also Malcolm N. Carter, "Great Private Collections: The Obsessions of Billy Wilder," *SR* (*Saturday Review*), December 1980: 60–64; and *A Selection of Paintings, Drawings, Collages and Sculpture from the Collection of Mr. and Mrs. Billy Wilder*, exhibition catalog for the Art Gallery of the University of California-Santa Barbara, intro. David Gebhard (University of California–Santa Barbara, October 11 through November 13, 1966).

235   **Accepting an award from the American Film Institute:** At the start of his acceptance speech for the American Film Institute (AFI) life achievement award in 1986, Wilder recalled that this is what Samuel Goldwyn, the master of malapropism, once told him when he was in a low mood after his latest picture flopped.

235   **Writing three years before:** Sikov, *On Sunset Boulevard*, ix.

235   **Swanson recalled in her autobiography:** Gloria Swanson, *Swanson on Swanson* (New York: Random House, 1980), 259.

235   **She did make one film:** Lawrence Quirk, *The Films of Gloria Swanson* (Secaucus, NJ: Citadel Press, 1984), 246, quoting from David Chierichetti, "Gloria Swanson Today," *Film Fan Monthly* (February 1975): 8.

236   **Even this high-powered cast:** Quirk, *The Films of Gloria Swanson*, 247–49.

236   **In 1952, she hired the newly minted:** See *Boulevard! A Hollywood Story*, a 2021 documentary by Jeffrey Schwarz about the failed attempt of Stapley, Hughes, and Swanson to convert *Sunset Boulevard* into a stage musical.

236   **In the early 1990s:** George Perry, *"Sunset Boulevard": From Movie to Musical*, foreword by Andrew Lloyd Webber (New York: Henry Holt, 1993).

236 **When he saw it:** Wilder quoted in Livingston, *A Front Row Seat*, 44.

237 **She bantered on air:** Tricia Welsch, *Gloria Swanson: Ready for Her Close-Up* (Jackson: University Press of Mississippi, 2013), 354.

237 **Even as early as the 1930s:** George Chauncey, *Gay New York: Gender, Urban Culture, and The Making of the Gay Male World, 1890–1940* (New York: Basic Books, 1994), 251–52; see also "Sepia Gloria Swanson and Sepia Mae West," as provided on the QMH (Queer Music Heritage) website: https://queermusicheritage.com/nov2014sepia.html.

237 **In a 1974 episode:** Carol Burnett, *In Such Good Company: Eleven Years of Laughter, Mayhem, and Fun in the Sandbox* (New York: Crown Archetype, 2016), 211–13, comments on Swanson's guest appearance on *The Carol Burnett Show* on September 29, 1973. In a recurring comedy sketch called "Sunnyset Boulevard," Burnett played "Nora Desmond" and Harvey Korman her servant Max. The movie has been parodied numerous times in popular culture, and its signature line, "All right, Mr. DeMille, I'm ready for my close-up," or simply, "I'm ready for my close-up," has entered the vernacular, so much so that people who say it are often unaware of its origins.

237 **Taping a segment:** "Swanson Discusses Sex after 70," *Time* 108, no. 16 (October 18, 1976): 54.

Epilogue: The Legacy of *Sunset Boulevard*

240 **Looking back:** Roger Ebert, retrospective view of *Sunset Boulevard*, dated June 27, 1999: https://www.rogerebert.com/reviews/great-movie-sunset-boulevard-1950.

240 **A week after Joe Biden clinched:** Maureen Dowd, "Goodbye, Golden Goose," *New York Times* (November 15, 2020), section SR: 9.

240 **His obsession with it:** Stephanie Grisham, *I'll Take Your Questions Now: What I Saw at the Trump White House* (New York: Harper, 2021), 76.

241 **In 2022, the business reporter:** Timothy L. O'Brien, "Trump's Final Scene Didn't Go According to Script," *Bloomberg* (June 28, 2022). See also Olivia Nuzzi, "The Final Campaign: Inside Donald Trump's Sad, Lonely, Thirsty, Broken, Basically Pretend Run for Reelection (Which Isn't to Say He Can't Win)," *New York* (December 23, 2022); and Karen Heller, "The Newly Relevant Relationship between Trump and 'Sunset Boulevard,'" *Washington Post* (December 30, 2022), style section; the

piece is subtitled, "As the former president's misfortunes mount, comparisons to Norma Desmond and the movie he loves seem increasingly apt."

241   **In a book on women, aging, and sexuality:** Lois W. Banner, *In Full Flower: Aging Women, Power, and Sexuality: A History* (New York: Knopf, 1992), 30–55.

241   **After viewing the movie:** Letter dated November 22, 1950, Harry Ransom Center, University of Texas at Austin, Swanson Series I, box 7, folder 7, fan mail.

242   **The seventeenth-century French aphorist:** François de La Rochefoucauld, Maxim 26: *Le soleil ni la mort ne se peuvent regarder en face* ("You cannot stare straight into the face of the sun, or death"). See title page of Irvin D. Yalom, *Staring at the Sun: Overcoming the Terror of Death* (San Francisco: Jossey-Bass, 2008). The maxim also translates as "Neither the sun nor death can be looked at steadily" in La Rochefoucauld, *Maxims*, trans. and introduction by Leonard Tancock (New York: Penguin, 1959), 21.

242   **In a poem of great poignancy:** Gerard Manley Hopkins, "The Leaden Echo and the Golden Echo" (1882). This poem was a favorite of Elizabeth Taylor, once considered among the most beautiful women in the world. She asked that it be read at her funeral. See Kate Andersen Brower, *Elizabeth Taylor: The Grit and Glamour of an Icon* (New York: Harper, 2022), 425.

PHOTO CREDITS

1, 2, 33, 37: Photofest

3–8: Paramount Pictures/Photofest

9: WPIX/Photofest

10: Universal Film Manufacturing Company/Photofest

11–19, 21–32, 34, 35: Paramount

20: Metro-Goldwyn-Mayer/Photofest

36: United Artists/Photofest

INDEX

A

Abbott and Costello Meet Frankenstein (film), 159

Abraham Lincoln (film), 82

Absent-Minded Professor, The (film), 220

absolution-seeking opportunist theme, in Wilder's films, 66

Academy Awards (Oscars)

of 1951, 208, 210–213

benefits of to film industry, 209–210

for "Buttons and Bows", 176

Chandler's critique of, 208–209

for *The Greatest Show on Earth*, 220

for Griffith, 83

for Head, 98

for Holden in *Stalag 17*, 224

for *Little Women*, 43

for *The Lost Weekend*, x, 75

for Mayer, 210

nomination for Holden in *Network*, 226

nomination for *Ninotchka*, x, 59

nomination for *A Star Is Born*, 46

nominations for Clift, 129

nominations for Swanson, 36, 211–212

for *Sunset Boulevard*, 210–213

for *The Ten Commandments*, 228

for *Titanic*, 228

winners of in 1950s, 214

Ace in the Hole (film), 231

Adler, Alfred, 6

Admirable Crichton, The (Barrie), 30

Adorno, Theodor, 16

Affairs of Anatol, The (film), 120

Africa Speaks (film), 162

Agee, James, 75, 206, 217

aging

female, depiction of in film, 210–211, 213

as theme in *Sunset Boulevard*, 239–242

alcoholism, 68, 71–72, 225

Alcott, Louisa May, 43

Aldridge, John W., 41

Algonquin Round Table, 41–42, 44

All about Eve (film), 98, 210, 212, 213

All My Sons (film), 156
All the King's Men (film), 186
Altman, Robert, 200
American dream, 163
American International Pictures, 218
Anderson, Bronco Billy, 3
Andy Hardy film series, 203
Ankerson, Ardis (Brenda Marshall), 134, 135, 192, 225
Anna Boleyn (film), 54
Anna Christie (film), 59
anonymity, studios enforcing, 21
anti-ornamental aesthetics, 8, 12
Apartment, The (film), 233
Arab-Israeli war, 81–82
architecture
   minimalism in, 8–9
   residential modernism, 141–142, 226–227
   revivalist, 141
Arise, My Love (film), 59
art department heads, 144–145
Arthur, Jean, 79–80
Artie character. *See* Green, Artie
Arts & Architecture (magazine), 142
Ashby, Hal, 200
assembly-line approach to screenwriting, 45–46
Austria
   The Death Mills screenings in, 73–74
   Wilder's time in, 6–9
Awful Truth, The (film), 56

B
Bacall, Lauren, 69–70, 219
Bach, Johann Sebastian, 161

Bad Seed (*Mauvaise Graine*) film, 13–14, 61
Balaban, Barney, 81
Ball, Lucille, 142
Ball of Fire (film), 59–60, 157
Banner, Lois, 241
Bardot, Brigitte, 236
Barnett, Lincoln, 63
Barrie, James M., 30
Barrios, Richard, 36
Barrymore, John, 212
Basinger, Jeanine, 164, 168
Battleship Potemkin (film), 222
Baxter, Anne, 212, 213
Baxter, John, 145
Bazin, André, 106
Beach Blanket Bingo (film), 218
Beatles, the, 221
Beauchamp, Cari, 221
beauty
   gendered norms of, 241–242
   manufacture of, 189
   Norma's regimen in *Sunset Boulevard*, 188–190
Beckett, Samuel, 218
Beedle, Bob, 134
Beedle, William, Jr. *See* Holden, William
Beedle, William, Sr., 131
Beek, Neill, 207
Beery, Wallace, 22–24, 25, 98
Belgian Museum of Fine Arts, 222
Bellini, Vincenzo, 198
Benchley, Robert, 41
Bergman, Ingmar, 200
Bergman, Ingrid, 173
Berkeley, Busby, 14

Berle, Milton, 90

Berlin, Germany
    Wilder's life in, 9–13
    Wilder's return to after World War
        II, 72–73

Berliner Zeitung am Mittag (B.Z.)
    daily, 11

Best Years of Our Lives, The (film), 218

Betty character. *See* Schaefer, Betty

Big Sleep, The (Chandler), 67

Big Sleep, The (film), 69–70

Billy the Kid, 3

Biograph Studios, 21

Birds, The (film), 145

birth control, 26–27

Birth of a Nation, The (film), 82, 104

Black Cat, The (film), 161

black comedy, 200

Black Dahlia (Elizabeth Short), 178

blacklisting of communist
        sympathizers, 124, 156,
        194–195, 219

bleak endings in films, 198

Blind Husbands (film), 104–105

Blue Angel, The (film), 17, 92

Bluebeard's Eighth Wife (film), 53–54,
        56–58

Body and Soul (film), 155–156

Bogart, Humphrey, 69–70, 219, 232

Boleslawski, Richard, 112

Boone, Pat, 229

Born Yesterday (film), 211, 212,
        224, 230

Boulevard! (musical version of *Sunset
        Boulevard*), 223, 236

Bow, Clara, 25

Bowker, Virginia, 95

Boyer, Charles, 61

Boyle, Robert, 144–145

Brackett, Charles. *See also Sunset
        Boulevard*
    and assembly-line approach to
        screenwriting, 45–46
    background and childhood of,
        39–40
    career after *Sunset Boulevard*,
        228–231
    death of, 230
    death of wife, 80–81
    early screenwriting endeavors of,
        42–44
    and F. Scott Fitzgerald, 193
    and formation of Screen Writers
        Guild, 48–49
    novels by, 44
    opinion of DeMille, 122–123, 125
    Parsons's words to, 195
    participation in Algonquin Round
        Table, 41–42
    partnership with Wilder
        and death of D. W. Griffith,
            82–84
        The Emperor Waltz, x, 77–79, 185
        A Foreign Affair, x, 79–80, 92
        formation of, 51–52, 53, 56–58
        Hold Back the Dawn, 61, 117, 134
        The Lost Weekend adaptation,
            ix–x, 65–66, 71–72,
            75–76, 140
        The Major and the Minor, 61–62,
            157, 180–181
        relationship after breakup,
            229–230
        rise to fame, 58–60

Brackett, Charles. *See also Sunset Boulevard* (cont.)
    search for actress to play Norma, 85–88, 91–96
    split during *Double Indemnity* adaptation, 67
    "swimming pool story" idea, xiii, 84, 85
    tensions in, 60, 63–64, 75–76, 81–82
    Wilder's shift from writer to writer-director, 60–62
    tension before filming *Sunset Boulevard*, x–xi
    theater reviews by, 40–41
    vanitas theme explored by, 3–4
    work with Leisen, 31
Brackett, Edgar, 40
Brackett, Elizabeth Barrows Fletcher, 44, 72, 80–81, 228–229
Brackett, Lillian "Buff" Fletcher, 228–229, 230
Brando, Marlon, 130–131
Breezy (film), 226
Bride of Frankenstein, The (film), 164
Bridge on the River Kwai, The (film), 214, 225
bridge scene, *Sunset Boulevard*, 166–168
Bringing Up Baby (film), 56
Briskin, Sam, 14
Bronson Gate (Paramount studios), 115
Brooks, Louise, 25
Browning, Tod, 158
Brownlow, Kevin, 122
Buddy Buddy (film), 233

Buffalo Bill, 2–3
Bull, Clarence Sinclair, 20
Burger, Hanuš, 73
Buster Keaton Story, The (film), 218
"Buttons and Bows" (Livingston and Evans), 176–177
B.Z. (*Berliner Zeitung am Mittag*) daily, 11

C
Cabinet of Dr. Caligari, The (film), 12, 17
Caged (film), 212
Cain, James M., 66–67
California ranch style, 141
Calleia, Joseph, 154
Campbell, Alan, 46, 47
Canadian Pacific (film), xii
capitalism, criticism of, 51
Capitol Records, 221
Capra, Frank, 14, 56, 166
Carol Burnett Show, The (TV show), 237
Carr, Larry, 28–29
Carson, Johnny, 237
Carson, Robert, 46
Casablanca (film), 62
"Case Study Houses" project, 142
Cavell, Stanley, 56, 58
Cerf, Bennett, 51
Chandler, Raymond, 71, 177
    alcoholism of, 68, 72
    collaboration on *Double Indemnity*, 67–70
    opinion of Oscars, 208–209
    on screenwriters in Hollywood, 46
Channing, Carol, 237

Chaplin, Charlie, 3, 35
    as icon of silent cinema, 167
    Limelight, 217
    Norma's imitation of, 183, 184
    relationship with Swanson, 22
Chateau Marmont, 15–16
Cheat, The (film), 122
Chekhov's Gun, 158
Chevalier, Maurice, 55
Christie, Agatha, 232
cinema. *See* Hollywood
CinemaScope, 90
Citizen Kane (film), 41, 105, 165
City Lights (film), 222
Clark, Fred, 152–153, 154
Clift, Montgomery, 128–130, 135, 190
close-ups, 172–173, 189
Cohan, Steven, 94–95
Cohn, Harry, 14, 133, 134, 135
Colbert, Claudette, 37
    in *Arise, My Love*, 59
    in *Bluebeard's Eighth Wife*, 54,
        57–58
    in *It Happened One Night*, 14
    in *Midnight*, 58–59
Cold War, 205–206
Coleman, Buddy, 140–141, 142
Collins, Floyd, 231
Columbia Pictures, 14, 133
comebacks, x, 19–20, 21
comedies of manners, 55
comedy, *Sunset Boulevard* as, 159,
        199–200
"Comedy's Greatest Era" (Agee), 217
communist sympathizers, blacklisting
        of, 124, 156, 194–195, 219
concentration camps, Nazi, 73–74

*Connecticut Yankee in King Arthur's
        Court, A* (film), 185
contraception, 26–27
Conversations with Wilder
        (Crowe), 234
Cooper, Gary, 122, 142, 219
    in *Ball of Fire*, 60
    in *Bluebeard's Eighth Wife*, 54,
        57–58
    in *Love in the Afternoon*, 232
Cooper, Merian C., 43
Coppola, Francis Ford, 233
Corliss, Richard, 156–157
cosmetic surgery, 29, 189
Crawford, Broderick, 211, 212
Crawford, Joan, 25
crime story, *Sunset Boulevard* as,
        148–149, 156, 200–201
crime-scene chaos in *Sunset
        Boulevard*, 193–194
Cronkite, Walter, 90
Crosby, Bing, x, 77, 78, 95
Crowe, Cameron, 234
Crusades, The (film), 123
Cukor, George, 42, 43, 88, 91
Curtis, Tony, 5, 232
cutting-in-camera, 61–62
cynicism
    atmosphere of in Vienna, 7–8
    towards love, in works by Wilder,
        4–6

D

"Dance of the Seven Veils" (Strauss),
    196
Danger Girl, The (film), 24–25
Darrieux, Danielle, 13

Davis, Bette, 37, 209, 210, 213
de Havilland, Olivia, 190
De Sica, Vittorio, 139–140, 236
Dean, James, 143
Death Mills, The (Die Todesmühlen)
    film, 65, 73–74, 80
D'Emilio, John, 120
DeMille, Cecil B., 83
    debacle at directors guild, 218–220
    description of Swanson by, 20–21
    exploitation of racial themes by,
        121–122
    Famous Players–Lasky, 119–120
    The Greatest Show on Earth, 214, 220
    marital comedies by, 26–27, 120–121
    personality of, 122–123
    politics of, 124–125
    relationship with Swanson, 117,
        118–119
    Samson and Delilah, 123–124, 184,
        185, 218
    sexy religious costume dramas by,
        123–124, 166
    in *Sunset Boulevard*
        audience reaction to, 218
        casting of, 118, 121
        Norma's visit to DeMille, 115–117,
            125–126, 184, 185–187
        Swanson's work with, 25–27, 30–31
    The Ten Commandments, 220,
        228
Dempsey, Jack, 42
Desmond, Norma (character in
    Sunset Boulevard)
    as avatar for Wilder, x
    as critique of views of women in
        modern society, 208

    in fifth act
        beauty regimen scene, 188–190
        crime-scene chaos, 194
        Norma's final descent of
            staircase, 195–198
    in first act
        Joe's arrival at mansion, 158,
            159–160
        monkey funeral scene, 160–161
    focus on writing career of, 39
    in fourth act
        Norma's performance for Joe,
            150, 183–184
        Norma's visit to DeMille, 115–117,
            125–126, 184, 185–187
    as inspiring compassion and
        sympathy, 72
    and location shooting, 138
    mansion of
        design of interiors, 144–147
        location shooting in, 137–138,
            140–144
    overview, ix
    resonance with modern audiences,
        240–242
    search for actress to play, 85–88,
        91–93
    in second act
        bridge scene, 166–168
        men's shop scene, 127
        scene of Joe and Norma
            watching old movies, 161–166
    similarities to Swanson, 19–20, 37
    similarity to Donald Trump,
        240–241
    Swanson's influence on
        development of, 93–96, 182

in third act
  Norma's New Year's party scene,
    170–174
  scene in Norma's bedroom,
    180–182
and transactional nature of love, 5
wardrobe design for, 98–100
Devil's Pass Key (film), 105
DGA (Directors Guild of America),
    218–220
Diamond, I. A. L. ("Izzy"), 232–233, 234
Dick Cavett Show, The (TV
    show), 238
Didion, Joan, 178
Die Fackel (*The Torch*) journal, 7
Die Stunde (*The Hour*) tabloid, 6–7
Die Todesmühlen (*The Death Mills*)
    film, 65, 73–74, 80
Dietrich, Marlene, 17, 92, 232
Dior, Christian, 98
Directors Guild of America (DGA),
    218–220
divorce, 26–27, 120–121
*Dr. Strangelove, or How I Learned to
    Stop Worrying and Love the
    Bomb* (film), 200
Dr. Jekyll and Mr. Hyde (film), 161
Don't Change Your Husband (film), 26,
    120–121
Doss, Erika, 70
Double Indemnity (Cain), 66–67
Double Indemnity (film), ix–x, 65–70,
    130, 140, 142
Douglas, Kirk, 231
Dowd, Maureen, 240
Dracula (film), 158
Dracula (Stoker), 157

Dragnet series, 178–179
dreams, Hollywood and, 162–163
Dreier, Hans, 144–146, 152, 155,
    184–185, 213
Dunne, Dunne, 48

E
Eames, Charles, 9, 142
Eames, Ray, 9, 142
Eastwood, Clint, 226
Ebert, Roger, 166, 240
Eisenstein, Sergei, 109
Eliot, T. S., 106
Emperor Waltz, The (film), x,
    77–79, 185
Entirely Surrounded (Brackett), 44
Essanay film studio, 21–23
Evans, Ray, 175–177
Executive Suite (film), 224
exploitation films, 218
expressionism, German, 12

F
facial beauty, manufacture of, 189
Fairbanks, Douglas, 35, 87
fame, fleeting nature of, 3–4,
    239–240
family planning, 26–27
Famous Players–Lasky, 119–120. *See
    also* Paramount Pictures
fan magazines, 20
Farber, Manny, 210–211
Father of the Bride (film), 212
Father Takes a Wife (film), xi, 89
Fedora (film), 226, 233
Fellig, Arthur (Weegee), 148
Fellini, Federico, 200

female aging, depiction of in film, 210–211, 213. *See also Sunset Boulevard*

Film (film), 218

film industry. *See* Hollywood

film noir, 70, 156, 201, 204

first-person narration, 200–201

Fitzgerald, F. Scott, 44, 72, 193–194

Fitzgerald, Zelda, 193

Five Graves to Cairo (film), 62

flappers (modern girls), 24–25, 26, 29

Flynn, Errol, 95, 134

Fontaine, Joan, 95

Foolish Wives (film), 106–107, 108

Footlight Parade (film), 14

For Better, for Worse (film), 27, 120

Force of Arms (film), 220

Ford, John, 218

Foreign Affair, A (film), x, 79–80, 92

Forgotten Paradise (film), 144

Four Horseman of the Apocalypse, The (film), 172

France

    von Stroheim's time in, 113

    Wilder's time in, 13–14

Frankenstein (Shelley), 157

Franz Josef I (Austro-Hungarian emperor), 3, 8, 78

Freeman, Estelle, 120

French, Brandon, 187

French New Wave, 200

Freud, Sigmund, 6–7, 110

Friedrich, Otto, 10

From Here to Eternity (film), 129, 214

Front Row Seat, A (Olson Livingston), 221–222

Funny Thing Happened on the Way to the Forum, A (film), 218

Futter, Walter, 162

G

Gable, Clark, 14

Garbo, Greta, 16

    manufacture of beauty of, 189

    in *Ninotchka*, x, 59

    Oscar nominations for, 36, 212

Garfield, John, 130, 136

Garroway, Dave, 237

Gaynor, Janet, 35

gendered beauty norms, 241–242

German silent cinema, 12–13

German-language salon, 16–17

Germany

    The Death Mills screenings in, 73–74

    Wilder's life in, 9–13

    Wilder's return to after World War II, 72–73

Germany—Year Zero (film), 79

Getty, J. Paul, 143

Ghost Breakers, The (film), 159

Gillis, Joe (character in *Sunset Boulevard*)

    choice of actor to play, 128–131, 135–136

    in first act

        arrival at mansion, 156–160

        Bel-Air Golf Club scene, 155–156

        chase scene, 156

        monkey funeral scene, 160–161

        narrative setup in, 152–154

        opening sequence, 149–151

        rats in swimming pool scene, 161

Schwab's Pharmacy scene,
154–155
focus on writing career of, 38, 39
in fourth act
Joe's visit to Betty's cubicle,
184–185
Norma's performance for Joe,
183–184
Holden's worries about role, xi
importance to story, 94
as kept man, 127–128
and location shooting, 137–138
overview, ix
Gillis, Joe (character in *Sunset
Boulevard*)
scenes with Betty in fifth act,
190–192
in second act
men's shop scene, 127–128,
168–169
scene of Joe and Norma
watching old movies, 161–166
similarities to Wilder, 15
in third act
Artie Green's New Year's Eve
party, 175–181
move from apartment to
mansion, 169–170
Norma's New Year's party scene,
170–174
scene in Norma's bedroom,
180–182
voice-over narration by, 149–150,
200–201
Gish, Dorothy, 189
Gish, Lillian, 29–30, 189
glamour photography, 20–21, 31

Gloria Swanson Hour (TV show), 89
Gloria Swanson Productions, 35–36,
110–113
Godard, Jean-Luc, 200
Gold Diggers of 1933 (film), 14
Golden Boy (film), xi, 131–134,
153, 154
Golden Globes ceremony, 208
Goldwyn, Samuel, 50, 51, 82–83, 95,
119–120
Gone with the Wind (film), 45, 59, 78,
163, 218
"Good Will Ambassador" for
Paramount, Swanson as, 205
Goodman, Ezra, 82
Goodrich, Frances, 49
Gough, Lloyd, 155–156
Grande Illusion, La (film), 113, 169, 222
Granger, Stewart, 213
Grant, Cary, 173
Great Gatsby, The (Fitzgerald),
193–194
Greatest Show on Earth, The (film),
214, 220
Greed (film), 107–109, 222
Green, Artie (character in *Sunset
Boulevard*), 128, 175,
178–179, 180
Greene, Graham, 79
Griffin, Merv, 237
Griffith, D. W., 35, 121, 189
The Birth of a Nation, 104
later life and death of, 82–84
True Heart Susie, 29–30
Grisham, Stephanie, 240–241
Gropius, Walter, 9
Gruen, Victor, 9

H

Habsburg, Otto von, 3–4

Hackett, Albert, 49

Haggard, H. Rider, 213

Haines, Billy, 95

Hall, Mordaunt, 36

Hamilton, Ian, 48

Hammerstein, Oscar, II, 18

Hammett, Dashiell, 49

Harlow, Jean, 37

Harold and Maude (film), 200

Harrison, Doane, 61, 180–181

Hart, Lorenz, 130

Hartwig, Hella, 13, 14

haunted house elements in *Sunset Boulevard*, 156–157, 158–159

Hawks, Howard, 56, 69, 128, 157

Hays, William, 33

Hays Office (self-censorship bureau), 33, 67, 69

Head, Edith, 34, 93, 96–99, 123, 179

Hearst, William Randolph, 195

Heerman, Victor, 43

Heiress, The (film), 129, 190, 205

Hellman, Lillian, 49

Hepburn, Audrey, 224, 232

Hepburn, Katharine, 43

Here Comes the Groom (film), 186

Hernandez, Helen, 63

Hess, Alan, 227

Heston, Charlton, 220, 224

Hetman, John (Hog-eye), 185–186

Hickock, Wild Bill, 3

High Noon (film), 214

Higham, Charles, 6

His New Job (film), 22

Hiss, Alger, 206

Hitchcock, Alfred, 121, 145

bleak endings in films of, 198

as implicating viewers in protagonist behavior, 197

notion of pure cinema, 164

Notorious, 173

Hitler, Adolf, 13, 14, 58

Hofmannsthal, Hugo von, 7

Hold Back the Dawn (film), 61, 117, 134

Holden, William, 142. *See also* Gillis, Joe

attempt to make play on Olson, 192

in *Born Yesterday*, 211

career after *Sunset Boulevard*, 220–222, 224–227

choice as actor to play Joe Gillis, 135–136

death of, 227–228

drunken driving incident, 225–226

in *Fedora*, 226, 233

in *Golden Boy*, 131–134, 153, 154

in *I Wanted Wings*, 134

limited success of, 134, 135

in *Sabrina*, 224, 232

tension before filming of *Sunset Boulevard*, ix, xi

time in army during World War II, 134–135

Holliday, Judy, 211–212, 213, 230

Hollywood

assembly-line approach to screenwriting, 45–46

avoidance of social issues in 1950s, 213–214

criticism of in *What Makes Sammy Run?*, 50–51

depictions of in *Sunset Boulevard*,
83–84, 187, 202–203, 240
effect of television industry on,
89–91
history of, 119–120
location shooting for *Sunset
Boulevard* in, 138–139
manufacture of beauty in, 189
opposition to Screen Writers Guild
in, 47–48, 49–50
self-censorship bureau, 33, 67, 69
state of film industry in 1948, 81
Sunset Boulevard as love letter to,
192–193
Swanson as "Good Will
Ambassador", 205
tension in before filming of *Sunset
Boulevard*, xii–xiii
Wilder's relocation to, 14–17
Hollywood (Kanin), 230
"Hollywood story" ("swimming pool
story") idea, xiii, 83–84, 85.
See also Sunset Boulevard
Hollywood the Dream Factory
(Powdermaker), 162–163
Holman, Libby, 129–130
Holocaust, 65–66, 73–74
Hoover, J. Edgar, 184, 206
Hope, Bob, 95, 142, 159, 176
Hopkins, Gerard Manley, 242
Hopper, Hedda, 91, 184, 194–195,
201
horror film, *Sunset Boulevard* as,
156–157, 158–159
Hour, The (*Die Stunde*) tabloid, 6–7
House Un-American Activities
Committee (HUAC), 156, 219

How to Stuff a Wild Bikini (film), 218
Howard, Sidney, 46, 48
Hughes, Dickson, 236
Hurrell, George, 20
Huston, John, 219
Hutton, Betty, 95

I

I Wanted Wings (film), 134
I'm No Angel (film), 86
Irma la Douce (film), 233
Irving G. Thalberg Memorial
Award, 15
Isotta Fraschini, in *Sunset Boulevard*,
115, 116
It Happened One Night (film), 14, 56
It's a Wonderful Life (film), 166
"I've Grown Accustomed to Your
Face" (Lerner and Loewe), 221

J

Jackson, Charles, 71
James, Henry, 190
Jannings, Emil, 17
Jazz Age, 25–26
Jazz Singer, The (film), 111
Jenkins, William O., 142, 143
Joe character. *See* Gillis, Joe
Jones, A. Quincy, 227
Joplin, Janis, 238
Journey to the Center of the Earth
(film), 229
Joyce, James, 106, 110

K

Kael, Pauline, 225, 226
Kaja the Dancer (play), 41

Kanin, Garson, 211, 230
Kaptur, Hugh, 226–227
Kaufman, George S., 41
Keaton, Buster, 3, 166–167, 216–218
Keim, T. Beverley, 142–143
Kelly, Gene, 130, 136
Kennedy, Jack, 36
Kennedy, Joseph P., 35–36, 110–111
Kennedy, Rose Fitzpatrick, 36
Kern, Jerome, 18
Kerr, Deborah, 213
Keystone Studios, 23
Killer Bees (film), 238
King and I, The (film), 228
King of Kings (film), 123, 166
King Solomon's Mines (film), 212–213
Kiss, The (film), 110
Kiss Me, Stupid (film), 233
Kiss of Death (film), 123, 204
Klemperer, Otto, 16
Knox, Margaret, 103–104
Kobal, John, 31
Kohner, Paul, 113
Koszarski, Richard, 105
Kraus, Karl, 7, 8
Kubrick, Stanley, 200

L
La Cava, Gregory, 56
"La Cumparsita" tango, 170
La Falaise, Henri de (Marquis de La
      Coudraye), 32, 33, 34, 35, 89
La Rochefoucauld, François de, 242
Laemmle, Carl, 104–105
Lake, Veronica, 97, 134
Lamarr, Hedy, 123
Lancaster, Burt, 130, 136

Lang, Anton, 73
Lasky, Jesse, 28, 119–120
Last Laugh, The (film), 17
Lawrence, Florence, 21
Le Corbusier, 8
Lean, David, 225
Lehár, Franz, 109
Leisen, Mitchell, 60
      Hold Back the Dawn, 61, 117, 134
      I Wanted Wings, 134
      and *Male and Female* fantasy
            sequence, 31
Lemmon, Jack, 5, 232, 233
Lemon Drop Kid, The (film), 186
Leonard, Maurice, 86
Lerner, Alan Jay, 221
Life Can Be Beautiful (soap
      opera), 180
Life in Photography, A (Steichen), 20
Lifetime Achievement Awards, 210
Limelight (film), 217
Little Sister, The (Chandler), 68
Little Women (film), 43
Livingston, Alan, 221
Livingston, Jay, 175–177
location shooting, in *Sunset Boulevard*,
      137–144
Loewe, Frederick "Fritz", 221
Loews, Inc., 204
Loos, Adolf, 8, 12
Los Angeles
      shifting residential aesthetics in,
            141–142
      swimming pools in, 177
      Wilder's move to, 14–17
Lost Weekend, The (film), ix–x,
      65–66, 71–72, 75–76, 140

Lost Weekend, The (Jackson), 71
Louise, Ruth Harriet, 20
Louvish, Simon, 123
love, cynical view of, 4–6, 12–13
Love in the Afternoon (film), 232
Love Is a Many-Splendored Thing
      (film), 224
Love of Sunya, The (film), 35
Loved One, The (Waugh), 81,
      159–160
Lubitsch, Ernst, 174
   background of, 54–55
   and *Bluebeard's Eighth Wife*, 52, 54,
      56, 57, 58
   and Dreier, 144
   and *The Emperor Waltz*, 78, 79
   Ninotchka, x, 59, 157
   "touch" as director, 55
Lucas, George, 233
Luft, Herbert G., 229, 231

M
*M*A*S*H* (film), 200
Mack Sennett Bathing Beauties, 150,
      183, 184
MacLaine, Shirley, 233
MacMurray, Fred, 69, 130, 136, 220
Madame Sans-Gêne (film), 32, 33–34
Major and the Minor, The (film),
      61–62, 157, 180–181
makeup, early twentieth century
      views of, 29–30
Male and Female (film), 30–31,
      118–119, 120, 186
Mamoulian, Rouben, 132, 133
Man Who Shot Liberty Valance, The
      (film), 2

Manhandled (film), 184
Mankiewicz, Herman J., 40–41, 49
Mankiewicz, Joseph, 49–50, 210–211,
      219–220
Mann, Thomas, 16
Marion, Frances, 48
marital comedies by DeMille, 26–27,
      120–121
Marshall, Brenda (Ardis Ankerson),
      134, 135, 192, 225
Marshman, Mac, Jr., 148, 213. *See also*
      Sunset Boulevard
Marty (film), 214
Marx, Harpo, 41
Mason, James, 82
Mason, Sarah Y., 43
Matthau, Walter, 233
Mature, Victor, 123–124
Maugham, Somerset, 35
Mauvaise Graine (*Bad Seed*) film,
      13–14, 61
Max (character in *Sunset Boulevard*).
      See Mayerling, Max von
May, Joe, 14, 15, 18
Mayer, Louis B., 130
   and Academy Awards, 208, 209,
      210
   end of career, 204
   on manufacture of beauty, 189
   reaction to *Sunset Boulevard*,
      201–204
   and Schulberg, 50, 51
   and Stroheim, 107, 109
Mayerling, Max von (character in
      Sunset Boulevard)
   choice of name for, 11–12
   and Joe's arrival at mansion, 158–159

Mayerling, Max von (character in *Sunset Boulevard*) (*cont.*)
　and Joe's move from apartment to mansion, 169–170
　in men's shop scene, 168
　monkey funeral scene, 160
　in Norma's New Year's party scene, 170
　organ playing scene, 161
　Stroheim's acceptance of role, 113–114
Mayerling incident, 11–12
McBride, Joseph, 80
McCarey, Leo, 56
McCarthy, Joseph, 206, 212
McMein, Neysa, 44
McTeague (Norris), 108
Meehan, John, 145–146, 151, 152, 155, 213
Meet Me in St. Louis (film), 78
meet-cute, 57, 79, 157
Menschen am Sonntag (*People on Sunday*) film, 12–13, 129, 139
Merry Widow, The (film), 78, 109
Merry-Go-Round (film), 107
meta-cinema, 200
Metropolis (film), 12, 17
MGM (Metro-Goldwyn-Mayer), 107–109, 130, 189, 203–204
midcentury modern designs, 142, 226–227
Midnight (film), 58–59
Mies van der Rohe, Ludwig, 9
Milland, Ray, 61, 75, 95, 140
Miller, Arthur, 156
Miller, John "Skins", 185–186
Mills, Hayley, 220

minimalism, 8–9
Minnelli, Liza, 237
Mio Figlio Nerone (*My Son Nero*, aka *Nero's Big Weekend*) film, 236
Mix, Tom, 3
modern girls (flappers), 24–25, 26, 29
modernism, residential, 141–142, 226–227
monkey funeral scene, 160–161
Monroe, Marilyn, 5, 228, 232
Moore, Jim, 72
morality clauses, 33
morgue scene, 150–151, 199–200
Morino (character in *Sunset Boulevard*), 155–156
Morley, Karen, 156
Motion Picture Industry Council, 124
Motion Picture Production Code, 67, 69
movie magazines, 20
movie stars
　as modern invention, 20–21
　Swanson's elevation to, 30–32
　use of former, in *Sunset Boulevard*, 166–168
　view of in *Sunset Boulevard*, 202–203
movie studios. *See* Hollywood
Much Ado about Nothing (Shakespeare), 56
Multiprises, 88–89
Murrow, Edward R., 90
music, in *Sunset Boulevard*, 149, 164, 190, 196
Music in the Air (film), 18, 37, 88, 92, 164
musicals. *See also specific musicals by name*

attempts to turn *Sunset Boulevard*
  into, 223, 236
avoidance of social issues in, 214
My Fair Lady (Lerner and Loewe),
  221
My Man Godfrey (film), 56
My Son Nero (aka *Nero's Big Weekend*
  or *Mio Figlio Nerone*) film, 236

N
Nash, Ogden, 49
National Film Theatre (Britain), 223
National Labor Relations Act
  (Wagner Act), 50
Naughty Riquette (play), 41
Nazi regime, 65–66, 73–74
Negri, Pola, 87
neorealist films, 139–140
Network (film), 226
Neutra, Richard, 141
New Hollywood, 200
New Look, 98
New Objectivity (*Neue Sachlichkeit*),
  in German arts, 12–13
New Year's scenes in *Sunset Boulevard*
  Artie Green's party, 175–181
  Norma's party, 170–174
New Yorker, The (magazine), 40–41
Niagara (film), 228
Nichols, Mike, 234
Night into Morning (film), 186
Nilsson, Anna Q., 166, 167
Ninotchka (film), x, 59, 157
Noble, Peter, 102
Norma (Bellini), 198
Norma character. *See* Desmond,
  Norma

Norris, Frank, 108
North by Northwest (film), 145
Nosferatu (film), 12
Notorious (film), 173

O
O'Brien, Timothy, 240–241
Oceanaire (Shorecliff Tower
  Apartments), 227
O'Connor, Donald, 218
Odets, Clifford, 131
Old Dark House (film), 158
Old World farces, 55
Olson Livingston, Nancy
  as Betty, 39, 153–154, 179–180,
    184–185, 190–192
  career after *Sunset Boulevard*,
    220–222
  excitement before filming *Sunset
    Boulevard*, xii
  on Holden's physique, 177
  on Stroheim's desire to direct
    Sunset Boulevard, 170
On the Waterfront (film), 214
One Hour with You (film), 78
O'Neill, Eugene, 184
opportunism theme, 66, 152, 168–169
"Ornament and Crime" (Loos), 8
Oscars. *See* Academy Awards

P
Paar, Jack, 237
Pacoima plane crash, 216
Pajama Party (film), 218
Pal Joey (Rodgers and Hart), 130
Paleface, The (film), 176, 185
Pam-Pam (film), 14–15

Paramount Pictures. *See also Sunset Boulevard*
  annual salary offered to Swanson by, 35
  assembly-line approach to screenwriting, 45
  Bluebeard's Eighth Wife, 53–54, 56–58
  Brackett and Wilder's rise to top in, 60
  depiction of studios in films, 115–118, 190–191
  Double Indemnity adaptation by, ix–x, 65–70, 130, 140, 142
  The Emperor Waltz, x, 77–79, 185
  formation of Brackett-Wilder team at, 52, 53–54, 56–58
  Golden Boy, xi, 131–134, 153, 154
  history of, 119–120
  house style of, 144–145
  Madame Sans-Gêne, 32, 33–35
  role of Edith Head at, 96
  state of film industry in 1948, 81
  Swanson as "Good Will Ambassador" for, 205
  twenty-fifth anniversary of, 95
  Wilder's shift from writer to writer-director at, 61–62
Parker, Dorothy
  disdain for screenwriting, 46, 47
  and *Entirely Surrounded*, 44
  and formation of Screen Writers Guild, 47, 48
  on Hepburn's acting skills, 43
  participation in Algonquin Round Table, 41–42
Parker, Eleanor, 212
Parsons, Louella, 195

Passion Play, 73
patriarchal values in early twentieth century, 29–30
peacock feather, in *Sunset Boulevard*, 185, 186
Peckinpah, Sam, 226
People on Sunday (*Menschen am Sonntag*) film, 12–13, 129, 139
Perelman, S. J., 101–102
pet burials, 159–161
Phantom House, 142–144
Philco Television Playhouse (TV show), 90
photography, glamour, 20–21, 31
Photoplay (magazine), 20, 28
Pickford, Mary, 35, 54, 87–88, 95
Picnic (film), 224
Pirandello, Luigi, 92
Place in the Sun, A (film), 129
plastic surgery, 29, 189
Play's the Thing, The (play), 41
Polan, Barron, 99
Pollyanna (film), 220
Pommer, Erich, 1–2, 16–18, 37, 92
Porter, Cole, 95
Pound, Ezra, 106
Powdermaker, Hortense, 162–163
Powell, Dilys, 207
Presley, Elvis, 229
preview audience reactions to *Sunset Boulevard*, 199–201
projection room chiaroscuro, 163–166
Pryor, Thomas M., 206–207
Psycho (film), 197, 198
Psychological Warfare Division, 72–74
pure cinema, 164

Q

Queen Kelly (film), xii, 35–36, 110–113, 162

R

racial themes, exploitation of by DeMille, 121–122

Rain (Maugham), 35

"Rain in Spain, The" (Lerner and Loewe), 221

Ramsaye, Terry, 208

ranch homes, 141

Rapf, Maurice, 213–214

rats in swimming pool scene, 161

Ray, Robert, 168

Reagan, Ronald, 124

Rear Window (film), 197

Rebel without a Cause (film), 143

Red River (film), 128–129

Red Wing (Lilian St. Cyr), 121–122

Redelings, Lowell E., 207–208

redemption-seeking opportunist theme, 66

Reed, Carol, 79

Reinhardt, Max, 54

Reisch, Walter, 59, 228

religious costume dramas by DeMille, 123–124

Renoir, Jean, 113, 169

residential modernism, 141–142, 226–227

revivalist architecture, 141

Reynolds, Zachary Smith, 130

Riefenstahl, Leni, 79

RKO, 42–43

Rodgers, Richard, 130

Rogers, Buddy, 87

Rogers, Ginger, 61

romance, cynical view of in, 4–6, 12–13

romantic comedy, *Sunset Boulevard* as, 157

Rommel, Erwin, 62

Rork, Ann, 143

Rose of the Rancho (film), 45

Rosita (film), 54

Ross, Harold, 40

Ross, Murray, 47–48

Rossellini, Roberto, 79, 139–140

Rosten, Leo, 45

rubble films (*Trümmerfilm*), 79, 129

S

Sabrina (film), 224, 232

Sadie Thompson (film), 35, 110

St. Cyr, Lilian (Red Wing), 121–122

St. Johns, Adela Rogers, 28, 36, 42, 43

Salomé (Strauss), 196

Samson and Delilah (film), 123–124, 184, 185, 218

Sanger, Margaret, 26–27

Sarris, Andrew, 66, 149

satire, *Sunset Boulevard* as, 156

Schaefer, Betty (character in *Sunset Boulevard*), 39

in Artie Green's New Year's Eve party scene, 179–180

Joe's visit to Betty's cubicle, 184–185

in narrative setup, 153–154

scenes with Joe in fifth act, 190–192

Schary, Dore, 124, 204

Schenck, Nicholas, Jr., 204

Schindler, Rudolph, 141

Schnitzler, Arthur, 6, 7
Schoenberg, Arnold, 16
Schorr, William, 189–190
Schulberg, B. P., 50
Schulberg, Budd, 50–51
Schwab's Pharmacy, 139, 154–155
Scorsese, Martin, 233
Screen Writers Guild, 47–50
screenwriting
    assembly-line approach to, 45–46
    competition in, 46–47, 48
    difficulty of making living in, 51–52
    importance to story of *Sunset
        Boulevard*, 38–39
    snobbery against, 46
screwball comedies, 55–60, 61
Sea Hawk, The (film), 134
Search, The (film), 129
Seitz, John F., 160, 164, 165, 172, 182
self-censorship bureau (Hays Office),
        33, 67, 69
Selznick, David O., 42, 43–44, 45,
        50, 202
semi-documentary style, 139–140
Sennett, Mack, 23, 150, 183, 184
Seven Year Itch, The (film), 232
sex
    changing views of after World War
        I, 120–121
    cynical view of in works by Wilder,
        4–6, 12–13
    in films by von Stroheim,
        109–110, 121
sex workers, 4–5
sexy religious costume dramas,
        123–124
Shakespeare, William, 56, 58

She Done Him Wrong (film), 86, 97
Shearer, Norma, 36
Sheldrake (character in *Sunset
        Boulevard*), 152–153, 154
Shelley, Mary, 157
Shorecliff Tower Apartments
        (Oceanaire), 227
Short, Elizabeth (Black Dahlia), 178
Sight and Sound (British
        publication), 222
Sign of the Cross, The (film), 123
Sikov, Ed, 64, 74, 159, 196–197, 235
silent cinema
    comedy in, 217
    former stars of in waxworks scene,
        166–168
    German, 12–13
Sinatra, Frank, 142
Siodmak, Robert, 12, 129
Sistrom, Joe, 67, 68
Skolsky, Sidney, 155
"Smiling Jim" role, 135
Smiling Lieutenant, The (film), 78
Smith, Darr, 207
social issues, in 1950s films, 213–214
Somborn, Herbert, 32
Some Like It Hot (film), 5, 232
Something to Think About (film), 120
Son of Flubber (film), 220
Sondheim, Stephen, 198, 218, 236
Sordi, Alberto, 236
speed, fascination with in early
        twentieth century, 24
Spiel, Hilde, 7
Spielberg, Steven, 233
Squaw Man, The (film), 119–120,
        121–122

Staggs, Sam, 181
Stalag 17 (film), 224, 232
Stanwyck, Barbara, 37, 95
    in *Ball of Fire*, 60
    in *Double Indemnity*, 69
    in *Golden Boy*, 133
    at VIP screening of *Sunset*
        Boulevard, 201
Stapley, Richard, 236
Star Is Born, A (film), 43, 46, 50, 202
star system
    as modern invention, 20–21
    Swanson's place in, 30–32
    use of former stars in *Sunset*
        Boulevard, 166–168
    view of in *Sunset Boulevard*, 202–203
Stars and Strikes (Ross), 47–48
State Fair (film), 229
Steichen, Edward, 20
Stern, Michael, 227
Sternberg, Josef von, 92, 123
Stevens, George, 129
Stewart, Donald Ogden, 46–47, 48
Stewart, James, 224
stingers, 128, 164
Stoker, Bram, 157
Story of Dr. Wassell, The (film),
    122–123
Strauss, Richard, 6, 96, 196
Stravinsky, Igor, 16
Streetcar Named Desire, A (Williams),
    130–131
Stroheim, Erich von, 83, 201
    career after *Sunset Boulevard*,
        222–224
    and depiction of sexuality in
        cinema, 109–110, 121

    directorial debut in *Blind*
        Husbands, 104–105
    Five Graves to Cairo, 62
    Foolish Wives, 106–107, 108
    Greed, 107–109, 222
    Legion of Honor awarded to,
        223–224
    length of films by, 105–108
    as master of self-invention, 102–104
    The Merry Widow, 78, 109
    opinion of DeMille, 122
    persona as villain, 101–102, 104
    Queen Kelly, xii, 35, 110–113, 162
    return to acting after directing
        career, 113–114
    in *Sunset Boulevard*
        acceptance of role, 113–114
        and Joe's arrival at mansion,
            158–159
        Joe's move from apartment to
            mansion, 169–170
        men's shop scene, 168
        monkey funeral scene, 160
        in Norma's New Year's party
            scene, 170
        organ playing scene, 161
        Oscar nomination for, 210
        relationship with Swanson
            after, 223
        reviews of, 207
        tension before filming, xi–xii
        as vestige of an earlier era in, 37
Struggle, The (film), 82
studios. *See* Hollywood
Sturges, Preston, 61, 117–118, 165
Submarine Command (film), 220, 224
Sullivan's Travels (film), 97, 117–118, 165

Sunset Boulevard (film). *See also*
Desmond, Norma; Gillis,
Joe; Mayerling, Max von;
Schaefer, Betty
and Academy Awards, 208, 210–213
Artie Green character, 175,
178–179, 180
casting of DeMille in, 118, 121
choice of actor to play Joe,
128–131, 135–136
choice of actress to play Norma,
85–88, 91–93
as comeback for Swanson, 19–20, 21
cynical view of love in, 5
fifth act
beauty regimen scene, 188–190
crime-scene chaos in, 193–194
Hedda Hopper's appearance in,
194–195
Norma's final descent of
staircase, 195–198
scenes with Joe and Betty,
190–192
first act
Bel-Air Golf Club scene,
155–156
chase scene, 156
Joe's arrival at mansion, 19,
137–138, 156–160
monkey funeral scene, 160–161
morgue scene, 150–151, 199–200
narrative setup in, 152–154
opening sequence, 148–152
rats in swimming pool scene,
161, 177
Schwab's Pharmacy scene,
154–155
fourth act
Joe's visit to Betty's cubicle,
184–185
Norma's performance for Joe,
150, 183–184
Norma's visit to DeMille, 115–117,
125–126, 184, 185–187
genre switching in, 156–157, 158,
200, 242
and Golden Globes, 208
key themes in, 4, 239–242
legacy of, 239–242
location shooting for, 137–144
as love letter to Hollywood, 192–193
mansion interiors, design of, 144–147
meet-cute in, 57
versus message avoidance in 1950s
films, 214
Morino character, 155–156
musical version, attempts to create,
223, 236
premier of, 205–206
preview audience reactions to,
199–201
rental of Phantom House for,
143–144
reviews of, 206–208
screenwriting, importance to story,
38–39
second act
bridge scene, 166–168
Max's playing organ scene, 161
men's shop scene, 127–128,
168–169, 215
scene of Joe and Norma
watching old movies, 161–166
similarities between real life and

as expressed in locations used, 138–139

Joe's similarity to Brackett and Wilder, 39

Swanson's intrigue with, 92

Swanson's similarity to Norma, 19–20, 34, 37, 96

Stroheim's acceptance of role, 113–114

suspense in, 207–208

Swanson's influence on character of Norma, 93–96, 182

tensions before filming, ix–xiii

third act

    Artie Green's New Year's Eve party, 175–181

    Joe's move from apartment to mansion, 169–170

    Norma's New Year's party scene, 170–174

    scene in Norma's bedroom, 180–182

view of film industry in, 187, 202–203, 240

VIP screening, reactions at, 201–204

voice-over narration in, 149–150, 200–201

wardrobe design for, 98–100

Swanson, Addie, 22, 23

Swanson, Gloria, 97. *See also* Desmond, Norma

abortions experienced by, 23, 33, 34–35

autobiography of, 21, 32, 34–35

in *Bluebeard's Eighth Wife*, 54, 56

career after *Sunset Boulevard*, 235–238

comebacks by, 21

in DeMille films, 25–27, 30–31, 118–119, 186

and F. Scott Fitzgerald, 193

in *Father Takes a Wife*, 89

Gloria Swanson Hour, 89

idiosyncratic appearance of, 28–30, 167

imitation of Chaplin by, 183, 184

in *Madame Sans-Gêne*, 32, 33–35

in *Male and Female*, 30–31, 118–119, 120, 186

marriages and divorces, 23–24, 27, 32–33

move into talking pictures, 36–37

Multiprises ownership, 88–89

in *Music in the Air*, 18, 37, 88, 92

Olson's lack of knowledge of, xii

opinion of DeMille, 122

as Paramount's "Good Will Ambassador", 205

as producer, 35–36, 110–113

and *Queen Kelly* production, xii, 35–36, 110–113, 162

reaction to death of Beery, 99

relationship with DeMille, 117, 118–119

stardom of, 20–21, 27–28, 30–32

start in movies, 21–23

in *Sunset Boulevard*

    choice as actress to play Norma, 88, 91–93

    enjoyment of role, 193

    Golden Globe won by, 208

    influence on development of character, 93–96, 182

    Oscar nomination for, 211–212, 213

Swanson, Gloria, 97. *See also*
    Desmond, Norma (*cont.*)
  photographs of in set design, 146
  relationship with Stroheim
    after, 223
  reviews of, 206, 207
  role in designing wardrobe for
    Norma, 98, 99–100
  screen test for, 91, 93–94
  similarities to Norma, 19–20, 37
  tension before filming, ix, xi
  VIP screening, 201
  "we had faces" scene, 164
  visit to Holden's house in Palm
    Springs, 227
  wardrobe of as integral to stardom,
    27–28
  work with Keystone Studios, 23–25
Swanson on Swanson (Swanson), 21,
    32, 34–35
Sweedie Goes to College (film), 22
swimming pools
  in opening sequence, 150–152
  rats in swimming pool scene, 161
  in scene where Joe arrives at
    mansion, 157–158
  "swimming pool story" idea, xiii,
    83–84, 85
  symbolisms related to, 177–178

T

taking advantage theme, in *Sunset
    Boulevard*, 152, 168–169
talk shows, xi, 89, 237
Taming of the Shrew, The
    (Shakespeare), 58
Tandy, Jessica, 131

tango scene, in *Sunset Boulevard*,
    170–173
Taylor, Elizabeth, 212
Taylor, Estelle, 42
Taylor, Robert, 133
Technicolor, 78
Teddy at the Throttle (film), 24
television
  as eroding film industry, xii–xiii,
    81, 89–91
  talk shows, xi, 89, 237
Ten Commandments, The (1923
    film), 123
Ten Commandments, The (1956 film),
    220, 228
Tetzlaff, Ted, 173
Texaco Star Theater (TV show), 90
Thalberg, Irving G., 48, 50,
    107–108, 109
Thin Man, The (films), 49
Third Man, The (film), 79
Thomson, David, 225
Three for Bedroom C (film), 235
Titanic (film), 228
Toccata and Fugue (Bach), 161
Toland, Gregg, 112, 165
Torch, The (*Die Fackel*) journal, 7
Tracy, Spencer, 212
trade unionism, 47–50, 209
transactional nature of love, in films
    by Wilder, 4–6
traveling close-ups, 172–173
Trespasser, The (film), 36
Triumph of the Will (film), 79
True Heart Susie (film), 29–30
Truffaut, François, 164, 173, 200
Truman, Harry S., 206

Trumbo, Dalton, 45
Trümmerfilm (rubble films), 79, 129
Trump, Donald J., 240–241
Turner, Lana, 155
Twentieth Century Fox, 228, 230
Twitchell, Archie, 127, 128, 215–216

U
UFA (*Universum-Film
        Aktiengesellschaft*), 11, 144
Ulback, Sylvia, 29
Ulmer, Edgar G., 12
Ulysses (Joyce), 106
Under the Lash (film), 27–28
unhappy endings, 198
Union Station (film), 220
unionism, 47–50, 209
United Artists, 35
Universal Pictures, 104–107

V
Valentino, Rudolph, 172
Valley of Fire (film), 186
vamp role, Norma's assumption
        of, 171
vanitas theme, 3–4, 239
velocity-mania in early twentieth
        century, 24
Vernac, Denise, 222, 223
Verne, Jules, 229
Vertigo (film), 197, 198
Vienna, Austria
    love-for-hire in, 4
    Wilder's time in, 6–9
Viertel, Salka, 4, 16–17
VIP screening of *Sunset Boulevard*,
        201–204

Visconti, Luchino, 222
voice-over narration, 149–150, 200–201
von Stroheim, Erich. *See* Stroheim,
        Erich von

W
Waggoner, Lyle, 237
Wagner Act (National Labor
        Relations Act), 50
"'Waiter, A Dancer Please!'"
        (Wilder), 11
Walsh, Raoul, 95
Warner, H. B. (Henry Byron), 166, 167
Warner Bros., 143
Washington Square (James), 190
Waste Land, The (Eliot), 106
Waugh, Evelyn, 81, 159–160
Waxman, Franz, 18, 164, 190, 196, 213
waxworks scene, *Sunset Boulevard*,
        166–168
Wayne, John, 129
Webb, Clifton, 95
Webb, Jack, 178–179
Webber, Andrew Lloyd, 236
Weegee (Arthur Fellig), 148
Weimar Republic, 9–10, 13
Weitz, Eric, 10
Welles, Orson
    on art department heads, 144
    Citizen Kane, 41, 105, 165
    poll on ten greatest films, 222
    in *The Third Man*, 79
West, Mae, 85–86, 97
West, Nathanael, 49
Whale, James, 158, 164
What Makes Sammy Run?
        (Schulberg), 50–51

What Price Hollywood? (film), 43, 88, 202

White Album, The (Didion), 178

Whiteman, Paul, 9

Who's Afraid of Virginia Woolf? (film), 234

Why Change Your Wife? (film), 26, 120

Wild Bunch, The (film), 226

Wild Rovers (film), 226

Wild West, 2–3

Wilder, Audrey, 9

Wilder, Billy, 199–200. *See also Sunset Boulevard*
    Ace in the Hole as turning point for, 231
    avoidance of politics by, 49
    Bad Seed, 13–14, 61
    in Berlin, 9–13
    bitter view of humanity, 6
    career after *Sunset Boulevard*, 224, 226, 231–233
    childhood of, 2–3
    coming of age in Vienna, 6–9
    cynical view of love, 4–6
    darkening worldview during World War II, 65–66
    The Death Mills, 65, 73–74, 80
    description of Brackett by, 49
    desire to learn English, 14–15
    Double Indemnity, ix–x, 65–70, 130, 140, 142
    and F. Scott Fitzgerald, 193
    freedom-of-speech petition signed by, 219
    as gigolo, 11
    on Holden's death, 227
    interest in musical after World War II, 77
    "invisible" editing, preference for, 180–181
    Irving G. Thalberg Memorial Award for, 14–15
    later life, 233–235
    on Lifetime Achievement Awards, 210
    on Lubitsch's work, 55
    and Mayer's reaction to *Sunset Boulevard*, 201–202
    modern art collection, 13, 234–235
    modernism and, 8–9, 142
    Music in the Air adaptation by, 18, 37, 88, 92, 164
    opinion of DeMille, 124–125
    Pam-Pam project, 14–15
    in Paris, 13–14
    partnership with Brackett
        and death of D. W. Griffith, 82–84
        The Emperor Waltz, x, 77–79, 185
        A Foreign Affair, x, 79–80, 92
        formation of, 51–52, 53, 56–58
        Hold Back the Dawn, 61, 117, 134
        The Lost Weekend adaptation, ix–x, 65–66, 71–72, 75–76, 140
        The Major and the Minor, 61–62, 157, 180–181
        relationship after breakup, 229–230
        rise to fame, 58–60
        search for actress to play Norma, 85–88, 91–96

and shift from writer to writer-director, 60–62

split during *Double Indemnity* adaptation, 67

"swimming pool story" idea, xiii, 84, 85

tensions in, 60, 63–64, 75–76, 81–82

partnership with Diamond, 232–233

People on Sunday, 12–13, 129, 139

poll on ten greatest films, 222

pool story told by, 1–2, 17–18

preference for voice-over narration, 149–150

profile of von Stroheim by, 108

in Psychological Warfare Division, 72–74

relocation to Hollywood, 14–17

as reporter, 6–7, 11

Some Like It Hot, 5, 232

Stroheim's interest in working with, 113

on studio house styles, 145

tension before filming *Sunset Boulevard*, ix–x

vanitas theme explored by, 3–4

views on film industry, 192–193, 202–203

work with Leisen, 31

Wilder, Eugenia, 2–3

Wilder, Judith, 60, 64

Wilder, Max, 2, 3, 5–6, 9, 11

Williams, Tennessee, 130–131

Winston, George, 237

wisecracking, role in audio cinema, 42

Witness for the Prosecution (film), 232

Wizard of Oz, The (film), 49, 188

Wolfe, Manny, 52, 53

Wood, Natalie, 143

Woollcott, Alexander, 41, 44

World of Yesterday, The (Zweig), 4

World War I

anti-German propaganda in films during, 104

culture in Berlin after, 10

marital comedies produced in wake of, 120–121

World War II

rubble films created after, 79, 129

Wilder's darkening worldview during, 65–66

Wilder's documentary on Nazi atrocities during, 65, 73–74, 80

Wright, Frank Lloyd, 141

writing, importance to *Sunset Boulevard* story, 38–39

Wyler, William, 129, 190, 219–220

Y

Young, Audrey, 191. *See also* Wilder, Audrey

youth, veneration of in cinema, 189

Z

Zaza (film), 166

Zinnemann, Fred, 12, 129

Zolotow, Maurice, 75, 76, 94

Zuckmayer, Carl, 10

Zukor, Adolph, 34

Zweig, Stefan, 4

ABOUT THE AUTHOR

David M. Lubin, a former writer for *Rolling Stone* and a professor at Wake Forest University, has published eight books on American art, film, and popular culture. His *Shooting Kennedy: JFK and the Culture of Images* won the Smithsonian Institution's Charles C. Eldredge Prize for distinguished scholarship in American art. Lubin is a Guggenheim fellow and an NEH Public Scholar.